Yiddish Empire

Yiddish Empire

The Vilna Troupe, Jewish Theater, and the Art of Itinerancy

DEBRA CAPLAN

UNIVERSITY OF MICHIGAN PRESS • ANN ARBOR

Published in the United States of America by the
University of Michigan Press
Manufactured in the United States of America
♾ Printed on acid-free paper

2021 2020 2019 2018 4 3 2 1

A CIP catalog record for this book is available from the British Library.

Library of Congress Cataloging-in-Publication data has been applied for.

ISBN: 978-0-472-13077-1 (Hardcover : alk paper)
ISBN: 978-0-472-03725-4 (Paper : alk paper)
ISBN: 978-0-472-12368-1 (ebook)

Additional photographs, video clips, and audio material related to the Vilna Troupe can be found at the following link: http://www.press.umich.edu/p/yiddish-empire.

To my father, Zev Caplan (1949–2003),
for introducing me to Yiddish theater,
and for giving me the keys to the kingdom.
May his memory be for a blessing.

The homeless, Jewish actor
Smiles to himself like a child in a dream.
Through London, Paris, Brussels,
New York, and Rio de Janeiro,
With a cigarette in his mouth
Sick on nostalgia
Drag, drag,
Day, night,
Jews—wanderers—actors.

—Irma Kanfer, "Żydowscy Aktorzy" [Jewish actors]

Dedicated to Vilna Troupe actress Miriam Orleska

Translated by Aniela and Jerzy Gregorek in *Native Foreigners: Jewish-Polish Poetry between the World Wars* (Merrick, NY: Cross-Cultural Communications, 2015), 25–27

Acknowledgments

As with all books, there are many people who made this project possible. I owe special thanks to Ruth R. Wisse, Martin Puchner, and Joel Berkowitz, who first inspired me to write about the Vilna Troupe, provided comments on early drafts, and were instrumental in shaping this book. Thank you for your commitment to this project and your willingness to always read another chapter draft.

My chair at Baruch College, Anne Swartz, supported a semester's teaching leave that enabled me to complete this book, and my colleagues in the Department of Fine and Performing Arts provided valuable feedback on the introduction. In particular, I am grateful to my Baruch colleagues Esther Allen, Cheryl Smith, and Susan Tenneriello for their comments on work in progress. A very special thanks is due to my Baruch colleague Elizabeth Wollman, who read many drafts of this manuscript. Her keen eye for detail was invaluable.

I am also grateful to LeAnn Fields at the University of Michigan Press, who believed in this project from the beginning, and to my two anonymous readers, whose suggestions greatly strengthened the argument of this book. I am also indebted to Jenny Geyer and Mary Hashman at Michigan for shepherding this book to publication.

Funding from the Baruch College Provost's Office and Dean's Office supported my research at critical junctures. My research was also supported by a PSC-CUNY award, jointly funded by the Professional Staff Congress and the City University of New York, and by the YIVO Institute for Jewish Research, Harvard's Center for Jewish Studies, Targum Shlishi, the Foundation for Jewish Culture, and the Memorial Foundation for

Jewish Culture. Special thanks are due to Amanda (Miryem-Khaye) Seigel and Doug Reside at the New York Public Library, Mila Sholokhova, Jesse Cohen, Gunnar Berg, and Vital Zajka at YIVO, James P. Rosenbloom at the Brandeis Judaica Collection, Michelle Chesner at Columbia University, the staff of the National Library of Israel, and Gregory Hahn in Solingen for helping me find Vilna Troupe materials scattered throughout the archives. I am especially grateful to Dr. Charles Berlin, Elizabeth Vernon, and Vardit Samuels at the Harvard College Library's Judaica Division for facilitating my access to the collections and granting me de facto office space for several months while I combed through the entirety of the Joseph Buloff Jewish Theater Archive.

Many scholars and friends offered advice as I worked on this manuscript, including Ingrid Anderson, Zachary Baker, Christopher Balme, Robin Bernstein, Katherine Biers, Shiraz Biggie, Gibson Cima, Judah Cohen, Emma Cox, Jeremy Dauber, Ofer Dynes, Sonia Gollance, Jean Graham-Jones, Stuart Hecht, Barbara Henry, Kate Hollander, Rebecca Kastleman, Agi Legutko, David Mazower, Bernadette Meyler, Derek Miller, Joanna Nizynska, Caraid O'Brien, Alyssa Quint, Magda Romanska, Rebecca Rovit, Rachel Rubinstein, Vardit Samuels, David Savran, Asya Schulman, Sebastian Schulman, Naomi Seidman, Sasha Senderovich, Laurence Senelick, Max Shulman, Matthew Wilson Smith, Claire Solomon, Michael Steinlauf, Anna Torres, Nick Underwood, Zohar Weimar-Kellman, Janet Werther, Stacy Wolf, and Sunny Yudkoff. I owe special thanks to Andrew Sofer for teaching me that a book is like a shark that must always keep moving. Your guidance made me a better writer.

I had the privilege of speaking with many descendants and friends of the Vilner who shared photographs, recordings, ephemera, and family lore. Dan Ben-Amos introduced me to his great-uncle Noah Nachbush over tea. Sharon Asro and Alexander Zaloum told stories that brought their grandparents and great-grandparents Alexander Asro and Sonia Alomis to life. Leonard Fein reminisced about his parents' friendship with Nachbush. I would also like to thank Barbara Buloff (daughter of Joseph Buloff and Luba Kadison), Madeline Friedman (granddaughter of Moyshe Feder), Carmela Rubin (daughter-in-law of Reuven Rubin), Craig Rapel (great-nephew of Ester Rapel and Zalmen Hirshfeld), Dr. Ziva Ben-Porta (daughter of Yehuda Ehrenkrantz), Michael S. Levy (grandson of Avrom Bell), Rosalind Wholden Thomas (friend of Noah Nachbush), Bill Katz (grandson of Chana Magidman), and Manny Azenberg (nephew of Wolfe Barzell). The late Charles Slucki also provided valuable perspective on the careers of the Vilner in Australia during and after the war. These conversations were the privilege of a lifetime.

Two research assistants, Ioana Costache in Bucharest and Zosia Sochanska in Warsaw, scoured the collections of the Romanian Academy Library and the Biblioteka Narodowa, respectively, for material and translated dozens of articles. I am also grateful to William Boletta, Daniel Dinsenbacher, Dorine Oz, Christopher M. Peterson, Katarzyna Sitkiewicz, and Lena Vanelslander for additional translation support. My research assistant and former student Rebecca Galpern spent countless hours piecing together biographical information. I would also like to thank Jessica Hamel, who turned a simple database into a beautiful data visualization that exceeded all expectations.

Though I did not know it at the time, the seeds of this project were planted on my first visit to Vilna under the auspices of the Vilnius Yiddish Institute. There I was privileged to study under Yitskhok Niborski, Avrom Lichtenboym, Pesakh Fishman (ז"ל), and Fania Bransovsky, who schooled me in Litvak dialect and taught me to fall in love with Vilna, that *shtot fun gayst un tmimes*. I have thought of them often while writing this book.

Special thanks are due to the friends and family members who provided me with the best support network any scholar could desire. Shauna Gordon-McKeon provided writing motivation when I needed it most. Orli Nativ offered detailed analysis of 1920s fashion and costuming. My mother reminded me why I started this project in the first place. My sister, Becky Caplan, was always there for me no matter what. Special thanks to Jerry and Sharon Teres, without whom none of this would have been possible. You are not just family, you are Family.

I could not have completed this project without the support of my husband, Nick Taft, who never questioned my desire to "have it all." Your patience and love carried me through the long process of writing this book. To my beautiful children Zev and Maya, my *yingele* and my *meydele* who came into the world alongside this project, it is you who make me who I am. This book is as much yours as it is mine.

This book is dedicated to the memory of my father, Zev Caplan, who introduced me to the Yiddish stage. My father loved books, and books about Yiddish culture most of all. Dad, this one's for you.

Contents

Prologue

The Sun Never Sets on the Yiddish Stage

> You could say of Yiddish theater at one time that it was like the British Empire—the sun never set on it.
> —Joseph Buloff

Consider an unlikely scenario. In the midst of World War I, a motley group of Jewish refugees in their teens and early twenties becomes obsessed with the idea of creating a Yiddish art theater, modeled upon Stanislavsky's famous Russian company. By day they work as laborers, storekeepers, and housepainters; by night they teach themselves the basics of acting and stagecraft from outdated Russian and German books. The only theater they can afford is a dilapidated former circus on the outskirts of Vilna, repurposed by the occupying German army as a military stable. The roof leaks. The stage reeks of horse dung. It is a bitterly cold winter and since there is no money for heat, the actors rehearse with frozen limbs and thaw their stage makeup over the footlights. They eat one meal per day—a single boiled potato—and rehearsals are regularly interrupted when actors faint from hunger.

Within a few months, however, these same actors are performing in the most extravagant theater in their city, a building that has never before permitted Jews upon its stage. Within a year, their company has become a household name across Eastern Europe. In less than a decade, they are a global sensation with a reputation that stretches across Europe, North and South America, the Middle East, Australasia, Africa, and beyond.

This was the improbable rise of the Vilna Troupe (1915–36), a Yiddish theater company that became the interwar equivalent of a viral sensation between the two world wars. Its founders were wartime refugees who came together only after a Russian military decree forced them to evacuate the cities where their families had resided for generations. Most were scarcely out of their teens and had no formal theatrical training. Yet in spite of these obstacles, the Vilna Troupe became one of the most famous and influential Jewish theater companies in history.

Yiddish, the primary vernacular of Eastern European Jewry, had always held a low position within the multilingual hierarchy of Ashkenazic Jewish culture.[1] Hebrew was the holy language of the Torah and prayer, while Aramaic was the intellectual language of the Talmud and rabbinic law. Yiddish, the everyday vernacular of the masses, did not have the same linguistic prestige. Accordingly, Jewish intellectuals regarded the first generation of professional Yiddish theaters in the late nineteenth century as unworthy of serious attention. They derided the Yiddish stage in unsparing terms: in the words of one such intellectual, the Yiddish theater was nothing more than "a sea of manure" and "a flood of trash."[2] The Vilna Troupe was the first Jewish theater to achieve the respect of both intellectuals and theatergoers, along with a diverse global audience that cut across religious, linguistic, and national divides with unprecedented ease.

It was through the productions of the Vilna Troupe that hundreds of thousands of theatergoers around the world first saw Yiddish theater. For many, the encounter was significant. In Berlin, Max Reinhardt visited the actors backstage and told them that their *Dybbuk* was more than just theater; it was akin to a religious rite.[3] Broadway director David Belasco frequently attended Vilna Troupe performances in New York and wrote the actors fan mail, which the company translated and reprinted as full-page advertisements in the Yiddish press.[4] In Warsaw, major Polish directors, including Juliusz Osterwa, Leon Schiller, Alexander Zelwerowicz, and Stanisława Wysocka, regularly attended Vilna Troupe productions. In Brussels, Queen Elisabeth of Belgium attended a Vilna Troupe performance and invited members of the company to visit her box after the show.[5] Other devotees included George Bernard Shaw, Israel Zangwill, Eugene Ionesco, and Albert Einstein.[6]

These responses are all the more surprising considering that the Vilna Troupe performed exclusively in Yiddish, a language with historic low-culture associations that many of its well-heeled audience members did not speak or even understand. So why did this unlikely experiment succeed?

How can we account for the meteoric rise of this Yiddish company from an obscure group of teenage amateurs to a central fixture of the global theatrical avant-garde?

Yiddish Empire is the first book, in any language, to tell the story of this plucky band of Yiddish-speaking theatrical innovators, their persistent homelessness over the course of two decades, and their encounters with other artists as they traveled. I argue that the Vilna Troupe's unlikely success can be attributed to the company's embrace of itinerancy as its central organizing principle, ideology, and marketing strategy. I call this approach "multimodal transnationalism," by which I mean a method of theater making that is predicated upon multiple kinds of frequent and sustained movement across a large geographic territory. Traversing countries and continents as a matter of course, the members of the Vilna Troupe encountered new techniques, repertoire, and theatrical ideas, then adopted these globally sourced models into their own productions.

The name "the Vilna Troupe" implies a singular theater company with a fixed location: the city of Vilnius in what is now Lithuania or, as it was called in Yiddish, *Vilne*. Any actor who performed in the Vilna Troupe became forever known as a "Vilner," which means "that person from Vilna." But the company's name was merely part of the performance. The Vilna Troupe may have started in Vilna but it performed there only a handful of times after departing for its first tour in 1917. In reality, the members of the Vilna Troupe belonged to the global artistic networks established by the company, not to the Eastern European nations with rapidly shifting borders from whence they came.[7]

For the Vilna Troupe was no discrete theater company. It was a global network of Jewish performers who all adopted the same repertoire, style, and brand identity. Beginning with the first of many quarrels between Vilner in 1918 (sparked in this case by a love triangle and a surprise elopement), there were always several Vilna Troupes operating simultaneously and performing across a vast geographical territory. Encompassing ten companies, hundreds of actors, and dozens of directors and designers, the Vilna Troupe was a world theater on a scale unparalleled in its era.

The Vilna Troupe could be anywhere or anyone. In fact, it was more like *every*where and *every*one, encompassing nearly every place where Yiddish was spoken and including virtually every major figure of the interwar Yiddish stage among its ranks. A Vilna Troupe actor could expect to have the same loyal audience base and high-art reputation no matter where he or she traveled. The existence of multiple Vilna Troupe branches gave the

Figure 1. Vilna Troupe members departing from Hamburg Port, 1924. YIVO Institute for Jewish Research.

company the illusion of omnipresence, enabling it to develop a global reputation in the span of just a few years.

Of course, Yiddish actors were not the only performers to travel widely between the wars. But unlike other theater artists of the period, Yiddish performers traveled virtually without regard to national borders. Like today's global theater producers who can expect to find an English-speaking audience almost anywhere they go, Jewish theater artists between the wars could count on finding an audience who spoke their language almost anywhere. There was no distinction between "at home" and "abroad" for these performers. There was only Yiddishland—an expansive, imaginary Yiddish-speaking territory that never appeared on any map but was more real than any nation for migrant Jews of the early twentieth century—and the open road.[8]

The Vilna Troupe's Global Yiddish Stage

This book considers the Vilna Troupe as a turning point in global theater practice. In the midst of a Europe that had spent centuries consolidating cultural capital in national institutions, including national theaters, Jewish artists developed an alternative, transnational mode of theater making.[9]

The term *transnational* refers to individuals, organizations, and phenomena that operate across national borders.[10] Scholars like Christopher Balme, Nic Leonhardt, Derek Miller, and others have begun to investigate the historical dimensions of transnational theater, most recently in the inaugural 2016 issue of the *Journal of Global Theater History*. As Balme writes, "In many periods of European theater history, the provision of performance was entirely reliant on itinerant troupes," and yet "with the exception of the Italian commedia dell'arte companies, these practices have been little studied in comparison to the metropolitan theatrical cultures."[11] Accounting for the significance of global theater travelers, Balme notes, "requires a revaluation of certain concepts of theater history."[12]

Like Balme's subject Maurice Bandmann, who established a worldwide theater circuit, the Vilna Troupe's extreme mobility is precisely what excised it from theater history. But even in comparison with other globally mobile artists like Bandmann, the Vilna Troupe stands apart. Bandmann was an individual who traveled widely and worked with many theater companies, each of which had its own name and identity.[13] The Vilna Troupe, on the other hand, was not centered on any one individual. It was a global brand.

It was this characteristic of the Vilna Troupe—its global dispersal along with a brand identity that operated independently from any one individual or group of individuals—that set it apart from other traveling theater companies of the period. Plenty of theater artists traveled across oceans and continents in search of fame and fortune in the early twentieth century.[14] But the Vilna Troupe was different. Sarah Bernhardt may have toured widely across Europe, South America, Australia, and the United States, but she did so as an individual, like so many traveling performers of her generation.[15] There were, of course, other theater companies that traveled. The Moscow Art Theater, for example, toured across Europe beginning in 1906 and to the United States beginning in 1923. Like the Vilna Troupe, the Moscow Art Theater also had multiple branches and associated studios.[16] However, the Moscow Art Theater's tours were sporadic and of limited duration, and the company still retained its home base in Moscow while it was on tour.[17] We could also compare the Vilna Troupe to Habima, which left Russia and toured widely in 1926 before splitting into two branches, one in New York and the other in Tel Aviv.[18] But unlike the Vilna Troupe, which maintained multiple simultaneous branches for decades, the American branch of Habima was short-lived. Habima also did not begin to tour until eight years after the Vilna Troupe began its travels. Indeed, it is likely that the success of the Vilna Troupe's tours inspired Habima to go on the road.[19]

The Ballets Russes, a name that refers both to a famous dance company that performed across Europe and North and South America between 1909 and 1929, and later to a series of offshoots, was more analogous to the Vilna Troupe.[20] Like the Vilna Troupe, the Ballets Russes carried in its name a location where it hardly ever performed.[21] Like the Vilna Troupe, the Ballets Russes was not about any one dancer; in the words of one Ballets Russes historian, the company was instead "defined by its artistic identity and a commitment to ballet as a fine art."[22] Still, there were differences. The Ballets Russes was a *dance* company whose performances could be equally understood by speakers of any language. The Vilna Troupe, on the other hand, performed exclusively in Yiddish, a language decidedly unfamiliar to many of its spectators.

In fact, the Vilna Troupe shares more similarities with contemporary trends in global theater than with other theaters of its era. David Savran is among those who have argued that the contemporary stage is a globalized site in which national identity is becoming less and less significant.[23] Even Broadway, "the most U.S. American form of theater," Savran writes, is increasingly "stateless," "one node in a global network of . . . performances that has little regard for national borders."[24] Much the same could be said about the Vilna Troupe over a hundred years ago.

Yiddish theater has never been included in the emerging discourse on transnationalism. And yet, Eastern European Jews could be considered the archetypal modern transnationals. As historian Rebecca Kobrin has argued, any positioning of transnationalism as a postmodern or contemporary phenomenon automatically excludes Ashkenazic Jewish culture, which came of age in the context of large-scale forced and voluntary migrations in the nineteenth and twentieth centuries. "Transnationalism is nothing new," asserts Kobrin. "East European Jews behaved like the quintessential transnational migrants."[25] If Kobrin is right, then it stands to reason that their theater would have much to offer the scholar of transnational performance.

Most studies of global theater must still contend with the particular national-linguistic context from whence its artists emerged. An Italian actor performing in France is still an Italian actor, and regardless of personal preference or citizenship, he or she retains an inextricable link to a particular place and national identity. But Yiddish theater between the wars operated in the total absence of a national infrastructure. This posed many challenges to Yiddish theater artists but also allowed for an unusual degree of flexibility and innovation.

Yiddish theater artists and audiences were scattered around the world, without access to government subventions, dramatic academies, gilded performance spaces, or any of the other resources nationally based theaters often have at their disposal. The Vilna Troupe did not "go on tour" like the Moscow Art Theater or Habima; instead, we might say that the Vilna Troupe was *always* on tour. There was rarely a stable home to which the actors could return after their travels, rarely a building, town, city, or even country that "belonged" to the Vilna Troupe. Instead of representing a particular nation or territory, the Vilner envisioned themselves as representatives of a global Jewish culture.

The Vilner were completely itinerant, which meant they had little to lose in an artistic gamble. If a play was poorly received, if a politician spoke out against them, if taxes or regulations were too onerous, or if local interest vanished, they could simply pack up and move on to the next town, country, or continent. For example, in the late 1920s when Polish lawmakers imposed a draconian ten percent tax on productions of all plays by "foreign" writers, automatically including all Yiddish playwrights whether or not they were Polish citizens, the Vilna Troupe responded by leaving Warsaw in protest.[26] The Vilna Troupe's existence was so precarious that there was little incentive to be cautious.

The case of the Vilna Troupe offers the theater historian insight into how audiences and critics responded to an early itinerant theater phenomenon and poses questions that have not yet been addressed in the emerging discourse on transnational theater. Without a nation, how do theatrical ideas travel across borders? What can an itinerant-by-design theater achieve that is different from other theater companies? What happens to theater in the crossing between countries and cultures, in the spaces between?

Multimodal Transnationalism

The Vilna Troupe developed a transnational theater practice that relied upon several simultaneous types of movement across borders: structural, aesthetic, and economic. In designating the Vilna Troupe's transnationalism as multimodal, I follow sociologists Waldinger and Fitzgerald in foregrounding the multidirectionality of transnational activity—that is to say, a sustained pattern of multiple exits and entries across national borders.[27]

The Vilna Troupe's transnationalism was not a one-way street. Instead, personnel, branches, theatrical ideas, and repertoire traveled back and forth across national borders.

The Vilna Troupe's transnationalism operated concurrently on three axes:

1. *Structural transnationalism*—the steady migration of bodies across borders.

   The Vilna Troupe relied upon the constant cross-fertilization of Jewish directors, performances, designers, and theater critics across geographical borders. In fact, the Vilna Troupe was a network of geographically dispersed artists and companies, all of whom claimed the same affiliation.
2. *Artistic transnationalism*–the global circulation of aesthetic ideas, techniques, texts, and/or stylistic elements.

   The Vilna Troupe envisioned its geographical precariousness as a source of theatrical creativity. The company's productions drew inspiration from the influences its members encountered as they traveled.
3. *Economic transnationalism*—a global marketing and branding strategy.

   The structural and artistic transnationalism of the Vilna Troupe was augmented by the company's creation of a brand identity that also operated on a global scale, with a singular name and logo, a fixed performance style, and a shared repertoire. Any Yiddish theater artist who could demonstrate his or her connection to the Vilna Troupe could use this brand to market their work virtually anywhere in the world where Yiddish-speaking Jews resided. In the 1920s and 1930s, this was a substantial global population. By 1939 there were nearly 12 million Yiddish speakers worldwide, with millions each in Europe and North and South America, hundreds of thousands in Asia, and tens of thousands in Africa and Australia.[28]

Taken together, these strategies allowed the troupe to experiment with theater in ways that often surprised and delighted their audiences. Even as each incarnation of the Vilna Troupe denied the existence of the others, all of the branches remained remarkably consistent in their repertoire and aesthetic. Indeed, the Vilna Troupe branches were in constant communication, as actors and directors frequently switched affiliations to settle artistic differences, to solve romantic quarrels, or to suit personal preferences. A successful production by any branch of the Vilna Troupe would often lead to a nearly identical production by the other branches in rapid succession. The Vilna Troupe's global reputation was a product of its seemingly uncanny ability to appear present in multiple places at once.

The Vilna Troupe thus bears a strong resemblance to precisely the kinds of global theater circulation that we see today—like Cirque du Soleil or Disney Theatrical Group or the global branding of international tours of Broadway musicals, which often run simultaneously in multiple countries with the same logo, staging, aesthetic, and design.[29] The Vilner were prescient in seeing the potential of global theater and recognizing the artistic and economic advantages it could offer. Today the methods of the Vilna Troupe—frequent back-and-forth travel, global branding, simultaneous performance—are common features of the contemporary stage. The Vilna Troupe thus represents a bridge between nineteenth-century models of theatrical travel, based primarily upon the voyages of individual performers and impresarios, and contemporary multimodal transnational theater.

Theater historians have traditionally regarded the Yiddish stage as a peripheral tradition on the outskirts of theater history. Yiddish theater does not appear even once in Oscar Brockett and Franklin Hildy's seminal *History of the Theatre*, nor is it mentioned a single time in John Russell Brown's *The Oxford Illustrated History of Theatre*, David Wiles's and Christine Dymkowski's *The Cambridge Companion to Theatre History*, or Phillip B. Zarrilli, Bruce McConachie, Gary Jay Williams, and Carol Fisher Sorgenfrei's otherwise relatively comprehensive *Theatre Histories: An Introduction*.[30] When included, more often than not, it is treated as peripheral, arcane, or a mere prelude to the rich history of American Jewish actors performing in English.[31]

This book challenges that stance by suggesting that Jewish performers were seminal in the development of twentieth-century theater. From the perspective of any one national theater history, the Vilna Troupe was indeed marginal. It is only when we reconsider the company through a "global optic" (as Margaret Werry has called for) that we can see how large these artists actually loomed.[32] The Vilna Troupe modeled the artistic and economic rewards of global theater before a diverse audience that included many of the most prominent artists of the twentieth century, including Reinhardt, Belasco, Clurman, Ionesco, and dozens of others. In arguing for the Vilna Troupe's centrality to modern theater history, I am suggesting that we cannot fully understand these artists or their work without accounting for the activities of these traveling Yiddish performers. The story of the Vilna Troupe, I contend, is no minority branch of theater history but rather one of its most central and little-known chapters.

Innovations and Influence

The Vilna Troupe forever altered the Yiddish stage. Prior to the Vilna Troupe, Yiddish theater revolved around its star actors. As Edna Nahshon described the first generation of Yiddish theater performers in New York, "At the heart of their world stood the actor, not the text, and acting was considered most commendable when it hoisted primal emotions to fever pitch."[33] Outsiders rarely came to the Yiddish theater, and audiences were almost entirely composed of Yiddish-speaking Jews.[34] Reformers like Y. L. Peretz and Jacob Gordin agitated for a "better" Yiddish theater, with less melodrama and more literary plays, but their efforts had limited success.[35]

Beginning in 1915, the Vilna Troupe dramatically expanded ideas about what Yiddish theater was, whom it was for, and what it could achieve. Inspired by the Moscow Art Theater, the Vilna Troupe introduced ensemble acting (in which each actor focuses on contributing to the group rather than on his or her individual performance) to the Yiddish stage. The Vilna Troupe also built new relationships between Yiddish theater makers and the Yiddish literary establishment and required actors to demonstrate their literary knowledge before performing. Later, the Vilna Troupe was responsible for introducing modernism to the Yiddish stage.

But the impact of the Vilna Troupe extended far beyond Yiddish theater. The Vilna Troupe produced the world premiere of *The Dybbuk* in 1920 and brought its production to hundreds of thousands of spectators around the world; today, *The Dybbuk* remains an iconic play that has inspired dozens of productions, with no decade since 1920 without a *Dybbuk* production happening somewhere.[36] The company served as a major transatlantic and transhemispheric conduit for dramatic repertoire between the wars: for example, as we will see in chapter 4, the company was the first to bring Eugene O'Neill to the Polish stage. The Vilna Troupe also pioneered the use of projection technology in Poland in the 1920s. In fact, an entire generation of groundbreaking scenic designers—including Mordecai Gorelik, Sam Leve, and Boris Aronson in the United States and Szymon Syrkus and Andrzej Pronaszko in Poland—learned their craft working alongside former Vilner.

The Vilna Troupe's impact also extended to the individuals and theater companies that it inspired. Dozens of Yiddish theater companies emerged between the wars inspired, directly or indirectly, by the Vilna Troupe. While most theater companies of the period had a relatively stable membership (Habima, for example, had 74 members over fifty years), the Vilna Troupe had 290 members, many of whom were involved with the company only briefly, in scarcely two decades.[37] Even the Moscow Art Theater, with its large membership rolls, retained "a solid kernel of permanence" in its personnel.[38] The unusually quick turnover in Vilna Troupe membership meant that veterans often had long careers in other theater companies after leaving. Among the Yiddish theater companies led by former Vilner were

- **In Poland**: Akord, Azazel, Balaganeydn, Bialystok State Yiddish Theater, Khad-Gadyo, FAKT (Fareynikter Idisher Kunst Teater), Folks un Yugnt Teater, Goldfadn Fareyn, Ida Kaminska Theater, Krokever Yidish Kunst Teater, Lemberg State Yiddish Theater, Lower Silesian Yiddish Theater, Melokhishe Yidishe Miniatur Teater, Moldovan State Jewish Theater, Nay Azazel, Orpheus Yiddish Laborers Theater, Vilner Yidish Folks Teater, VYKT (Varshever Yidisher Kunst Teater), VNIT (Varshever Nayer Idisher Teater), Yiddish Folk Theater, Yung Teater
- **In Latvia**: Nayer Yidisher Teater, Riger Yidishn Meutim Teater
- **In Romania:** BITS (Bukhareshter Idisher Teater Studiye)
- **In Russia**: Birobidzhan State Yiddish Theater
- **In the United States**: Bronx Art Theater, Chicago Dramatishe Gezelshaft, Ensemble Art Theater, Jewish Art Theater, New Yiddish Art Theater, Nit Gedayget!, Second Avenue Theater, Unzer Teater, Yiddish Theater Unit of the Federal Theater Project
- **In France**: PYAT (Parizer Yidisher Arbeter Teater)
- **In Belgium**: Yiddish Folk Theater, Brussels
- **In Brazil**: São Paulo Dramatic Circle
- **In Australia**: Dovid Herman Theater
- **In South Africa**: Cape Zionist Society Amateur Drama Club, Fareynikter Yidisher Kultur Front Studio, Idisher Folks Teater, Johannesburg Dramatic Studio, Paarl Dramatic Circle

Many of these companies adopted the Vilna Troupe's repertoire and/or elements of its aesthetic. Others featured numerous actors, directors, or designers who were also Vilner. Maurice Schwartz's Yiddish Art Theater in New York City included a total of thirty-one former Vilna Troupe members.[39] Seven individuals started their careers in the Vilna Troupe before joining the Moscow State Yiddish Theater (better known by its Russian acronym, GOSET).[40] Leyb Kadison, Dovid Likht, Jacob Ben-Ami, Joseph Buloff, Leon Liebgold, Mordechai Yachson, Leola Vendorf, and Jacob Rotbaum all worked with the Vilna Troupe before joining the Folksbiene.

Former Vilner were also involved with dozens of non-Yiddish theater companies and cultural organizations. After fleeing Poland in 1940, Zygmunt Turkow directed Portuguese productions for several prominent Brazilian theater companies.[41] In Tel Aviv, former Vilner acted in Habima and the Zavit Theater, directed for the Cameri Theater, designed for the Ohel Theater, founded and danced in the Israel Ballet Company, and played in the Israel Philharmonic Orchestra.[42] In Poland, designer Andrzej Pronaszko followed his Vilna Troupe period by designing productions for Teatr Reduta and the National Theater of Warsaw.[43] No other company in the history of Jewish theater ever had such a wide-ranging impact.

The Art of Itinerancy

Yiddish Empire asks how itinerancy influences what gets produced on stage. What are the artistic outcomes of travel? Of exile? Of diaspora?

The Vilna Troupe reimagined Jewish geographical insecurity as a gateway to the global, cosmopolitan theater of the future. Inspired by the Vilna Troupe, Yiddish theater between the wars became known as much for its artistic inventiveness as for its global scope. Indeed, these two characteristics were inextricably linked.

The Vilna Troupe's embrace of itinerancy was a radical inversion of the accepted logic of the economics of theatrical production. While other theaters of the period were growing their subscribers, cultivating wealthy donors, and building permanent buildings for their companies, the Vilna Troupe traveled virtually nonstop.[44] Conventional wisdom told theater producers that traveling theater was both difficult and costly. Travel meant time not performing; being on the road meant spending without earning. This explains why the Vilna Troupe never achieved financial stability, despite its many critical successes. And yet, the Vilna Troupe continued to travel, demonstrating how a fully itinerant theater could survive and thrive.

The Vilna Troupe had to design all of its productions to travel across great distances. Each set piece had to fit, dismantled, into a train car. Props and costumes were designed to be lightweight and to occupy the minimum space possible. Every lighting design had to be reproducible in a range of performance spaces, from grand proscenium stages in Europe's urban capitals to converted barns and hastily erected tents in rural hamlets. As the vernacular theater tradition of a nomadic people, Yiddish theater had always required its artists to improvise, but actors, directors, and critics had long lamented that all of this wandering prevented the Yiddish stage from reaching the artistic heights of its peers. The Vilna Troupe was the first Jewish theater to leverage its itinerant circumstances as creative fodder.

The Vilner drew upon everything that they encountered in their travels and fused it together to create unique and memorable productions. The stylistic elements that critics lauded as "innovative" were more often than not borrowed from other theater artists: the ensemble-based style of the Moscow Art Theater, the romanticism of Stanisław Wyspiański, the directing style of Max Reinhardt, the stylized modernism of the experimental Polish stage, the flexible staging of Adolphe Appia and his followers, the constructivism of Meyerhold, and repertoire drawn equally from Eastern Europe, Western Europe, and the Americas—all combined with elements drawn from liturgical melodies, synagogue aesthetics, and the gestural vocabulary of traditional Jewish religious practice.

This strategy of global borrowing, in which elements from a wide range of non-Jewish avant-gardes were fused together with distinctly Jewish influences, enabled the Vilna Troupe to attract unprecedentedly diverse audiences to the Yiddish theater. It was not unusual for a Vilna Troupe audience to include impoverished rural Jews sitting side by side with prominent non-Jewish intellectuals, Russian and German military commanders seated next to Yiddish-speaking refugees, or religious Jews in dark coats and fur hats next to politicians and even European royalty. Vilna Troupe programs typically included fully bilingual cast and crew listings, playwright biographies, and extensive scene-by-scene plot summaries for non-Yiddish speakers.[45] The Vilna Troupe's highly theatrical, visually arresting production style also contributed to its appeal.

The Vilna Troupe was a theater of itinerancy that thrived on movement, a theater that viewed cultural hodgepodge, amalgamation, and fusion as artistically inspired. The Yiddish theater of the Vilna Troupe was an artistic response to the diasporic dispersal of the Jewish people. It was also a coping mechanism that allowed nomadic performers to access a sense of belonging no matter where they traveled.

Individually, the actors may have longed for a home, but collectively, the Vilna Troupe was able to create innovative theater because of its perpetual homelessness. Simply put, these performers believed that the Yiddish theater—itinerant, global, teetering on the edge of economic and political precariousness—was, precisely for these reasons, ideally positioned to stand at the vanguard of the modern stage.

Methodology

A book about the Vilna Troupe is a study in contradictions. The Vilna Troupe was founded in Vilna but had only the most tangential connections to the city. The Vilna Troupe was simultaneously a discrete cultural institution and a cluster of independent theater companies. In repertoire and aesthetic, the Vilna Troupe was equal parts Jewish, European, American, transcontinental, and transhemispheric. Like the subtitle of *The Dybbuk*, the Vilna Troupe's greatest hit, the company was perpetually "between two worlds."

This book evaluates the Vilna Troupe from several methodological angles. I draw heavily upon archival material, primarily reviews, programs, photographs, letters, and other documents preserved by the actors. Many of these documents have never before been explored; on several occasions I found myself opening boxes of archival documents that had been taped shut decades earlier. The obscurity of many of these artists also required digging beyond traditional archives. I contacted relatives of dozens of Vilna Troupe descendants, who graciously shared programs, posters, photographs, scrapbooks, clippings, and stories not present in any library. Along the way, I collected oral histories, examined family photo albums, and watched home videos of aging Vilner. I gleaned small details about their personalities through the objects they preserved. I held Joseph Buloff's shaving kit and makeup case, still in impeccable shape decades later, and imagined the actor looking into the mirror as he prepared for a role. I drank tea next to Noah Nachbush's samovar, a giant metal contraption that he carried with him across oceans and continents. Each find added a piece to the puzzle.

In addition to archival material and interviews, this book also draws upon digital methodologies, including data visualization and digital mapping. These methodologies enable a macrohistorical account of the Vilna Troupe that takes the individual stories of all of its artists into consideration. I used digital tools to find and analyze patterns in data in order to zoom out on the story of this massive theater company and visualize its scope and impact. I collected and analyzed data about Vilna Troupe members, their geographical movements, and their personal and professional connections from Zalmen Zylbercweig's seven-volume reference work *Leksikon fun yidishn teater* (*Encyclopedia of the Yiddish Theater*); from listings of names, dates, plays, and locations from hundreds of Vilna Troupe programs found in the archival collections of individual actors at the YIVO Institute for Jewish Research, the Harvard Library Judaica Division, the Billy Rose Theater Division and the Dorot Jewish Division of the New York Public Library, and Columbia University's Jewish Studies Collection; from the Internet Broadway Database and the Internet Movie Database; and from interviews that I conducted with the living descendants of Vilna Troupe members.[46]

Structure

Yiddish Empire consists of five chronological chapters interspersed with narrative interludes. A companion website (www.vilnatroupe.com) provides visualizations of the Vilna Troupe's travels and its members' personal and professional networks. By providing multiple points of entry into the story of the Vilna Troupe, I hope that readers will emerge with the fullest possible sense of its complexity, its global scope, its larger-than-life personalities, and its historical significance.

I begin by introducing the cultural and historical dynamics that shaped Jewish theater and consider the conditions that enabled the Vilna Troupe's emergence. First I examine the fraught historical relationship between Jews and theater. Next I turn to the Vilna Troupe's primary precursor: the early twentieth-century theater reform campaign of the Yiddish writer Y. L. Peretz. In the last decade of his life, Peretz became obsessed with revolutionizing the Yiddish stage. The result was a series of failed attempts that, nonetheless, started an important new conversation about the role of theater in modern Jewish life.

Chapter 2 considers the geographic dislocation of Jews during World War I as the primary catalyst for the Vilna Troupe's formation. I show how wartime displacement shaped the company's every move in its first years, from repertoire selection and rehearsal process to production aesthetics and audience, and examine why this set of circumstances enabled the Vilna Troupe to succeed where other ambitious Yiddish theaters had failed. Finally, I trace how the Vilna Troupe discovered its signature formula of itinerancy and artistic innovation during its first tour.

Chapter 3 examines the production history of An-sky's *The Dybbuk*, first staged in 1920 by the Vilna Troupe. *The Dybbuk* is arguably the most influential Jewish play of the modern period. The Vilna Troupe's world premiere production of *The Dybbuk* (with two nearly identical productions by two distinct branches) propelled the company to international acclaim and secured its reputation as an avant-garde theater of significance. More than any other production, *The Dybbuk* enabled the Vilna Troupe's rapid global expansion, from Eastern Europe to Western Europe and North and South America. I discuss how the Vilna Troupe's *Dybbuk* inspired other Jewish theater companies, including Habima and the Yiddish Art Theater, to stage *Dybbuk*s of their own and trace how the Vilna Troupe's success sparked the formation of dozens of new Yiddish art theaters with strikingly similar repertoires and aesthetics. This chapter also considers a second, equally iconic and experimental, Vilna Troupe production of Osip Dimov's *The Singer of His Sorrows* in 1924.

The fourth chapter examines the theatrical innovations of the Vilna Troupe during the company's most creative period: the late 1920s. I argue that these avant-garde contributions were accidental byproducts of the unique economic, political, and social position of Jewish theater artists during this period. Finally, *Yiddish Empire*'s fifth chapter assesses the Vilna Troupe's lasting impact against the backdrop of the company's decline and dissolution in the 1930s.

The interludes tell the stories that fill in the gaps. The Vilner led fascinating lives—full of intrigue and romance, ambition and folly, heady ideals and crushing disappointments—lives so dramatic that at times they seem almost like fiction. In the four interludes, you will learn what inspired young Jewish men and women across Eastern Europe to leave their homes and families behind and become traveling performers. You will read of the dramatic elopement of the Vilna Troupe power couple Sonia Alomis and Alexander Asro and of the many others who fell in love backstage, along with the romantic trysts on trains, heartbreaking affairs, and onstage weddings that followed. You will catch a glimpse of the backstage atmosphere, the long train rides, and the rivalries and intrigues that took place in these spaces. You will hear the stories of the actors' children, of how some traveled the world with their parents, doing homework backstage during shows, and how others were left behind. The final interlude documents the fates of Vilna Troupe actors during the Holocaust; those who survived and those who perished, those whose careers saved them when they happened to be on tour when the war broke out, and those who kept on performing amid the worst horrors, even in Auschwitz. In presenting these individual stories alongside the collective experience of the company, I aim to document how the large political, social, and economic forces described in the chapters affected individuals.

Theater without Borders

In 1919 two longtime Vilna Troupe members, Mordechai Mazo and Isaac Samberg, along with a few other Yiddish actors and directors, founded Poland's first Jewish Actors' Union (Yidisher Artistn Fareyn, also known by its acronym, YAF).[47] Officially, according to its registration with the Polish government, the YAF was simply the Jewish equivalent of the Union of Polish Theater Artists. But in practice, the YAF's activities extended far beyond Poland.

According to correspondence found in the archives of the YAF, both the Polish union and the YAF appear to have been members of a short-lived International Union of Theater Artists, a federation of twenty-one theater unions from across Europe and the United States, based in Vienna.[48] Every other organization in the federation represented artists from a single country. The Dansk Skuespillerforbund represented Danish actors, the Svenska Teaterförbundet represented Swedish actors, and the Budapesti Színészek Szövetsége represented Hungarian actors. Only in Yiddish did actors unionize across national borders.

In official documents, the YAF maintained the fiction that it was a national actors' union just like the others, but its membership rolls reveal a different picture. At any given time, nearly a quarter of the YAF's active members resided outside of Poland. In 1926, for example, there were 324 actors registered as members of the YAF, 62 of whom resided abroad.[49] The union's correspondence with its actors and directors reveals that even those who provided permanent addresses in Poland were out of the country more often than not. The YAF thus maintained active correspondence with members in twenty-five countries.[50]

There could be no such thing as a national actors' union for the artists of the interwar Yiddish theater. Theirs was a stage with outposts everywhere that Ashkenazi Jews resided. More than any other group, the Vilna Troupe was responsible for transforming the Yiddish stage into a global theater. Indeed, the Vilna Troupe's supporters cultivated the notion that the company's success heralded a new era of cosmopolitanism for the Yiddish stage. As one imagined,

> Soon there will be such a strong link between the Yiddish theaters of America and Europe that companies will travel from Warsaw to New York, just as today actors set out on a tour from New York to Boston or from Chicago to Detroit. *The very notion of great distance*

> *is vanishing altogether*, and soon there will come a time when, if a Yiddish theater company from America is on their way to Europe and realizes that somebody forgot to bring along Dovid Moyshele's beard, they will simply send the stage manager on an airplane from the middle of the ocean, and he will meet the company in Europe with the beard.[51]

There is a prescience to this vision; today actors do set out on tour from Warsaw to New York (and to and from places far beyond) with the same regularity and expectations as an actor in the 1920s booking a train from Cleveland to Milwaukee. This vision of a globally interconnected theater has indeed come to pass.

As members of a diasporic theater tradition that was most at home traveling between nations, the Vilner were uniquely able to transmit theatrical ideas across borders in a period long before advances in transportation and communication would enable virtually any theater artist to exert a global presence. This is the story of their unlikely theatrical revolution.

CHAPTER 1

Spectacular Failures

Jewish Theater as Cultural Frontier

This is a thing that I didn't understand. Why I was drawn to it. My environment naturally was against it all.
—Jacob Ben-Ami, 1973

Baruch Lumet was a cantor's son who planned to follow in his father's footsteps. But when he was just six years old, his father died suddenly in an accident.[1] The boy was sent to live with his uncle in Warsaw and apprenticed to a tailor. Baruch was too little and clumsy to do much in the tailor's shop, so the tailor's wife tasked him with taking care of their baby. The boy took long walks through the streets of Warsaw, pushing the baby carriage and taking in the sights and sounds of the big city. It was on one of these walks that Baruch first discovered the theater.

The boy started showing up at the Yiddish theater in his new neighborhood every day, feeding the baby bottles while he peered in from the doorway. One day, the show was short a few extras. A kindly stage manager offered Baruch and the baby free admission in exchange for joining a crowd onstage.[2] The boy with the baby carriage followed directions and did well. The actors asked him to come back and be an extra again, but by the time he returned, the troupe had already moved on to another city.[3]

But the boy had caught the theater bug. He made it his goal to find another theater and somehow save enough money to buy a ticket. When Baruch finally managed to see his first full play, he was mesmerized:

> Little boys walked with the Sefer Torahs, with the scrolls up to the stage, singing "La-ta-ta-tam-ta-ta, *pintele yid*, La-ta-ta-tam-ta-ta, *pintele yid*." That's something unusual, and then the scene changed to another place, the woods. I mean, my God, how can they do. . . . Here's a house, here's the woods, how do they do it? And then they changed back to a synagogue. I didn't realize that it's all scenery. . . . Scene changes. I didn't know a thing about it. And everything was like magic to me.[4]

A few years after attending his first performance, Baruch Lumet would join the Vilna Troupe and become a professional Yiddish actor. Later, his son and protégé, Sidney Lumet, would go on to become one of the most prolific filmmakers of the twentieth century. But when Baruch was a child, the Lumet family's involvement in theater and film was no foregone conclusion. It was the product of a complete revolution in Jewish cultural life.

Yiddish theater came of age in a single generation. When the first professional Yiddish theaters emerged in the 1870s, Jewish intellectuals were quick to dismiss them. A few decades and a world war later, Yiddish actors were brushing arms with the global cultural elite. How did this transformation happen?

Between 1905 and the beginning of the First World War, what became known as the *teater-frage* (theater question) became the subject of vigorous debate among Jewish writers and intellectuals. A group of writers based in Warsaw organized to create a new kind of Yiddish theater modeled upon the Moscow Art Theater—a "Yiddish art theater" with educated actors, a literary repertoire, lengthy rehearsal periods, thoughtful designs, and well-behaved audiences. For too long, these writers lamented in the pages of Warsaw's Jewish newspapers, intellectuals had neglected the Yiddish stage in favor of Yiddish literature. In relegating theatrical activity to the background of Jewish culture, these critics argued, writers had allowed the Yiddish stage to become contaminated with *shund*—a pejorative term for trashy, raucous, poorly written, melodramatic, and anti-intellectual entertainment.[5] The Yiddish stage did not merely need reform, they contended. It required a total revolution.

This chapter introduces the historical and cultural dynamics that shaped Jewish theater prior to World War I along with the first attempts of Jewish writers to reform it, most of which failed. These writers may not have achieved their goals in the short term, but their all-too-public flops drew attention to the state of Yiddish theater and ultimately laid the groundwork for the Vilna Troupe's subsequent emergence. Like any good spectacle, these failures made audiences take a closer look.

The Problem with Yiddish Theater

Yiddish theater was an upstart enterprise that came to the table exceptionally late compared to other European theaters. It was also a double exile. Internally, theater was confined to the outskirts of Jewish culture; externally, Yiddish culture was on the margins of European society. From both angles, Yiddish theater was what sociologist Everett C. Hughes has called a "bastard institution" that lay "outside the realm of respectability."[6]

Decades after the emergence of modern Jewish literature in Yiddish and Hebrew, there was no professional Jewish theater in either language. The first professional Yiddish theaters were founded in the mid-1870s, while there was no professional Hebrew theater until Habima was founded in 1918.[7] According to Alexander Mukdoni, one of Baruch Lumet's Warsaw contemporaries, Jewish theater in the mid-nineteenth century was like a waiter at a wedding to which he had not been invited.[8] The metaphorical marriage was that between Jewish culture and modern literature. For the first generation of modern Jewish writers, the stage was a source of embarrassment. For those who followed, however, the stage would become their frontier.

Yiddish, the primary vernacular of Eastern European Jewry for nearly a thousand years, had long been associated with low culture by Jews and non-Jews alike. But until the late nineteenth century, Yiddish was considered inappropriate for art, literature, scholarship, or anything more serious than everyday banter. True, there were Yiddish books, but the cultural elite thought of them as suitable only "for women and the uneducated masses."[9] To Jewish intellectuals, Yiddish was an impure, bastardized form of German, a *zhargon* (jargon) and not a language. Indeed, *zhargon* was what most people called the language well into the first years of the twentieth century, including many of its first modern writers.[10] The name Yiddish (meaning "Jewish") became popular only later with the emergence of a younger generation of writers who wanted more legitimacy for their literature. In the late nineteenth century, these writers succeeded in building a thriving Yiddish literary culture.[11]

But Jewish theater lagged behind. To begin with, stringent religious prohibitions had hindered its development for centuries. In the Talmud, the ancient rabbis called the theater *moshav letsim*, or "the seat of scoffers."[12] Traditional Jews frowned upon women singing in public, upon male cross-dressing, and upon Jews dressing like gentiles.[13] Theatrical activity was officially permitted only one day per year, on the Jewish holiday of Purim, when bands of amateur players performed semi-improvised plays based on biblical stories in private homes.[14]

The first professional Yiddish theater artists—beginning with Avrom Goldfaden in Romania in the 1870s—were thus transgressors who disrupted long held antitheatrical prejudices. The very act of writing a play in Yiddish—the vernacular at the bottom of the multilingual Jewish linguistic hierarchy—went against dominant cultural norms.[15] Most Jewish writers were fluent in many languages, including Hebrew and Yiddish as well as European tongues like German, French, Polish, and Russian. Writing in Yiddish was a choice, not a default. Performing that Yiddish play—against the advice of Talmudic sages and contemporary Rabbinical authorities alike—was even more transgressive. Staging a play in Yiddish drew attention and provoked objections. Though this opposition softened over time, Yiddish performers always remained hyperconscious of their stage's early associations with illegitimacy.

These associations came simultaneously from within the Jewish community and from the outside world. Without a nation to call its own, Yiddish theater was subject to the unpredictable political, social, and economic currents of Jewish life. Less than a decade after the emergence of the first professional Yiddish companies, the Russian imperial government enacted a blanket ban on all Yiddish performances in 1883. Still, Yiddish theater continued, albeit underground. The ban's enforcement depended upon the whims of local officials and censors, and some were stricter than others.[16] Though it failed to prevent Yiddish theater entirely, the ban deepened the chasm between Jewish literary culture and the popular theater of the masses. For Jewish writers who sought to build a culture that would be recognized by their European neighbors, the illegal Yiddish theater could not be included or even acknowledged. Jewish intellectuals thus ignored the covert Yiddish performances that existed in pockets of the empire between 1883 and 1905, preferring instead to attend the legal Polish- and Russian-language theaters.[17]

Largely due to the ban, Yiddish theater was geographically dispersed almost from its very inception. After the assassination of Tsar Alexander II in 1881, the Russian government imposed repressive anti-Jewish measures that spurred performers to become increasingly nomadic, fleeing pogroms and mass evictions along with the rest of Russia's millions of Jews. Between

1881 and 1903, to cite just one example, Avrom Goldfaden opened productions in Lemberg, Paris, Bucharest, and New York.[18] As actors and audience members traveled, they brought their theater with them. By the turn of the century, there were Yiddish theater companies from Warsaw to London to New York, and even further outposts like Johannesburg and Kyrgyzstan.[19] These companies operated independently from one another. In the late nineteenth century, the global Yiddish press that would later enable close communication between migrant performers was still in its infancy.

In 1905, in the aftermath of the first Russian Revolution, the ban on Yiddish theater was relaxed. Though it was not officially lifted, the overall weakening of tsarist absolutism led many to believe that the ban no longer applied. Russian and Yiddish newspapers mistakenly reported that the ban had been withdrawn, and most local authorities stopped enforcing the law.[20] This perceived retraction had an immediate impact on urban Jewish intellectuals. For the first time in twenty-two years, they began to seriously consider the role of the stage in Jewish culture. Inspired by the revolutionary atmosphere of 1905, Jewish writers began to imagine a theatrical revolution that would bring modern Yiddish culture to the world.[21]

As the Yiddish theater ban was relaxed, the Russian government also loosened its censorship of the Yiddish press. Less than a year after the government loosened its publishing restrictions, Warsaw had five Yiddish dailies, with a combined circulation of nearly one hundred thousand readers.[22] A debate over the future of the Yiddish stage soon emerged in the pages of these new publications, providing an unprecedented opportunity for Jewish intellectuals to discuss Yiddish theater with the masses.

Spectacular Failures

In 1905 the writer Yitskhok Leybush Peretz (1852–1915) was *the* central figure of modern Yiddish literature.[23] Aspiring literati flocked to Warsaw to earn his approval. Teenagers who loved Peretz's writing would follow him on his daily walks through Warsaw's Saxon Garden.[24] We might imagine Peretz, as the leading architect of Yiddish literary culture, resting on his laurels as he aged. Instead, in the last decade of his life, Peretz became obsessed with reforming the Yiddish stage.

In order to properly stage literary work, Peretz decided, he would first need to reform what he saw as the excesses of the Yiddish stage. As with all of Peretz's projects, a group of intellectuals followed his lead. They dedicated their careers to Yiddish theater reform, creating what amounted to an unofficial school of theater criticism. Beginning in 1905, this group—which included playwright Yankev Dinezon, writer A. Vayter, director Dovid Herman, and theater critic Alexander Mukdoni—expounded their demands in articles, letters, and reviews in the Warsaw Jewish press. To these writers, reforming the Yiddish stage was a matter of urgent import upon which the very future of Jewish culture depended.

Their first task would be to convince readers that Warsaw's well-attended Yiddish theaters needed improvement. This was no simple charge. Within a few months of the relaxation of the ban, Warsaw was home to three thriving Yiddish theaters.[25] And yet, to Peretz and his friends, these theaters produced nothing but *shund*.[26] A few years later, Dovid Pinski, an American Yiddish playwright and friend of Peretz's, would analogize the development of the Yiddish theater to the three-act structure of a play. The first "act" of Yiddish theater was *shund*—theater with the sole purpose of entertaining the audience. With Peretz's efforts, Pinski argued, the Yiddish theater had entered the second act of its development: an era hovering on the border between *shund* and art, when content became more important and the characters more lifelike; yet the plays still drew upon melodramatic elements to entertain audiences. In the third act yet to come, Pinski told readers, these *shund* characteristics would disappear entirely and Yiddish drama would be based upon pure artistic principles.[27]

Of course, the distinction between literary theater and *shund* was subjective. Indeed, Peretz was never able to provide a clear definition of what distinguished "artistic" Yiddish theater from its trashier counterparts. And what of work that straddled the border, like the occasional melodrama penned by a self-styled "literary" writer like Jacob Gordin?[28] Peretz and his colleagues shied away from these questions. In practice, *shund* was, to a large extent, anything that Jewish intellectuals thought of as beneath them.

Peretz launched his campaign against *shund* theater in Warsaw's Yiddish newspapers. The Yiddish stage was "like a pot of stew in the marketplace," he wrote in 1906, "and whatever you throw in, cooks; what's yours, what's stolen, what's fresh, what's old, even what's tainted."[29] Worse still, Peretz charged, Warsaw's Yiddish theaters were steeped in "impurity": the haphazard jumbling of dramatic genres; the unattributed amalgamation of original and plagiarized material; the mixing of various staging techniques and styles in performance.[30] Yiddish theater, he charged, was "like Noah's ark with all of the animals, a catchall of song, dance, movement, screaming, and crying."[31] Peretz's colleagues followed his lead, writing scathing reviews that referred to the productions of Warsaw's Yiddish theaters as "a flood of trash."[32]

Peretz's articles, some under his own name and others under the sardonic pen name "Lucifer," described the Warsaw Yiddish stage in unsparing terms: a "disgrace," "dangerous," "inappropriate," and "diseased." When an educated Jew attends a Yiddish play, Peretz wrote,

> He feels that it is a lie! That it is a spider web and that everything is foreign to him, tremendously and impossibly foreign, every word, every gesture, every movement. . . . As soon as he can, he runs to the truth—to the real Gentile theater, where every word has its real meaning. . . . Where those who move about the stage are living people, not talking mannequins, and in their veins flows blood, not colored water; where you cry because it hurts, and you laugh when it is truly enjoyable![33]

For Peretz, the greatest crime of the contemporary Yiddish stage was its nonrealistic theatricality. Ironically, Peretz and his colleagues located the authenticity missing from Yiddish theater on the European stage, where realism was in vogue. Peretz's campaign for reforming Yiddish theater was in part a plea for theatrical realism in the guise of Jewish "authenticity."

Paradoxically, Peretz continued attending the same melodramatic productions that he disparaged, staging demonstrative protests from the audience. He often invited colleagues to join him in storming out of *shund* performances whenever something offended him. The young writers who accompanied him on these outings were often shocked to find their mentor enjoying parts of the show. As the Yiddish writer Yankev Dinezon told the actor Boaz Young,

> Peretz swelled with pride at the singing and the dancing. But when the melodrama came to its dramatic section, he stood up and demonstratively left the theater. With us went a quarter of the audience. Peretz came back in when they began to sing and dance again.[34]

If Peretz's goal was simply to agitate against *shund*, then why did he return for the big musical number? Moreover, why did the Yiddish theater's most vehement critic continue to attend production after production? Peretz's answer depended on who was asking. To playwright Peretz Hirschbein, he replied that he enjoyed the "folksy" musical numbers but remained offended by the lowbrow quality of the dialogue.[35] To the Yiddish actor Boaz Young, Peretz proclaimed, "I would rather see a nice joke in the Yiddish theater than the . . . much-advertised non-Jewish literary plays."[36] Peretz's continued attendance at these productions reveals that even he was not immune to the charms of Warsaw's Yiddish theaters, though he would never admit it.

Others were less forgiving of *shund* theater's faults. When Alexander Mukdoni first arrived in Warsaw in 1909 after several years in Western Europe, he took Peretz's advice and reviewed productions at each of Warsaw's three Yiddish theaters. He was appalled by what he observed.

> I left the theater depressed. The play, the acting, and the audience—especially the audience—made the most dreadful impression on me. This audience laughed with their mouths pried open and sobbed crudely. . . . Between the acts was a gluttonous buffet, a drunken orgy, people flung glasses of whiskey into their mouths, they gnawed on chicken drumsticks, they swallowed roasted gizzards, they ate standing up, and everyone's mouths were stuffed full with entire goose gizzards and livers. Their faces became terribly coarse, their eyes gluttonous, and their necks swollen. I left the theater in such a miserable mood that I could not even begin to write my review.[37]

By invoking anti-Semitic tropes of vulgar Jewish physiognomy and behavior, Mukdoni positioned *shund* as a dangerous contaminant that had the potential to undermine the very legitimacy of Jewish culture. In another review, Mukdoni called the spectators at the Muranover Theater "the most primitive in the world."[38] Mukdoni ended his tour of the Warsaw Yiddish theaters at the Elysium, a building that, in his description, accosted the theatergoer with the smell of rotten food upon entering. "I could not imagine that 'my people,' my Jews could enjoy themselves in such a sea of manure," a horrified Mukdoni told readers.[39]

Of course, this notion of a diametrical opposition between *shund* theater and "artistic" theater was not entirely accurate. In addition to the melodramas and operettas derided by the critics, the three so-called *shund* theaters in Warsaw also staged plays by venerated literary writers, including Peretz, Sholem Asch, and Jacob Gordin, as well as translations of European dramas by Molière, Gorky, Octave Mirbeau, and others.[40] Even the Muranover Theater, reputedly the *shund*iest of them all, staged Sholem

Aleichem's play *Scattered and Dispersed* along with several of Peretz's one acts, in what one historian called "a wink in the direction of literature."[41] Warsaw's Yiddish theaters were far more receptive to new ideas about theater than their critics were willing to admit. Yet while these categories of "art" versus "trash" did not accurately capture the offerings of Warsaw's Yiddish theaters, Peretz and his colleagues were successful in establishing a strict art/*shund* polemic in the imaginations of their readers. They hoped that this flood of criticism would leave spectators hungering for a new theater that would satisfy their theatrical appetites while also refining their aesthetic tastes, a theater that would make their favorite writers proud.

A Temple of Art

Yiddish theater emerged at a time of revolutionary ferment in the history of the modern stage, a moment when artists around the globe were questioning what it meant to make theater. Art theater—aggressively noncommercial theater devoted to artistic integrity—was all the rage. In Europe, artists like Gordon Craig, André Antoine, and Adolphe Appia had generated a public conversation about what it meant to create theater with "an earmark of higher art upon it," as one contemporary called it.[42] By 1905, art theater was thriving from Moscow to Munich, from London to New York.

Turn-of-the-century Yiddish writers were also interested in art theater. But while Peretz and his colleagues were able to articulate what was wrong with the Yiddish theater of the present with precision, they were less certain about what a Yiddish art theater ought to be. The criteria expressed in their essays tended to be either negative (no melodramas, no preferential star treatment) or comparative (a better repertoire, a more educated actor, a more serious rehearsal process). The art theater imagined by Peretz and his followers was one perpetually engaged in battle with its *shund* adversary. A 1910 editorial by Mukdoni was typical in its combative desperation:

> We are on the cusp of a danger that this theater will cultivate a wild Jewish population that will have no ear for a beautiful word, no eye for colors and lines, no sense of what is ideal, no curiosity to think, no ability to speak respectably. . . . We must take a look around us, we must do something before it is too late.[43]

With its potential to create an abyss between Jewish intellectuals and the masses, *shund* theater seemed to threaten the entire notion of a Yiddish culture led by writers. With this in mind, Peretz and his coterie framed Yiddish theater reform as a project of national significance. "Why should Jewish talents play *Bar Kokhba* and *The Evil Woman*?" Peretz pleaded with readers. "Art is the soul of the people, the national personality."[44] Mukdoni accused Jewish society of not noticing "how the theater—one of our most important national institutions—became a travesty."[45]

In positioning Yiddish theater as an essential ingredient for Jewish cultural, linguistic, and national legitimacy, Peretz drew upon established European ideas about the theater as a site of protonationalism.[46] This was the same period when William Butler Yeats, Lady Gregory, and other writers founded the Irish National Theater Society (better known as the Abbey Theater), which spurred a revival of interest in Celtic culture and inspired a nationalist movement.[47] Like these Irish writers, Peretz and his circle also sought to create a theater that would spur national cohesion.

For Jewish intellectuals, theater seemed an ideal arena to demonstrate the validity of modern Yiddish culture. Peretz saw in the theater a means of bringing his writing to a less elite audience that included everyday Jews. As Tea Artsishevska, a Polish and Yiddish actress who was one of Peretz's young followers, later recalled, "He dreamed of seeing his work in theater, believing that the word of the stage had a wider reach and a deeper impact on *dos folk* [the people]."[48] Moreover, theater offered a means of transmitting Yiddish literature and culture to audiences outside of the Jewish community. Even the best Yiddish writers could scarcely hope to attract a non-Jewish readership because of the barriers of language and alphabet. But theater, as a spoken and visual medium, could access a broader audience. If Yiddish theater could succeed with non-Jewish spectators, Peretz reasoned, the legitimacy of Yiddish literature and culture would be permanently assured.

In addition to establishing an art/trash polemic and starting a conversation about theater and Jewish nationalism, Jewish intellectuals also followed the lead of European writers in envisioning theater as the modern, secular equivalent of a holy space. Whereas Polish poets and playwrights had compared their national theaters to churches, Peretz and his compatriots transposed the "priestly mission" of the Polish theater into a Jewish context.[49] Their new Yiddish art theater, they hoped, would replace the social and cultural functions of the antiquated synagogue for modern Jewry. "A theater is a synagogue," Peretz wrote in 1907, "where no imperfection, no individual lacking in merit may enter."[50] He pleaded with readers to abandon the *shund* theater and "come into our 'Temple', as it were, of—art!!!"[51]

In the aftermath of the chaotic upheavals of 1905, Peretz and his circle of theater critics were certain that their reformation of the Yiddish theater was well underway. With high hopes, Peretz and his colleagues launched the second phase of their campaign: a plan to launch a Yiddish art theater company. With the most influential figure in Jewish Warsaw at the helm, how could they possibly fail?

First Failure: Peretz's *Temptation*

In May 1905 a Yiddish theater director named Avrom-Yankev Kaminski brought his company of actors to the Winter Garden Theater on the outskirts of Warsaw. At the time, Kaminski's troupe consisted of his immediate family; cofounder Misha Fishzon and his family; another director, Mark Arnshteyn; and twenty actors.[52] Kaminski and his talented actress wife, Esther Rokhl Kaminska, had been following the theater debates in the Yiddish press and decided to answer Peretz's call for a literary Yiddish theater. They joined forces with Fishzon, a director known for his productions of operettas and melodramas—the very sort of plays that Peretz and his colleagues had been attacking in their editorials. In coming together as partners, the Kaminskis and Fishzon hoped that their productions would bridge the gap between the literary theater that Jewish intellectuals sought and the popular entertainment beloved by the masses.

While Peretz and his colleagues were expounding their theories about Yiddish art theater in the press, the Kaminski-Fishzon Troupe was actively trying to bring literary theater to Jews in one of the city's poorest neighborhoods. The company soon disbanded, but not before it attracted Peretz's attention. In addition to publishing editorials and reviews, Peretz was also writing new plays. When he learned about the Kaminski-Fishzon Troupe, he was just putting the finishing touches on *Der nisoyen* (*The Temptation*), a Yiddish reworking of his Hebrew play *Khurban beit tsadik* (*The Fall of the Sage's House*) (1903). A subsequent 1907 Yiddish version of this play would later become famous under the title *Di goldene keyt* (*The Golden Chain*). With the ban no longer in effect, Peretz began to search for artists who could help him produce *Temptation*. Between Kaminski's directorial ambitions and Fishzon's eye for spectacle, the Kaminski-Fishzon Troupe seemed a perfect fit.

If a production of a literary drama like *Temptation* could succeed, Peretz hoped that it would shake the foundations of *shund*. Moreover, he began to dream that *Temptation* could bring Yiddish theater to the attention of non-Jewish spectators.[53] Peretz might have been inspired by news of the Moscow Art Theater's first European tour, in 1906, which established the international reputation of Stanislavsky and his company. As he read of German theater critics proclaiming, "We know the Russians are a hundred years behind politically, but dear God how far they are ahead artistically," we can imagine Peretz wondering if a Yiddish theater company with ambitious artistic goals might be able to elicit similar sentiments.[54]

When Kaminski returned to Warsaw at the beginning of 1906, Peretz was prepared.[55] He went to meet with the directors, armed with a handwritten copy of *Temptation*.[56] When Kaminski and Fishzon agreed to stage the play, Peretz took part in every aspect of the production. Not only did he insist on casting the entire show himself, but he also attended every rehearsal, occasionally even taking over for the directors. As Peretz's secretary remembered, "He did not tire of repeating a phrase even ten times so that the artist would pick up the correct tone of the Rabbi."[57] While Fishzon and Kaminski were ostensibly the directors of *Temptation*, Albek's recollection suggests that Peretz's involvement extended beyond his official role as dramatic advisor. Instead, he took on tasks that would ordinarily fall within a director's purview, like coaching actors on their interpretation of specific lines.

On opening night, April 26, 1906, the auditorium was packed. But when the curtain rose, the audience was appalled. Even the best actors struggled to embody Peretz's abstract characters, the critics agreed. The next day's reviews were unrelenting in their criticism. Writer Yente Serdatski wrote of a production suffused with impoverishment. "We sat on simple wooden benches. The cheaper tickets were terribly far from the stage and you could not hear a word. There was hardly any lighting or heat. This poverty had an effect on the actors, and they wandered about the stage as if they were in an alien world."[58] The only lively moment in the production, wrote Serdatski, was during the intermission, when Peretz walked around the theater greeting friends. Literary critic Bal-Makhshoves blamed shoddy playwriting:

> There was no sky, no meadow, no river, no strength of the Hasidim, no body and no soul. The *sukkah* was an ugly *sukkah*, wall upon wall without a separation. The Rebbe Mendl seemed like a magician in a Purim play, and the Hasidism around him like clowns. There was no emotion to consider. And so far as the poetic crept in, it was nothing more than the kind of cheap effects that hold no interest for the edu-

> cated spectator. Peretz gave his *Temptation* the subtitle "a drama." This is a false title. We see very little that befits a drama here.[59]

For Bal-Makhshoves, *Temptation* was precisely what Peretz had promised to change: scenes, sets, and characters that bore no relation to their real-life counterparts, no emotional authenticity, overly exaggerated characters, and cheap effects. Rather than supplying the Yiddish theater with a new model, the critics charged, Peretz had produced a flawed melodrama with literary pretensions.

Most of *Temptation*'s critics blamed Peretz for the debacle and excused the actors. Bal-Makhshoves's assertion that the actors "did not perform Peretz's play well, [because] they could not perform it well" was typical.[60] Indeed, the play itself was part of the problem. Reading *The Temptation* today, what is most striking is its utter lack of dramatic tension.[61] The first act opens with a group of Hasidic Jews reading and praying in the synagogue. Their language as they discuss the Torah portion of the week is lofty and poetic, but dramaturgically, the scene is completely flat. The Hasidim drone on and on about religious matters, other worshippers recite psalms, and virtually nothing happens. It is a conceptual piece with too many characters to keep track of that never really goes anywhere. To be fair, there are moments of great theatrical writing scattered throughout the text, particularly in the third act when Yonatan, the secular renegade son of a devout father, is put on trial by local religious leaders and begs his dead father and God for forgiveness ("I am the last link in the chain. I am the last one here").[62] God and the assembled masses remain silent in spite of his exhortations, and the play ends ambiguously without the audience knowing for certain if Yonatan was actually excommunicated. But the first two acts are more atmospheric than theatrical. Peretz may have been a great Yiddish poet, essayist, and storyteller, but in 1906 he was not yet a competent dramatist.

As the critics blamed Peretz, the playwright accused the actors of sabotaging his masterpiece. He demanded that the company's star actress, Esther Rokhl Kaminska, return his manuscript and cease performances immediately. Kaminska protested that perhaps they could rehearse for a few more weeks and try again, but Peretz thundered that he would never permit the Kaminski-Fishzon Troupe to perform his work again—not even the scheduled second-night performance of *Temptation*. He was convinced that *Temptation* had failed because the actors did not understand his work. It was symbolic, Peretz raged, that Kaminski had to write Misha

Fishzon's part out in Cyrillic letters because the actor could not read the Hebrew alphabet.[63] He swore that he would never again work with actors so unschooled.

Yet though it failed with the critics, *Temptation* demonstrated that there was indeed an audience—and a large one at that—interested in Yiddish art theater. *Temptation*'s failure may have mortified Peretz, but it did not diminish his resolve to continue advocating for a "better" Yiddish theater. At the same time as he withdrew his play and broke off all contact with the Kaminski-Fishzon actors, Peretz started reaching out to younger writers with practical stage experience, among them the young playwright Peretz Hirschbein. Peretz would convince Hirschbein to form a new Yiddish theater company under his watchful guidance, only to find that the same humiliating scene from the *Temptation* premiere would repeat again and again.

Second Failure: The Hirschbein Troupe

Unlike most Yiddish writers of his generation, Peretz Hirschbein (1880–1948) was born and raised among farmers in the countryside.[64] In 1905 Hirschbein published *Miriam*, a drama about a destitute young woman forced into prostitution after being jilted by her rich lover. Hirschbein originally wrote the play in Hebrew, but he also published his own Yiddish translation of it a year later, establishing a pattern that he would follow for the next several years in which Hebrew originals preceded Yiddish translations.[65] Though the first professional Hebrew theater company was not established until 1917, over forty years after the founding of the first professional Yiddish theater, Hirschbein, like most Jewish writers of the period, viewed Yiddish theater as unsuitable for literary drama.[66] As was common among turn-of-the-century Jewish intellectuals, Hirschbein was an avid attendee of Russian theater and cited his experiences attending Russian-language productions as his inspiration:

> The [Russian] language sounded clear and musical. Sitting in the theater, I learned from the actors how to speak Russian beautifully. Yiddish troupes often traveled to Vilna, and when I went to see what they performed, going with the same eagerness with which I went to the Russian theater, I emerged ashamed, spiritually bereft.[67]

At the age of twenty-four, Hirschbein traveled to Warsaw and, like most young Yiddish writers, went straight to Peretz's house. He was so anxious that he forgot to bring a sample of his work. Peretz, however, was intrigued and hired a driver to take the young man home to retrieve his writing.[68] From this inauspicious first meeting emerged a close mentorship. The two began to take long walks together to discuss symbolist drama. Peretz suggested that Hirschbein take a look at the work of Belgian playwright Maurice Maeterlinck and solicited the younger writer's input on a revised version of *Temptation*.[69] Peretz also introduced Hirschbein to other Jewish dramatists around his age, including Sholem Asch. Hirschbein was surprised to learn that Sholem Asch had written several plays in Yiddish.

Though Peretz encouraged him to stay in Warsaw, Hirschbein returned to Vilna. The Warsaw trip inspired him to experiment with two new approaches: first writing symbolist dramas modeled on Maeterlinck and later writing in Yiddish.[70] In 1906 Hirschbein wrote his first original Yiddish play *Af yener zayt taykh* (*On the Other Side of the River*), along with several Yiddish one acts. He sent them to publishers and was promptly rejected.[71]

Disappointed, Hirschbein briefly returned to Warsaw, where Peretz again tried to convince him to stay and start a theater company. By 1907, Warsaw's literary circles were abuzz with theater frenzy. Another of Peretz's protégés, a young director named Dovid Herman, had just enrolled in the local Polish drama school with Peretz's blessing. Staged readings organized by Peretz were held nightly in the homes of prominent Warsaw literati.[72] By the time Hirschbein met with Peretz, the latter had largely recovered from his disappointment with *Temptation* and had begun to work in the theater again, collaborating with amateur performers to organize small-scale productions around the city.[73] But eager for new experiences, Hirschbein left and became an itinerant playwright. When that work dried up, he moved to Odessa in the spring of 1908.

Odessa was hardly a natural choice for a budding Yiddish playwright. To begin with, there were no professional Yiddish writers in Odessa, a city heavily steeped in Russian and, to a lesser extent, Hebrew culture. All of Odessa's Jewish writers had secondary occupations: S. Y. Abramovitch (better known by his pen name, Mendele Moykher Sforim) was the director of a Talmud Torah school, Chaim Nakhmen Bialik worked as a printer, and Berl Shafir always stank of Turkish tobacco from his day job as a cigarette manufacturer.[74] Yet Odessa was also a Jewish community founded by adventurers that never quite lost its frontier-town feel.[75] In Odessa, Hirschbein discovered Jewish cultural organizations more nimble and experimental than in Warsaw. Far from Warsaw, the cultural center of Jewish Eastern Europe, Hirschbein decided to start a Yiddish theater company, inspired by his conversations with Peretz. In Odessa, however, the company would have true autonomy.

Just a few weeks earlier, the movement to develop modern Yiddish culture had hit its apex with the Czernowitz conference. Convened by writers from across Jewish Eastern Europe, the Czernowitz conference sought to assess the place of Yiddish language and culture in Jewish life.[76] The conference attracted hundreds of Jewish writers, intellectuals, and leaders, including Peretz, who delivered the keynote address. "Jews are one people whose language is Yiddish," Peretz proclaimed.[77] One of the many hoped-for cultural institutions mentioned by Peretz in his speech was a Yiddish theater that would unite European Jewry—a reference that could not have escaped Hirschbein's attention. The Czernowitz conference and Peretz's opening plea for Yiddish cultural autonomy received extensive coverage in the Jewish press.[78]

In 1908 Odessa was a small enough city to have only one Yiddish theater, which played primarily melodramas.[79] Odessa also boasted a prestigious Russian-language drama school with many Jewish students. Caught between *shund* and the anti-Semitism of the Russian stage, many of these Jewish students were delighted to have an alternative and signed on to Hirschbein's project.[80] All of the actors were young: few were past their twenties and none were over forty. In keeping with the socialist politics of most of the members, they agreed that everyone would have equal access to the best roles and nobody's name would be billed in larger type than any of the others. This was a far cry from the "star system" that dominated the Yiddish stage, in which leading actors often exerted near-complete control over productions.[81] Almost immediately, the company became known around Odessa as "the literary theater."[82] Indeed, according to its founder, the Hirschbein Troupe's primary goal was to develop a mass readership for modern Yiddish literature. Later in life, Hirschbein loved to give examples of how his company had inspired young Jews in Odessa to become avid Yiddish readers and writers.[83]

Still, the Hirschbein Troupe faced many challenges. To begin with, there were not enough extant Yiddish plays that met the company's high standards. Moreover, the company did not have complete control over its repertoire selection. Of those plays that the actors could agree upon, only a handful were approved by the Russian censors. The Hirschbein Troupe thus never had more than fifteen plays in its repertoire.[84] Second, Hirschbein started his company with virtually no money. High-minded ideals often had to take a backseat to financial considerations. The Hirschbein

Troupe's first play, *Shadkhonim* (*Matchmakers*), was a second-rate piece written by a wealthy Odessa lawyer who agreed to fund the initial productions if the company performed his plays.[85] With few alternatives, Hirschbein accepted the compromise.

A second production soon followed of Hirschbein's own *Tkies-kaf* (*The Handshake*). This time the Hirschbein Troupe was able to fill the theater. The next evening the Hirschbein Troupe performed another Hirschbein drama, *Di neveyle* (*The Carcass*), to another full house.[86] In the summer of 1909 the Hirschbein Troupe toured southern Russia and Bessarabia to local acclaim.[87] When a group of influential writers (Peretz among them) invited the company to perform in Warsaw that winter, Hirschbein accepted. This would be his chance to demonstrate his achievements before the most prominent Jewish intellectuals of the era.

In 1910 Warsaw was the hub of a thriving Yiddish culture. The city's two largest Yiddish newspapers (*Haynt* and *Der Moment*) printed over two hundred thousand copies a day.[88] Meanwhile, the debates over the future of Yiddish theater had only grown. Literary clubs held nightly lecture series where locals could study theater history. Writers started new periodicals devoted entirely to Yiddish theater. The members of Peretz's circle spoke of a *teater-shturem*, a "theater storm" brewing in Warsaw.[89]

The previous year, 1909, marked the year that the Yiddish daily *Der Fraynd* moved from Moscow to Warsaw, and Mukdoni convinced the editor to run a regular feature on Yiddish theater, with himself as lead contributor. Peretz's campaign now had the official approval of one of Warsaw's most popular Yiddish newspapers. A group of writers began to gather regularly in *Fraynd*'s offices to discuss theater reform. In addition to Peretz's original circle, this group included playwright Sholem Asch, poet Avrom Reyzen, critic Bal-Makhshoves, writer H. D. Nomberg, and *Fraynd*'s editor, Shmuel Rosenfeld.[90] In the pages of *Fraynd*, their new press organ, Warsaw's most prominent literary figures declared their support for Peretz's vision.

Feeling hopeful, Peretz decided to organize a symposium on Yiddish theater and rented the Philharmonia, Warsaw's finest concert hall. Peretz's friends could hardly believe that he had the nerve to ask the Polish landlord to rent the Philharmonia for a Jewish gathering. There were frightening rumors of anti-Semitic reprisals.[91] Nevertheless, Peretz and his colleagues publicized the symposium with daily ads in *Fraynd*. Entitled "About Theater," the symposium would feature four lectures: Mukdoni on acting, Vayter on audiences, Nomberg on Yiddish theater history, and finally, Peretz on the Yiddish art theater to come.[92]

The publicity worked. When the speakers arrived, they found a crowd numbering in the thousands. The Philharmonia could seat over two thousand spectators, and Peretz had never imagined that his theater symposium would fill it. Instead, the lines were so long that tickets sold out an hour before the symposium began and hundreds were turned away. Inside, every seat was occupied. Hundreds more crammed into the gallery, the balcony, and every corner. The Yiddish press reported that twenty-four hundred attended the symposium.[93]

Peretz was the last to speak. "The Yiddish theater is lowly," Peretz insisted, "The holiest place, trampled underfoot."[94] Who, then, was to blame? Not writers, Peretz told those gathered, for even without enough literary Yiddish dramas, the theater still could have produced work by European playwrights in translation. Nor was it fault of the actors, those "unlucky artists who work day and night."[95] Peretz never did explain who or what was to blame for *shund*. Instead, he concluded with a battle cry: "Let no Jewish foot cross the threshold of the old Yiddish theater. We will destroy it, and upon its ruins we will build the new Yiddish art theater!"[96] Thunderous applause filled the hall. It was against this backdrop that Peretz invited the Hirschbein Troupe to Warsaw.

The Warsaw Yiddish press anticipated the Hirschbein Troupe's arrival with a rush of enthusiasm, though none of the journalists had actually seen it perform. Bal-Makhshoves called the Hirschbein Troupe "the first company of intelligent theater-lovers."[97] Avrom Reyzen praised Hirschbein for hiring only actors who were fluent in Russian and educated in Yiddish literature.[98] Mukdoni was also delighted by the actors: "young, lively people. . . . All were well-read in Russian literature."[99]

Yet the company's arrival also brought ominous surprises. The actors seemed too young and immature, their clothes were tattered, and they were virtually penniless. Instead of the refined actor-intellectuals they had been expecting, Warsaw's writers found a ragtag group of young actors who, as Mukdoni recalled, "did not make the best impression on all of us, neither on the stage nor in private life."[100]

Still, Warsaw's Jewish intellectuals hoped that the first performance would compensate for the troupe's lackluster arrival. As with *Temptation*, Peretz took part in the preparations, and rehearsals were held in his living room.[101] On February 26, 1910, the Hirschbein Troupe opened at Warsaw's Muranover Theater with a sold-out production of two one acts: Sholem Asch's *Mitn shtrom* (*With the Current*) and Sholem Aleichem's *Mentshn* (*People*). Virtually every Jewish writer in Warsaw was present. Sitting in the front row, Peretz was so excited that he hardly noticed when his colleagues next to him, Mukdoni and Vayter, tried to engage him in conversation. The lights dimmed and the audience hushed. As Mukdoni recalled,

> Peretz, who sat next to me, let out an audible groan of bitter disappointment. The stage was prepared so tastelessly, so asymmetrically, and the setting was so drably pedantic that you simply had to avert your eyes. The performance itself was no better. Tedious, long, and unfilled pauses struck a nerve. We could hardly wait until the play ended.[102]

Many did not wait and abruptly left during intermission. Peretz remained seated, rigid with disappointment. He did not say a word.[103]

The Hirschbein Troupe continued its residency in Warsaw for another week. Mukdoni and others published daily reviews arguing that Hirschbein's "new" Yiddish theater was no better than *shund*.[104] Peretz, for his part, was silent on the subject, perhaps out of a desire to maintain his friendship with Hirschbein, perhaps out of embarrassment or fury. A few writers with a vested stake in Hirschbein's success, including Dinezon, Bal-Makhshoves, and Nomberg, rushed to the troupe's defense, but soon they too stopped attending performances. The audience that had initially filled the theater beyond capacity dwindled to almost nothing.[105]

The Hirschbein Troupe had come to Warsaw flush with a success among Jewish intellectuals unprecedented in the Yiddish theater to date. Yet in spite of this achievement, Hirschbein's literary idols had unequivocally rejected his company's offerings. This was a bitter pill for Hirschbein and his actors to swallow.[106] To make matters worse, they were running out of money. They appealed to the Warsaw Jewish community for financial assistance, to no avail. In desperation, Hirschbein sold his beloved writing desk to pay the troupe's outstanding bills and the company left Warsaw.[107] After a few dozen unsuccessful performances in Minsk, Kovne, and Bobruisk, the actors decided to go their separate ways. On July 7, 1910, the Hirschbein Troupe gave its last performance in Dvinsk before a miniscule audience.[108]

Though the Hirschbein Troupe failed to live up to its audiences' expectations, it was the first Yiddish theater company to receive serious and sustained attention from Jewish intellectuals. The Hirschbein Troupe may have been short-lived, but it generated a lasting interest in Yiddish theater that extended far beyond Warsaw. When Mukdoni toured the Polish countryside in late 1910, he was pleased to discover "a great interest in the theater, which had arisen in a very short time."[109] Economic desperation and the search for new audiences had compelled the Hirschbein Troupe to travel far and wide throughout the Pale of Settlement. Future Yiddish theater companies would follow the Hirschbein Troupe's lead, traveling to find Jewish audiences wherever they resided.

The Hirschbein Troupe, as one Yiddish theater historian put it, "laid the foundations for a Yiddish art theater with European theater culture."[110] Hirschbein was even more specific. "Our Troupe," he wrote, "laid the groundwork for the Vilna Troupe, which emerged a few years later. . . . Each branch of Vilna Troupe carries the mission to fight for a better theater; to separate themselves from *shund* as much as possible, and to maintain a relationship to the Yiddish word and to literature. This was *our* tradition."[111] Though a failure in its time, the Hirschbein Troupe was ultimately the most successful part of Peretz's campaign.

Third Failure: The Gezelshaft Theater

With Peretz's hopes dashed once again, Warsaw's Jewish writers did not dare to speak about Yiddish art theater—for a time. In the spring of 1910, Mukdoni wrote, Warsaw was "quiet, the quiet after the great storm that we had started."[112]

The silence did not last long. A few weeks later, the members of Peretz's circle began writing about theater again. In one article published in April 1910, writer Noyekh Prilutski called upon his colleagues to watch over the theater's development like one safeguards a child who is learning how to walk:

> We approach the Yiddish actor with revolver-criticism [*revolverkritik*] and boycott-agitation [*boykotagitatsye*] . . . but isn't our theater still just a suckling babe—barely out of his swaddling clothes—who takes his first steps with weak, shaky feet? His parents and the entire household watch over the baby fearfully, for he cannot yet hold his balance. They guard him as you guard your own eye, they hold his hands to steady him. The tragedy is that the so-called "Jewish intellectual" is not capable of feeling for our young theater what parents feel for a child. Has he worried about the Yiddish stage? Has it ever occurred to him that the play that the wandering actors "practice" has a national-cultural significance and is part of our living cultural

> present? . . . The solution must be: *go to the Yiddish theater, regardless of how terrible it may be*.[113]

Meanwhile, Peretz had recovered enough from the Hirschbein Troupe debacle to start thinking about his theater campaign again. He gathered his colleagues and they debated their options. Instead of relying on others, they decided, why not create a company themselves under the auspices of Warsaw's Yiddish literary society? The Literarishe Gezelshaft, founded in 1909, included all of the members of Peretz's theater circle among its ranks, and the "theater question" was often a subject of discussion at its meetings. The Literarishe Gezelshaft would provide the theater with financial security and a permanent affiliation; the company would provide the literary society with a Yiddish art theater.

This time it was a younger writer, A. Vayter, who was the driving force behind the project. With Peretz's blessing, Vayter drafted a plan. The Gezelshaft Theater, according to Vayter's outline, would be a joint-stock company with individual investors purchasing shares. Vayter wrote hundreds of letters and traveled across Eastern Europe soliciting funds.[114] But few were interested in contributing. There was no established culture of theater philanthropy among Jews in Eastern Europe. Previous Yiddish theaters had been funded exclusively by ticket sales, and potential donors were unmoved by Vayter's pleas that this theater could not survive on that alone. As the year wore on, an increasingly desperate Vayter began to contribute his own meager salary to the empty coffers, even starving himself for days on end to pay for the train tickets and stamps necessary to continue fundraising.[115]

In March 1911 Peretz and his wife set off on a fundraising trip to Russia. Their local sponsor, the Yiddish Literary Society of St. Petersburg, had organized a banquet in Peretz's honor and invited local Jewish writers and business leaders to attend. Initially, the attendees seemed enthusiastic. Prominent writers gave speeches praising Peretz's theater campaign. But all of the speeches were in Russian, which rankled Peretz. Forgetting both his fundraising mission and his manners, he snapped at the speakers and stormed out of the banquet hall. As one attendee recalled,

> The guest [Peretz] was silent the entire time. His thick lower lip hung down sullenly, and his cold and tired eyes wandered about. . . . Suddenly, after one of the Russian speeches, Peretz hastily stood up, eyes blazing and agitated, and shouted: "I cannot, I will not . . . you

offend me with your Russian speeches. It is insulting that you speak to me in a foreign language! It is a disgrace to our people."[116]

When Peretz returned to Warsaw, he recounted the incident to the horror of Vayter, Mukdoni, Asch, and the entire Literarishe Gezelshaft. Peretz was convinced that he had responded correctly. "Jews who welcome a Yiddish writer with Russian speeches will not build a Yiddish culture," he told Mukdoni. "They will not build a Yiddish theater. They will not even build a Yiddish stable, because even a Yiddish stable must be built in Yiddish."[117] For Peretz, his campaign was first and foremost about the elevation of Yiddish literary culture. But his younger colleagues were crushed. The fate of their project had hinged upon the success of Peretz's fundraising trip. His failure to raise the necessary funds was its death knell.

Aftermath

As Peretz's campaign came to a close, melodrama grew ever more popular in Warsaw as an influx of performers arrived from New York.[118] American melodramas were a hit with audiences, and the few Warsaw theaters that had once attempted to produce literary work turned to *shund* to compete. The most popular Warsaw production of the period was Moyshe Zeifert's *Dos pintele yid* (*The Essential Spark of Jewishness*), which ended with a star of David descending from the ceiling while the play's title was illuminated in glowing electric lights.[119] *Essential Spark* played over two hundred times in Warsaw to packed houses.[120] Echoing Peretz's activities in years past, young writers tried to sabotage the performances by shouting at the actors that they were poisoning the audience.[121] But this time, an older Peretz did not take part in the anti-*shund* antics. One by one, the former members of Peretz's theater circle also turned their backs on the Yiddish stage: first Dinezon, then Nomberg, and finally Mukdoni and Vayter. Mukdoni, who had wanted to become a professional Yiddish theater critic, was especially bitter. For years, he carried the proposal for the Gezelshaft Theater in his breast pocket as he migrated from Warsaw to St. Petersburg to Kovne and, finally, to Berlin. It was not until 1923, on the eve of his emigration to the United States, that Mukdoni finally let go of the proposal, burning it to rid himself of the unhappy memories.[122]

On April 3, 1915, during the intermediary days of Passover, Peretz died at his home in Warsaw. For over a decade, he had fought—unsuccessfully—to develop a Yiddish art theater. Ironically, the fulfillment of Peretz's vision would come to pass just a few months after his death; not in Warsaw, the great metropolitan center of Yiddish culture, but hundreds of miles away, in a nearly unrecognizable Vilna ravaged by war, with an unlikely group of starving, inexperienced amateur performers at its helm.

Peretz the playwright is not the successful writer that we so often encounter in Jewish literary history. He is all too human, a man wounded again and again by rejection. Why did Peretz, the most prominent Jewish writer of his generation, fail so spectacularly? Khone Shmeruk has argued that "over the whole Yiddish literary world, his approval was cited as the principal justification for any writer's claim to fame."[123] Why was he unable to translate his influence into theater reform?

First, Peretz lacked practical experience in the theater. Without even the most cursory knowledge of directing method, acting style, or how to run a rehearsal, Peretz's approach to theater was that of a frustrated audience member. Similarly, despite his literary talent, Peretz lacked a finely tuned sense of dramaturgical structure. Shmuel Niger described Peretz as "more of a subjective lyricist than a powerful playwright," and others concurred that writing for the stage was perhaps not his greatest strength.[124] Peretz was baffled as to why so few wanted to perform his plays. Like Antoine Artaud, Alfred Jarry, and so many other leaders of the European avant-garde theater, Peretz was perhaps more effective as a proclaimer of manifestos than as a playwright.[125] Hobbled by theatrical inexperience, Peretz could not create the theater he sought.

Second, Peretz wanted his plays to be at the center of the Yiddish art theater, and he struggled to collaborate. Despite his theatrical inexperience, the famous writer was not interested in accepting advice. Never once did Peretz admit that he was at fault for the failure of his endeavors. Instead, he laid blame upon actors, directors, critics, and investors. It would ultimately take a company of younger performers committed to collaborative theater making to enact Peretz's revolution.

Third, Peretz was never able to articulate precisely what he envisioned for the Yiddish art theater. He adapted the term to fit his needs at any given moment. Turkow-Grudberg compared Peretz's role in the theater campaign to a doctor who sought to assess the "diseases" of the Yiddish theater but "did not always present the same diagnosis."[126]

Shifting historical forces and contexts also played a role. When Peretz pursued his theater campaign, Yiddish theater had only recently become legal again. Not everyone was convinced yet that theater was an important avenue for Jewish literary culture. Moreover, even after 1905, Yiddish theater in the Russian Empire was still under the control of the censors. This created logistical challenges. Jewish actors were also subject to strict residency restrictions that limited their ability to travel. For example, the Hirschbein Troupe received permission to perform just outside of the Pale of Settlement in Poltava but had to leave the city every night to sleep in a place where Jews were permitted to reside.[127] A few years later, the relaxation of censorship and movement restrictions during and after the First World War would enable Yiddish theater to travel at will.

Finally, Peretz's campaign was weakened by its geographical limitations. His campaign occurred in the midst of the great age of Jewish migration, yet his efforts were limited to the small Yiddish-speaking corner of the Russian Empire where he presided as cultural leader. In a period when Eastern European Jews were leaving the Russian Empire in unprecedented numbers, the lack of international support weakened Peretz's campaign. Peretz's campaign was disconnected from similar efforts to reform the Yiddish theater in the United States.[128]

Yet the campaign was not without its achievements. While Peretz failed to achieve any of his practical goals, he succeeded in starting a conversation among Jewish intellectuals about the future of the Yiddish stage. Unbeknownst to Peretz, his efforts would ultimately lay the groundwork for a Yiddish art theater movement. Several actors who got their start in the Hirschbein Troupe—including Jacob Ben-Ami, Reuven Vendorf, and Leah Naomi—would later join the Vilna Troupe. Peretz's campaign also contributed the writers and critics of his theater circle: Mukdoni, Dinezon, Vayter, and Herman. These critics (with the exception of Vayter, who was murdered in a 1919 pogrom) would all make significant contributions to developing and promoting the Vilna Troupe and the Yiddish art theater movement that it inspired.

Posthumously, Peretz's call to arms became the inspiration for a new generation of artists. Vilna Troupe cofounder Leyb Kadison later recalled how the actors chose one of Peretz's lines from his symposium lecture as their unofficial motto:

> We remembered Y. L. Peretz's decree at a meeting in the Philharmonia before an audience of thousands: No Jewish foot shall cross the doorstep of the old Yiddish theater. We will destroy it, and upon its ruins we will build the new Yiddish art theater.[129]

A. H. Bialin considered all of the members of the Vilna Troupe to be "directly or indirectly ignited with the same blaze that the Hirschbein Troupe made widespread."[130] Peretz may have died thinking that his campaign was a failure, but its effects were lasting.

Between 1905 and 1911, an aging Peretz sought to revolutionize the Yiddish stage by creating a European-inspired art theater in Yiddish. Unable to create the theater he sought, Peretz spent the last decade of his life consumed with frustration. Yet for the first time in history, Peretz had convinced writers to take responsibility for the state of Jewish theater. After Peretz's theater campaign, the Yiddish stage could no longer be relegated to the outskirts of Jewish intellectual discourse.

CHAPTER 2

Jargon Art

From Refugees to Artistic Visionaries

> Hungry, they thought that by art, you know, they'll feed themselves with art. Maybe only in the imagination of starving hungry people, you see, can come an idea like this.
> —Joseph Buloff, New York, 1980

Genesis

While Peretz fretted over the failures of his theater campaign in Warsaw, while Hirschbein sold his beloved writing desk, while Mukdoni burned his lecture notes from Peretz's symposium, the first stirrings of something new were brewing hundreds of miles away in the mind of a young housepainter and amateur theater hobbyist in Kovne (today Kaunas, Lithuania), on the northernmost outskirts of the Pale of Settlement.

Leyb Shuster had always wanted to be an artist. As a child, he was always drawing, painting, and making collages out of anything that he could find. When he was seven, his father was mistaken for a scab during a strike at the factory where he worked and was murdered. His mother remarried a rabbi—a strict traditionalist who threw away the boy's crayons and drawings. Leyb ran away from home and became an apprentice in a sign-making shop.[1] There he learned to produce signs for bakeries, factories, and shops, embellished with drawings. He became known for his excellent craftsmanship.

Meanwhile, young Leyb was developing an interest in theater. He became fascinated with opera and hung around the Kovne State Opera House until the stage crew taught him how to design and build sets.[2] Inspired, he started an amateur Yiddish theater club, the Kovne Yiddish Dramatic Society, with friends.[3] The club staged a few Hirschbein and Asch plays and Leyb struck up a friendly correspondence with both playwrights, who often visited his home when in Kovne. Leyb subscribed to Russian theater magazines to read about the Moscow Art Theater.[4] He continued painting signs. He fell in love, got married, and had three children. Life went on.

Amateur Yiddish drama clubs like Shuster's had a long history. The first amateur Yiddish company on record started in Lodz in the 1890s. By 1910 there were over 360 amateur groups in Poland.[5] Collectively, these efforts were known in Yiddish as *libhober bines* and their actors as *libhobers*—which (like the French *amateur*) could be translated as "those who love the stage." Others deemed the amateur clubs *di yugntlekhe bine*—"the youthful stage," referring to the teenagers and young adults who dominated them. These clubs, with their young actors and literary orientation, differed significantly from the professional Yiddish theaters. Despite tiny budgets and few resources, it was not uncommon for amateur clubs to stage work by highly regarded Yiddish writers (Gordin, Peretz, and Pinski were favorites) or their own translations of contemporary European playwrights (like Ibsen, Molière, and Gorky) while professional companies were more likely to produce melodramas like Lateiner's *The Jewish Heart*, Hurwitz's *Mother Love*, or Shomer's *The Coquettish Ladies*.[6]

The amateur clubs across Eastern Europe and the United States functioned as an unofficial school of drama in a culture without dramatic academies or any other formal pathways to theatrical training. The clubs filled this institutional gap by providing a means for aspiring Jewish actors to acquire a theatrical education that was otherwise inaccessible.[7] In addition, the amateur clubs were instrumental in developing a new audience for Yiddish theater. Amateur performances were social occasions where actors and spectators built communities around a shared interest in Yiddish theater. Actors sometimes even invited audience members to give feedback at the end of shows.[8]

The Vilna Troupe had its roots in this tradition of amateur Yiddish theatrics. Leyb Shuster was not the only future Vilna Troupe member to begin his career in an amateur club. Dovid Herman, who would later direct the Vilna Troupe's world premiere of *The Dybbuk*, spent decades working with amateur groups before turning to the professional stage. Herman actually introduced many of his trademark innovations—extensive rehearsal periods, the elimination of the prompter's booth, individual coaching sessions with actors—as an amateur director.[9] Several other future Vilna Troupe actors began their careers with Jacob Ben-Ami's amateur company, a short-lived offshoot of the Hirschbein Troupe.[10] Indeed, many Vilner (including Leyb himself) would eventually return to the amateur stage.[11]

The Shuster family—Leyb, his wife, Khane, and their young children—were among the many members of Eastern Europe's thriving amateur Yiddish theater scene, and they likely would have happily remained anonymous, amateur actors had historical forces not intervened and uprooted their comfortable existence in an instant.

When the Russian Empire entered the First World War and Germany became an enemy, the Russian government feared that Yiddish-speaking Jews with their Germanic language would turn traitor. As the front approached the Russo-German border, the Russian army ordered all Jews in the area to evacuate within twenty-four hours. With a single decree, tens of thousands of Jews woke up one morning to find out that they were refugees. The Shusters were among them.

Forced to leave the city where their ancestors had resided for generations, the family fled to nearby Vilna, which was just far enough east to be excluded from the resettlement order. Vilna was already overcrowded and disease ridden, but there were few nearby cities where Jews were now permitted to live. Jewish refugees flocked to Vilna by the thousands, most of them penniless.[12] As Leyb's daughter Luba recalled,

> When we came to Vilna, it was hunger. It was terrible. Because the Russians were losing the war. There were outbreaks of pogroms. And we were hiding, and we didn't know what to do. Finally, my mother, [who] was a very energetic and wonderful person, and she would never lose herself in any situation, and she found somewheres [*sic*] an apartment . . . and we started to live again. And she got some food, she kept the potatoes under lock in a special little room because they were like precious diamonds.[13]

They were lucky to find even a meager apartment. By the summer of 1915, as the front pressed eastward, thousands of homeless and starving refugees wandered the streets of Vilna. By the fall, twenty-two thousand Jewish and ten thousand Christian refugees had entered Vilna seeking asylum.[14]

In Kovne, Leyb had been content to stage amateur productions as a hobby. But unemployed in Vilna, he decided to make theater the center of a new life. Together with a group of fellow migrants and a few locals, Shuster and his new friends founded the Fareyn fun Yidishe Dramatishe Artistn (better known by its acronym, FADA) in the kitchen of Leyb and Khane's cramped apartment. They idealized the Moscow Art Theater, which they knew about from subscriptions to theater magazines, and vowed to produce only artistic work—never a "cheap play" just to bring in money.[15]

FADA, a ragtag company made up primarily of displaced refugees, would later become famous as the Vilna Troupe. Its roots, however, were not in Vilna but in the border towns from which Jews were forcibly evicted during the war. Like most of the FADA actors, Leyb ironically "became a Vilna resident [Vilner] against my will," only later to become famous as a Vilner.[16] The Vilna Troupe was not a company of actors from Vilna; it was the product of a chance wartime encounter between refugees and starving locals. Without the Russian government's paranoia about Jewish loyalties, the founders would most likely never have even met.

But Leyb and his new friends could not start a theater company immediately—at least, not outside of the confines of the apartment. At the start of the war, the Russian commander of Vilna had outlawed Yiddish theater, causing all of Vilna's local Yiddish theater companies to dissolve and their actors to seek work in other cities.[17] In wartime Vilna, Yiddish theater was illegal again, as if 1905 had never happened.

Meanwhile, conditions continued to decline by the day. When the Russian army suffered military setbacks, they held Vilna's Jews to blame and introduced repressive measures against them. As the German army approached Vilna's borders, the city was under siege for months on end, further exacerbating difficult living conditions.

On the morning of Yom Kippur (September 18, 1915), the Jews of Vilna learned that the Russians had retreated overnight and the Germans had occupied their city.[18] After suffering under oppressive anti-Semitic Russian legislation and surviving a siege, Vilna's Jews welcomed their new rulers. Every Jewish organization in the city sent representatives to greet the German soldiers. Even though his company was still just an idea, Leyb joined the delegates, billing himself as the representative of Vilna's Yiddish theater.[19] After all, there were no other Yiddish theaters left in Vilna.

German military commanders found themselves in charge of a city that was on the brink of collapse. Vilna's municipal infrastructure was ill equipped to deal with the refugee crisis. The German army was overwhelmed with requests for food, medicine, and housing for homeless and starving residents while war raged nearby on the Russo-German front.[20] Still, the German army treated the Jewish community kindly. The army began publishing daily announcements in Yiddish alongside bulletins in German, Polish, and Lithuanian and granted permission for Jews to run their own Yiddish-language schools.[21] In a sharp reversal of the language policies enacted by the Russians, the German commanders promised to support Yiddish culture. Yiddish seemed politically neutral and even potentially pro-German to the German officers who were largely unacquainted with the Jewish vernacular. After all, it was simply "German, with many, many unintelligible words," as one army commander quipped.[22] Russian, on the other hand, was the language of the enemy. The German army immediately enacted a campaign to rid the city of its Russian influences. The army repainted Russian street signs in German, forbade Russian-language education in Vilna's schools, and ordered the closing of every Russian theater within the city limits.[23]

Between the Yiddish theater ban under the Russians and the Russian theater ban under the Germans, the language politics of the First World War had created a theatrical vacuum. By September 1915 there was not a single theater company left in Vilna. The army tried to fill the void by inviting artists from Berlin to give guest performances. Still, these performances were intended for the German soldiers, not for the locals, who were left with no theatrical entertainment of their own.[24]

It was against this backdrop of war, military occupation, linguistic conflict, and a theatrical vacuum that a pair of would-be Jewish actors decided to make their pitch for a Yiddish art theater. Their first task would be to secure permission from the military commanders. With the help of community leaders from the Jewish Aid Committee and sympathetic German-Jewish officers, Shuster and Alexander Orliuk, a Vilna-born actor with some experience in amateur Yiddish and professional Russian theater, managed to secure a private meeting with the new German commander of Vilna. The artists outlined their proposition for a Yiddish theater that would stage only plays of the highest literary quality. The commander responded with incredulity.

> He looked at us as though we were mad. His "*Waaas!?*" scared us half to death. He led us to the window and showed us: "*Sehen Sie meine Herren!* My soldiers roam about the streets without a place to live, all of the local representatives have come to ask us to help the downtrodden and starving masses, and you come to spin me some nonsense about a Yiddish theater?"
>
> We were a little ashamed, but we quickly came to our senses and

> explained to him in high German [*Hochdeutsch*] that the local Jewish population was starving just as much for a theater as for bread.[25]

Before the war, Vilna had been famous for its rich Jewish literary culture, earning the city the nickname "Yerusholayim d'Lite" (Jerusalem of Lithuania).[26] However during the war, Vilna's greatest artists, scholars, and writers, along with most Jews of means and nearly half of the Jewish population, fled the overcrowded city just as the flood of homeless refugees arrived.[27] Shuster and Orliuk hoped that their theater might restore Vilna's Jewish cultural glory and bring hope to the starving Jewish refugees who now made up a sizable portion of the city's population.

When the commander sent them away, the actors were undeterred and continued to lobby other military personnel, who were likewise astonished by such a daring request for scarce wartime resources. As one Baron von Stolzenberg told Dr. Jacob Wygodski, a representative of the Vilna Jewish Aid Committee who appealed to the military on behalf of the artists, "In the vicinity of Vilna flows the heroic blood of our soldiers and—you want to play theater!"[28] Yet to the astonishment of Stolzenberg, Wygodski, Shuster, Orliuk, and the entire German military establishment, the commander published a decree a few days later granting the artists exclusive permission to open a Yiddish theater in occupied Vilna. It was a brilliant publicity maneuver for the German army. With a single decree, they had won the support of Vilna's Jews.

Feeling like they had won the lottery, Leyb and his friends began to seek out every aspiring Jewish actor they could find in occupied Vilna. Most of the recruits were amateurs from prewar Yiddish theater clubs. Some had no stage experience at all. A few were experienced Russian actors of Jewish descent, graduates of prestigious Russian drama schools who found themselves stranded in a German-occupied city where performing in Russian was forbidden. Finally, they recruited Matisyahu Kovalski, the only professional Yiddish actor left in war-torn Vilna. Kovalski, at the age of twenty-one, was the most seasoned Yiddish actor among them.

The actors could hardly have been more different. Some had been raised with a traditional Jewish education, while others had attended the state-run Russian gymnasia or a secular Yiddishist or Bundist school.[29] Most had no formal theatrical training, while a few had performed in professional Russian-language companies. Leyb later wrote that the bulk of his work as director involved teaching basic acting techniques and theater terminology: how to walk, how to project, what a director was, and so on.[30]

Even language was no equalizer. While most were fluent in Yiddish, several spoke no Yiddish at all and had to learn the language from scratch. For months, these actors were limited to nonspeaking roles while they studied grammar tables and vocabulary lists.[31] Only two actors, Orliuk and Sholem Tankhus, bridged the divide between the company's twin organizational and cultural heritages: between amateur and professional and between Yiddish and Russian theaters.

These were decidedly less than ideal conditions for the founding of a theater company: a ragtag assortment of mostly untrained actors without even a common language. Adding to the chaos, the political status of the company was anything but secure. Right away, nearly all of the actors adopted stage names, just in case the Russians took back Vilna and tried to punish them for breaking the wartime Yiddish theater ban. Alexander Orliuk became Alexander Asro, Noyekh Bushlewicz became Noah Nachbush, and Leyb Shuster and his family became the Kadisons.

Only under a particular set of political conditions—the defeat of the Russians, the continued occupation of the Germans, the end of the war that they had begun to doubt would ever come—could FADA continue without putting the actors' lives at risk.

Table 1. Actors of the Original Vilna Troupe, 1915

Birth name	Stage name	Place of origin	Theater experience
A. Lerer	—	unknown	Amateur Yiddish
Alexander Orliuk	Alexander Asro	Vilna	Amateur Yiddish and professional Russian
Frida Blumental	—	Vilna	Amateur Yiddish
Khane Shuster (née Mogel)	Khane Kadison	Kovne	none
Leyb Shuster	Leyb Kadison	Kovne	Amateur Yiddish
Matisyahu Koval	Mateus Kovalski	Luninets	Professional Yiddish
Noyekh Bushlevits	Noah Nachbush	Minsk	Amateur Yiddish
B. Kalen	—	unknown	Amateur Yiddish
R. Rivkina	—	unknown	Amateur Yiddish
Pola Shroder	Pola Valter	Riga	Professional Russian
Rivke Hanenzon	Yehudis Lares	Vilna	Professional Russian
Shneyer-Chaim Gamerov	Chaim Shniur	Osveya	Amateur Yiddish
Sholem Tankhus	Sholem Tanin	Kovne	Amateur Yiddish and professional Russian
Sonia Lubotski	Sonia Alomis	Vilna	Amateur Yiddish
Yankev Sherman	"Hamacabi" (The Maccabee)	Lubawa	Amateur Yiddish

The company's full name ("Federation of Yiddish Dramatic Actors [FADA] under the Direction of Mateus Kovalski") signified one of its first innovations: the merging of amateur and professional Yiddish theater traditions. Originally, Leyb Kadison (né Shuster) and Alexander Asro (né Orliuk) sought to create an umbrella organization for amateur performers that would be both a theater company and a quasi-union.[32] But when professional Russian actors like Pola Valter and Yehudis Lares joined, the founders abandoned the federation plan. The twenty-one-year-old Kovalski, as the only professional Yiddish actor among them, was officially charged with running the company, but his leadership was in name alone. Kovalski never directed a single FADA (or later, Vilna Troupe) production, and the memoirs of the other actors scarcely mention his name. Kovalski's nominal positioning as artistic director was a strategic gesture to invoke professional legitimacy.

FADA was a cooperative in which every member had a vote on all company decisions. Theoretically, actors were supposed to be elected to join a rotating leadership committee.[33] In reality, however, individual members took on semipermanent roles. Kadison, as the most experienced director and the most skilled visual artist among them, was almost always chosen by the committee to direct the productions and to design and build FADA's sets. Asro took charge of the actors. Soon, the committee brought in Mordechai Mazo, a former gymnastics and fencing teacher, to serve as FADA's business manager.[34] Mazo was an avid theatergoer who shared Kadison and Asro's goals about elevating the quality of the Yiddish stage. A charismatic and savvy leader with a deep-rooted knowledge of the local Jewish community, and over a decade older than the others, Mazo's influence far exceeded his nominal role of business manager and he quickly became one of the company's leaders. Mazo was an uncompromising idealist who refused to let anything get in the way of making great art. He supported Kadison's push for lengthy rehearsal periods and complex set designs even when they were costly. If the company did not have the necessary funds, he raised them. For Mazo, "there was one thing," Luba Kadison later recalled: "the performances had to be perfect."[35] Somehow, Mazo always managed to make the money stretch just far enough.

Still, although FADA was primarily managed by a few key individuals, ensemble performance with a focus on the collective over the individual was a core part of the company's approach. Every actor and every character, no matter how small the part, was supposed to be equally significant. This was a new concept in Yiddish theater, a tradition that had long been dominated by talented, vocal, and often egotistical star performers in what was colloquially known as the "star system." In theory, FADA challenged this entrenched model with a collective approach to theater making that matched the socialist politics of its members. In addition to an executive committee, there was a statute committee that crafted rules for the company members, a repertoire committee that was responsible for selecting plays, and a building committee to secure performance locations.[36] In practice, the socialist ethos of FADA was imperfect. Actors with small parts may have been treated equally by FADA's directors, but those with larger roles were often paid higher salaries.[37] Still, the collectivist attitude of FADA was a major departure from previous Yiddish theater companies. This was an ideological choice, certainly, but it was also a necessity. As the actor Chaim Shniur recalled, FADA had little choice but to operate as a collective.[38] With more than half of the company made up of untested amateurs and the rest struggling to master basic Yiddish grammar, the actors had to rely upon one another to fill in the gaps. There was nobody with enough authority or experience to guide the company according to his or her whims alone. Individually, the actors struggled to overcome the gaps in their linguistic and artistic backgrounds; collectively, they made an impressively talented ensemble.

Around the Kadisons' kitchen table, FADA's members voted on the central tenets of their company. Khane Kadison would prepare for each actor his or her only meal of the day—a single boiled potato—and they would carry on debates about Yiddish art theater late into the night. "In those days, a potato was a luxury," Luba Kadison recalled, but "it was under these conditions that our idealism developed."[39] Ultimately, the actors agreed on their goals:

> Fight against the star system, place the greatest emphasis on ensemble performance, pay attention to even the smallest roles, strict discipline in rehearsals and performances, do away with the prompter (i.e. the actors must learn their roles by heart), a true artistic relationship to set design, lighting effects, costumes, and makeup, and not to go out during the intermission to bow to the audience, because this ruins the totality of the performance.[40]

Moreover, every member of the company would be responsible for maintaining his or her reputation as an educated intellectual. Asro was particularly stubborn on this point, swearing that no actor would be granted a speaking role until he or she could prove an ability to speak, read, and write a proper literary Yiddish. A formal demonstration of one's knowledge of modern Yiddish literature before the entire company was required to be eligible for the best parts.[41] Finally, the company members agreed upon a rigorous rehearsal process, in which no play would be performed until its director deemed the production perfect. Each of these was by itself a major innovation; taken together, FADA's goals were a complete overthrow of Yiddish theatrical norms.

The FADA founders hoped that their venture would be so successful that it would also attract Russian and European intellectuals. FADA was modeled on the work of Russian and European troupes like those of Max Reinhardt, Gordon Craig, Vsevolod Meyerhold, and, most importantly, Stanislavsky and the Moscow Art Theater. Though FADA drew from a range of European art theater models, the Moscow Art Theater was its primary influence. The actors idolized Stanislavsky and his company. Late-night discussions after rehearsals focused on how to best emulate the Moscow Art Theater's ensemble techniques, stylistic innovations, training, and repertoire.[42]

At times, the Yiddish actors felt themselves at a disadvantage compared to their Russian idols. "Stanislavsky's troupe was educated by the best Russian playwrights, while the Vilna Troupe educated the 'best' Yiddish playwrights," lamented FADA member Chaim Shniur. "The Muscovites were brought up on the best theaters of their era. It was not the fault of the Vilner that the 'best' Yiddish theaters didn't exist."[43] The Moscow Art Theater could call upon the Russian literary establishment and could draw upon a network of reputable Russian theater companies for inspiration and collaboration. FADA, on the other hand, was on its own. Its task was not only to create a Yiddish art theater but also to develop the institutional infrastructure, critical apparatus, and audience base that the company needed to survive from the ground up.

The members of FADA thus envisioned their project as having two aims. As Jewish culture builders, they would bring art theater, à la Russian and European models, to the Jewish intelligentsia and ultimately, they hoped, to the Yiddish-speaking masses. At the same time, they hoped to introduce non-Jewish art theater aficionados to the Yiddish stage and, by extension, to the achievements of modern Jewish literature and culture. One function was almost never mentioned: entertainment. FADA sought to elevate the Yiddish stage. Entertainment was beside the point.

While FADA was fashioned on a Russo-European model, the actors never wrote a formal manifesto. For European artists in the early twentieth century, it was the manifesto that defined—and more often than not, preceded—the movement. Why didn't FADA write a manifesto? FADA's founders did not appear to reflect on this question. Perhaps Yiddish actors were wary of aligning themselves with the politically explosive—and, within a politically unstable Jewish context, potentially dangerous—genre of the artistic manifesto. Or perhaps FADA's lack of a stabile home base, its wartime origins, and the actors' lack of leisure time made the production, publication, and dissemination of a manifesto a daunting task.

Instead, FADA's leaders crafted a logo. Both Kadison and Asro were visual artists before they became theater artists. Both had trained as painters, while neither had received any formal training in acting, directing, or stagecraft. While FADA's founders were ideologically committed to Peretz's vision of a literary Yiddish theater, in practice their approach to theater was highly visual. Their goal was not merely to stage literary dramas, as Peretz had sought, but to render them onstage in three dimensions. The FADA actors were not writers with a side interest in theater like their predecessors. They were theatergoers for whom the appeal of Yiddish drama had to do with its stage viability. FADA's visual orientation would later enable the company to embrace the theatricality that became its trademark. Initially, however, we can see FADA's interest in the visual in a meticulously designed logo that served as its manifesto, brand marker, and visual mission statement.

This logo, designed jointly by Kadison and Asro and dated 1915, is the first recorded document referring to FADA's existence and may have even predated the official founding of the company. The logo features a picture-frame proscenium stage with Yiddish letters spelling out "FADA" emblazoned at the top. The curtains are drawn back to reveal a wooden stage lit not with ordinary gas or electric footlights but with a row of seven ancient lamps, each with a single burning flame. These lamps evoke the seven-branched menorah that stood before the ark of the ancient Temple in Jerusalem. Like the Temple, this theater is also a holy space. The presence of a menorah, the unofficial symbol of Jewish peoplehood, at the base of the stage suggests that Yiddish theater is a central element of Jewish life. Beyond the menorah-like footlights, the stage turns into an open road leading to a rising sun—the future. The flat platform of the stage becomes a ramp that rises upward, elevating the audience and the actors to new heights. Come to the Yiddish theater, the logo suggests, and join us en route to the future of Jewish culture.

FADA's logo illustrates the company's aims in visual terms. Letters and

Figure 2. *A.* (left) Kadison and Asro's original logo sketch, 1915. *B.* (right) Logo from an early FADA program, 1916. YIVO Institute for Jewish Research.

images are fused together in seamless harmony, symbolizing the integration of literature and visual artistry. The upward tilt of the stage toward the sun echoes the imagery of vertical ascent that was often associated with the company.[44] FADA's Yiddish theater sought to demonstrate—to Vilna Jewry, to their Gentile neighbors, and to the occupying German army—that Yiddish deserved a place at the table of modern European culture.

In the fall of 1915, FADA selected its first play: Sholem Asch's 1911 lighthearted comedy *Der landsman* (*The Compatriot*). It was an unlikely choice for the first production of a self-styled art theater. Set in New York, *The Compatriot* tells the story of an upwardly mobile Jewish American immigrant named Jack (né Yankl) Levi (played by Kovalski) whose wife has recently died. Jack decides to remarry a high-society assimilated German Jewish woman. But at the end of the first act, Jack gets a surprise visit from an elderly Eastern European Jew and his wife who have just arrived in America. It is Moyshe (Noah Nachbush) and Blume, the couple from Jack's old shtetl who raised him after his parents died. They have brought his former fiancée Sheyndele (Yehudis Lares), whom Jack had abandoned when he decided to come to America to seek his fortune. Sheyndele is now widowed and has a daughter of her own, Feygele (Pola Valter), who is the same age that Sheyndele was when Jack abandoned her. When his assimilated in-laws-to-be make fun of his shtetl kin and former fiancée, Jack breaks off the engagement and decides to marry his jilted fiancée's daughter instead. In *The Compatriot*, Old World Jewish authenticity trumps high society New World ambitions.

As a play about a Jew rejecting the assimilatory trappings of German culture and rediscovering his true Jewish identity, *The Compatriot* was a bold choice given the context and timing of FADA's production. After all, Jack rejects snobbish German culture in favor of Jewish identity, and FADA was performing under German military occupation in front of an audience full of German soldiers. Perhaps Kadison and Asro reasoned that the Germans in attendance would understand only a portion of the dialogue and might not pick up on the full extent of the play's anti-German sentiments. But the Jews in the audience would hear their message loud and clear: even under German occupation, FADA would not be complicit in any project to assimilate Vilna's Jews. *The Compatriot* was a not so thinly veiled declaration of FADA's independence from the city's German military overlords, beneath the surface of a heartwarming domestic comedy.

The actors elected Kadison as their first director. Rehearsals were held at night in the Kadisons' living room and often lasted until dawn. Legend has it that Kadison rehearsed the company at this breakneck pace for forty nights, with scarcely an evening off.[45] Actors arrived at rehearsals on the verge of starvation, struggling to maintain their energy after a long day without sustenance. Still, they respected Kadison's grueling schedule and faithfully attended night after night, with or without food.

Once the rehearsal process was underway, Kadison began to seek an adequate performance space. This was no simple task, as the German army had requisitioned every decent theater building in the city. Yet had the Germans never occupied Vilna, the company still would have struggled to find a suitable space, since, as a rule, the managers of Vilna's best theaters did not allow Jews to perform on their stages. Vilna's Yiddish companies had traditionally performed in two locations on the outskirts of the city: a small makeshift theater located in a Jewish cafeteria and a dilapidated former circus.[46] These buildings were also repurposed when the Germans occupied Vilna. Deeming both stages unfit for visiting German performers, the army converted the cafeteria theater into soldiers' quarters and the circus theater into a stable for military horses. Furniture and sets from the old Yiddish theater productions were burned to heat the buildings.[47]

At the request of the horrified Jewish owner of the circus, Kadison managed to convince the Germans to move the horses elsewhere and rent him the building. The owner was so relieved at the departure of the horses that he gave Kadison the space for free. Overjoyed, the actors entered their new home only to discover thick layers of dust mired in horse dung between the boards of the stage, an auditorium littered with broken chairs and half-burnt set pieces, footlights with broken lamps and chewed-up electrical wires, and layers of ice in every corner from buckets of water that were left behind when the army departed and turned off the heat.[48] The actors scrubbed the boards and hauled furniture during rehearsal breaks. In his memoirs, Kadison recalled his disappointment upon finding the building that was supposed to be his "Jewish Temple of Art" converted into a horse stable. Like the ancient Maccabees restoring the Temple in Jerusalem to its former glory, Kadison wrote, the members of FADA took up the task of purifying their theater.[49] By connecting FADA's restoration of the circus theater to the cleansing and resanctification of the ancient Temple, Kadison framed their cleanup as an act of Jewish national heroism.

Still, as Kadison admitted to his colleagues, the circus theater was not the proper site for a Yiddish art theater. Even before the war it had never been a respectable performance space, hindered first by its associations with lowbrow circus entertainment and, second, by the inadequacies of the building itself. In Kadison's words,

> The circus theater was not suitable even for melodramas and operettas. A dreadful stage and terrible acoustics. Cold and uncomfortable. The circus was particularly ill-suited to our repertoire, but, as I said, we had no choice.[50]

FADA's literary repertoire and subdued realism would have been better suited to a small, intimate space with good acoustics. Instead, the circus theater was a massive building perhaps better suited to housing horses than an art theater. It was difficult to hear the dialogue from almost any seat in the house, and the actors had to resort to shouting in order to be heard. The stage was literally falling apart, the lighting primitive, the dressing rooms barren, and the roof leaky whenever it rained or snowed. Even worse, the company did not have enough money to heat such a large space for both rehearsals and performances, so they rehearsed through the bitter cold of a Vilna winter without heat, their hands swelling from the frosty air as they built and painted sets late into the night.[51]

By the winter of 1916 Vilna was a city teetering on the verge of starvation. Food was so scarce that mothers routinely abandoned their children in the streets, knowing that they would receive more food in the military-run orphanages than at home.[52] Rampant cholera and contaminated food exacerbated the hunger problem. The extreme poverty that permeated the city was particularly noticeable among Vilna's Jews. More than half of the city's Jewish population depended upon charity for their food.[53] Over two thousand Vilna Jews died in 1915, nearly two-thirds from starvation.[54] Many of Vilna's starving residents turned to prostitution or illegal smuggling to provide for their families. It was within this context of a city cowed by starvation and disease that Kadison announced FADA's opening performance.

Perhaps acknowledging the incongruity of asking starving people to buy theater tickets, Kadison asked Mordechai Mazo to handle publicity. Mazo was well liked in the Jewish community for his advocacy work to help those who had lost their homes or livelihoods because of the war. He put up posters, distributed flyers, set up ticket discount programs, and perhaps most importantly, convinced the destitute Jews of wartime Vilna that a Yiddish art theater was no luxury, just as Kadison and Asro had managed to convince the German commander that Vilna's Jews needed theater even more than they needed bread.[55]

The Compatriot opened on February 18, 1916, on the rotting wooden stage of the decrepit circus building. Between donations from the community and meager loans from the actors' own pockets, FADA had raised just enough money to heat the auditorium during performances. The actors were not so lucky: there was no money left over to heat the dressing rooms.

Mazo's publicity campaign was successful and opening night brought a packed house with a diverse audience. There were, in Kadison's words, "'aristocrats' who customarily frequented the Russian theaters and wrinkled their noses at Yiddish, the sincere Jewish intelligentsia, the common folk—craftsmen, shopkeepers, traders, laborers. And so too came many of our new rulers—German officers and soldiers."[56] With the exception of the German soldiers, this was precisely the audience that Peretz had dreamed of a decade earlier. On opening night of its first production, FADA had already managed to attract the kind of public that Peretz had never quite been able to secure: the intelligentsia and *shund* theatergoers, Russianists and Yiddishists, and, for reasons peculiar to Vilna's wartime situation, Jews and non-Jews.

A special commission of German military and communal leaders arrived in uniform: the German censor, the field rabbi, the German police chief of Vilna, and the generals who commanded the city. Each had brought his field binoculars, and Asro remarked to his colleagues that perhaps the commission had come to see "the wild animals, the *Ostjuden* [Eastern European Jews] who recently went crazy and decided to play theater in a time of hunger and war."[57] Jewish Vilna was also well represented by journalists, writers, and community leaders. While the majority of the audience consisted of Jews, the Germans were accorded front-row seats. FADA's desire to please its German audience members was also reflected in the program, where large-print German text appeared above the Yiddish.[58] Moreover, the program opened from left to right, following the European custom, rather than right to left, as was standard for Yiddish theater programs. There was little choice in these gestures. FADA needed German support in order to continue to operate.

Ovation after ovation followed the final curtain, to the astonishment of the actors, who remained frozen in disbelief during the curtain call. The next day brought glowing reviews. "Our Vilna amateurs have taken their test and have passed," crowed one Yiddish reviewer.[59] The company stayed up all night after the first few performances, critiquing their work and debating how they could improve. These all-night debates would become a Vilna Troupe tradition (occasionally this would prove troublesome on tours, when hotel management would receive calls complaining about actors shouting all night).[60]

The company quickly developed a local following. The German writer Sammy Gronemann became one of FADA's strongest advocates. Gronemann was a German-Jewish soldier whose company was stationed in Vilna in 1915.[61] He was deeply moved by what he observed at his first FADA performance. "In a large unheated room, in front of a small, highly uneducated audience," Gronemann reflected, "they offered a remarkable and wonderful surprise. . . . There, perhaps for the first time, it dawned on me the beauty and intimacy of the Yiddish language."[62] Though the actors were "quite literally starving," wrote Gronemann, "they were strong enough to avoid making any concessions to popular taste in terms of the repertoire, such as chasing after cheap hits."[63] Gronemann and his army friends, including the painter Hermann Struck, the poet Herbert Eulenberg, the journalist Hans Goslar, and others, began attending FADA's performances in earnest.[64] Many of FADA's German army fans were—like Gronemann, Struck, and Eulenberg—themselves of Jewish descent.[65] After performances, these young German Jewish artists would gather to celebrate in a local restaurant with the actors. On Friday evenings, Gronemann recalled, they would join the FADA actors in singing Yiddish songs and Hasidic *nigunim* (wordless melodies). For many of the German Jewish soldiers who were wholly secular, these gatherings were an education in Jewish culture.[66]

Initially, FADA had scheduled two matinee performances a week, but it soon added performances on Saturday and Sunday nights to accommodate the demand.[67] Because it was a repertory theater with a different play nearly every night, fans could attend FADA performances two or three times in a single week and see only new material. In its first season alone, FADA presented twenty-eight plays, most of which were only ever performed a handful of times.[68] To keep up this pace, the company had to prepare a new production every two weeks. This meant an arduous schedule for the actors, who often rehearsed straight through the night after performances. Their success also did not ease the company's financial difficulties, and expenses continued to outpace income in spite of strong ticket sales. The circus building was massive and wood was exceedingly expensive to procure during wartime, even in small quantities. Nearly all of FADA's profits went directly to heating the space, leaving the actors to cover the costs of props, costumes, furniture, and sets out of pocket.[69] The dressing rooms remained unheated. Heating the auditorium was non-negotiable, since heat was a major draw for impoverished spectators in a cold winter.

In FADA's first season, a handful of playwrights were its standbys: Sholem Asch, Dovid Pinski, Peretz Hirschbein, Mark Arnshteyn, Leon Kobrin, Y.L. Peretz, and Jacob Gordin. There were few other options. Unlike Europe's high-art theaters, FADA was working in a language without a fully developed dramatic repertoire. There were few Yiddish plays that met FADA's requirements of literary authorship and "serious" subject matter without necessitating overly complex sets. The company relied on their own translations of European plays to fill the gaps: from Russian, Mikhail Artsybashev's *Jealousy* (produced by the Vilna Troupe in 1917) and Evgeny Chirikov's *The Jews* (1916); from German, Hermann Sudermann's *Battle of the Butterflies* (1916) and Ludwig Fulda's *School Friends* (1916), and others. Soon, however, the dearth of repertoire became less of a pressing concern. As FADA's popularity expanded, so did the repertoire as young Yiddish writers tried playwriting. Rather than preceding the development of the drama, as was the case in most European contexts, FADA's success spurred the development of a robust Yiddish dramatic literature.

Initially, FADA's performances were animated by a fierce commitment to realism, which was already passé on the European stage. Still, FADA's productions represented a step forward for a Yiddish stage where melodrama dominated and realism had never taken hold. During rehearsals, Kadison told the actors that their goal was to exorcise melodrama from the

Yiddish theater, to "get rid of the unnatural onstage" by not "speak[ing] in a singsong manner with too much pathos."[70]

Kadison's entreaties asking the actors to avoid pathos, superfluous gestures, and excessive face making reflects an underlying anxiety about Jews being perceived as improperly theatrical. Anti-Semitic rhetoric of the period often portrayed Jews as excessive in speech, gesture, and affect—and thus dangerous in their ability to lead the righteous astray. Similarly, European popular culture associated Jews with melodrama. A common trope in nineteenth-century European literature was the odious Jewish owner of the melodramatic theater: for example, Mr. Isaacs in Oscar Wilde's *The Picture of Dorian Gray* (1890). Dorian's first description of Mr. Isaacs typifies how many Europeans thought of Jewish theater artists during this period:

> A hideous Jew, in the most amazing waistcoat I ever beheld in my life, was standing at the entrance, smoking a vile cigar. He had greasy ringlets, and an enormous diamond blazed in the centre of a soiled shirt. "Have a box, my Lord?" he said when he saw me, and he took off his hat with an air of gorgeous servility. There was something about him, Harry, that amused me. He was such a monster.[71]

FADA's emphasis on realism was partially a rejection of all Yiddish theater that had come before, but it was also a response to communal anxieties about Jewish excessiveness and performativity. In the guise of realism, FADA sought to reimagine the theatrical Jewish body as refined.

While FADA professed its allegiance to realism, its productions also included a few nods to German expressionism, which may have been inspired by conversations with the company's young German supporters.[72] For example, Leyb Kadison's set design sketches for Sholem Asch's *Got fun nekome* (*God of Vengeance*), a play about a Jewish brothel owner and the coming of age of his innocent daughter, in 1916 had a decidedly expressionist feel. Kadison built the entire set around the strange angles and sloping ceilings of the circus building, lending the space an aura of contrasting proportions and exaggerating the shapes of the actors' bodies. A crooked staircase led into the main room of the brothel, with a window framed by exaggerated, cartoonish beams of light, while bedrooms were cleverly nestled into oddly shaped alcoves.[73] Perhaps these choices were simply a function of the theater space, perhaps Kadison was inspired by pictures of German expressionist sets he saw in newspapers and magazines, or perhaps the designs were influenced by his conversations with German soldiers.

In addition to reviews in Yiddish newspapers, numerous articles about FADA appeared in the German press, beginning with the local army newspaper *Zeitung der 10. Armee*. The first announcements made a point of emphasizing that the building had heat.

> On Friday the 18th and Saturday the 19th of February, the first performances of the Jewish theater in the Circus Theater building on Lukas (Lukitshki) Street will take place. . . . The theater building is repaired and well heated.[74]

A few days later, this announcement was followed by a review of *The Compatriot* by soldier-journalist Carl Winter, who described his visit to the Circus Theater to see Jewish theater as "a leap into the unknown." Still, Winter continued, the actors "knew how to speak the Jewish idiom so that it captivated all of our hearts, with such depth that the foreign language was more understandable to us with our hearts than with our minds." By the end of the play, Winter reported, many in the audience had tears in their eyes. The applause continued long after the actors finished taking their bows.[75] A few weeks later, another army journalist described FADA's production of Nomberg's *The Family* as "an exemplary performance" with "clever direction." The audience was delighted, wrote the reporter, and "thanked the artists with an ovation."[76]

These reviews marked the first time in history that major non-Jewish newspapers and magazines regularly reviewed Jewish theater. Some of these early German articles were authored by Gronemann and his army friends Goslar, Struck, and Eulenberg; others were written by army journalists reporting on current events for fellow soldiers. Some appeared in the local army newspapers and magazines published in Vilna, Kovne, Minsk, and Bialystok.[77] Others were written for readers back home in Germany. For example, Hans Goslar's article in the Berlin magazine *Zeitbilder* included a lengthy description of the company alongside reprints of photographs from FADA productions. "Our soldiers have learned many wonderful things on their Eastward march," Goslar told Berlin readers:

> For many who came to Poland and Russia, one of the greatest surprises in these small cities was the Jewish theater. . . . Performers like Asro, sometimes dreamy and sometimes shaking with storm-

> tossed passion, or like Miss Alomis . . . or Mrs. Vitalin who showers her mother characters with pure womanly charm, have such great talent that they could hold their own upon Western Europe's great stages.[78]

Army reporters also attended Lithuanian, Latvian, and Belorussian performances and published reviews of them in army press organs. However, only FADA's performances received such accolades.[79] In part, this had to do with the accessibility of Yiddish to German speakers. But the journalists were also genuinely impressed with what they viewed as the high quality of FADA's performances.[80]

In addition to expressing surprise at the quality of FADA's performances, German journalists read FADA's realism as a demonstration of Eastern European Jewish authenticity. Indeed, German reviewers were far more interested in FADA's realism than the Yiddish writers who reviewed the same productions. Herbert Eulenberg described FADA as "inimitable, exactly the archetype of a second life. . . . Nowhere do actors perform so naturalistically, with absolutely everything on the stage in such a natural mood, as in today's Jewish theater."[81] Friedrich von Wilpert wrote of FADA's early productions, "This is life in its fullest and deepest feeling. What those upon the stage are saying is no longer poetry, but truth itself. . . . The portrayal seems as realistic as humanly possible."[82] It was not unusual for German reviewers to confuse FADA's realism with Jewish authenticity, as in this 1918 review for the Berlin newspaper *Tageblatt*: "Their acting, which developed directly out of the soil of authentic Jewish life, seeks to be interpreted and understood under its own conditions."[83] This conflation of realism with Jewish authenticity allowed FADA to adopt a style long out of fashion in Western Europe while still appearing cutting edge. These reviews also underscore the fact that Jews and Germans in wartime Vilna often attended FADA productions for different reasons. Jews wanted an art theater to demonstrate the achievements of Yiddish literature and culture before the world. German military spectators were more interested in seeing "authentic" depictions of Eastern European Jewish life to better understand the people who surrounded them.

As press attention mounted, the German army offered FADA the ornate Vilna Municipal Theater in November 1916.[84] The actors transported their sets and props from the dilapidated Circus Theater to the grandest theater building in Vilna. This was a major event for Vilna Jewry, marking the first time in the city's history that Jews had ever been allowed to perform on the Municipal Theater's magnificent stage. The invitation to the Municipal Theater, and FADA's subsequent geographical move from the outskirts of the city to its center, was a symbol of the company's growing import and recognition among Jews and non-Jews alike. Accordingly, the company added several European plays in the actors' own Yiddish translations to the repertoire. The new repertoire—by Mikhail Artsybashev, Semyon Yushkevich, Arthur Schnitzler, and others—consisted primarily of naturalist dramas by German and Russian playwrights of Jewish descent. Many of these plays were familiar to the soldiers stationed in Vilna and attracted more Germans to the audience. FADA's German attendees were often surprised to discover that, as speakers of a Germanic language, they could understand a significant portion of the dialogue despite not knowing Yiddish. Most of the German soldiers—even those who were Jewish—had never heard Yiddish before coming to Vilna.[85] Yiddish theater offered them an opportunity to learn about Eastern European Jewish life, which seemed to many more authentic than the Jewish identity they knew.[86]

But in spite of their achievements, the actors continued to struggle to feed themselves and their families. The economic crisis in Vilna was only getting worse. By the start of FADA's second season in the fall of 1916, the desperation of Vilna's Jewish community was palpable. The German army regularly requisitioned food and commodities from impoverished families to support its soldiers. Family heirlooms and religious objects, including thousands of menorahs and Sabbath candlesticks, were confiscated and smelted for cash. Colonels and generals, short on voluntary recruits, began seizing men in the streets for forced labor and military conscription.[87] These seizures were disproportionately targeted at Vilna's Jewish neighborhoods. Many of FADA's fans spent days or weeks on end hiding in cellars and attics to avoid forced conscription. To make matters worse, with the onset of winter typhoid and dysentery epidemics broke out across the city, killing tens of thousands. Hospitals and morgues were overwhelmed, and there were long waiting lists for ambulances, hospital beds, and even hearses and coffins.[88] Again, Vilna's Jews were particularly hard hit by these epidemics, and the death toll surged in Jewish neighborhoods. By March 1917 the death rate of the Jewish population was 97.5 per 1,000, about five times as high as before the war.[89] Essentially, every tenth Jew in Vilna was doomed.

As the situation worsened by the day, FADA continued to perform in the Municipal Theater, albeit to smaller and smaller audiences. Kadison considered shutting down, but the Germans convinced him to keep the company running by offering additional support. Vilna's German military commanders were proud of the Jewish theater company that was attracting so much attention and sending positive news back to Berlin. Throughout 1917, the German army provided the actors with occasional food, shoes, and most importantly, exemptions from forced labor, which were nearly impossible to procure otherwise.[90] Compared to the rest of Vilna's residents, the FADA members were living like royalty. The company grew and grew.

Still, the additional amenities provided by the army did not fully alleviate the company's problems. Actors often arrived at rehearsals poorly dressed and famished. As Asro recalled,

> I remember one time, I shudder to recall it, how during a rehearsal . . . at three o'clock in the afternoon one of our most talented actresses suddenly went down like a felled tree, with a resounding slap against the hard boards of the stage and with an unspoken line still lingering on her pale lips. . . . She lay there unmoving. . . . Three in the afternoon, and she hadn't yet had a single meal. We all stood there frozen in place. . . . A glass of water and a baked potato . . . brought our actress back to life.[91]

When German officials suggested that the company leave Vilna and go on tour, the actors quickly agreed. The German army envisioned a FADA tour as an antidote to the pervasive anti-Semitism that had spread through its ranks during the war.[92] The actors had their own reasons for wanting to leave. Ticket sales had begun to decline in Vilna as people became more wary of public gatherings during the epidemics. The actors too were ready to leave their disease-ridden city for safer territory. Moreover, after nearly two years of preparing new repertoire at a breakneck pace, the actors were thrilled at the prospect of temporarily forgoing their exhausting rehearsal schedule and adopting the more relaxed pace of a tour, where they could simply present already prepared productions. And so, in May 1917, FADA set out for Kovne with a fourfold goal: to combat anti-Semitism for its German army friends, to recoup its financial losses, to escape the epidemics in Vilna, and to take a break from rehearsals while bringing a repertoire of reliable hits to new audiences.

Exodus

When the actors arrived in the rural Polish provinces, they found local residents eagerly awaiting their arrival. Reports of FADA's productions had traveled far, and Jews throughout war-torn Poland were excited to meet the young actors who had caused such a stir. Never before had a Yiddish theater company received such enthusiastic reviews from both the Jewish and non-Jewish press, and never before had a traveling Yiddish troupe been welcomed with such fanfare. Crowds of admirers met the actors as they entered each town. Audiences continued to include local Jews alongside German soldiers. "In Bialystok, the Troupe won its first great success," wrote Gronemann of one of the first stops on the tour, "Then the German officers began to stream into its theater, and the company's fame spread even further."[93]

With a new audience every few weeks, FADA had the luxury of presenting only its greatest hits. For Jews in small shtetls and villages, the company performed plays about the triumph of Jewish identity over external influences, including Leon Kobrin's *Der dorfsyung* (*The Village Lad*), Hirschbein's *Di puste kretshme* (*The Abandoned Inn*), and Osip Dimov's *Shma Yisroel* (*Hear O Israel*) and *Der eybiker vanderer* (*The Eternal Wanderer*). In larger cities where audiences were more diverse, FADA favored European dramas by Leonid Andreyev, Mikhail Artsybashev, Ludwig Fulda, and Tolstoy.

On tour, FADA discovered that its work had an appeal beyond hyperliterary Vilna. Audiences in small towns were, if anything, even more enamored. In smaller cities and towns, local audiences had fewer options than theatergoers in larger cities for quality entertainment, which made the Vilna Troupe's arrival all the more exciting. Unlike major urban centers such as Vilna or Warsaw, which hosted the best Yiddish theater companies in Eastern Europe, cities like Grodno or Kovne housed only midrate companies if they had any permanent Yiddish theaters at all. In a larger city, there was always the possibility of Jews going to see Russian or Polish theater instead of Yiddish theater; in a smaller town, this was not always an option. As one small-town youth described FADA's visit,

> It was the first great theater in my life. The first time I trembled before great, serious dramatic art. I saw them on their tour of the provinces in a small *shtetl* called Tomashov, by the river Pilitsa. We waited for them like they were Messiahs. Our hearts almost stopped twenty times from the anxiety: will they or won't they avoid our *shtetl*? Until at last they came.[94]

The whole town "ate theater, drank theater, slept theater" for the duration of FADA's stay. When there were not enough seats in the theater to accommodate the entire shtetl, spectators "stood around the stage, like in Shakespeare's time."[95]

Cities and towns across Poland invited FADA to visit. When the company could not accept all of the invitations, locals were disappointed. In Lodz, the Jewish community pined for FADA for nearly a year before their invitation was accepted. As one Lodz writer wrote when FADA finally arrived, "The Jewish and German press was filled with songs of praise for them. The lucky ones who purported to have . . . seen them with their own eyes used to come and speak about them with humility. And we sat here a whole year and waited until they finally came to Lodz."[96]

As the company traveled, the press continued to praise production after production. But FADA's first tour was not at all glamorous. The actors stayed at second-rate hotels and ate at third-rate restaurants, sleeping on the train when they could not afford accommodations. One time in Lodz, the troupe could not afford dinner until a sympathetic waiter allowed them to order gefilte fish juice—sans the fish. Bread dipped in fish juice was enough to temporarily satisfy their hunger, and the troupe continued on.[97]

No longer a local Vilna organization, FADA began to define itself as a traveling troupe. The company would continue to travel constantly for the next twenty years, rarely spending more than six months in any given locale. This was not entirely unique among European performers of the period. Max Reinhardt and Stanislavsky traveled extensively with their companies, and Sarah Bernhardt was better known for her Parisian tours than her performances at home in London. But for FADA, traveling was instrumental and an integral part of its development. FADA did not become the Vilna Troupe in Vilna, its starting point. It became the Vilna Troupe on the road, in Warsaw.

Warsaw in 1917 was indisputably the capital of modern Yiddish culture.[98] It was a metropolis of over a million people where Jews made up more than a third of the population, the largest concentration of Yiddish speakers in all of Europe.[99] Fondly referred to as *kleyn Pariz* (little Paris) by its Jewish inhabitants, Warsaw had five daily Yiddish newspapers and dozens of theaters.[100] Across the Atlantic, Yiddish writers in New York looked to Warsaw for approval. In the words of one literary historian, Warsaw was "the center of all of the centers of Yiddish literature."[101] With more Yiddish-speaking Jews than any other city, Warsaw had the largest potential audience for any aspiring Yiddish writer or theater artist and could thus support more Yiddish newspapers, publishing houses, journals, and theaters than any other city in the world.

Like Vilna, Warsaw was also under German occupation during most of the First World War, and like their Vilna counterparts, Warsaw's Jewish actors had also tried to capitalize on German officers' interest in Yiddish theater, which was more intelligible to them than Polish-language theater. With the encouragement of the German army, Warsaw's five Yiddish theaters flourished during the war, attracting mixed audiences of Jews and German soldiers.[102]

It was in German-occupied Warsaw that the members of FADA, still giddy from their success in the Polish provinces, adopted the name under which their company would become famous: the Vilna Troupe. Prior to its arrival in Warsaw, FADA—unprecedented as its successes may have been—was still a minor regional phenomenon. It was only in Warsaw that the company began to develop an international reputation.

FADA arrived in Warsaw in September 1917. On tour, the actors had encountered the Warsaw-based actress Esther Rokhl Kaminska traveling with her theater company. After attending a FADA performance, Kaminska was enamored and invited the actors to return home with her.[103] The actors agreed, in spite of their anxiety about performing in a city known for its unsparing cultural critics. "We had behind us many artistic successes," recalled Asro, "but a terror fell upon us as we neared our arrival in Warsaw. Warsaw, a city with a million Jews! . . . Warsaw, where in every Jewish corner the towering spirit of the great Peretz still loomed!"[104] Though Peretz had died two years prior to their arrival, the actors still felt like they were auditioning for his posthumous approval. Perhaps they were also remembering the Hirschbein Troupe debacle. Like the Hirschbein Troupe a decade earlier, FADA was a regionally successful theater company that came to Warsaw seeking approval. Like Hirschbein's company, FADA was also primarily comprised of amateurs with big ambitions who sought to be crowned as the representatives of Peretz's art theater project. For opening night, Kadison, Mazo, and Asro chose what they hoped would be a surefire crowd pleaser: an adaptation of Leon Kobrin's play *Yankl Boyle* staged under the new title *Der dorfsyung* (*The Village Lad*) to avoid attracting the attention of the censors, who had rejected the play under its original title.[105]

The Village Lad is a naturalist drama about a doomed love affair between a Jewish boy, Yankl, and a Russian girl, Natasha, in a rural fishing community. The central conflict of the play is between Yankl's Jewish identity and his love for Natasha. He wishes to marry her without converting to Christianity, but her anti-Semitic drunkard father will not allow it. Meanwhile, Yankl's father is sick and dying. On his deathbed, he begs his son to marry

Khayke, a local Jewish girl, and swears to haunt him from beyond the grave if Yankl does not obey his dying wish. After his father's death, Yankl begins to go mad. He hears his father's voice everywhere and decides to marry Khayke to put the voices to rest. But just before the engagement, he learns that Natasha is pregnant with his child. Marry me, Natasha begs him, or else my father will kill me. Yankl refuses and runs away. Having abandoned his pregnant beloved, he hangs himself out of guilt, while Natasha's father drinks himself into a stupor as the curtain falls.

On opening night, the FADA actors were petrified, their fingers trembling as they applied their makeup. As the audience entered the theater and found their seats, the terrified actors peered out through a hole in the curtain ("like a cluster of flies upon a piece of sugar," recalled one actor) and counted the famous writers seated in the front row: H. D. Nomberg, Hillel Zeitlin, Dovid Einhorn, Noyekh Prilutski, Yankev Dinezon, and other literary giants whose pictures they recognized from newspaper clippings.[106] Unlike most theater companies coming to Warsaw for the first time, FADA's reputation had preceded it. "Nomberg is in the theater, Nomberg is here!" the actors anxiously announced. Nomberg was a former member of Peretz's theater circle who was known as an exacting theater critic.[107] The company's recognition of these figures speaks to the success of Kadison and Asro's efforts to educate the actors in Yiddish letters. All of the actors were by this point well versed in Yiddish literature, and they idolized Warsaw's Jewish literary elite.

As the curtain rose and the play began, the actors, intimidated by the caliber and size of their audience, were unsure what to expect. To their surprise, they were enthusiastically received by many of the same Warsaw critics who had eviscerated the Hirschbein Troupe just a few years earlier. As Asro described the opening night performance,

> From the stage the audience hears the first notes of the famous Russian song *Vniz po matushke po volge* ["Down the Mother Volga"]. A few seconds later, and the curtain rises slowly. On the floor, in a real Russian cottage, the village fishermen weave a large net. As the curtain rises, their song grows stronger and bolder. They begin to converse while singing, and upon the threshold of the open door appears [Sonia] Alomis in the role of the Russian village girl Natasha. Her entrance brings thunderous applause. The audience is truly surprised by her authentic Russian appearance. Before the theater audience stands an eighteen-year-old peasant girl, a village beauty, in

> colorful realistic Russian clothes, with two long blond plaits braided through with fiery red ribbons and a samovar glistening in her tan and healthy bare arms.[108]

In contrast to the hastily prepared melodramas that dominated the Warsaw Yiddish stage, the Vilna Troupe presented a meticulously constructed spectator experience suffused in realism. The tempo was measured and purposeful, adding to the power and gravity of the script. The costumes, sets, and music were carefully chosen. Lines were fully memorized and there was no prompter, enabling the actors to imbue their words with layered meaning. The characters were fully realized. It was the realistic portrayal of the Gentile Natasha and her "authentic" Russian surroundings that seemed to impress the audience most of all. In an era when Jewishness and Russianness tended to be positioned as diametrically opposed by both parties, a Jewish actress who could convincingly portray a Russian maiden was striking.

The actors performed with strict realism in mind, but at times, their enthusiasm and youthful exuberance took over, as evidenced by these publicity stills. The audience seemed particularly responsive to moments when the actors' energy took hold: for instance, *The Village Lad* featured a scene where Natasha dances with Yankl at a local fair. The company transformed this brief scene into an extended and rousing group dance number.[109]

When the final scene of *The Village Lad* ended, according to Asro, the applause lasted so long that the curtain was raised and lowered fifteen times.[110] The critics, wrote Gronemann, who had accompanied the troupe on its trip to Warsaw, "were beside themselves with enthusiasm and the performances all sold out."[111] The same writers whom the actors had nervously spotted in the front row insisted on meeting with the entire company backstage after the curtain call. There the actors learned that several had traveled from afar just to see them perform. Lazar Kahan had come from Lodz, journalist Shaul Stupnitski had journeyed from Lublin, and Zalmen Reyzen and Beynish Mikhalevitsh had traveled from Vilna to see "their" art theater take Warsaw by storm.[112] The actors, having braced for the worst, were thrilled to receive such a warm welcome from the leaders of modern Yiddish culture.

The reviews were effusive. Even the notoriously acerbic Nomberg was charmed. In the opening lines of his review for *Moment*, he likened the performance to a spiritual transformation:

Figure 3. *A.* (left) Alex Stein in *The Village Lad*, 1917. YIVO Institute for Jewish Research. *B.* (right) Sonia Alomis in *The Village Lad*, 1916. Sharon Asro and Alexander Zaloum.

> I walked into the theater *a vokhediker* [a workaday person] and emerged a *yontevdiker* [in holiday spirits]; I entered a skeptic and left a believer. This is how I would describe the feeling aroused by the first appearance of the Vilna Troupe, which is currently visiting Warsaw in the Elysium Theater.[113]

For Nomberg, watching the performance was a metaphysical experience that elevated everyday Jewish reality to the specialness of a holiday celebration or Sabbath observance. Watching the performance, Nomberg told readers, he nearly forgot that there was a war raging nearby. Even better, he noted, there were no stars and no "starist" behavior on display. "There is no famous name to find among the actors," Nomberg crowed. "I consider this an advantage. A very great advantage." For Nomberg, the greatest achievement of this company was its complete rejection of the norms of Yiddish theater.

> The Vilna Troupe performs together like a whole, like an organism that was simply created that way. If I tried to list the other virtues

> of the Vilna Troupe, I would have too much work. I would have to count up all of the defects and crudities and coarseness and tastelessness of the Yiddish theater and then say that the Vilna Troupe *possesses none of it*.[114]

It was Nomberg too who crowned the company "the Vilna Troupe" in this first review, a title quickly embraced by the actors.[115] A connection with Vilna, the city known as "a citadel of Jewish religious and secular high culture," gave the young company credibility.[116] For the next few years, their playbills included both names, though "Vilner trupe" (the Vilna Troupe) was always foregrounded in large type at the top, followed by "Fareyn fun Yidishe Dramatishe Artistn" or "FADA" in tiny print below it.[117] Soon they would abandon the FADA name altogether in favor of the streamlined moniker that evoked both the high literary culture of their former hometown and the extent of their success. Vilna had played host to dozens of Yiddish theater companies over the years, but it was only this company that people called *the* Vilna Troupe.

The newly designated Vilna Troupe quickly became a major presence in Warsaw. *The Village Lad* was the company's signature piece, and it played several times a week in rotation with old favorites like Hirschbein's *The Abandoned Inn* and Artsybashev's *Eyferzukht* (*Jealousy*), alongside newer additions like Hirschbein's *The Handshake* and a Yiddish translation of Gorky's *The Lower Depths*. As in Vilna and other cities, German army officers continued to attend. Indeed, as Sammy Gronemann noted, local German government officials would even bring visiting guests of honor from Berlin to see the Vilna Troupe.[118]

The histories penned by Yiddish theater critics and the recollections of the members of the Vilna Troupe present a seemingly unified narrative in which the company earned only glowing reviews in Warsaw.[119] To some extent, this was true. Writers held banquets and galas in honor of the Vilna Troupe, treating the actors to expensive dinners and praising their work in speeches. Effusive reviews continued to appear in the Yiddish press, many of which credited the Vilna Troupe with finally realizing Peretz's goals. "How many times did we try to make an art theater here?" wrote one journalist in *Der Moment* after the company's second performance in Warsaw. "And here—take a look! Young people, without dramatic academies, amateurs, without publicity, to become 'darlings' in such a short time—it makes the heart light up and fill with joy."[120] The actors, in turn, viewed their success in Warsaw as the reward for two years of struggling under difficult circumstances. "Warsaw honored us with an outstretched hand and gave the Troupe its first laurel wreath for the two years of hard labor, superhuman courage, hunger and need, that FADA experienced in Vilna," recalled one actor.[121] With ticket sales on the rise, the members of the Vilna Troupe could suddenly afford what had once seemed inaccessible luxuries: enough food and clothing for their spouses and children, new shoes, and suitable—albeit crowded—housing. These "luxuries," as the actors called them, were modest at best. For example, the Kadisons, a family of five, shared a two-bedroom, one-bathroom apartment with another family of three, a maid, a seamstress, and an upright piano. Luba Kadison recalled that with ten people in a small apartment, space was tight.[122] Still, compared to homelessness and potato rations in Vilna, it was a significant improvement. Not only did Warsaw provide a steady income that allowed the actors to support their families for the first time, but their literary idols also took an interest in their artistic development. The actors' memoirs are full of tales of the close relationships that formed between them and Warsaw's Jewish intelligentsia in 1917 and 1918. Yankev Dinezon, a writer and another former member of Peretz's theater circle, grew particularly close to the actors, who nicknamed him their *heyser khosid* (passionate follower). At one point, Dinezon even tried to adopt an orphaned Vilna Troupe actor as his own daughter.[123] The ties between the actors and their literary mentors were indeed close.

However, a closer examination of the sources reveals a more complicated relationship between the Vilna Troupe and Warsaw's Jewish literary establishment. While many writers and journalists did voice unconditional support of the Vilna Troupe's productions, there were those who disagreed. One Yiddish journalist, writing for *Dos Folk* in 1918, penned an article entitled "Good and Bad about the Vilner," in which he argued that the intelligentsia had poured all of their hopes into a single company while unfairly ignoring other talented actors. Still, the author ultimately conceded that the Vilna Troupe had more combined talent than any other company in Yiddish theater history.[124] Others were less enamored. An anonymous journalist writing for *Arbeter Tsaytung* argued that the Vilna Troupe had nothing to offer beyond their admittedly impressive production of *The Village Lad*. They were a one-hit wonder, he continued, whose other productions were like "the last drops that remain on the bottom of the cup you've just recently drained."[125] Another *Dos Folk* journalist, Yankev Vaserman, criti-

Figure 4. Yankev Dinezon (*rear, center*) with members of the Vilna Troupe, Warsaw 1918. YIVO Institute for Jewish Research.

cized the troupe for not having a distinct style of its own and accused the company of imitating outdated European realism:

> They [the Vilner] lack a style. That which at first glance seems to been their artistic logic is actually nothing more than a bad copy, and furthermore, of a theater specialty that long ago fell out of favor.[126]

Vaserman's critique of the Vilna Troupe's initial offerings was not entirely inaccurate. If we were to periodize the Vilna Troupe, following the lead of Yiddish theater historians of the 1920s and 1930s, the company's arrival in Warsaw marked a second, more mature period in its development.[127] In FADA's early years (what we might call its "Vilna period"), it was little more than a Yiddish-language imitation of the Moscow Art Theater. Between the company's 1917 arrival in Warsaw and its production of *The Dybbuk* there in 1920 (the "Warsaw period"), the company gained its name and its actors became fully fledged creative artists in their own right. In Vilna, intellectuals tended to frequent the Russian theaters and worship Stanislavsky. In Warsaw, it was the Polish-language stage that was considered preeminent. When the Vilna Troupe added eight Warsaw-based members to the company in 1917–18, it both increased the physical size of the company and expanded its theatrical models to include recent developments on the Polish stage.[128]

In Warsaw, the company brought in several new members who had trained extensively in Polish theater schools, where they had been exposed to a range of theatrical innovations and staging techniques. Mazo managed to convince several talented Jewish students to quit the Polish Warsaw Drama School (Warszawska Szkoła Dramatyczna), learn Yiddish, and join his company. Among these students was Miriam Orleska, who quickly mastered Yiddish with Asro's help and, shortly thereafter, originated the role of Leah in *The Dybbuk*. Other new members brought years of experience in Warsaw's professional Yiddish theaters, including Leyzer Zhelazo, who had performed and toured extensively with Esther Rokhl Kaminska's ensemble. Another actress who joined the Vilna Troupe in Warsaw, Leah Naomi, had once been a member of the Hirschbein Troupe. Not only was Naomi a talented actress with decades of professional experience but her association with the Hirschbein Troupe also symbolized the company's inheritance of Peretz's theater campaign. Finally, Dovid Herman, Warsaw's most talented Yiddish director and a former member of Peretz's theater circle, also joined.

Soon, the actors tired of Warsaw and decided to embark on another tour. The Vilna Troupe began its second tour in March 1918, traveling first to Lodz, then to Kazimierz to train the new recruits and rehearse. After a brief respite, they were off again, visiting dozens of shtetls and towns on the way to Lublin, before returning to Lodz for a second visit.

On their first tour, the actors had suffered through uncomfortable travel arrangements, mediocre accommodations, and insufficient food. This time was different. After its success in Warsaw, the Vilna Troupe had become a household name. The actors traveled in style, renting private train cars to carry the company and their sets and properties. According to Nahma Sandrow, crowds of admirers met them at every train station and people fought over the honor of carrying the actors into town on their shoulders.[129]

Reviews of the second tour echoed the glowing appraisals the company had received in Vilna and Warsaw. Local journalists praised the Vilna Troupe for its ensemble style, which made the company seem more like "a living organism" composed of a "harmonious family of artists" than "a machine where every worker is a wheel driven along a fixed track."[130] Others, like Zvi Cahan, described the Vilna Troupe as a "Temple of Art," praising the company's "serious and holy relationship to the stage."

> When they venture out to perform, they go to create, to poeticize, they feel as if they are *Kohanim* [high priests], and they know that this holy work must not be desecrated. So they do not go onstage too early, but only after lengthy preparation, and when they do show themselves on stage, they do not see the audience at all. They do not perform for the audience, they are creating now, they are poeticizing, they are perfecting a world of poets, placing souls in dead bodies. They perform with youthful vigor, passionately, with reverence, never mechanically or perfunctorily, never cheerlessly or professionally."[131]

To Cahan, the Vilna Troupe's theater was sacred, even holy work, akin to the function of the Kohanim in maintaining the ancient Temple in Jerusalem. The Vilner, Cahan argued, were different from other actors because they approached every performance with palpable kinetic energy—not as bored professionals, but like the enthusiastic amateurs they once were. For Cahan, the actors seemed to infuse new vitality into the "dead bodies" of dramatic texts, bringing them to life.

The second tour also secured the company's reputation as a traveling theater. During the first tour, the members of the Vilna Troupe had still conceived of their company as belonging to a fixed physical space: first Vilna, where they initially intended to return; then Warsaw, as they dreamed of putting down roots in the capital of Yiddish culture. With its second tour, however, the company gained repute as traveling performers.

During the second tour, Jewish theater aficionados speculated in the Yiddish press about where the Vilna Troupe would visit next as hundreds of towns and cities competed to woo the newly famous actors. Though the company had not yet traversed great distances, it was already an international sensation. The Vilna Troupe's reputation preceded it, often years in advance. When the Vilna Troupe returned to Lodz in 1918, the critics proclaimed "Finally!" as though they had been waiting for decades. Indeed, on some level, they had been. As one Lodz journalist wrote,

> For many years we have waited for you. . . . Jealous and pained at learning of your novel richness while becoming aware of our own poverty, our longing for you grew. [It was] a longing for our own beauty, for our own art. Not an art of imitating others, not a tired art, not the kind of art from which you take away a feeling of inepti-

> tude like from an unsuccessful joke. [A longing for] pure, restorative art, art that is truth, harmony and beauty.[132]

The Lodz Jewish intelligentsia's longing for the Vilna Troupe was an expression of the same pining for a better Yiddish theater that had been present in Jewish intellectual circles for decades.

In the German and Polish coverage of the second tour, reviewers expressed surprise that a Jewish art theater could actually exist. One German journalist who was sent to Lodz was initially skeptical that there could be an artistic theater in a language that grated on his nerves, but he emerged from his first Vilna Troupe production a believer. "I was thoroughly cured of my skepticism. Even the very first evening was a profound experience," he wrote. "There was no trace of the swollen pathos that has so often annoyed me when I sit in the theater. True art was displayed here—pure, noble art presented by people who regard their work as a mission." He remained bothered by the sound of the Yiddish language ("the beauty of the language escaped me") but ultimately conceded that in spite of this flaw, the production was great art.[133] This narrative of a symbolic conversion from Yiddish culture skeptic to believer, with the Vilna Troupe as the transformative hinge, became a hallmark of the company's reviews in the non-Jewish press.

Jewish journalists also echoed this astonishment that Yiddish culture could produce such high-caliber theatrical artistry. In Lodz, a critic described his mounting disbelief while watching the Vilna Troupe's performance of *The Village Lad*: "It was simply unbelievable that our Yiddish theater art already contains such psychological authenticity and dramatic truth," he marveled.[134] Another journalist reveled in the company's negation of prevailing stereotypes about Yiddish theater. With "love and seriousness" the Vilna Troupe "has proven for the first time that the Yiddish theater is not merely a milking cow or a spice shop, but a cultural institution with specific aesthetic and artistic aims."[135] In other words, the Vilna Troupe demonstrated that Yiddish theater could produce more than cheap entertainment. In Lublin, another Jewish writer admitted that he entered the theater prepared for an unpleasant evening, as he generally had little patience with the theater in general and with Yiddish theater most of all. Instead, he was surprised to find a "Yiddish art theater" that exceeded every expectation. This was a theater "without pepper or salt, without *kupletn* [comic couplets], without dancing like Cossacks, without vehement cursing, without immature pranks." In the place of flashy spectacle and comic antics was "pure art, where everything is present, where everyone speaks like a person, and moves like a human being rather than a wild animal. A pure theater, beautiful, refined, tender, without pretensions, without publicity."[136] Of course, the Vilna Troupe did, in fact, have a rather sophisticated publicity campaign orchestrated by Mordechai Mazo. What this reviewer was describing was the Vilna Troupe's perceived organic quality, its seemingly inherent authenticity.

Critics considered the Vilna Troupe's realism as a marker of its artistic integrity. Reviewers praised the actors for their ultrarealistic portrayals. "The people on the stage sit in real dwellings . . . with a roof above them and a carpeted floor beneath them," glowed one Lodz critic. "And when (as in *Yankl the Blacksmith*) the iron ought to glimmer in the smithy, it glimmers, and when sparks should fly, they fly. This is the artistic seriousness with which the Vilner work."[137] Another reviewer made a similar distinction between the Vilna Troupe's realism and the work of other Yiddish companies. "This is not acting. I am fed up with 'acting,'" he wrote of *The Village Lad*. "Life itself, wrapped up in the heightened material of art, seemed present to me, compressed and concentrated in the eternal young sorrows of a Yankele and a Natasha."[138] While the non-Jewish press continued to express surprise at encountering serious artists on the Yiddish stage, Jewish critics praised the Vilna Troupe for adopting a theatrical style that was long out of fashion.

At the close of the second tour in 1918, the Vilna Troupe triumphantly returned to Warsaw. The company had transformed itself from a ragtag group of unknown amateurs and non-Yiddish-speaking actors into a thriving professional theater troupe with a growing reputation. Less than three years after rehearsing through a Vilna winter with no heat and with only a daily boiled potato to fill their stomachs, the actors found themselves courted by admirers in cities and towns across Eastern Europe, where they were treated to lavish banquets in their honor and provided with luxurious accommodations. By the time the Vilna Troupe returned to Warsaw, it was a cultural institution.

Even more significantly, the company had survived its first major internal crisis, though perhaps not in a way that satisfied everyone involved. The source of this crisis was neither artistic nor financial. It was romantic. Tensions had been building for years between the manager, Mordechai Mazo, and leading lady Sonia Alomis. Mazo was in love with Alomis, but she was in love with her childhood sweetheart Alexander Asro, who often played opposite her as leading man. When Asro and Alomis eloped, a jealous quarrel broke out that split the Vilna Troupe in two.[139] Asro, Alomis, and those who sided with them left Warsaw and returned briefly to Vilna, where they formed a second Vilna Troupe. Those who remained with Mazo carried on in Warsaw as planned. Both branches continued to use the same Vilna Troupe logo and performed an identical repertoire. Both also claimed sole authenticity as the "real" Vilna Troupe and refused to publicly acknowledge the existence of the other branch.

But instead of crippling the Vilna Troupe, the existence of two branches only furthered the company's international reputation. Journalists and audience members were often unaware that multiple Vilna Troupes existed. As press attention mounted, it seemed as though the Vilna Troupe was famous everywhere. In addition, both branches were forced to bring in new talent to make up for the departure of those who had left. These new recruits only strengthened the artistic talent of each branch of the company.

Still, at the end of 1919, both branches still struggled to find a unique artistic voice. The Vilna Troupe's productions were, stylistically, scarcely distinguishable from the first FADA performances in the Circus Theater. In the first years of its existence, the Vilna Troupe had two goals: to bring literary texts to the Yiddish stage and to stage them as realistically as possible. This initial style, as Kadison explained, was an explicit rejection of *shund* conventions:

> Our goal was to create living characters upon the stage, who move and speak like living people, and most importantly—to feel and experience the roles not by staring vacantly with our eyes and throwing our hands about, but with silence, with the pauses and movements that are necessary.[140]

The Vilna Troupe's initial repertoire was drawn equally from Yiddish and European plays. From the Yiddish canon, they chose Leon Kobrin's *The Village Lad*; Mark Arnshteyn's *Dos eybike lid* (*The Eternal Song*), a one-act drama about working class life, and *Der Vilner balebesl* (*The Vilna Householder*), a drama based on the life of a tormented cantor who became a success on the Warsaw Opera stage; Jacob Gordin's *Got, mentsh, un tayvl* (*God, Man, and Devil*), a tragedy about a good man's downfall, based loosely on the Faustus legend, and *Khasye di yesoyme* (*Khasye the Orphan Girl*), a social drama; Peretz Hirschbein's pastoral dramas *A farvorfn vinkl* (*A Forsaken Corner*) and *The Abandoned Inn*, in which the playwright dramatized family conflicts and romance among Jewish peasants living in the rural countryside; Sholem Asch's *God of Vengeance*, a drama about a brothel owner's misguided efforts to preserve his daughter's innocence and purity; and Dovid Pinski's *Yankl der shmid* (*Yankl the Blacksmith*), a psychological drama about a proletarian blacksmith who falls in love and tries to reform his womanizing ways. The Vilna Troupe's initial Yiddish repertoire also included Jacob Gordin's *Di shvue* (*The Oath*) and *Di kreytser sonate* (*The Kreutser Sonata*), Osip Dimov's *Shma Yisroel* (*Hear O Israel*), H. D. Nomberg's *Di mishpokhe* (*The Family*), Sholem Asch's *Mitn shtrom* (*With the Current*) and *Yikhes* (*Pedigree*), a dramatic adaptation of Y. L. Peretz's story "Din-toyre mitn vint" (A Legal Argument with the Wind), and Dovid Pinski's *Di gliks-fargesene* (*The Luckless*). The company's first Yiddish plays tended to feature stories of working-class Jewish laborers, and with the exception of Hirschbein's symbolist dramas, realism dominated. There were very few comedies in the repertoire. The actors who were good at playing realistic tragic heroes and heroines, like Asro and Alomis, got one leading part after another, in spite of the company's avowed insistence on distributing parts equally. Still, an ensemble spirit prevailed. Chaim Shniur remembered that from the earliest days of the Vilna Troupe, the actors all informally directed one another and helped each other to put on makeup and change costumes backstage.[141] Every actor was a part of the stage crew, whether he or she had a leading role or not.

Not all of these Yiddish plays were equally beloved by the members of the Vilna Troupe. But with literary Yiddish playwriting still in its infancy, there were few options to choose from. European plays would have to fill in the gaps. Though the Vilna Troupe initially turned to European dramas out of frustration with the dearth of Yiddish plays, the actors quickly embraced them as the source for a full half of their repertoire. This often attracted criticism from Jewish audiences, who wanted the company to perform only Yiddish material. "There are not enough Jewish-milieu plays to perform," a frustrated Mazo told critics again and again.[142]

European plays helped the Vilna Troupe to attract non-Jewish and non-Yiddish-speaking audiences. Between 1916 and 1918 the actors chose Austrian playwright Arthur Schnitzler's *Anatol*, a drama about a bourgeois playboy and his many romances; Herman Sudermann's *Battle of the Butterflies*, a German comedy about a love triangle in a middle-class family; Tolstoy's tragedy of seduction and murder *The Power of Darkness*; Evgeny Chirikov's philosemitic *The Jews*, which glorifies the role of radical revolutionaries as defenders of the Jews during the pogroms; Russian naturalist Mikhail Artsybashev's *Jealousy*, a tragedy about romantic entanglements gone wrong; Semyon Yushkevitch's *Miserere*, a play that depicts the effects of extreme poverty on urban Jewish families; and Ludwig Fulda's witty comedy of errors *School Friends*; among others. Many of these plays (including *The Power of Darkness* and *Miserere*) had been famously staged by the Moscow Art Theater a decade earlier.[143] Evgenii Chirikov's plays were frequently produced by the Moscow Art Theater, while Herman Sudermann's were staples of the Freie Bühne in Berlin, where playwright Ludwig Fulda was one of the founding company members.[144] In choosing plays closely associated with prominent art theater companies, the Vilna Troupe consciously positioned itself as a member of that same scene.

Even after Asro and Alomis left Mazo's company to form their own Vilna Troupe, both branches still shared a single repertoire. In spite of each group's insistence that their branch was the only authentic Vilna Troupe, the existence of a shared repertoire testifies to the ongoing conversation between them. Actors frequently switched allegiances between the two wings of the company, bringing information about the other group's productions along with them. The shared repertoire also indicates that each branch followed the press about the other. Between 1918 and 1920, both branches added dozens of new plays that were performed in rotation alongside old standbys, including, most famously, Peretz Hirschbein's pastoral drama *Grine Felder* (*Green Fields*) and his "cellar drama" *Neveyle* (*Carcass*). *Carcass* became an instant sensation in both branches and one of the Vilna Troupe's signature plays. Indeed, the two versions of *Carcass* were remarkably similar because the same director—Dovid Herman—directed both productions.

Carcass typifies the Vilna Troupe's early repertoire in its gritty depiction of working-class family life, its dark subject matter, its coarse everyday language, and its imitation of the techniques of European naturalist playwrights. The protagonist is Mendl Abrusch, the son of an impoverished horse trader whose career and health have been ruined by alcoholism. Mendl lives with his father, his stepmother, and her daughter, Reyzl, in a dark, dank cellar. Uneducated and forced into poverty by his father's addiction, Mendl becomes a skinner of animal carcasses in order to support his family. Dually despised for his socially unacceptable job and his ugly appearance, he cannot lead a normal life or have a normal relationship with anyone. He seeks affection from his depressed stepmother and alcoholic father, but they are unable and unwilling to love him in return; likewise, when Mendl declares his romantic attraction to his stepsister Reyzl, she rejects his advances, repulsed by the stench of carrion that he carries on his body. "You smell like animal hides . . . like dead horses," she tells him.

"I wouldn't eat from the same spoon as you! Do you understand?"[145] The climax of the play occurs in the final act when Mendl, spurned, desperate, and on the verge of madness, strangles and kills his drunkard father.

Carcass was as naturalist a play as any. One German critic lauded the Vilna Troupe's productions of *Carcass* as a "true proletarian piece" reminiscent of Gerhart Hauptmann's *Das Friedensfest* (*The Reconciliation*; 1890), a naturalist drama of family conflict and the violent rejection of paternal authority, albeit with a happier ending; and Maxim Gorky's *The Lower Depths* (1901–2), which depicts the destitute urban lives of a group of lower-class social outcasts living together in a cellar lodging house and culminates in an emotionally charged murder scene.[146] Both of these plays were associated with European art theaters: *The Reconciliation* had premiered at the Freie Bühne in 1890 under the direction of Otto Brahm, while Stanislavsky's production of *The Lower Depths* at the Moscow Art Theater in 1902 was one of the most successful plays in the company's history.[147] By drawing a connection between the Vilna Troupe's *Carcass* and these renowned productions at two of the foremost theaters in the world, this critic implicitly suggested that the Vilna Troupe belonged to the European art theater scene.

Negative reviews were few and far between and often reflected the prejudices of their writers. In one, a Berlin-based German journalist called the Vilna Troupe's work *jarkonkunst*—"jargon art," full of "degenerate naturalism, dripping sentimentality, and scandalous, lurid buffoonery."[148] The obvious anti-Semitism aside, this journalist saw "jargon art" as a contradiction in terms, something ridiculous and impossible that could never be. Art theater in Yiddish? Like the forces of modernity that assail Tevye in *Fiddler on the Roof*, it was once "unheard of, absurd! Unthinkable!"[149] The Vilna Troupe challenged dominant notions of what could be achieved in Yiddish so successfully that this line of criticism soon disappeared.

For nearly four years, the Vilna Troupe had flourished by making choices about repertoire and aesthetic that followed the lead of established European art theaters. This would all change in 1920, when both Vilna Troupe branches finally found their own aesthetic with two back-to-back productions of *The Dybbuk*. The year 1920 signified the end of the company's initial period of aesthetic imitation and the beginning of an era in which the Vilna Troupe (no longer the name of a single company but a global phenomenon) would become renowned for stylistic innovation. It was this turn away from imitating its Russian idols and toward a new ethos of theatrical experimentation that would inspire others to follow the Vilna Troupe's lead.

INTERLUDE I

Rogues and Rebels

Why would a Jew choose to become an actor in a theater tradition that virtually ensured lifelong itinerancy? The actors of the Vilna Troupe followed many paths to their careers, but they had one thing in common. They were all rebelling against someone or something.

Avrom Bell's parents wanted him to go to medical school and become a doctor. Avrom obeyed for a time, until a traveling Yiddish theater troupe came to town and he ran away for good. His family was horrified, which was precisely the point. As Avrom's grandson remembers,

> He was a bit of a rogue in conjunction to the rest of his family. He was a rebel and he liked going to the theater. It was like running away with the circus. He was somewhat rebellious and he didn't want to go to medical school, so he joined the circus—in this case, the Yiddish theater. And he loved it.[1]

For young Jewish men and women rebelling against family and religious obligations, Yiddish theater offered a way out of their present circumstances and into a new life of travel and adventure.

Model citizens these future Yiddish actors mostly were not. Jacob Ben-Ami was thrown out of his yeshiva after smacking a child prodigy with a wet towel. He was sent away to a Russian school in Minsk, where he lived with his aunt. There he discovered theater at the local Russian circus and was captivated. Eight-year-old Ben-Ami would pay five kopeks for one show, then stay for the entire day. When the circus owner caught him, the boy negotiated his way into playing the barrel-organ musical accompaniment in exchange for free tickets.[2]

When Ben-Ami decided to join a Russian theater company at the age of fifteen, his family was appalled. "Oy, a clown. He's going to be a clown," they complained to anyone who would listen.[3] On tour, Ben-Ami traveled to Odessa, where he met a young Peretz Hirschbein, who was just starting his company. Ben-Ami immediately joined. It was Hirschbein who came up with his regal-sounding stage name (up until then, he had been Yankev Shtchirin).[4]

The Hirschbein Troupe came to Minsk, the same city where Ben-Ami had been sent to live after his expulsion from school. After the first performance, the young man was shocked to find his aunt waiting for him. She enjoyed the show so much that she revealed a long-held family secret. Ben-Ami had been raised without a father and he had always been led to believe that his parents got divorced because his father went out dancing with girls on the Sabbath. That night in Minsk, he learned the real truth. His parents divorced because his father became an actor and his mother was ashamed to be associated with him.[5] Ben-Ami was floored. Now he knew why he had always been drawn to the theater. "It was solved then and there and I knew why," he realized. "I got it through my father."[6] Apparently, roguishness and rebellion ran in the family.

Joseph Buloff was a class clown who was expelled from school several times for his antics before finally dropping out altogether. "Listen here, young man, I'm losing my patience already with all these stunts," teachers would tell him. "This isn't a circus."[7] After dropping out of school, the young man became a furrier's apprentice, a hospital orderly, a smuggler, a refugee, and a prisoner of war in quick succession.[8] Finally he ended up where he had belonged all along, at the Circus Theater with FADA/the Vilna Troupe.

As a child, the orphaned Baruch Lumet lost one apprenticeship after another for clumsiness, misdeeds, and other mishaps. One time he lost a job after accidentally discovering his boss on a rendezvous with a mistress.[9] At the age of fourteen, he was an unemployed school dropout with no prospects. The teenaged Lumet decided to start his own vaudeville theater in Otvosk, a resort town just outside of Warsaw. He gathered a group of actors, rented a space, and started Otvosk's first vaudeville theater. But when Lumet fired an actor unceremoniously, the jilted actor retaliated by burning down the building. That was the end of his vaudeville career. "All my episodes ended in disaster," Lumet later recalled. "Why, I don't know, but it's a fact that very little joy did I have in my youth."[10]

Before discovering the theater, many of the Vilner were outsiders, misfits, and nonconformists. The theater was the only place where they felt at home, their refuge from a world that did not understand them. The theater became their home and their family.

Simkhe Natan began his career as a prompter with the Kaminskis. For Natan, what happened on stage was just as real as anything else in his life, and he often got in trouble for his emotional outbursts on the job. One day, during a production of *Mirele Efros*, he sobbed so hard in the prompter's box that he lost his place in the script and ruined the performance. Esther Rokhl Kaminska took him aside and told him that a prompter must not act. Natan tearfully replied, "Then I don't want to be a prompter. I want to perform instead."[11] Kaminska took pity on him and invited him to join her company.

As an actor, Natan was obsessed with always getting the best role. If another actor got the part he wanted, he became horribly depressed and would make himself physically sick with jealousy.[12] "Natan was so united with the stage that it was incredibly difficult for him to tear himself away," his colleague Yonas Turkow recalled. "He wanted, as one says in the theater, to make love to the stage. The man would have wanted to play every role."[13] Natan was not a healthy man; he had problems with his liver for most of his professional life. Between shows, he was sickly and depressed. But on stage, he would forget all about his chronic illness.[14]

Big egos were common. Isaac Samberg demanded that the other actors refer to him as *der keyser* (the tsar) because he was so popular with audiences.[15] In his post–Vilna Troupe career, Samberg refused to be billed below any other actor on theater posters and publicity materials, which infuriated his colleagues. Many a producer tried to convince him to accept an alphabetical billing system, to no avail; Samberg had to be first. Younger actors often caved in, but Samberg's fellow Vilner were nothing if not stubborn. One time when Samberg and Avrom Morevsky were both cast in a production of *Danton's toyt* (*Danton's Death*) in Warsaw (directed by fellow former Vilner Mikhl Weichert), Samberg refused to perform if Morevsky had first billing. Morevsky, who was playing the title role of Danton, vowed to quit if Samberg's name appeared first. Finally, they agreed to a compromise. Two posters would be printed—one with just Samberg's name and the other with just Morevsky's—and they would be distributed equally around the city. The show went on.[16]

None of the Vilner were "supposed" to become actors, and they knew it. Except for those who had actor parents, a career in the theater went against everything they had been raised to do. It also typically did not pay a living wage. Years after the Vilna Troupe's founding, the Yiddish Actors Union in Poland required every aspiring young actor to answer the question "Do you understand the economic position of the Yiddish actor?" before joining. These young men and women knew exactly what they were getting into—a life of poverty and travel. They became actors anyway. Here's how future Vilner Hersh Poznanski answered the questionnaire:

> Q: Do you understand the economic position of the Yiddish actor?
> Poznanski: All too well!
> Q: What are your reasons for wanting to become a professional actor?
> Poznanski: I want to perform in the theater so I can redeem it.[17]

A bold response for a teenager with scarcely any acting experience.

The Vilna Troupe was full of men and women just like Poznanski—young, untrained rebels who had rejected their upbringing and run away from home looking for a new purpose. The Vilner welcomed them with open arms.

CHAPTER 3

Between Two Worlds

The Dybbuk *Goes Global*

A few years ago I sat down with Dan Ben-Amos, a professor of Jewish folklore at the University of Pennsylvania, to listen to some old records. Ben-Amos happens to be the great-nephew of the Yiddish actor Noah Nachbush, the man who originated the role of the enigmatic Messenger in the Vilna Troupe's 1920 world premiere of *Der dibek* (*The Dybbuk*). Thirty years later, Nachbush struggled to make ends meet in Brooklyn. He traveled around the country giving monologues from his old Vilna Troupe repertoire and selling self-produced records of Yiddish songs under a homemade label. I listened to these records in Ben-Amos's living room in Philadelphia, drinking tea and staring at the gigantic gold-plated samovar that Nachbush had carted across all of Europe.

Among the many gems on the records are several recordings of Nachbush performing the *Dybbuk* monologues that once made him a household name. They are the only surviving recordings of an actor from the original Vilna Troupe production performing an excerpt from *The Dybbuk*. Nearly one hundred years later, Nachbush's Messenger still takes my breath away.

In one excerpt, Nachbush performs the scene at the end of the play in which Sender, Leah's father, is put on trial by her lover Khonen's dead father from beyond the grave, with the Rabbi and the Messenger mediating between the living and the dead.[1] This was no standard theatrical monologue. In the recording, Nachbush delivers this speech entirely in song, cantorial style. He sings the words in *Magein Avot*—a minor mode that uses the relative major at key moments for emphasis.[2] In the second monologue Nachbush begins in *Ahava Rabbah* (a mode with an augmented second) before shifting back to *Magein Avot*.[3] Nachbush's voice bespeaks a quiet intensity, as if singing these monologues requires a full-body effort. It is as if he is pouring every fiber of his being into these notes, his voice heaving and cracking with emotion.

The Dybbuk, as seen by its first theatergoers in Warsaw and Berlin, was no ordinary play. The same cantorial inflection of the dialogue in Nachbush's recordings was used throughout the production, supplemented by extensive musical underscoring, full-cast choral numbers, and ritualized stage choreography. All of this was intended to replicate the effect of praying in a synagogue—albeit in a secular theater scene in which Shabbat and holidays were popular nights for performances.[4] In short, *The Dybbuk* in its initial production was actually something of an edgy, experimental musical.

The Dybbuk is arguably the most influential Jewish drama of the modern period. In the first year of performances alone, the Vilna Troupe performed *The Dybbuk* over 390 times to a cumulative audience of over two hundred thousand theatergoers.[5] Two years later, a Hebrew production of the same play directed by the Russian director Yevgeny Vakhtangov would make Habima's name on the world stage. Today, *The Dybbuk* remains the most frequently produced Yiddish play of all time and has inspired adaptations by artists including Aaron Copland, George Gershwin, Jerome Robbins, and Tony Kushner.[6]

The Vilna Troupe's *Dybbuk* marked the moment when Yiddish theater began to play a significant role in the modern theater at large. As actor Jacob Waislitz would later write, *The Dybbuk* marked when Yiddish theater earned its "citizenship rights among the theaters of the world."[7] It was also a turning point in the Vilna Troupe's development. Prior to *The Dybbuk*, the Vilna Troupe's production style was basically a low-budget, portable imitation of the Moscow Art Theater's. But with this production, the Vilna Troupe introduced its own distinct aesthetic that brought together staging practices inspired by the various theaters and artists that Vilna Troupe actors encountered on their travels. In the case of *The Dybbuk*, it was a fusion of the Moscow Art Theater's ensemble style combined with the German expressionism of Max Reinhardt merged with the modernist neoromanticism of the Young Poland movement, all blended together within a decidedly Jewish framework. It was this transnationally sourced aesthetic that made *The Dybbuk* a twentieth-century landmark.

This chapter examines *The Dybbuk*'s original appeal to audiences and demonstrates how the play's success enabled the Vilna Troupe's rapid global expansion, from Eastern Europe to Western Europe to the Americas. The

Vilna Troupe's *Dybbuk* literalized the overarching ethos of the European art theater movement: the stage as sacred cultural space. The young idealists of the Vilna Troupe symbolically converted their *bine* (the stage) into a *bime* (the podium in a synagogue) and their audiences into supplicants. The Vilna Troupe's *Dybbuk* struck a nerve among theatergoers that had more to do with its ritualistic stage interpretation than with the actual content of the play. For Jews, the cantorial melodies of *The Dybbuk* evoked nostalgia and sparked communal connection. The production offered a space for secular Jews to engage with a romanticized Jewish past and reminded them of the experience of attending synagogue services with a talented cantor. For non-Jews, however, the experience was unlike anything else that they had ever seen or heard before, an invitation into the inner sanctum of Jewish religious practice in a secular public space.

In Jewish folklore, a dybbuk is a dislocated soul of a dead person that inhabits the body of a living person (typically male dybbuks possess female bodies, with few exceptions).[8] *The Dybbuk* was written in 1914 by Shloyme Rappoport, a Russian Jewish ethnographer better known by his pseudonym, S. An-sky, who based the play on his ethnographic research.[9] Between 1912 and 1914 An-sky and a team of ethnographers traveled to over sixty towns and villages across the Pale of Settlement, gathered two thousand photographs, eighteen hundred folktales, fifteen hundred folk songs, and one thousand wordless melodies, and recorded five hundred wax cylinders of music.[10] Before their work was cut short by the outbreak of World War I, An-sky and his team prepared an elaborate questionnaire (*The Jewish Ethnographic Program*) that they intended to use to interview Jews in more communities.[11] Though the questionnaire was never deployed, it offers insight into Jewish customs and beliefs throughout the Pale. *The Jewish Ethnographic Program* included many questions about dybbuks that give a sense of what An-sky and his fellow researchers encountered on their expedition.

> 2035. What does a dybbuk normally say and shout?
> 2036. Because of what sins does a dybbuk enter a person?
> 2037. Does a male dybbuk ever enter a female and vice versa?
> 2038. Do most dybbuks enter a male or a female, a young person or an old person?
> 2039. What antidotes or remedies can be effective in such a case?
> 2040. Does a dybbuk ever harm other people [outside the person it enters]?[12]

The Dybbuk was directly inspired by the folkloric material that An-sky collected on his ethnographic expeditions.[13]

Apropos its subtitle, *Between Two Worlds*, the play's central theme is the desire of its characters to build bridges across seemingly insurmountable divides: wealth and poverty, tradition and modernity, choice and destiny, and ultimately, life and death. Two lovers named Leah and Khonen are betrothed by their fathers before birth. As young adults, they subconsciously fulfill their destiny by meeting and falling in love. But Khonen's father is long dead and, in his absence, Leah's father breaks his vow and finds a wealthy groom for his daughter. When Khonen learns that Leah is engaged to marry someone else, he turns to Kabbalah (Jewish mysticism) in order to win her back, but the dark power he raises is too great for him to control and it consumes him. Yet the bond between these lovers is so inextricable that Khonen is able to haunt his beloved from beyond the grave, inhabiting her body on her wedding night as a dybbuk. Khonen's challenge to paternalistic authority is seemingly thwarted when the local wonder-working Hasidic rabbi exorcises Khonen's dybbuk from Leah's body against the collective will of the entwined lovers. But even exorcism cannot break their bond, and the play culminates with Leah and Khonen reuniting not in life but in death, transcending all of the barriers that had heretofore kept them apart.

The Vilna Troupe's *Dybbuk* began as a publicity stunt. An-sky had spent the last few years of his life trying desperately to get the play staged: first in its original Russian version at the Moscow Art Theater under Stanislavsky, then in a Hebrew version at Habima, and later, when both of those plans fell through, in a Yiddish version.[14] In readings before Jewish intellectuals in Kiev, St. Petersburg, Moscow, Odessa, and Vilna, An-sky presented his play to audiences who insisted that it was too literary and folkloric for the stage.[15] Especially in its earliest drafts, it was more like the ethnographic museum that An-sky dreamed of building than the kind of play readers were accustomed to. Indeed, as Gabriella Safran has noted, *The Dybbuk* "stressed display over narrative, education over catharsis, genuine artifacts over interpretation."[16] When An-sky proposed a production to the actor Avrom Morevsky, who would later perform the role of Reb Azriel in the Vilna Troupe's production, he declined because there were no "great roles" in the play ("God, blessed be He, in the heavens laughed without end and the angels cried," Morevsky later remarked ruefully).[17]

Still, An-sky continued to seek backers for a production of *The Dybbuk*, writing again and again to friends in the theater asking for their help, to no avail. When An-sky heard about the Vilna Troupe and its successes in Warsaw, he wrote to Leyb Kadison and suggested a meeting. The core members of Mazo's Vilna Troupe traveled to a sanatorium in Otvosk, a town just outside of Warsaw, where An-sky was convalescing after an illness.[18] Kadison and Mazo were captivated by An-sky's reading of the play, and they agreed to prepare the script for production. But a few weeks later, before they had even begun work on the script, the actors learned that An-sky had died suddenly of a heart attack.

The Vilna Troupe attended An-sky's funeral, carrying a banner that referenced *The Dybbuk*: "On the path between two worlds, a last greeting to Sh. An-sky."[19] At the graveside, Mordechai Mazo, the company's business manager, gave an impromptu speech before the crowd of eighty thousand mourners. According to Avrom Morevsky, Mazo shouted, "Wait a minute!" just as cemetery workers began to shovel earth into An-sky's open grave. Without consulting his colleagues, he made a dramatic vow that the Vilna Troupe would stage the world premiere of *The Dybbuk* in exactly thirty days, at the close of *shloshim*, the traditional period of mourning prescribed by Jewish law. "If I do not raise the curtain at the premiere of *The Dybbuk* at the end of *shloshim*," Mazo promised, "I will leave the Vilna Troupe!"[20]

Many were furious with Mazo, but there was no time to quarrel. The actors soon realized that they had a problem: the play was steeped in the culture of Hasidic Jewry, a branch of Jewish religious practice that emphasized strict observance coupled with mystical spirituality. The members of the Vilna Troupe, on the other hand, were secularists whose idea of holiday observance involved adding extra shows to their schedule instead of going to synagogue. Given the company's reputation for realism and dramaturgical rigor, the actors were concerned that audiences might balk if they staged *The Dybbuk* without the proper Hasidic context. Compounding the problem were the peculiar circumstances of the production. Most of the actors did not learn of their company's plan to produce *The Dybbuk* until Mazo's eulogy. By then, they had only thirty days to prepare.

And so, desperate for Hasidic expertise and extremely pressed for time, the Vilna Troupe asked Dovid Herman to direct the production. Herman had once been Peretz's protégé and was then an established Yiddish director who had previously directed two of the Vilna Troupe's Warsaw productions, *Carcass* (a new staging for Warsaw) and *The Handshake*, in 1919. Both productions had done well, though neither had been stylistically different from the troupe's previous offerings. For *The Dybbuk*, however, the Vilna Troupe asked Herman to develop a distinctive production that would live up to the hype of Mazo's speech. Herman was the ideal candidate for the task: raised and educated in a traditional Hasidic home, he had the proper religious credentials, but as a secularist who had left the fold decades earlier, he could also identify with the Vilna Troupe's insistence that Yiddish theater—done right—could replace the synagogue as the central institution in Jewish communal life.[21]

The Vilna Troupe may have turned to Herman for his religious expertise, but Herman was more interested in introducing the actors to new ideas culled from his encounters with avant-garde theater artists in Poland, Austria, and Germany. For the founding members of the Vilna Troupe, who had grown up in the Russified Jewish communities of the Pale of Settlement, Russian theater was synonymous with high culture. But Herman had begun his theatrical career as one of the first Jewish students to enroll in the Warsaw Drama School, where he trained under major Polish actors and directors of the period, including Wincenty Rapacki (1840–1924) and Mieczysław Frenkiel (1858–1935).[22] After graduating in 1907, he moved to Vienna, a major center of turn-of-the-century theatrical modernism.[23] There he founded a German-language theater company.[24]

In inviting Dovid Herman to work on *The Dybbuk*, the Vilna Troupe inadvertently gave the project a modernist director. Herman was able to exert an outsized influence on *The Dybbuk* because the actors considered his ideas more authentic than theirs due to his Hasidic background, which none of them shared. During rehearsals for *The Dybbuk*, Herman introduced the Vilna Troupe to the latest currents in German and Polish theater: on the one hand, German expressionist experiments with stagecraft and expressionism; on the other, the mystical neoromanticism of the avant-garde Polish stage. It was this idiosyncratic aesthetic, a fusion of Hasidic ritual atmosphere with trendy avant-garde elements drawn from Polish and German theater, that would enable the Vilna Troupe's *Dybbuk* to appeal to uncommonly diverse audiences around the globe.

With a strict thirty-day deadline, rehearsals for *The Dybbuk* were frantic. This was a mammoth project for any company to undertake in a single month, let alone a group of semiamateur newcomers accustomed to long rehearsal periods. Never before had the actors tackled such a complex script. Moreover, their new director had a reputation for being difficult and for pushing actors to the limits of their endurance.[25] Accustomed to the minimum three-month rehearsal period that he always insisted upon, Herman's anxiety was palpable. Some actors began to doubt whether they would be ready in time, but Mazo was committed to the deadline, swearing repeatedly that if they delayed the production by even a single day the others would find his dead body on top of An-sky's grave in the very spot where he had made his vow.[26]

Opening night arrived all too soon for the nervous actors: December 9, 1920. The Vilna Troupe's *Dybbuk* production introduced many changes to An-sky's play: cutting dozens of lines and even entire sections, combining the third and fourth acts into a single finale, inserting an expressionist dance of death just prior to Leah's wedding-night possession, and adding a musical theme underlying the entire play based on the biblical Song of Songs, which heightened the erotic tension between the thwarted lovers at key moments. Many of these modifications, especially the dance of death, would become integral parts of most future productions. The 1937 film of *The Dybbuk*, for example, features the same Song of Songs musical motif from the Vilna Troupe production. In the film, the song symbolizes the betrothal promise made and then broken by Leah and Khonen's fathers, reminding the audience that their love was preordained. The film also features an extended dance of death sequence at Leah's wedding, as introduced in the Vilna Troupe's production. Critics have long considered this scene to be one of the film's most central, evocative, and iconic moments (indeed, J. Hoberman's seminal Yiddish film history *Bridge of Light: Yiddish Film between Two Worlds* features that very scene as its cover image).[27]

Stylized set and lighting designs also contributed to the modernist effect. *The Dybbuk* began in candlelight with the stage curtain opening to reveal a secondary curtain—a gigantic oversized tallis (a Jewish prayer shawl) that framed Kadison's gigantic Reinhardt-inspired expressionist set and the entire action of the play. As the American Jewish composer Joseph Rumshinsky described the opening moments,

> The theater Elysium, in which they performed *The Dybbuk*, was long and narrow with bare benches; it gave off the impression of a Russian barracks. I sat upon one of the hard benches. It was pitch black. I saw before me an old tallis, soaked in tears. In the thick darkness, I saw a tall, Hasidic young man with a religious book and a light. He looked far into the distance, towards the nothingness. When the second curtain rose and I saw the synagogue, I heard wrenching voices singing a mysterious wordless melody; voices that moaned, that communed with God, voices that drew themselves nearer to the generations that came before. They sang slowly, very slowly, and rocked themselves with nervous intensity. A considerable amount of

Figure 5. The Vilna Troupe in *The Dybbuk*, Paris, 1923. Private collection of Laurence Senelick.

> time went by before they uttered the first word. It was like a long overture, but without an orchestra.[28]

This framing added a visual layer to the religious framework of the dialogue. For Jewish spectators, the opening and closing of the curtain at the beginning and end of each act invoked familiar rituals: the opening and closing of the synagogue ark to reveal the Torah, the wrapping of one's body in a prayer shawl during silent prayer, the ceremonious shrouding of a Jewish corpse in the tallis of the deceased, and so on. It seems that no theater company since has ever reproduced this frame, which is visible in only a handful of photographs.

In addition to referencing Jewish religious practice, the tallis curtain also connected the production to the mystical and ritualistic style that Warsaw theatergoers were accustomed to seeing on the avant-garde Polish stage in a Christian context.[29] The tallis curtain was thus both a reminder of *The Dybbuk*'s Jewish landscape and of its aesthetic connection to experimental theater.

As Rumshinsky recalled, Herman also added a prologue that depicted how Leah's and Khonen's souls were unconsciously drawn to each other before they were born. According to one reviewer,

> Just as the first curtain opened, we saw before us a *tallis* curtain. The two wandering souls of Leah and Khonen, each drawn towards the other, entered accompanied by the Messenger. This immediately put us into a symbolic-mystical mood and exposed us to the proper perspective on the play. The entire first act was carried out through and through in this same tone. The singing, the conversations of the *Batlonim*, the mystical dance, the Messenger, all of the visual elements, the music, and the rhythm—everything was thoroughly covered with a veil of mysteriousness.[30]

In addition, the Vilna Troupe made significant modifications to *The Dybbuk*'s final scene. Whereas An-sky's play ends with the reunion of Leah and Khonen in the spiritual realm and the Rabbi's distress upon discovering Leah's dead body, Herman followed the closing of the final curtain (the giant tallis) with an epilogue in which all of the actors chanted the biblical Song of Songs together, hand in hand.[31] By adding a new finale in which living and dead characters join hands and sing in chorus, the Vilna Troupe's *Dybbuk* dangled the possibility of a reconciliation between the binary divides that are the source of the play's major conflicts—an attractive suggestion for spectators torn between traditional Jewish culture and modern European life.

The ceremonious atmosphere of *The Dybbuk*'s staging was reinforced by the stylized mannerisms that Herman required of the actors as they sung the liturgically inflected dialogue. By weaving music into the play, Herman evoked the "sacred act" performance style that was common in Juliusz Osterwa's Polish productions during this period, in which spectators were invited to bear witness to "holy rituals"—i.e., ritualized performance embedded in modernist productions. For example, Osterwa's 1926 production of Juliusz Słowacki's *The Constant Prince* (adapted from Calderón) framed the entire play as a sacrificial ritual with the tragic hero as a Christ-like martyr.[32] As the Polish theater historian Kazimierz Braun describes, Polish audiences saw a link between the Polish stage and the Catholic Church, and Polish theater thus always had a "peculiar, semi-religious character."[33] Yiddish theater adopted these modalities from the Polish stage and transposed them into a Jewish landscape.

By all accounts, *The Dybbuk* was an extraordinary success. The actors played before full houses in sold-out performances for months. Numerous anecdotes describe how the influx of people coming to the Elysium Theater from all parts of the city was so great that the Polish tram conductor whose route passed by the building took to calling out "An-sky" or "Dybbuk" in place of the street name.[34] These anecdotes suggest the extent to which *The Dybbuk* permeated a new kind of Yiddish theatergoing public that cut across ethnicity, religion, and class. The working-class drivers of the Polish tram system knew about *The Dybbuk*, as did the city's most respected theater artists. At the time, Leyb and Khane Kadison's daughter Luba was enrolled at the Warsaw Drama School where she was studying acting with Stanisława Wysocka, one of the most renowned actresses of her generation.[35] Wysocka had heard about *The Dybbuk* and mentioned it to Luba, who promptly invited her teacher to a production and sat beside her translating the dialogue. Wysocka was delighted. In *The Dybbuk*, she told Luba, she saw something that she had never seen before on the stage, "something new, a new kind of tone brought into the theater."[36]

The Polish director Juliusz Osterwa also attended a production of *The Dybbuk* in early 1921. Like many Polish attendees, it was his first introduction to Jewish theater and he was impressed.[37]

> I was delighted with the interpretation of *The Dybbuk* by the director Herman. My admiration grew even stronger when I became familiar with the unbearable conditions and primitive means that the actors and the director had to work with.[38]

Osterwa noted that the Vilna Troupe's *Dybbuk* brought together a range of artistic styles and influences, including German theatrical training methods ("greatly developed enunciation and astonishing attention to detail," wrote Osterwa), the exaggerated pathos of the Polish stage, and "the acting style of artists from Stanislavsky's school, with an extraordinary intuition for pauses" (Avrom Morevsky, Osterwa wrote, was particularly good at the latter).[39] Nachbush as the Messenger, on the other hand, performed in a style that struck Osterwa as thoroughly original.[40] Osterwa was so inspired by seeing his first Yiddish production that he asked Mazo if he could collaborate with the Vilna Troupe on a bilingual staging of Wyspiański's *The Judges*, a play in which a Jewish innkeeper is tried for murder, with the actors of the Vilna Troupe playing the Jews and the Polish actors from his experimental company Teatr Reduta playing the Christian characters.[41] The production never materialized, but Osterwa remained a fan.

Figure 6. Joseph Buloff (*left*) as Henokh and Alex Stein (*right*) as Khonen in a publicity still for the original *Dybbuk* production, Warsaw 1921. YIVO Institute for Jewish Research.

The American Jewish theater composer Joseph Rumshinsky, who saw *The Dybbuk* while visiting Warsaw from New York, described how he had heard people talking about "the brilliant production of *The Dybbuk*" nonstop "for the entire time since I left America."[42] Reflecting upon the production a quarter of a century later, Rumshinsky wrote, "It lives in my memory as though it happened only yesterday, this is how much this production is engraved in my mind."[43] "I speak not of the actors," he continued, "because I do not consider them as actors, but as more than actors. I did not feel as though I sat in a theater. I felt as though I was encountering something that I had never before seen or heard."[44] Rumshinsky was so excited by the matinee performance he attended that he and a friend returned that same night to see the evening show.[45] The production made a similar impression on Osterwa, who told a reporter in 1925, "Even though I saw *The Dybbuk* many years ago, I remember all of the details with full clarity. . . . It was a masterpiece of directorial work."[46] Even theater journalists beyond Poland took notice. In February 1921, just two months after *The Dybbuk*'s opening, the *Berliner Tageblatt* sent a foreign correspondent to Warsaw just to review the production. "Hidden Art in Warsaw," proclaimed the headline.[47] In the press, in the lecture halls, and in the streets, Warsaw's Jews described their city as having been *fardibekt*—that is to say, possessed by the haunting play that had attracted so much attention.[48]

Experimentation and Its Critics

Unlike in Jewish literature, where there are many contenders for the title of first literary modernist, the emergence of Jewish theatrical modernism can be traced precisely to the Vilna Troupe's *Dybbuk*.[49] The Vilner did not gradually adopt modernism; they stumbled into it by choosing Herman as their director. The first performances of the Vilna Troupe's *Dybbuk* sparked a debate among Jewish intellectuals about whether or not modernism belonged on the Yiddish stage. In the aftermath of *The Dybbuk*'s success, however, these initial debates over the production's appropriateness were quickly forgotten as the Vilna Troupe became synonymous with avant-garde experimentation.

Many critics were initially ambivalent about the use of stylized theatrics on a Jewish stage. Wasn't modernism a Gentile sensibility, some wondered? Jewish intellectuals were slower to warm to *The Dybbuk* than the masses. Peretz and his disciples had envisioned a Yiddish art theater founded by Jewish writers. Their ideal theater was one steeped in Jewish literary culture, where educated actor-intellectuals would bring the best of Yiddish literature to life upon the stage. The Vilna Troupe had initially emulated this model, to the delight of writers, who were thrilled by the company's requirement that its actors pass a battery of examinations in Yiddish language and literature before performing. With Herman's departures from *The Dybbuk*'s script, however, some Jewish writers felt betrayed by the theater company they had come to think of as their own.

The tallis curtain, the revised act structure, the distorted expressionist sets, the dance of death, the elaborate musical score, and the symbolic prologue were all significant departures from An-sky's play. The goal was no longer to produce an accurate representation of the text but to create a theatrically evocative production that stressed emotion, physicality, and the senses. In the first few weeks of performances, critics accused Herman of betraying the recently deceased playwright. Indeed, during his lifetime An-sky himself had expressed concern about theater directors who changed scripts too much. When An-sky began to correspond with the Vilna Troupe about a *Dybbuk* production, he suggested that perhaps they could do without hiring a director at all. To the actor Avrom Morevsky, he explained his belief that theater required a clear hierarchy between a playwright and the actors. A director could only get in the way.

> "Spectacle" always was and is for me—and will continue to be until my last breath—*playwright* and *actor*. A thousand factors can aid them and hinder them, from the painter to the heating system, from the musicians to a rainy day. But the "essence" is the *player*, fertilized and guided by the *author*! So why should a third party approach the pearls of the literary work and try to alter them? Who is he? And why do we need him?[50]

Morevsky was deeply affected by An-sky's argument. A few months later, when Morevsky joined the Vilna Troupe and began rehearsals for *The Dybbuk* under Herman's direction, he fought against each departure from the script, arguing to anyone who would listen that each one conflicted with the author's intent. "Every step, every note, every detail stood in harsh opposition to the author," wrote Morevsky of Herman's rehearsals. The production was ultimately a success, he conceded, but it was not An-sky's *Dybbuk*—"Not by the most minimal measure, not for one second An-sky's style, and not for one millimeter An-sky's world."[51] To Morevsky, the Vilna

Troupe's *Dybbuk* was the product of a director who wrongly subordinated the script to his own agenda.

Initially, Warsaw's Yiddish critics were silent about the production. Neither *Haynt* nor *Moment*, Warsaw's primary Yiddish dailies, published a single article about *The Dybbuk* for over a week after the premiere. However, both did print small advertisements for *The Dybbuk* alongside large ads for concurrently running melodramas like *Shimshon hagibur* (*Samson the Strong*) at the Apollo Theater, *Di nekome fun a gefalene* (*Revenge of the Fallen*) at the Tsentral Theater, and the similarly themed *A dibek oder a malakh?* (*A Dybbuk or an Angel?*) at the Kino Forum Theater. Advertisements for *The Dybbuk* during the first performances were buried in small type on the back page beneath notices for jewelry sales, travel opportunities, and private Hebrew tutors.[52]

The first *Haynt* article about *The Dybbuk* appeared on December 17, well over a week after the opening. Buried on the last page, the review was highly critical. An-sky's play, wrote the journalist Aron Aynhorn under the pseudonym Eyner (Someone), was indeed a literary masterpiece. But the Vilna Troupe had distorted the play with its stylized modernism. Aynhorn told readers that realism, and realism alone, was the only appropriate style for the Yiddish stage.

> If one wanted to completely spare the spectator, then there is not a single moment that could not be played realistically. The director of the Vilna Troupe, however, has done exactly the opposite. Not only did they draw out the symbolic moments as much as possible, but they also simply inserted several things that were not in the play itself. So, for example, they inserted into the second act a "dance of death" where there is no trace of such a thing in the play. The Messenger (Mr. Nachbush) who is in An-sky's play a living person with only the smallest wink towards mysteriousness becomes on the stage a living mannequin, who goes about stretched out like a broken violin string, with empty eyes, a frightening figure. . . . But drawn towards symbolism, the director did not find it useful to sharpen the clearly realistic moments.[53]

Aynhorn suggested that the Vilna Troupe ought to have staged *The Dybbuk* using psychological realism, with the dybbuk symbolizing Leah's descent into madness rather than a literal spirit. Problematic too, Aynhorn said, was Herman's choice to insert elements that were not in An-sky's script.

Ironically, the additions that Aynhorn cited as especially egregious would later become two of the most iconic elements in future productions of *The Dybbuk*: the dance of death and the expressionist Messenger.

Aynhorn's article sparked a contentious debate in the pages of *Haynt* and its primary competitor, *Der Moment*. The following week, Yehezkel-Moyshe Nayman (under the pseudonym A. Foygl) published his take on *The Dybbuk* in *Haynt*. Symbolism, Nayman countered, was the very soul of the play and ought to play a major role in any production. While the Vilna Troupe's version was imperfect (Nayman criticized what he saw as Herman's overuse of the Song of Songs), it was "the best play that we have ever seen in the Yiddish theater."[54] Still, Nayman countered Aynhorn's accusations of infidelity by suggesting that An-sky had personally sanctioned every one of Herman's deviations from the script: "It is a fact known to everyone that *all of the improvements that Dovid Herman added to Dybbuk were done with the permission [hekhsher] and with the involvement of the author*."[55] Even those who initially advocated for the Vilna Troupe's production argued that it was the playwright, and not the director, who had final authority.

If *The Dybbuk* was really about the symbolic elements (such as the "lunatic Messenger" and the "bizarre" dance of death), retorted Aynhorn, then "we ought to be permitted to say openly that *The Dybbuk* is on the same [artistic] level as Zolotorevsky's *Yeshive bokhur* [*The Yeshiva Student*, a melodrama playing in Warsaw at the time], with the only difference being that Zolotorevsky is less pretentious."[56] For Aynhorn, melodrama and theatrical modernism were one and the same, linked by their preference for the visual over text. Herman's *Dybbuk*, Aynhorn concluded, imported ill-fitting European modernist ideas into Jewish culture: "In fundamentally Jewish plays, like *The Dybbuk*, one should not import any non-Jewish [*goyishe*] elements, even if they come directly from Wyspiański!"[57]

The reluctance among *The Dybbuk*'s first Jewish critics to approve of Herman's modernist approach reflects the degree to which realism was entrenched in the idea of a Yiddish art theater. As *The Dybbuk*'s popularity with audiences grew, however, Jewish critics changed their tone. Gradually, they softened their critique and began to accept—and even demand—modernism on the Yiddish stage.

A few Yiddish reviewers, writing for minor papers with smaller circulations, argued from the beginning that the Vilna Troupe ought to be praised for its daring aesthetic. I have been able to find only one review of *The Dybbuk*'s opening night, from a minor Yiddish paper, preserved in a tattered clipping in the archives of the YIVO Institute for Jewish Research (the fact that I have been able to find only one review of the premiere lends further support to my claim that *The Dybbuk* was not immediately accepted among Jewish intellectuals).

> The tragedy is that An-sky wrote this play in an acutely realistic form. If the director had staged the play in *this* genre, its characters would have been far too mundane and clichéd, which would have obliterated the mystical elevations that cry out during the entire play. Mr. Dovid Herman demonstrated a tremendous artistic sensibility in staging the entire play as an enigma, casting off the burden of the superfluous realism and enlivening it here and there with a mysterious wink towards the luminous allusions.[58]

In contrast to most of the Yiddish press, *The Dybbuk*'s modernism was embraced early on in the Polish-language Jewish press. Many of these critics, who were accustomed to reviewing avant-garde Polish theaters, actually criticized Herman for not being modernist enough. In a review published in the daily *Nasz Kurier*, Jakób Appenszlak accused the Vilna Troupe of being overly loyal to a flawed literary text.

> Reverence flowed through the veins of this work like hot blood. As a stage manager and director, Mr. Dawid Herman should have, in my opinion, solved the dilemma of the author, the dilemma of drama and mystery. He hesitated and aimed at a compromise. . . . Mr. Herman tolerated realistic scenes next to those wrapped in the shroud of legend. Some episodes he simply spruced up, but on the whole the director did not demonstrate a dominant idea.[59]

In the Polish-language Jewish press, Herman's modernist approach was hardly controversial. Unlike the first Yiddish critics, who accused the Vilna Troupe of disloyalty, Jewish critics writing in Polish were inclined to charge Herman with the opposite crime: *too much* reverence for the text.

The major Yiddish press organs lagged behind their Polish-language and smaller Yiddish-language counterparts in embracing *The Dybbuk* as a positive development for Yiddish theater. But a few weeks later, as public acclaim for *The Dybbuk* grew and grew, a new consensus began to emerge. On December 24, more than two weeks after opening night, Ber Karlinski published an article in *Moment* praising the production. Jews have traditionally been wary of theatricality, Karlinski argued, in part because of its associations with lowbrow melodrama and in part because of an aversion to the theater inherited from rabbinic culture. This antitheatrical prejudice had prevented the Yiddish stage from reaching the artistic level of its European peers. According to Karlinski, *The Dybbuk* was historically significant because it put Yiddish theater into dialogue with European artists for the first time.

> The stage stands on the verge of bankruptcy, and the only way that it can provisionally keep itself alive is with that which is traced in broad outlines in the production of *Dybbuk*—the path that compels the artist to bring out of human language the maximum value of the expression together with the maximum of its visual, rhythmic, and especially, musical beauty; the path of stylizing the action while simultaneously internalizing and deepening it, of keeping the action within the framework of the picturesque, the purest beauty and the finest discretion. This is no directorial whim—this is a question of "to be or not to be" for the [Yiddish] stage.[60]

Other critics followed suit. A *Haynt* article by Ben Levi [Avrom Levinson] in mid-January turned An-sky's playwright-actor-director hierarchy on its head. It was the Vilna Troupe's modernist aesthetic, Ben-Levi argued, that transformed An-sky's ordinary play into something greater.

> *The Dybbuk* is not a great play: the dramatic content is a bit overwrought, the fable too naive, the effects too cheap, the characters too simple, and only a few good scenes, a few successful dialogues (or more accurately, monologues), a few sharply defined characters to commend the play. In general, however, it is actually not even a drama precisely, but what they call in Russia a "*bitova drama*" [domestic drama]: scenes from folk life with a naive dramatic fable and a small dose of childlike mysticism in the guise of Hasidism. If the author were not An-sky, and if the play were not being performed by the Vilna Troupe, it would certainly not have caused such a commotion in our Warsaw Jewish world. The Vilna Troupe, though, demonstrated that one could make something out of this play, something truly out of the ordinary, a masterpiece.[61]

This shift in the critical consensus was motivated by *The Dybbuk*'s popularity. As spectators scrambled for sold-out tickets, Yiddish critics began to praise *The Dybbuk*. But as *The Dybbuk*'s reputation continued to grow, the critics stopped commenting on its innovations and began focusing instead on its reception. An article published in *Moment* on January 18 detailed admiring reviews of *The Dybbuk* in Polish and European newspapers in disbelief, as if the production had wrought a possession: "A dybbuk, a headstrong dybbuk, has taken over the workers of the *Gazeta Warszawska*!"[62] At times, these tales of non-Jewish spectators embracing *The Dybbuk* were fiction. In the case of *Gazeta Warszawska*, for instance, its workers may have attended productions but the paper never ran a single review of the Vilna Troupe's *Dybbuk*.

Still, whether true or false, press coverage of *The Dybbuk*'s reception continued. Some used humor to counter the sacred atmosphere that seemed to surround every mention of the play. In March a critic for *Moment* complained, "Warsaw has begun to take ill due to two factors: we run to see *The Dybbuk* and we gorge ourselves on chocolate."[63] Another journalist imagined that he had seen a Dybbuk wandering the streets of Warsaw, chased by an opportunistic Herman and the Vilna Troupe actors, hoping for another lucrative business opportunity.[64] Others emphasized the play's sacrosanct reception by comparing its audiences to devout worshippers.[65] Literary critic Nakhmen Mayzel described spectators making "a true holy pilgrimage" to see *The Dybbuk* from cities and towns across Europe.[66] Actor Avrom Morevsky wrote of the throngs of "*kosher*, god-fearing, sincere believers" who were obsessed with *The Dybbuk*.[67] Others described how *The Dybbuk* had taken over Warsaw: how the play was a primary topic of conversation in cafes and literary salons, how the Vilna Troupe actors were celebrities, how the streets were filled with Jews and non-Jews alike singing Hasidic *nigunim* (wordless melodies) that they had learned from the play.[68] By the winter of 1921, critics were focusing almost exclusively on the popularity of the production. Herman's modernist techniques, first derided, then quietly accepted, were no longer a matter of debate.

The program booklet for *The Dybbuk* offers insight into how the Vilna Troupe redefined itself as an avant-garde company.[69] The booklet, which features a drawing (likely by Kadison) of Leah embracing Khonen's ghostly spirit, contains several lengthy essays in addition to the customary cast list, playwright biography, and list of scenes. The Vilna Troupe's previous programs were typically single-sheet documents that included little more than the names of the cast and crew.[70] A booklet-length program was a major departure from the company's norms.

In actor Avrom Morevsky's essay "Spektakl tsu shloshim" (Spectacle in honor of the thirty-day anniversary [of An-sky's death]), he described *The Dybbuk*'s power in bringing together seemingly opposed worldviews.

> Two worlds, two worlds—
> Heaven and hell,
> Body and soul,
> Truth and illusion,
> Content and form—
> The contradictions grapple with each other, and this shapes the powerful process
> that we call "life."
> And when the quarrel ends, when one world has annihilated the other and rules in
> eternal victory over the contradiction—then there is eternal peace, but no life. . . .
> Life is the threshold between two worlds
> Life is the fusion of both contradictions
> Life is the point where both worlds have intersected one another and each will not
> yield even one sliver of its own existence to the other. . . .
> Theater is life.[71]

By 1920 decades of upheavals—years of pogroms, urbanization, forced migrations during the First World War, and the emergence of a thriving secular Jewish culture—had wrought rapid changes upon Eastern European Jewish life, and Jews struggled to adapt to this sudden entry into modernity. At the same time, they were drawn toward the promise of what a modern urban life could offer in the newly reconstituted Polish Republic, which promised Jews equal civil and cultural rights, though it did not always deliver on these assurances. *The Dybbuk*'s theme of being pulled between two opposing worlds captivated Jewish audiences, who identified with the metaphysical predicament of the tormented lovers.While breakage with the past tended to be cast in a positive light by European modernists, Morevsky described a more complicated Jewish relationship to tradition.[72]

> We stand upon the threshold between two worlds, as the falling columns rumble and crack.

> As our bodies grow weary and our souls tremble with deep longing for that which is disappearing while pining for that which is yet to come—
>
> We are a generation split in two, a tormented generation, a bewildered generation.
>
> And upon our lips blessings mingle together with curses.
>
> Lamentations are bundled together in our hearts with shouts of cheerful greeting.
>
> We wander and we never find where the beginning is, or the end.[73]

The Dybbuk, according to Morevsky, perfectly captured the challenges of living in this historical moment and offered a compelling solution. In the world of this play, tradition is simultaneously rejected and embraced, and there is a tremendous amount of ambivalence in depictions of both the old and the new. The Miropoler Rebbe, the dominant representative of traditional Jewish culture, is both sympathetic and problematic, as are the parents, Leah's friends and relatives, and even Khonen, with his terrifying descent into the dark side of Jewish mysticism. By adding a final scene in which all of the characters join Khonen and Leah in transcending the boundaries between worlds, Herman's direction emphasized the supreme clarity of the young lovers' position.[74]

Morevsky also described *The Dybbuk* using religiously inflected language. *The Dybbuk*, he argued, was a return to the theater's ancient association with Jewish religious life.[75]

> Theater was once a place of prayer and ecstasy, of tremendous exaltation, of spirituality. The elders used to go to the theater in order to praise God—during the holiest days of the year. . . .
>
> Theater became a place of vulgar recreation, of overindulgent physicality, of spiritually bereft amusement that played upon lowly desires—
>
> This is what has become of the theater under its current sovereigns—the gluttons, the exploiters. . . .
>
> And their world is disintegrating!
>
> A new world is on the way, it is coming, it is almost here—
>
> A world of builders and creators
>
> A world where entertainment is a form of spiritual service to the divine [*avoyde*].[76]

Morevsky called on theatergoers to "piously remember the holy spirit of Shloyme Zalmen, son of Aharon the Cohen An-sky" and concluded by invoking the opening lines of the Mourner's Kaddish, the traditional Jewish prayer for the dead, thus suggesting that the entire production was a memorial prayer in the playwright's honor.[77] Furthermore, Morevsky asked readers to join the Vilna Troupe in a blessing for An-sky and for the future of the Yiddish stage as they watched *The Dybbuk*. The prayer suggested by Morevsky is a modified version of the Rabbis' Kaddish (Kaddish D'Rabbanan), the prayer traditionally recited after a public reading of the Talmud or other rabbinical writings on behalf of all those who study and teach Torah. In the following excerpt, lines from the original prayer appear in quotation marks, interspersed with Morevsky's additions.

> Mourning and entertainment??
> "To all those who engage in the study of the Torah"
> All who are engaged in metaphysical pursuits, in spirituality of every kind,—
> "In this holy place or in any other place"
> Offer in mourning their heartfelt blessing:
> "Grace, kindness, compassion, and long life"
> The Yiddish theater brings to An-sky's work new life. . . .
> Trembling before the task, bent beneath the yoke of moldy archaic forms, Jewish actors move towards the new era in the ancient Temple of beautiful art.
> Around us is the theater's clamor—"only life, life through and through"
> In our hearts is An-sky's unforgettable image
> "May there be grace, kindness, and compassion."[78]

Morevsky employed a familiar linguistic device that draws a connection between Yiddish theater and classical Jewish modes of textual exegesis. The echoing of each Aramaic line with a Yiddish "equivalent" invoked the tradition of *taytsh*, a method of studying Jewish religious texts in which students would first read aloud a line of the Talmud, then repeat an interpretive translation of that same line in Yiddish vernacular.[79] Here Morevsky's *taytsh* translation was not simply between high Hebrew and vernacular Yiddish but between ancient liturgy and the modern Yiddish theater. The implication is that Yiddish theater is the contemporary equivalent of ancient liturgy and that *The Dybbuk* could serve the same function as the Kaddish: memorializing the departed by magnifying the divine presence.

More than the sold-out performances in Warsaw, it was the Vilna Troupe's tour of *The Dybbuk* that introduced theatergoers around the globe to the Yiddish stage. The explosion of *The Dybbuk*'s international reputation was enabled by the existence of multiple versions of the production that toured simultaneously with different branches.

After over one hundred performances in Warsaw, Mazo's Vilna Troupe took *The Dybbuk* across Eastern Europe. Over the next few months, the company toured Lodz, Bialystok, Lublin, Grodno, Lida, Vilna, Lemberg, and other Polish and Lithuanian cities and towns. It was not uncommon for impoverished rural Jews to travel great distances to see the Vilna Troupe perform, bringing items to barter for tickets. Luba Kadison recalled poor Jews coming to the theater and saying, "I'll give you this chicken if you let us into the theater. We want to see *The Dybbuk*!"[80]

In late 1922 Mazo's Vilna Troupe brought *The Dybbuk* to Vienna, along with its other hit productions of An-sky's *Tog un nakht* (*Day and Night*) and *Amnon un Tamar*, Hirschbein's *The Abandoned Inn* and *Green Fields*, Sholem Aleichem's *Shver tsu zayn a yid* (*Hard to Be a Jew*), Leonid Andreyev's *Der vos krigt di petsh* (*He Who Gets Slapped*), Mikhail Artsybashev's *Jealousy*, A. Vayter's *Di shtime* (*The Voice*), and Mark Arnshteyn's *The Vilna Householder*.[81] *The Dybbuk*, in particular, received an overwhelmingly positive reception.[82] Among those who attended during the first week of performances were major Yiddish literary personages, including the New York–based playwright Dovid Pinski, who happened to be visiting Vienna, and notables from leading Austrian and German theaters, including the opera singers Enrico Caruso and Leo Slezak, the playwrights Arthur Schnitzler and Richard Beer-Hoffman, and the director of Berlin's Deutsches Theater, Max Reinhardt. Reinhardt was so deeply affected by *The Dybbuk* that he insisted on visiting the Vilna Troupe actors backstage to congratulate them in person. "Das ist nicht kein Schauspiel" (This is no mere play), he told them, echoing the sentiment of Warsaw's critics. "Das ist ein Gottesdinst" (It is a religious rite).[83] Reinhardt was so impressed with Morevsky's portrayal of Azriel Miropoler, the wonder-working Hasidic rabbi, that he invited the actor to star in *King Lear* and to play Shylock in *The Merchant of Venice* at the Deutsches Theater. Morevsky was flattered but turned down the offer.[84] The Austrian composer Alban Berg was urged by friends, both Jews and non-Jews, to attend the Vilna Troupe's *Dybbuk*. According to the journalist Soma Morgenstern, a friend of Berg's, the composer was so impressed with the performance that he attempted to secure the German-language rights to produce it and was disappointed when he learned that the rights were already taken.[85] Arthur Schnitzler, it was reported, was a fan of the Vilna Troupe and attended every premiere in Vienna.[86]

Vienna's critics were likewise enthusiastic. For German-speaking Jewish intellectuals, *The Dybbuk* was a revelation about the "flowering of [a] new Jewish art."[87] For the Hebrew writer Moshe Ya'akov Ben-Gavriel, a prominent Viennese Jew, *The Dybbuk* demonstrated that theater was an important component of modern Jewish life. "I have had no relationship with the theater in the past, and nobody could convince me otherwise," wrote Ben-Gavriel, "but when they played *The Dybbuk*, I forgot it was theater. I was shaken to the depths of my soul, truly shaken, the ten or fifteen times that I attended the production."[88] Months later, Ben-Gavriel was still writing in his diary about *The Dybbuk*. "Jewish theater is not just European theater," he wrote. "It is a part of us all. . . . And *The Dybbuk* remains an experience forever and ever!"[89] Like many in the audience, Ben-Gavriel did not speak Yiddish, but this did not dissuade his enthusiasm for the Vilna Troupe's *Dybbuk*. In a review published in Vienna's *Neue Freie Presse* under his birth name, Eugen Hoeflich, Ben-Gavriel called *The Dybbuk* "a play of original, pure Judaism" in which "the highest goals of theater are achieved even when the spectator now and then does not understand the language."[90]

For non-Jewish critics, *The Dybbuk* was even more surprising. As Lisa Silverman has written, *The Dybbuk* succeeded in Vienna because "the play's narrative, aesthetic appeal, and language successfully transformed the stage into a platform upon which they could project the ideas they sought: a Jewish culture with an eye to the past, expressed in modern terms."[91] Indeed, Silverman argues, in Vienna a lack of Yiddish knowledge did not hinder spectators' enjoyment of Vilna Troupe productions. On the contrary, she suggests, "the unfamiliarity of the language allowed them to appreciate [these productions'] more 'spiritual' or 'irrational' qualities."[92]

The Austrian writer Robert Musil reviewed the Vilna Troupe's *Dybbuk* in December 1922. Musil found the politics of Yiddish confusing ("if I am correctly informed, it is actually a corrupted language," he pondered) but praised the actors for their performances. He compared Miriam Orleska (as Leye in *The Dybbuk*) to Eleanor Duse, calling her "the most beautiful actress since Duse appeared upon the stage" and adding, "One wishes to see this actress in a great role on the European stage, perhaps Desdemona." Musil called Noah Nachbush (as the Messenger) a "word architect of auditory fairytale castles."[93] Another anonymous reviewer was similarly effusive about the Vilna Troupe's production of Artsybashev's *Jealousy*, comparing the company positively to other European art theaters:

> They did not disappoint. It ought to be recognized that the Vilna Troupe is on par with the new Western European theaters. Both the direction and the technical elements are excellent. This proves the seriousness and dedication of the young actors.[94]

In addition to the *Neue Freie Presse*, reviews appeared in *Wiener Morgenzeitung*, *Arbeter-Zeitung*, *Der Nachmittag*, and a special issue of the Austrian theater magazine *Komödie: Wochenrevue für Bühne und Film* dedicated to the Vilna Troupe.[95] The special issue included dozens of photographs of the Vilna Troupe alongside articles about its history and its productions in Vienna.[96] Ben-Gavriel wrote another article on *The Dybbuk* for this special issue. "About the Vilner," he exclaimed, "one can certainly say that their art is an event."[97]

A Second *Dybbuk*

Hundreds of miles from Vienna, the second group of actors who called themselves "the Vilna Troupe" watched as their former colleagues catapulted to international fame. Asro and Alomis's Vilna Troupe, in contrast, had met with little success since their elopement and hasty departure. The Vilna they found upon their return was not the same city they had left. While Asro and Alomis were touring Poland with the troupe, their hometown had changed hands six more times after the departure of the German army in 1918, its jurisdiction passing back and forth between Lithuanian independence fighters, the Polish army, and military forces from the newly established Soviet Union.[98] In a city steeped in political uncertainty and economic desperation, Asro and Alomis struggled to convince their fellow renegade actors that they had made the right choice. In the summer of 1920 they somehow managed to bring aboard new defectors who had tired of Mazo's strict leadership, among them director Dovid Herman.[99] Herman approached Asro and Alomis about staging a production of An-sky's *Dybbuk*, and together they began preparing the script. At this point, An-sky was still alive and Mazo's Vilna Troupe had not even begun to discuss *The Dybbuk*. Had Asro and Alomis's plan worked, the world premiere of *The Dybbuk* might have happened with their branch in Vilna, not in Warsaw.

But the new branch's continued existence was suddenly thrown into question when, following a brief peaceful respite, the Bolsheviks invaded Lithuania and the Poles fled. Faced with the all-too-familiar scenario of living under a military occupation, several of Asro and Alomis's new troupemates (including Herman) returned to Warsaw and rejoined Mazo's branch.[100] The reworked *Dybbuk* script went with them. When the Bolsheviks turned over power to the Lithuanians five weeks later, three of the remaining actors followed them to Moscow.[101] Fearing the return of the Polish army and the inevitable bloody battles that would follow, Asro, Alomis, and their remaining small contingent of actors fled inland to Kovne, where they tried without success to restart their twice-exiled branch of the Vilna Troupe.[102]

Imagine the emotional turmoil of Asro and Alomis upon learning of their former colleagues' stunning success with *The Dybbuk* in the aftermath of their own company's dissolution. Jealous, the couple watched from the sidelines as their former castmates garnered a level of international acclaim that none of them had imagined possible for a Yiddish theater. As Asro and Alomis dreamed of reconvening their branch and starting over, they began to plan their own *Dybbuk* production that would capitalize on Mazo's hit.

In the summer of 1921, nearly a full year after the dissolution of their company, Asro and Alomis left Kovne for Berlin. In 1921 Berlin was an emerging center of Jewish culture that was home to many who had fled Eastern Europe during the war, including Yiddish and Hebrew writers like Dovid Frishman, H. D. Nomberg, Chaim Nakhmen Bialik, and Dovid Bergelson.[103] It was in this burgeoning cultural milieu that Asro and Alomis encountered an enthusiastic circle of German-Jewish intellectuals who had followed the press about Mazo's Vilna Troupe and vowed to help the couple reestablish their own branch in Berlin. These supporters included the German writers Sammy Gronemann, Hermann Struck, Hans Goslar, and Arnold Zweig, who had helped Asro and Kadison found the original Vilna Troupe in German-occupied Vilna, as well as the German theater and film directors Henrik Galeen and John Gottowt, both of whom had trained under Max Reinhardt, and Leo Winz, the editor of the illustrated monthly Jewish journal *Ost und West*.[104] These figures used their influence to raise funds and to secure a building: the Herrnfeld Theater.[105] They also began to drum up support among local cultural leaders before Asro and Alomis had even recruited a single actor.

Armed with a beautiful theater space, adequate finances, and the support of Berlin's cultural elite, Asro and Alomis reached out to current and former members of the Vilna Troupe and invited them to come to Berlin.

Most of the former members from their short-lived branch in Vilna joined them, as Asro and Alomis had hoped; more surprisingly, however, several more actors defected from Mazo's company in Warsaw and joined the group organizing in Berlin.[106] Among the renegades was—once again—Dovid Herman, now internationally renowned as the director of *The Dybbuk*. With a company that featured several actors and directors made famous by Mazo's company and a repertoire that consisted primarily of Vilna Troupe hits imported straight from Warsaw, it was no wonder that many in Berlin believed that Asro and Alomis's company was in fact the famous—and only—Vilna Troupe.

And so a new organization of actors operating under the now-famous name "the Vilna Troupe" developed its own productions of the Warsaw Vilna Troupe's classics with the cultured tastes of Western European audiences in mind: Hirschbein's *The Abandoned Inn*, *Carcass*, and *Green Fields*; Dovid Pinski's *Yankl the Blacksmith*; Leon Kobrin's *The Village Lad*; H. D. Nomberg's *The Family*; and, of course, *The Dybbuk*. The company also adopted a second, German name: Jüdisches Künstler Theater (Jewish Art Theater). The company used both names on its programs, advertisements, and even business cards, which Asro and Alomis had made for the actors.[107] The press used the two names interchangeably.

Opening in September 1921, this second *Dybbuk* production was a virtual copy of the original, albeit with a different cast. Herman, fresh off the heels of an extraordinary success that he hoped to repeat, kept his original blocking intact and trained the actors to emulate the mannerisms, speech patterns, and gestural language that Morevsky, Orleska, and the other members of Mazo's company had made famous. Herman also hired the German-Jewish painter and graphic artist Jakob Steinhardt (who later became the director of the Bezalel Academy of Arts and Design in Jerusalem) to copy Kadison's expressionist sets.[108] For the next eight months, Berlin theatergoers flocked to see Asro and Alomis's Vilna Troupe perform what appeared to be the famous *Dybbuk* production from Warsaw.

Audience members and critics responded enthusiastically.[109] In Berlin, Jewish critics agreed that *The Dybbuk*'s modernist staging was the primary reason for its success and that Herman's staging rehabilitated a flawed play. Without Herman's modernist staging, An-sky's *Dybbuk*, lamented a typical review in the Yiddish press, was

> Hastily thrown together with naive, childish devices, without tension, movement, or expression. . . . The best that is in *The Dybbuk* is

> the excellent direction of Mr. Dovid Herman. He correctly staged the play not as a drama but as a film-like performance and, as much as possible, put aside the language of the play and drew back out that which was silent.[110]

"I have strong doubts about the dramatic-artistic worth of this play," agreed another Yiddish reviewer.[111] *The Dybbuk* seemed to succeed in spite of the play, not because of it. Indeed, according to this reviewer, An-sky's dialogue was ill suited to the play and required modification:

> He [Herman] also fragmented the pace of the monologues and dialogue with a half-declamatory, whispering, ecstatic, and storybook tone. The wordless melodies seem accidental, interrupted, fragmentary, the theatrical imagery seems primitive and semi-cohesive, in a futuristic-modernist style, as a modern story requires. From these efforts, the entire play becomes spiritual, otherworldly, visionary, just like, for example, Gerhart Hauptmann's *The Sunken Bell*, Ibsen's *Peer Gynt*, . . . and the like.[112]

For German Jews, Herman's modernist *Dybbuk* transformed a Jewish folk legend into a universal play that was on par with the work of famous European playwrights.

Many German critics agreed. Alfred Kerr, the esteemed drama critic for the *Berliner Tageblatt* who was nicknamed "Der Kulturpapst" (The culture pope) for his role as arbiter of Berlin's theatrical and literary scene, described a "first rate" production that "bustles like a grisly ballet" despite being in a "strange language" that he scarcely understood.[113] Felix Stössinger, writing for *Die Freiheit*, called *The Dybbuk* "marvelous folk poetry" representing only "the merest scintilla of the beauty and creative wisdom of the Ghetto."[114] Norbert Falk, in *Berliner Zeitung*, wrote of Sonia Alomis's performance as Leah in *The Dybbuk*: "The storm of emotions that comes out of her—of love and fear, rebellion and decline—rending the heart to pieces—is so original and so passionate that there is a growing desire to make this warm flame useful for our Western theater."[115] A reviewer for the *Berliner Börsen-Kurier* told readers that the actors "have the talent of heavenly spirits."[116] The German writer Alfred Döblin wrote that the Vilna Troupe was one of the two best theaters in all of Berlin and its actors were so talented that they would be noticed on any stage in the city.[117] "Extremely reliable and nuanced ensemble performances," concluded Döblin.

"This art is serious."[118] A journalist for *8 Uhr Abendblatt* gushed of *The Dybbuk*, "It is a theater no longer but high—be still my enthusiasm—the highest art!"[119] Within a year there were two independent German translations of the play.[120] The press coverage of the Vilna Troupe's time in Berlin was not only limited to the German and Yiddish press. For instance, foreign correspondents stationed in Berlin wrote reviews of Vilna Troupe productions for several Dutch newspapers. In *Het Vaderland*, the paper's first review of the Vilna Troupe even made the front page.[121]

German critics were also struck by the Vilna Troupe's depiction of Eastern European Jewish folklore and religion, a world that seemed to them exotic. Felix Stössinger wrote in *Die Freiheit* that *The Dybbuk* brought audiences into a world that "not only the anti-Semite but even the assimilated Jew knows nothing about."[122] A journalist for the *Berliner Lokalanzeiger* remarked that *The Dybbuk* exerted a "soul-quaking" power on its "largely sophisticated public" that captivated spectators, regardless of their religious background, with "the living power of religious feeling alive in this drama, a force saturated with a thousand-year-old tradition, filling the everyday with meaning and sanctity."[123] This sentiment was not limited to non-Jews. The Austrian Jewish critic Otto Abeles wrote of a Vilna Troupe production of An-sky's *Day and Night*: "If it were possible to assemble together all Jewish people who have ever been weighed down by alienation or strange feelings of repugnance or by hatred aimed at Jewish characteristics, and bring them to this performance, they would go home feeling purified, delighted, and richer."[124]

Still, not every German reviewer was so enthused. The drama critic Fritz Engel sneered in *Berliner Tageblatt* that the Vilna Troupe's *The Abandoned Inn* was nothing more than "mystical manure"—at least in the morning edition of the paper.[125] By the evening edition, however, after reading the reviews of other theater critics, Engel had softened his critique.[126] Others struggled to determine their opinion, given the language barrier. "One can say nothing about the play if one does not understand the language," one reporter for the *Berliner Tageblatt* complained. "Perhaps it is very good that one does not understand the words, for perhaps the play is painfully weak and only becomes so strong through the acting."[127] Others criticized Herman's direction and the circumstances of the production. "The work is much weaker when we see it performed than when we read it," complained a Hamburg reviewer of *The Dybbuk*. "Pauses are tangible. . . . There is no central focus. The sympathies of the audience are fragmented, with attention pulled first in one direction, then another."[128] A reviewer in Chemnitz complained that *The Dybbuk* started half an hour late and was too long and demanding. "By the time the curtain went down for the last time amidst a torrent of applause and everyone left the oppressively hot atmosphere of the hall," he complained, "it was exactly 12:00 midnight."[129]

Still others responded negatively to the sound of the Yiddish language itself or struggled to overcome the language divide. As Julius Hart wrote in his review of the Vilna Troupe's *Green Fields* for *Der Tag*, he panicked when he realized that the production would be entirely in Yiddish:

> My God! I don't understand any Yiddish at all. . . . If only it were possible to know what they are talking about up there. During the intermissions, I seek help and assistance from the others, from every one of my colleagues who are also critics. And they don't completely agree either. One of them points out one thing. The other something different. I look pleadingly up at the ladies around them. A few times they laughed very knowingly. Gracious, noble, helpful and good ladies—have mercy on me in my critical misery. Tell me what's going on.[130]

In some cases, however, the strength of the actors' performances overcame linguistic aversion. As Max Alexander Meumann wrote of the Vilna Troupe's *Carcass* in *Hamburger Fremden-Blatt*,

> As the curtain rose, our ears began to struggle with the unfamiliar, guttural, and rushed jargon of "Yiddish." Again, we sat here feeling somehow indignant, filled with a slight aversion and inner reluctance, cold and dismissive of this realistic setting. And again, brilliant theatrical art forced us irresistibly and against our will under the spell of an artistic adventure, as flames burst forth where there was only smoke and soot—a smoldering work: *Carcass*.[131]

On the whole, the German press responded positively to the Vilna Troupe. Many followed the lead of the Yiddish press in naming Herman, and not An-sky, as the artistic genius behind *The Dybbuk*'s triumph and in praising its modernism. As Michael Brenner has written, the "unusual enthusiasm" of German audiences cannot be explained by the Vilna Troupe's production quality alone.[132] Instead, Brenner argues, it was *The Dybbuk*'s aesthetic that enabled critics (especially German Jews) to "express their emotional attachment to the cultural products of their East European kin while expressing their preference for modernism."[133] Modernism, in a play steeped in Jewish folk and religious content, allowed German Jews to engage in nostalgia for a mythical Jewish past while simultaneously proclaiming their allegiance to current artistic trends.

Among the German Jews who attended Vilna Troupe productions in Berlin was Albert Einstein. Einstein was so moved by the Vilna Troupe's production of Hirschbein's *The Abandoned Inn* that he wrote to Herman directly, thanking him for the performance.

> I feel the urge to thank you for the sublime delight your wonderful performance of the piece *The Haunted Inn* [an alternate translation of the title] gave me. Seldom have I seen human passion and human destiny in general so grippingly portrayed and coming so much from the heart, without being run-of-the-mill. I particularly admired the perfect interaction and the commitment with which all the actors subordinated themselves to the spirit of the piece.[134]

Herman was very proud of this letter and made it available to the press, where it was widely reproduced.[135]

After eight months of playing to packed houses, Asro and Alomis's Vilna Troupe left Berlin in May 1922 and embarked on a tour of Western Europe, beginning with other German cities. The troupe encountered an unusually chilly reception in Cologne, where their posters were defaced and few showed up for the performance.[136] In other German cities, however, the company inspired enthusiastic reviews from non-Jewish spectators, and ticket sales were so strong that they extended the length of their stay in Chemnitz, Leipzig, and Hamburg.[137] "The ear will get accustomed strangely quickly to the language of the guests," wrote Fritz Mack for the *Leipziger Neueste Nachrichten*. "By the end, one can follow along effortlessly, supported by the extraordinary eloquence of the gestures and facial expressions of the Jews."[138] The troupe continued on to England, France, Belgium, and the Netherlands, and *The Dybbuk* continued to be a sensation, inspiring lyrical accolades among spectators and critics who, more often than not, did not speak Yiddish.

The Vilna Troupe's success with non-Jewish audiences in Austria and Germany can be explained, in part, by the linguistic overlap between Yiddish and German. German-speaking spectators did not need to speak Yiddish to follow the plot of a Vilna Troupe play, and the company could count on audiences getting the basic gist of the story. But upon leaving Germany, the members of Asro and Alomis's Vilna Troupe had to contend, for the first time, with performing for audiences wholly unacquainted with a Germanic language. This only cemented the company's commitment to staging visually oriented, modernist productions that emphasized gesture, movement, color, emotion, and mood over plot and dialogue. This strategy was by and large successful, and the company quickly attracted a significant following across Western Europe.

In London, performances at the Kingsway Theater sold out so quickly that the Vilna Troupe was invited to move to a larger space within days of its arrival.[139] "The fame of the company had, it seems, preceded it," noted one London reviewer, "for the theater was crowded."[140] French intellectuals who attended the Paris premiere of *The Dybbuk* included the poet and art critic André Salmon and the French Jewish writer Edmond Fleg.[141] Commenting on the prevalence of noteworthy figures among the spectators, one Yiddish journalist wrote that it felt as though one were at the premiere performance of a major French play rather than a production by a traveling Jewish company.[142] In Antwerp, a journalist for *Die Schelde* effused about *The Dybbuk*,

> It was a revelation of beauty. I am forever grateful to the actors for the beautiful epiphany that they brought us. They are at the forefront of the cleansing of dramatic art. They are the apostles of their art and it almost seems as if they are the writers of their plays. We take note, we listen and admire. They have inspired in us a belief in stage art once again.[143]

In the Netherlands, performances were standing room only and reviews of the Vilna Troupe appeared in *Het Vaderland*, *Haagsche Courant*, *Algemeen Handelsblad*, *Arnhemsche Courant*, *Het Volk*, *De Telegraaf*, *Rotterdamsch Niewsblad*, and *Niuwe Rotterdamsche Courant*.[144] One Amsterdam newspaper stated that the Vilna Troupe actors "were as good as the very best in Europe" and that they "attain the level of the Comédie-Française or the Vienna Burgtheater."[145] The Dutch magazine *Het Masker* published a special issue on Jewish theater featuring multiple articles about the Vilna Troupe, including a lengthy article on *The Dybbuk* by Dovid Herman himself, translated into Dutch.[146] Asro and Alomis's Vilna Troupe was a sensation in Western Europe—to an equal or perhaps even greater extent than Mazo's company in Warsaw.

For Asro and Alomis, who had languished in obscurity just a few months earlier, the response was astonishing. They had never imagined being embraced by such a large non-Jewish and non-Yiddish-speaking audience. Years later, the actors would speak of this tour as the highlight of their theatrical careers. "[It was] a triumphant march of Jewish art over the temples of Yefes [Noah's second son, traditionally regarded as the biblical ancestor of the Greeks and the Europeans]," wrote the actor Chaim Shniur, echoing the general feeling among company members that their success symbolized the triumph of minority Yiddish over dominant Western European culture.[147]

Assimilated European Jews (most of whom did not speak or understand Yiddish) also attended Vilna Troupe productions. There were some unlikely conquests. On his deathbed, Max Nordau, cofounder of the World Zionist Congress and the second most famous Zionist leader in the world, defied his doctor's orders of bed rest and ventured to the theater to find out, as one of the actors wryly commented, "if Yiddish art and Yiddish theater were not a paradox."[148] After the show, he assured the actors that they had his support. Albert Einstein returned to see the Vilna Troupe perform again in Paris and gave the actors one of his books as a present, in which he inscribed the dedication "You are the sculptors of the human spirit."[149]

European critics, in turn, declared that the Vilna Troupe's productions transcended linguistic boundaries. In London, a reviewer for the *Era* wrote of *Carcass*, "One did not need a knowledge of Yiddish to grasp the significance of it all. It was there, stark and cold, a memorable picture."[150] The Welsh painter Augustus John, who frequently attended Vilna Troupe performances in London along with his friend, the painter Walter Sickert, wrote, "Though I had no Yiddish, such was the excellence of the acting that it was easy to follow the gist of what was said."[151] A journalist for the *Star* wrote, "I am completely ignorant of Yiddish, . . . but much of the meaning was clear to me, and I was held by the performance. The skill of the actors prevails over the barrier of language."[152] "They are amazing. They stun one with their artistry," wrote a reviewer for London's *Sunday Times*. "The people establish once and for all that truth in acting is the main thing in the theatre. . . . The Yiddish that they speak does not trouble you in the least."[153] In Hamburg, another wrote,

> Again, as the curtain rose, our ears began to struggle with the unfamiliar, guttural, and rushed jargon of Yiddish. Again, we sat here feeling somehow indignant, filled with a slight aversion and inner

> reluctance, cold and dismissive of this realistic setting. And again, brilliant theatrical art forced us irresistibly and against our will under the spell of an artistic adventure, as flames burst forth where there was only smoke and soot.[154]

Journalists frustrated by the language barrier were few and far between.[155]

Not only did Western European drama critics argue that the appeal of Asro and Alomis's Vilna Troupe extended beyond the Jewish community but many also suggested that these Jewish actors were more advanced than their European contemporaries. "My wildest dreams of the Moscow Art Theater never conjured up such a performance," wrote one critic of the Vilna Troupe's London visit.[156] The Dutch critic Simon Koster wrote of the Vilna Troupe, "They have taught us what acting actually is, as opposed to what is usually called acting."[157] Another Dutch critic wrote, "We must ask ourselves the most important question: What has this ensemble from Vilna taught us and how can this benefit our theater in the Netherlands?"[158]

The London critics were particularly vocal in calling upon local actors to emulate the Vilna Troupe. J. T. Grein, the founder of London's Independent Theater Society, hailed the Vilna Troupe as cutting edge. "If you are seeking something fresh in the field of art," he advised readers in the *Illustrated London News*, "you will find it here."[159] Even more astounding, many Western European reviewers concluded that the Vilna Troupe could teach European actors a lesson in technique.

> If the Vilna Troupe could give a special matinee for London actors and actresses, they would be doing good work. I should like our players to see the methods of this Yiddish company. What our players should note is the strength of the comedy acting, which never becomes exaggerated or unnatural.[160]

> The Vilna company are perfect actors. Those who care about the art of acting can still seize a rare pleasure. I have seldom seen individual acting so precise and vigorous, and never better orchestrated into a complete harmonious event. . . . We often heard three or four men and women speaking at once, as people do when they are quarreling or in moments of excited discussion. How often do you hear that done on the English stage? Here one can observe how it ought to be done.[161]

In asking English actors to follow the lead of the visiting Yiddish players, these reviewers suggested a new hierarchy in which the "advanced" Yiddish theater could serve as a model for the "backwards" European stage. This was a sharp contrast to the old anxieties of Jewish intellectuals about a Yiddish theater that lagged behind its peers. Predictably, the Yiddish critics following the Vilna Troupe's tour of Western Europe trumpeted this new hierarchy. "Dozens of English artists have become great devotees [*khasidim*] of the Vilna Troupe and of the Yiddish theater!" boasted a journalist for the London Yiddish press, likening the enthusiasm over the Vilna Troupe to religious fervor.[162]

The Vilna Troupe emerged during a period of relative European tolerance for Jewish culture. Still, anti-Jewish sentiments were rampant in parts of Western Europe, and the Vilna Troupe was not immune. One of their first Parisian reviewers was the journalist Jean Dreux of the notoriously anti-Semitic paper *La Libre Parole*. In a venomous review, Dreux suggested that *The Dybbuk* was part of a joint Jewish-Freemason conspiracy to infiltrate French culture and criticized the manager of the Théâtre des Champs-Élysées for allowing Jewish performers into the building. Without understanding what the actors were saying, Dreux wondered, how could critics be sure that they were not mocking French culture?[163] Hostile and anti-Semitic reviews like Dreux's were unusual, though there were occasional lapses into subtle anti-Semitic invective even among those who embraced the Vilna Troupe. "The language does not matter. The skill of the artists overcomes its harshness and oddities," wrote one English journalist, implying no small measure of astonishment that such a high level of "perfectly artistic" theater could overcome the bizarre sounds of the actors' language.[164] Another London reviewer, who called the company an "extraordinary troupe," also suggested that perhaps their manager had strategically lengthened the intermissions between the acts to enable members of the audience to conduct business, invoking old anti-Semitic accusations of Jews obsessed with money.[165]

Still, support for the Vilna Troupe was remarkably consistent during this Western European tour, and the company received few negative reviews in spite of the significant linguistic and cultural barriers between the performers and their audiences. This raises the question, Was the praise justified? Were the Vilna Troupe's productions really as good as the critics described? The reviews seem to suggest that these questions were irrelevant to many of the Vilna Troupe's supporters. The very existence of a Yiddish art theater, its actors' familiarity with European drama and contemporary theatrical trends, their ability to hold the attention of non-Yiddish-speaking spectators—this surprised and delighted critics, regardless of the artistic value of the productions. For most of these reviewers, unfamiliar with the rise of a sophisticated, modern Yiddish culture in Eastern Europe, astonishment was part of the Vilna Troupe's enigmatic attraction. As one Dutch critic put it,

> Where do these miracle-makers come from? Are they Polish, Russian, Lithuanian? What language do they speak? Who inducted them into the deepest and yet most intelligible secrets of the art of theater? Do they come from an old generation of actors or did they learn all this on their own? Yes, what is their name and where do they get their repertoire?[166]

This aura of mystery was part of the Vilna Troupe's allure, compounded by the fact that its language and culture were so unfamiliar to Western European audiences.

Critics also described the Vilna Troupe as an alternative to traditional European ideas about Jewish culture. "A brand new, friendly image comes to us of these Eastern Israelites, which the West Europeans had considered a people only of trading and peddling," read one Berlin review of a production of Hirschbein's pastoral drama *Green Fields*. "Here we see fresh, vigorous, unspoiled people working on the land and in their family life."[167] In Hamburg, another critic wrote that the Vilna Troupe's *Dybbuk* offered audiences "a wonderfully poignant insight into the folklore of Eastern European Jewry, which certainly does not deserve popular contempt, but is as good as any other."[168] *The Dybbuk*, with its depictions of a traditional Jewish life that seemed exotic to many, challenged Western European assumptions about Jewish culture.

By the time Asro and Alomis's branch returned to Germany in May 1923 to develop new repertoire, their fame had so far outpaced the Eastern European Vilna Troupe that they were able to recruit seven of Mazo's best actors (Noah Nachbush, Sholem Tanin, Matisyahu Kovalski, Pola Valter, Leah Naomi, Miriam Veyde, and Moyshe Feder).[169] After three months of intensive rehearsal, they returned to Holland, Belgium, and London before setting sail for New York, becoming the first branch of the Vilna Troupe to journey to the United States.

The Vilna Troupe's success during this first Western European tour was propelled by the ongoing positive press about Mazo's branch, which was simul-

Figure 7. (*left to right*) Alexander Asro (Khonen), Noah Nachbush (Messenger), and Sonia Alomis (Leye) in *The Dybbuk*, Berlin, 1923. YIVO Institute for Jewish Research.

taneously performing first in Austria, then in Romania and Poland. Though each refused to acknowledge the other's existence, press about both branches only reinforced the Vilna Troupe's growing pan-European reputation.

A Movement Emerges

Just as the Vilna Troupe had become an international presence in only a few years, so too did the idea of a Yiddish art theater—modeled upon the Vilna Troupe's repertoire and practices—spread rapidly throughout the global Jewish diaspora. After the First World War, self-proclaimed "Yiddish art theater" companies sprang up around the world. In New York, Maurice Schwartz founded the Yiddish Art Theater in 1918.[170] Jacob Ben-Ami, a former member of the Hirschbein Troupe, formed a rival New York company, the Jewish Art Theater, in 1919.[171] In Warsaw, director and actor Zygmunt Turkow and actress Ida Kaminska, both former Vilner, began to recruit actors for their Warsaw Yiddish Art Theater company (known by its Yiddish acronym, VYKT) in 1922; the company began performing in 1924.[172] Dozens of other "Yiddish art theater" companies were founded in the 1920s, including the Varshever Nayer Yidisher Teater (VNIT, Warsaw), Davke (Vilna), the Khaveyrim Trupe (Lublin), and the Chicago Dramatishe Gezelshaft, also known as the Jewish Art Players of Chicago, among others. Who were the members of these companies? In many cases, they were former Vilna Troupe members. In VYKT, besides Turkow and Kaminska, were Klara Segalovitch, Meir Melman, Yankev Mansdorf, Khavel Buzgan, A. Sandu, Pepi Urich, Wolf Zilberberg, Yoysef Shlivniak, and others. VNIT had Dovid Herman, Hersh Poznanski, Isaac Samberg, Klara Segalovitch, and Yoysef Shlivniak. The Vilna Troupe played a seminal role in training young actors for careers in a burgeoning Yiddish art theater movement.

Most of these companies modeled themselves on the Vilna Troupe, inspired by coverage in the international press. When the Vilna Troupe held fast to realism and performed plays by Hirschbein, Kobrin, Asch, and Pinski alongside those of Tolstoy, Hauptmann, Moliere, and Ibsen, the new Yiddish art theaters followed its lead. Maurice Schwartz opened the first season of his Yiddish Art Theater with Hirschbein's *A farvorfn vinkl* (*A Forsaken Corner*), a play that had first become famous in the Vilna Troupe's 1917 production. In 1919 Jacob Ben-Ami opened his Jewish Art Theater with Hirschbein's *The Abandoned Inn*, another play made famous by the Vilna Troupe. Ben-Ami himself acknowledged the Vilna Troupe's influence on the staging of his production of *The Abandoned Inn*.[173] When the Vilna Troupe introduced a modernist aesthetic in *The Dybbuk*, the other Yiddish art theaters followed its lead.

For years, the Yiddish art theaters had a shared repertoire. New plays staged by the Vilna Troupe often reemerged at the Yiddish Art Theater, the Jewish Art Theater, the VYKT, and other companies just a year or so later. Maurice Schwartz's Yiddish Art Theater copied the Vilna Troupe's repertoire more than most. To cite just a few examples: the Vilna Troupe staged Dovid Pinski's *Ayzik Sheftel* and Theodore Herzl's *Dos naye geto* (*The New Ghetto*) in 1918; Schwartz's productions of the same plays opened in 1919 and 1920, respectively. In 1919 the Vilna Troupe staged a Yiddish version of August Strindberg's *The Father* in Warsaw; Schwartz's version opened in New York a few months later. Later that year, the Vilna Troupe produced Fishl Bimko's *Ganovim* (*Thieves*)—and so did Schwartz's Yiddish Art Theater in 1920. This pattern continued for many years. In 1928 Mazo's Vilna Troupe opened its adaptation of Sholem Asch's novel *Kidush Hashem* (*Sanctification of the Holy Name*) in May 1928, to rave reviews in Warsaw. The curtain went up on Maurice Schwartz's version in New York just four months later.[174] The Vilna Troupe also influenced the creation of new companies that adopted similar methods and repertoire. The Yiddish theater historian Nakhmen Mayzel explicitly credited the Vilna Troupe's *Dybbuk* (and its subsequent departure from Warsaw to "pluck the fruit from that unexpected success") with inspiring Zygmunt Turkow and Ida Kaminska to organize their Warsaw Yiddish Art Theater.[175] The Vilna Troupe paved the way for the explosive growth of a global Yiddish art theater movement.

The Moscow State Yiddish Theater (Moskovskii Gosudarstvennyi Evreiskii Teatr, known by its acronym, GOSET), on the other hand, was distinct from the Vilna Troupe. Unlike the Yiddish art theaters in Europe and America, which had no financial support outside of the Jewish community, GOSET was a state-funded institution under the auspices of the Soviet Union. As such, GOSET interpreted the idea of a Yiddish art theater differently than its peers and developed its own set of goals and artistic practices that bore little relation to the model established by the Vilna Troupe.[176] Still, there was some personnel crossover. Actors Morits Norvid, Sara Rotbaum, Yosef Shayn, and Yankev Shidlo were all Vilna Troupe members before joining GOSET.[177]

What did "Yiddish art theater" signify for the companies that adopted its mantle? When asked about the *art* in the name of his company, William Mercur, the business manager for Schwartz's Yiddish Art Theater in New

York, responded, "Plays were produced meticulously, not like in the old days. We did them with great care, we discussed them thoroughly in advance."[178] For many, art theater simply meant productions that were superior to standard Yiddish theater fare. Following the Vilna Troupe's model, the actors and directors of these Yiddish art theater companies often spoke of being inspired by the Moscow Art Theater.[179] Over time, each Yiddish art theater gradually developed its own distinct repertoire and aesthetic outlook. The Yiddish art theaters in the United States tended to define *art theater* in terms of literary merit, even when directors incorporated modernist strategies. When asked to define Yiddish art theater, Maurice Schwartz replied with one word: "literature."[180] In Europe, Yiddish art theater companies tended to focus more on experimental styles and avant-garde aesthetics. Both strands of the movement were equally represented within the Vilna Troupe branches that traveled among them all.

Maurice Schwartz's New York *Dybbuk*

In September 1921, just nine months after the premiere of Mazo's *Dybbuk* in Warsaw and only weeks before the opening of Asro and Alomis's version in Berlin, Maurice Schwartz's Yiddish Art Theater opened its own *Dybbuk* in New York.[181] No doubt, this production was inspired by the international coverage of the Vilna Troupe's version. Indeed, New York Jewish intellectuals had been holding heated discussions about the Vilna Troupe's *Dybbuk*, based on the European reviews.[182] When Schwartz announced that he would be staging the play as the opening production of his 1921–22 season, the debates grew even more intense.

American Jews wondered whether Schwartz would follow the Vilna Troupe's controversial modernist staging. Some hoped for a realistic production. Others hoped that Schwartz would copy Herman. "It is perhaps no accident that *The Dybbuk* was embraced only after it was produced on the stage," commented one New York critic.[183] Still others encouraged Schwartz to make the play even more avant-garde by adopting futurism or surrealism.[184]

Schwartz capitalized on the conversation surrounding his production by publishing an essay on the morning of *The Dybbuk*'s opening night. Titled "Impressionism and Realism: Which of These Two Methods Should Be Applied to the Production of An-sky's Dramatic Legend *The Dybbuk*?" the editorial took up the question that New York's Yiddish theater critics had been speculating about for months. "Other directors" of *The Dybbuk*, he wrote, tended to model their work either on Stanislavsky's realism or on Reinhardt's expressionism.[185] The implied reference was, of course, to Herman—for in the fall of 1921, no other director had yet staged a production of *The Dybbuk*, in any language. Schwartz's condemnation of "other directors" who relied on Stanislavsky or Reinhardt for inspiration was a thinly veiled reference to the Vilna Troupe. Instead, he promised a different approach.

> The mission of the director for a work like *The Dybbuk* is to bring out the essence of the poetic Jewish legend, with its stimulating realism, its resonant mysticism, and its heartfelt folksiness. The director must ensure that the production has artistic charm, but it must be Jewish charm, and not an imitation of Maeterlinck's *The Blue Bird* or of a Reinhardt *Hamlet* production. First and foremost comes loyalty to the spirit of the work, and that is what I seek to provide.[186]

Schwartz's belabored assurances that his *Dybbuk* would correct for the mistakes of past directors are full of oblique references to the Vilna Troupe. His approach to the play, in contrast to Herman's, adopted the arguments of *The Dybbuk*'s first Warsaw Yiddish critics. Like those critics, Schwartz highlighted the characterization of the Messenger as a prime example of the fallacies of the unnamed "other *Dybbuk* directors." In "some *Dybbuk* productions" (i.e., the Vilna Troupe's), he wrote, the Messenger had been transformed into an enigmatic figure outside of the world of the play. Instead, Schwartz promised, his production would portray the Messenger as a simple man with a prophetic voice, evoking the familiar Jewish trope of Elijah the Prophet disguised as a beggar.[187]

Schwartz's *Dybbuk* opened at the Irving Place Theater on September 1, 1921. It was a moderate success, but no runaway hit. Decades later, Schwartz wistfully wrote, "I wanted to be as successful as the Vilna Troupe had been, perhaps even more so."[188] Still, the Yiddish Art Theater's *Dybbuk* drew large crowds and earned a panegyric from none other than the *New York Times*, which raved that Schwartz's production had a "Rembrantesque quality" that rendered the play "extraordinarily vivid" and "unforgettable."[189] Yiddish critics were less enthusiastic, comparing Schwartz's production unfavorably to Herman's Warsaw and Berlin sensations. The Messenger was so lifelike that his role in the play was confusing, argued one Eastern European Jewish critic who had traveled to Berlin and New York to compare Schwartz's *Dybbuk* to the Vilna Troupe's. Schwartz's realism had led him away from the play's essence, the reviewer concluded, and the result was a production where "the play's spiritualism was sacrificed to materialism."[190] Disappointed by the tepid response, Schwartz cut *The Dybbuk*'s run short and moved on to other productions.[191]

Schwartz's *Dybbuk* is a classic example of how the Vilna Troupe influenced other Yiddish theater directors around the world, though Schwartz never openly admitted to it. Indeed, Schwartz repeatedly and falsely claimed that his company was the first to produce *The Dybbuk*, including in an editorial for none other than the *New York Times* in 1940.[192] In fact, the Yiddish Art Theater's New York production was conceived as a direct response to the controversy over Herman's modernist techniques; its reception was likewise colored by the Vilna Troupe's version. The Vilna Troupe's influence was everywhere. Perhaps Schwartz's *Dybbuk* would have been more successful had reviewers not known about the Vilna Troupe's version. Nevertheless, in seeking to define how his production differed from Herman's, Schwartz ironically demonstrated just how deep the Vilna Troupe's influence actually ran.

Habima and *The Dybbuk*

In January 1922 the Moscow-based Hebrew-language theater Habima opened its own version of An-sky's play. *The Dybbuk* was Habima's breakthrough production, spurring its reputation as the premiere Hebrew theater in the world. Just as Habima ultimately became the national theater of Israel, so too would Habima's *Dybbuk* become a national icon for Yishuv culture in British Mandate Palestine, and later, in Israeli culture.[193]

The members of Habima never spoke openly of the Vilna Troupe. Their publicity for *The Dybbuk* did not mention that the play had originally been staged in Yiddish.[194] In choosing to disregard the play's Yiddish roots, Habima's production implicitly suggested that *The Dybbuk* belonged to the Hebrew-language stage, a claim that carried increased resonance after the company resettled in Tel Aviv and became the de facto protonational theater of the Zionist movement. The members of Habima wanted to create a Jewish art theater in Hebrew, and they sought to distance their work from the Yiddish stage as much as possible. Historians by and large followed their lead, crediting Habima's *Dybbuk* with total originality.[195] As Shelly Zer-Zion has written, acknowledging the Vilna Troupe's role as a forerunner "disrupts the narrative of Habima as modern and wholly new in the field of Jewish theater in Eastern Europe."[196]

To be fair, the tone of Habima's *Dybbuk* did differ from both Herman's and Schwartz's earlier Yiddish versions. Directed by the Russian Jewish avant-garde director Yevgeny Vakhtangov, Habima's *Dybbuk* was a fully fledged expressionist production with an emphasis on the grotesque. The paupers wore cubist masks, each of which depicted a different animal: a fox, a bird, a hyena, a wolf, a monkey.[197] Every gesture, costume, and set piece was larger than life and constructed to highlight visual contrasts. In Habima's *Dybbuk*, Leah's pale face (artificially emphasized with white makeup) and white dress contrasted with her long black braid and the dark kaftans of the men surrounding her. This visual contrasting, combined with expressionist choreography and design, superseded the plot as the dominant element of the production (a sensible choice, since the first audiences for Habima's *Dybbuk* were, like Vakhtangov himself, non-Hebrew speakers and relied upon visual cues to make sense of the play).[198] Unlike in Yiddish theater, there was no modernist crisis for the modern Hebrew stage. It was brazenly modernist from the beginning.

Still, in spite of these differences, elements of Habima's *Dybbuk* were still inspired by the Vilna Troupe. While Habima had long considered producing *The Dybbuk*, even beginning rehearsals as early as 1918, the company did not bring the production to fruition until after the Vilna Troupe demonstrated the play's viability as a vehicle for modernist experimentation.[199] Moreover, Habima's version incorporated elements drawn directly from the Vilna Troupe's production, including a dance of death during the wedding scene.[200]

Indeed, although Habima refused to acknowledge the Vilna Troupe's influence, the two companies were remarkably similar. Both were explicitly modeled on the Moscow Art Theater, and both sought to create a prestigious Jewish theater. Habima and the Vilna Troupe shared much of the same repertoire, as Habima's first productions were mostly literary Yiddish plays (often initially staged by the Vilna Troupe) in Hebrew translation.[201] Like Schwartz's *Dybbuk*, Habima's rise to prominence was largely predicated upon the Vilna Troupe's earlier successes. The Vilna Troupe was thus not only the inspiration for the emergence of a Yiddish art theater movement but also a catalyst for the development of the modern Hebrew stage.

"That's Marvelous! Who Wrote It?"

The Vilna Troupe's metamorphosis into a modernist theater company was initially incomplete. While both Vilna Troupe branches turned increasingly to modernist approaches after *The Dybbuk*, for the next few years they tended to produce this work alongside more traditional fare.

But for a new generation of Yiddish actors, including the youngest members of the Vilna Troupe, being on the cutting edge was more important than producing literary dramas. Among them was an ambitious twenty-four-year-old aspiring director named Joseph Buloff, who convinced Mordechai Mazo to allow him to stage an experimental production of Osip Dimov's *Der zinger fun zayn troyer* (*The Singer of His Sorrows*) in Bucharest in 1924. This production signified the culmination of the aesthetic shift that had begun with *The Dybbuk*. Many Vilna Troupe productions in the early 1920s either reverted to the company's initial realism or tried to reproduce the tone of *The Dybbuk* with little success (indeed, both Mazo's and Asro and Alomis's Vilna Troupes were heavily criticized in the years after *The Dybbuk* for incorporating elements from An-sky's play into other productions where they did not belong).[202] Buloff wanted to take Mazo's branch in a new direction.

The play was a hard sell. *Singer* was a rather simplistic play about an impoverished musician and his unrequited love, and Mazo questioned the wisdom of staging it. But Buloff was persistent, explaining to Mazo that the subject matter was unimportant. His staging would use Dimov's script only as a vehicle for creating a completely new piece that he had invented in his mind. Mazo was hesitant, but he had few other options. Leyb Kadison had recently left the company along with his wife, Khane, to take up jobs with Maurice Schwartz's Yiddish Art Theater in New York, and Dovid Herman was with Asro and Alomis's branch. Mazo's branch no longer had a director. Reluctantly, Mazo accepted Buloff's offer to direct and hired the Yiddish poet Yankev Shternberg to write an adaptation of Dimov's play.[203]

The Singer of His Sorrows centers around a love triangle and a touching, if predictable, tearjerker plot about a poor musician named Yoshke who is in love with a maid named Sheyne. Sheyne, in turn, is in love with her master's son Solomontshik, who is about to be betrothed to a wealthy bride. Yoshke agrees to write letters from Sheyne to Solomontshik to help her win his heart. Suddenly, Yoshke wins the lottery. He gives all of the money to Sheyne, hoping to win her love, but Sheyne instead promptly uses the money to snare her upper-class beau. At the end of the play, having lost both his fortune and his bride, Yoshke goes mad, gives away all of his clothes and possessions, and becomes a homeless beggar.

Buloff and Shternberg's version recontextualized this simple plot with an elaborate prologue. The Vilna Troupe's *Singer* opened with a grandmother telling her grandchild a story. Suddenly, the grandmother transformed into Yoshke (Joseph Buloff), the story came to life, and the play began. Everything was larger than life, abstract, and dream-like, as if seen through the eyes of a young child. An old chicken vendor was costumed as a hen. A chimney sweep made all of his entrances and exits through the stove. Yoshke's makeup resembled the shape of the fiddle he always carried. Larger-than-life facial features (extra eyelashes drawn on his face with dark eyeliner, exaggerated eyebrows and lips, and bright red spots on both cheeks) completed the clown-like effect. The actors wore big, exaggerated costumes and colorful masks with huge, overpowering features.

To further intensify the dream-like quality, Buloff staged the entire play in the kitchen, where the grandmother's story began. Each wall of the set had dozens of holes in it, through which countless pairs of anonymous eyes, with long, painted, wing-like lashes, could observe the characters' every move. Two large group scenes involving the entire cast, one when crowds gather to tell Yoshke that he has won the lottery, the other when the beggars make Yoshke one of their own, were tightly choreographed and employed grotesque facial expressions and movement.[204]

Like Herman with *The Dybbuk*, Buloff faced significant opposition early on. The Vilna Troupe actors, particularly the older members, were skeptical about taking part in such an unconventional production of a play that seemed to border on melodrama. The actors grumbled, and even Mazo questioned whether he had made the right choice in allowing Buloff to direct. But the complaints disappeared after the first performance. At one of the last rehearsals, one Vilna Troupe actor (who asked to remain anonymous) told a Romanian reporter, "I wouldn't like you to write about me playing this part. To tell you the truth, I'm not so happy about it." When interviewed again less than a week later, the actor admitted he had experienced a change of heart. "I was wrong, I'll admit it, *mea culpa*," he confessed, "I couldn't possibly have imagined that the play would be so successful."[205] Even the playwright himself was taken aback. When Dimov learned of the production's success, he reportedly exclaimed, "How marvelous! Who wrote it?"[206]

The Singer of His Sorrows attracted diverse audiences (35 percent non-Jews, in Buloff's estimation) in Bucharest, where it was hailed by critics as a masterpiece.[207] Victor Eftimiu, the former director of the Romanian National Theater, called the production "a model of stylized realistic drama" and suggested that the Vilna Troupe ought to be invited to stay in Bucharest, "as it brings over some of the momentum that drama has gained in other countries, some of the striving for perfection that we find in Russian and German theater."[208] Eftimiu went on to suggest that the Romanian government ought to lower the Vilna Troupe's taxes to incentivize an extension of its stay in Bucharest.[209] "This performance seemed to me the most accomplished artistic event that we've seen these past few years, not only here, but also in Western cities," wrote another Romanian critic. "We urge all theater lovers not to miss this play, which is a landmark in artistic performance from every point of view. . . . These actors now represent the epitome of pure art in our capital."[210] "[Buloff] has broken the molds, he has created *another* art and heroically opened the window to unexpected points of view," wrote another reviewer. "With this performance, the Vilna Troupe has made itself indispensible and should never be allowed to leave."[211] Still another Romanian journalist described the opening moments of the play:

> The grey curtain is trembling, and in the dim light I can recognize the familiar faces that I usually see through the windows of Capşa, past and present state dignitaries, and countless artists, all drawn here by the magnet of pure Art that has overcome all petty prejudice. . . . Then the scenes follow: here comes the sublime embodiment of Yoshke: shy, gentle, dreamy eyes gazing at his beloved; every gesture is infinitely varied, with every look he pours out his feelings and his soul, and the feelings and the soul are those of a great artists who belongs to no race, people, or nationality, for he is the son of a creative muse, the son of mankind's eternal genius. He speaks in Yiddish, true, but what do we care? He is love itself, sacrifice itself, pain itself throbbing, breaking, bending, groveling under our enchanted gaze.[212]

Other Romanian drama critics made similar assessments, calling the actors "half-gods, sublime beings endowed by nature not with one soul but with many souls."[213] The playwright and journalist Solomon Weitzendorf called the production "a sway of emotion, a harmonious vibration of inner light, a pure and crystalline spring, a music as yet unsung. Something weightless that escapes cold analysis, something dissipated among the infinitesimal atoms of your soul like the eternal scent of a perfect flower."[214] Romanian theatrical modernism seemed almost primitive in comparison. "Buloff has begun a new era," the critics crowed.[215]

Many commented on how the Vilna Troupe overcame poverty and adversity to stage *Singer*. Yiddish critic Khayim Geler wrote of Mazo's initial struggle to secure travel permits to bring the company to Romania after an anti-Semitic government official fired the head of the Culture Foundation and hired an unsympathetic individual in his place. Moreover, wrote Geler, the Zhignitza Theater in Bucharest—the only local theater where the Vilna Troupe could afford to perform—was no more than "a large courtyard with a small stage and terrible acoustics" suitable only for "cabarets of a middling sort."[216] Romanian journalists agreed. "Every other theater in Bucharest has had better circumstances this year: more comfortable and luxurious halls, sets and costumes as needed, state subsidies, and entire companies of actors," remarked the Romanian novelist, playwright, and critic Felix Aderca. "The Vilna Troupe has a theater which lacks all creature comforts, the number of artists is low, the stage is beyond inappropriate—so insufficient that it is downright hostile to any performance. Mr. Bulow . . . has overcome all of these difficulties and given Bucharest the most astonishing artistic performance this city has seen so far."[217] As the reviewer Jan Pos described the atmosphere,

> The actors are young and poor. The stage is no more than three cubits wide and deep, the hall has no comfortable seats and terrible acoustics. But here upon these boards, amongst sets made of the poorest cloths and material, there struggles a noble, courageous soul whose emotions exert a power over the unaesthetic theater and transfer its vibrations to the spectator, whether or not they know Yiddish.[218]

Others compared *The Singer of His Sorrows* to better-known theatrical modernists. "Buloff is not just an actor, but a thinker," wrote a Bucharest journalist in *Gazeta Sporturilor*, "an explorer of traditions, a spokesperson for [Edward Gordon] Craig, a living image of Stanislavsky."[219]

By the twenty-fifth performance, *The Singer of His Sorrows* had already broken Bucharest's record for performances of a play in a single season.[220] The fiftieth performance was attended by the former Romanian minister Mihai Popovici, two princesses and a prince, and Corneliu Moldovanu, director of the Romanian National Theater.[221] The Vilna Troupe's production of *Singer* played in Bucharest for a full year, culminating in a royal command performance before King Carol II and his entourage.[222] This was the first time in history that a Jewish theater company had been invited to perform before a monarch—a significant benchmark for a theatrical tradition that had always struggled to prove its legitimacy. It would not be the last time that the Vilna Troupe would perform before royalty.

The actors were astonished by the transformative impact that *Singer* seemed to have on the attitudes of Bucharest locals about Jewish culture. As Buloff described it,

> The secret of our success lies in the Romanians' attitude towards the show. From the most insignificant writer to the greatest poet or artist, they all feel it's their duty to speak publicly of their admiration for Jewish art and for the Yiddish language. One of the best Romanian actresses, Tanzi Cutava, said that a French version of the play would not sound nearly as beautiful as the Yiddish. When they get together for a glass of wine, Romanian writers diligently sing "*Yoshke mitn fidl, Berl mitn bas*," the leitmotif of Dimov's *Singer of His Sorrow*. . . . We're invited to work with Romanian theaters and to stage Yiddish plays in Romanian translation. The climax was reached when a group of Romanian poets invited us to read from Yiddish literature at one of their literary meetings. It was the greatest satisfaction that the barren soil of Jewish Bucharest could produce. Seeing the hall filled with army officers, students, poets, priests (and the occasional curious Jewish face), I could feel myself trembling as I got onto the stage. But the silence and rapt attention that accompanied the reading were much more intense than I had ever seen at a Jewish literary gathering, and the applause and the "bravos" were conspicuously loud. The book *Arabesques* (I had been reading [Alter] Kacyzne's "Eyeless") was snatched from my hand and passed from hand to hand by people who held it upside down and gazed in admiration at the square and "mysterious" Jewish letters.[223]

Just as with *The Dybbuk*, the reaction of non-Jewish spectators to *Singer* was the offstage drama that secured the production's onstage reputation. Spectators came to the theater ostensibly to see the Vilna Troupe perform *Singer*, but also to witness how other audience members responded. Indeed, Bucharest's Jews became interested in *Singer* only after members of the Romanian elite began to attend. Had Romanian intellectuals not taken to *Singer* so strongly, the production would likely not have been as successful with local Jewish theatergoers.

The Singer of His Sorrows secured for Mazo's Vilna Troupe a reputation for being "experimental."[224] In 1929 the Yiddish writer Moyshe Broderzon wrote that he considered the Vilna Troupe's *Singer of His Sorrows* a turning point in the history of Jewish theater and one of "the two best productions with the greatest theatrical-artistic worth that we have seen in Poland," second only to Habima's *Dybbuk*. "A masterful production," wrote Broderzon of *Singer*. "A date to remember for all of us who have endured Yiddish theater."[225]

Indeed, like *The Dybbuk*, *Singer* also inspired other theater artists to adopt a more aggressively modernist stance in their work. Maurice Schwartz invited Joseph Buloff and Luba Kadison to join his Yiddish Art Theater in New York based largely on *Singer*'s success, hoping that they would bring their experimental ideas to his company.[226] *Singer* may have even inspired a young Eugene Ionesco, who was living in Bucharest at the time. The Yiddish literary critic and director Yankev Botoshansky and Joseph Buloff both claim that Ionesco attended a production of *Singer* in Bucharest.[227] Years later, according to Buloff, Ionesco called him on the phone, thanked him for *The Singer of His Sorrows*, and credited the production with inspiring his early ideas about playwriting.[228]

The Singer of His Sorrows marked the culmination of the Vilna Troupe's introduction of modernism to the Yiddish stage. This ethos of theatrical experimentation, in which the text was simply the first stage in a lengthy creative process, took hold among Yiddish theater artists throughout the world, inspiring companies like Schwartz's Yiddish Art Theater and Habima to incorporate an increasingly modernist approach while also spurring the development of dozens of new companies, many of which were founded by former Vilna Troupe members. The Vilna Troupe's productions of *The Dybbuk* and *The Singer of His Sorrows* were the catalyst for this modernist embrace.

INTERLUDE II

Love and Romance on the Road

Acting in the Vilna Troupe was a full-time job and then some. Every day there were rehearsals all through the morning and afternoon, followed by evening performances and late-night discussion sessions. The actors lived in close quarters and spent nearly all of their time together. There were no weekends or days off. Then there was the grueling travel schedule. When the Vilna Troupe could not afford to rent hotel rooms or sleeper cars (which was often), the company would sleep overnight on wooden benches on the train. The actors carried miniature pillows so they could rest on long train rides from Kishinev to Bucharest or Odessa to Minsk.[1]

Romance was inevitable under these circumstances. Twenty-three percent (69 out of 290) of the actors were romantically involved with fellow Vilner at one point or another. Some married, some dated briefly then broke up. Others had affairs. The Vilna Troupe offered members the chance to meet young Jewish idealists like themselves, and many found romantic partners through the company. Here are a few of their stories.

Bella Bellarina and Chaim Shniur would likely never have met without the Vilna Troupe. Before she took on her stage name, Bella Rubinlicht was the fifth child in a well-to-do Warsaw Jewish family. Her father was a real estate broker, her mother a homemaker.[2] She received a thorough secular education, and her Polish was flawless.[3] At seventeen, she studied to become a teacher at the local university.[4] But the stage beckoned. In 1916 Bella enrolled in the Warsaw Drama School against her parents' wishes, imagining that she would become a Polish actress. A chance meeting with future Vilna Troupe director Dovid Herman changed her mind.[5]

Her future husband Chaim Shniur's life could hardly have been more different. Chaim was a poor, working-class boy from a small town who dreamed of something bigger. At age thirteen he was sent to Vilna to become a tailor's apprentice. He was a mediocre tailor but quickly became fascinated with the city's amateur Yiddish drama scene.[6] Soon he joined FADA.

Chaim met Bella during the Vilna Troupe's first trip to Warsaw in 1917, and both were smitten.[7] They carried on a brief romance until a fight caused them to break up on the eve of Chaim's departure. Bella was heartbroken. A few months later, she ran away from home to find him. She packed a suitcase, left a note for her parents, and hopped on the next train to Lodz, where she knew from the newspapers that she could find the Vilna Troupe. Bella found out where Chaim was staying and confronted him, offering to share her life with him in a "free love" arrangement without the restrictions of marriage.[8] Somehow, she thought this would win him back. Chaim was shocked and countered that they should be married by a rabbi instead. Bella agreed. Upon marrying, she immediately became a member of the Vilna Troupe, though some of the other actors felt that she would never have been admitted were it not for her relationship with Chaim. To them, she would always be an interloper.[9]

Chaim Shniur and Bella Bellarina remained happily married for the rest of their lives, but many backstage romances did not go so smoothly. Leyzer Zhelazo was an up-and-coming young actor in Avrom Fishzon's traveling company; Ester Lipovska was a beautiful chorus girl. They had a brief fling, but when Ester got pregnant, Zhelazo abandoned her.[10] Soon he would join the Vilna Troupe. When Ester gave birth to her son, she refused to give him the Zhelazo last name and gave him her maiden name instead.[11] Ester later married the theater director Nokhum Lipovski, who adopted the boy and gave him his last name. Little Sasha Lipovski would ultimately follow in his father's footsteps and become a member of the Vilna Troupe a decade and a half later, to his mother's dismay.

Meanwhile, Leyzer Zhelazo had found a new romantic interest: another young actress named Roza Birnboym. Roza had run away from her traditional religious upbringing to become a Yiddish actress and was nearly twenty years younger than him. Zhelazo recruited Birnboym to the Vilna Troupe, and they become first lovers, then husband and wife.[12] One can imagine that when the Vilna Troupe encountered Ester and Nokhum Lipovski on the road, it was acrimonious.

Love triangles were common. There was Ida Kaminska and Zygmunt Turkow's tumultuous romance, marriage, and divorce, followed by Kaminska's remarriage to fellow Vilner Meir Melman. There was Yosef

Kamen and Dina Koenig's marriage and Kamen's rumored involvement with another Vilner, Nadia Kareni, when he fled to Uzbekistan during World War II.[13]

And then there was the story of Sonia Alomis and Alexander Asro. Asro and Alomis first met when he was eleven and she was seven. "An angel was standing on a chair reciting a Hebrew poem . . . could I not love her?" Asro recalled.[14] They were childhood friends who grew up, fell in love, and started the Vilna Troupe. By all accounts, Asro and Alomis were deeply in love for their entire lives. A candid photograph from early in their relationship shows the happy couple embracing backstage at a dress rehearsal in Berlin, 1921. Alexander is twenty-nine, Sonia is twenty-five. If anything, they look even younger. They cling to each other tightly, madly in love.

"He idolized her," their granddaughter told me. "He just thought she was the most amazing actress. She was his leading lady, on the stage and in life."[15] The feeling was mutual. When Asro was cast in a touring production of the hit Broadway musical *Leave It to Me!* in 1939, Alomis refused to stay behind in New York. "My grandmother wouldn't allow her husband to go alone on tour, with all those beautiful Broadway starlets, so she came along."[16] Clearly, Sonia had seen enough actors having affairs while traveling with the Vilna Troupe. Luckily, the company welcomed her, and the couple spent the next year and a half traveling across the United States by train with Sophie Tucker and a young Mary Martin, who had just made her Broadway debut in the show.[17] Alomis became close with Sophie Tucker, and they roomed together for most of the tour.[18]

Another Vilna Troupe power couple brought together by the company was Joseph Buloff and Luba Kadison. When Joseph Buloff found himself homeless and hungry in Warsaw, he decided to find the Vilna Troupe that he had heard so much about. Leyb Kadison found the young man waiting for him in the empty theater. Buloff introduced himself as an actor, and Kadison invited him home for dinner. When Buloff knocked, thirteen-year-old Luba Kadison answered the door. "I saw a person with a wrinkled suit and an odd little hat and a pair of big eyes that looked at me with fear," Kadison later recalled, "and I said, 'Mama, come here and see who it is.'"[19] So began a romance that would last for more than sixty years.

When Boris Thomashefsky came to Mazo's Vilna Troupe a few years later with an invitation to America and Mazo turned him down, Leyb and Khane Kadison independently decided to take the American producer up on his offer. They wanted their daughter to join them in America, but Luba preferred to stay in Europe with Joseph. Leyb and Khane gave her

Figure 8. Alexander Asro and Sonia Alomis, Berlin. Sharon Asro and Alexander Zaloum.

an ultimatum: "Either you go with us or you get married."[20] Luba decided to marry and stay with the Vilna Troupe. She was sixteen.

Luba Kadison and Joseph Buloff's wedding, like so much of their lives, happened onstage. During the day, the couple had a traditional ceremony. But on their wedding night, they performed Hirschbein's *Green Fields*, with Luba as the female lead, Tsine, and Joseph as her beloved, Levi-Yitskhok. At the end of the play, Tsine and Levi-Yitskhok get married. That night, all of the characters celebrated their wedding with greater fanfare than usual. "To us," Luba recalled, "the real wedding took place on the stage."[21]

CHAPTER 4

Nomadic Chutzpah

The Vilna Troupe's Accidental Avant-Garde

When Joseph Buloff attended his first Samuel Beckett production decades after the Vilna Troupe's dissolution, he was not impressed. "Modern style, my foot!" Buloff trumpeted. "I pioneered Theater of the Absurd back in the twenties!"[1]

> By its nature, the infant Jewish theater had to be absurd because it grew out of the absurd situation of the Jews in Czarist Russia. . . . When [Jewish actors] recognized spies entering the makeshift theater and infiltrating the audience, they would send a signal to the stage. Then, abruptly, the actors would switch from the Yiddish script they were performing. An actor from Poland would begin declaiming in Polish. A Hungarian actress would answer him in Magyar. A couple of actors who only knew Yiddish would carry on a dialogue in meaningless gibberish—"Nov shmoz kapop . . ." And so on. The audience, in on the ruse, would listen to this babble impassively. . . . There you have it: a dozen actors on a bare stage, each one speaking a different language. Alienation, failure of communication, absence of objective meaning—all the elements of Theater of the Absurd. And it was invented a century ago by Jewish actors out of grim necessity.[2]

Coy though it may be, this description of a renowned playwright unconsciously hewing to an artistic sensibility invented by Eastern European

Jews reflects how the Vilner thought of their work. Simply put, they saw themselves as modernist innovators.

But unlike other modernists of the period, the Vilna Troupe's innovations were hardly intentional or even conscious. Often, chance mishaps during travel led to new techniques. Once while traveling in the Polish countryside, a Vilna Troupe branch unexpectedly ran out of cash and could no longer afford electricity to light the stage. In desperation, the actors spent hours manually rigging wires to tap into the grid and override the theater's electrical system, producing an eerie lighting effect. Spectators and critics were delighted.[3]

More often than not, the Vilna Troupe's greatest contributions were accidental byproducts of the unique social, economic, and political position of Jewish artists between the two world wars. Spurred by precarious circumstances, Yiddish performers were often more artistically nimble than their peers. Indeed, the ability to adapt was often necessary for survival.

Between 1924 and 1930, in the aftermath of the sensational success of *The Dybbuk*, the Vilna Troupe became a global brand signifying that Yiddish theater could be on par with other European theaters, that it was an integral part of Jewish culture, and finally, that Yiddish theater was aesthetically innovative. This chapter considers the Vilna Troupe's contributions to the theatrical avant-garde between 1924 and 1930, including advances in staging techniques and technical breakthroughs, alongside the company's role in disseminating repertoire and connecting experimental artists around the globe. Travel was an essential ingredient in the Vilna Troupe's recipe for artistic ingenuity. Within the borders of any one country, Jewish theater artists could create sophisticated repertoire, cultivate talented performers, and develop thriving urban theater scenes. But it was only when these agile actors took to the road and were exposed to new theatrical ideas that they began to seriously innovate.

"The Wizards of Dramatic Art!" rang the headline in the daily Yiddish newspaper *Der Forverts*.[4] "They are a completely different type of actor than we've ever seen before," proclaimed another journalist, sharing "every important detail" of "how they dress, what they look like, how they talk."[5]

An intellectual revolution for the Yiddish stage. A brand that signified artistic ingenuity. Celebrities whose every gesture, outfit, word, and deed captivated fans across Europe and beyond. Thus was Asro and Alomis's Vilna Troupe received by the American public in the winter of 1924. The press tracked their every move. Journalists detailed the hotels they stayed in, the restaurants they ate at, the shows and banquets they attended, and the clothing they wore in the weeks leading up to the troupe's American premiere. In dozens of articles in the American Jewish press, journalists marveled at the actors' refined manners, their youthful features, their intellectual acumen, and their knowledge of Yiddish literature. With the sole except of *Forverts* editor Abraham Cahan, no American journalist had actually seen these actors perform, but this did not stop them from hailing the Vilner as "high priests of art" who would transform the American stage.[6]

An ocean and a continent away, the Warsaw Jewish public's obsession with the Vilna Troupe continued. "Are you from Vilna? If so, you can make a living in Warsaw," wrote Pinkhas Katz, a Warsaw-based journalist, in a foreign dispatch for the *Forverts*. Instead of sending a few dollars back home to help your poor relatives in Poland, he joked, why not send Polish Jews a Vilna Troupe actor instead?

> For the best, most up-to-date currency, the thing that is worth more than the very best stocks, the thing that people are willing to pay the highest prices for . . .—it's the Vilner, the Vilna actors of the American Vilna Troupe! Ah, Vilner, Vilner, Vilner! When somebody here sees a Vilna Troupe actor, he chases him down the street. For everyone wants to see a Vilna Troupe actor with his own eyes or, better yet, to touch him.[7]

Tongue in cheek, Katz suggested that the Polish government ought to capitalize on the Vilna Troupe's celebrity by offering the actors as lottery prizes. Instead of a million marks, why not make the grand prize a Vilna Troupe member, the country's most valuable export?

The year 1924 was a watershed for the Vilna Troupe that marked the beginning of its cross-continental presence and its establishment as a global brand. In 1915 the Vilna Troupe was a small, discrete company of fifteen actors who performed in a limited region of Eastern Europe. By 1920, at the time of *The Dybbuk*'s premiere, there were forty-eight performers in two companies, one in Eastern Europe and one in Western Europe. In 1924 a branch of the Western European contingent departed for the United States and a third Vilna Troupe formed in its absence. By the end of that year there were sixty-two Vilna Troupe actors performing across two continents, from Odessa to Los Angeles. The events of 1924 permanently expanded the troupe's geographical reach and firmly established its identity as a global enterprise.

By the late 1920s there were six Vilna Troupe branches, all of which were on the road more often than not. Between 1923 and 1930, they performed in dozens of cities, including

1. Mordechai Mazo's Vilna Troupe: Warsaw, Lodz, Krakow, Czernowitz, Radom, Lublin, Bialystok, Baranovitch, Bucharest, Jassy, Kishinev, Vilna, Riga, Transylvania, Lviv, Belgrade, Prague, Vienna
2. Alexander Asro and Sonia Alomis's Vilna Troupe: Berlin, Paris, London, Brussels, Amsterdam, The Hague, Harzburg, New York, Bridgeport (CT), Wilmington, Baltimore, Paterson (NJ), Fall River (MA), Worcester (MA), Boston, Lawrence (MA), Providence, Hartford, Rochester (NY), Toronto, Buffalo, Cleveland, Detroit, St. Louis, Cincinnati, Pittsburgh, Philadelphia, Newark (NJ), New Haven, Brownsville (PA), Youngstown (OH), Chicago, Montreal, Los Angeles, San Francisco
3. American Revival Troupe #1: New York
4. Belgium Vilna Troupe: Antwerp
5. Waislitz, Buzgan, Shapiro Troupe: Lviv, New York
6. Bronx Vilna Troupe: New York, Chicago, Philadelphia, Boston, Baltimore, Los Angeles, Cleveland, Detroit, Toronto, Montreal, Winnipeg[8]

By 1930, 241 theater artists could claim that they had once performed with "the" famous Vilna Troupe. By 1936, a total of 290 artists, including 29 designers, 24 directors, 10 composers, and 2 choreographers across five continents claimed affiliation with the Vilna Troupe. Many of these artists went on to start theater companies of their own. The Vilna Troupe was no longer a single company or even a group of companies. It was a cultural phenomenon.

A Global Brand

Identifying the Vilna Troupe was no simple matter by the mid-1920s. Loyal fans, casual spectators, and professional theater critics were equally befuddled by the elusive company that seemed to be everywhere at once. The simultaneous existence of multiple Vilna Troupes gave the company the illusion of omnipresence, enabling it to quickly develop a global reputation.

During the 1920s, a Yiddish-speaking Jew almost anywhere in the world could open up a newspaper and find conflicting reports of the Vilna Troupe's geographical presence. In a single week, a Warsaw reader in 1924 might have come across:

- a telegram announcing that the Vilna Troupe had finished its tour in Yugoslavia, was performing in Czechoslovakia, and would soon arrive in Vienna;
- a letter to the editor about a current Vilna Troupe production in Lviv;
- an advertisement for the Vilna Troupe's upcoming season in Warsaw;
- a review of the Vilna Troupe's tour of Belgium and Holland;
- a review of recent Vilna Troupe productions in New York; and
- an announcement that the Vilna Troupe would soon be performing in Philadelphia, Boston, and Baltimore.[9]

Even for the most avid Yiddish theater fans, the company was a puzzle. Each branch followed the others in style and repertoire. Adding to the confusion, reviews of the company's productions tended to be remarkably similar. One Warsaw correspondent for the *Forverts* commiserated with his American readers:

> Early one beautiful morning you wake up and read in the paper:
>
> "THE VILNA TROUPE IN BERLIN: For the past week, the Vilna Troupe has performed to enormous acclaim in Berlin. They presented *The Dybbuk* for their first performance, and on the second night they performed *The Abandoned Inn*. The third night—*The Family*, and they are currently preparing *Day and Night* and *Amnon and Tamar*. Their performances were attended by the most eminent German artists and critics of Berlin."
>
> But then you pick up a second paper and read:
>
> "THE VILNA TROUPE IN VIENNA: The Vilna Troupe, which has been performing here for a week, has had extraordinary success. Besides *The Dybbuk*, *The Abandoned Inn*, *The Family*, and *Day and Night*, they are preparing a production of *Amnon and Tamar*. Their performances were attended by the most prominent Christian critics and artists of Vienna." . . .
>
> Another paper: THE VILNA TROUPE IN PARIS

> And yet another: THE VILNA PLAYERS IN HOLLAND
>
> You leap up as if scalded. What the heck is this?? At the same time as they are performing in Amsterdam, they are a hit in Paris, and on the very same day that they are a sensation in France—their performance delights the Dutch press?[10]

This uncertainty about the Vilna Troupe's identity did not tarnish its reputation. On the contrary, it only served to enhance it.

The Vilna Troupe created a brand identity that operated on a global scale. Each branch employed practices that conveyed a fixed identity: a shared name, logo, style, and repertoire. Any artist could use these brand markers to instantly attract an audience anywhere in the world where Yiddish-speaking Jews resided—and many former Vilner did. When Asro and Alomis toured Mexico in the 1940s, they billed their repertoire as "Masterpieces of Jewish Literature from the Vilner Yiddish Theater."[11] In Glasgow, they advertised their show as featuring "Founders and Principals of the Vilna Troupe."[12] In Buenos Aires, they advertised "a performance by the founders and leading actors of the world famous VILNA TROUPE Sonia Alomis and Alexander Asro."[13] Nokhum Melnick and Devorah Rosenblum did the same, advertising their duet performances in Argentina and Brazil as "Vilna Troupe" productions and referring to themselves as "Vilner."[14] The press often followed suit. "After a successful tour with the Vilna Troupe, across the great Jewish communities of Belgium," wrote one São Paulo Jewish journalist, "this pair of actors separated from them temporarily, in order to bring the masterpieces of the Vilna Troupe's theater art to the Jewish communities of South America."[15] Indeed, in addition to performing as a couple, Melnick and Rosenblum restaged several Vilna Troupe productions in Argentina and Brazil, including an ambitious version of the company's 1928 hit *Bay nakht afn altn mark* (*At Night in the Old Marketplace*) with local amateur actors.[16] Of course, Melnick and Rosenblum had not left the Vilna Troupe "temporarily" in 1939; by then, there were no more Vilna Troupe branches anywhere in the world. But the narrative that they were bringing Vilna Troupe repertoire, aesthetic, and productions with them was an effective way to market Melnick and Rosenblum's personal projects to Jewish communities around the world.

To borrow from Douglas Holt's theory of cultural branding, the Vilna Troupe became a "cultural icon" for Ashkenazi Jews dispersed around the world and functioned as a kind of shorthand for Yiddish culture's successes during the interwar period.[17] "Vilna," as one journalist reflected on the fifteenth anniversary of the company's founding, "is no mere name but, rather, an idea."[18]

Just as a consumer approaches a brand-name commodity because of past associations, the name *Vilna Troupe* carried expectations that impacted spectator experiences. Every production was colored with the memory of how past productions had been received. When people heard that the Vilna Troupe was coming to town, wrote one journalist, the reaction was the same:

> Who? The Vilna Troupe? Ah, yes. We know them already . . . and we will attend! Nobody asks: who is performing? What are they performing? What difference does it make who or what? This is the Vilna Troupe! It's a sure thing, a brand.[19]

Or, in the words of another critic,

> He who buys a ticket for a Vilna Troupe performance wants to see something different, something that he would never see done by another theater group. It is thus unimportant if "the others" are actually better or not, just as the consumer of a particular type of tea or chocolate wants precisely that one kind and not another.[20]

Articles about the Vilna Troupe appeared throughout the global Yiddish press, not just in the places where the company was currently performing. These articles enabled Jewish theatergoers in the Americas to participate, albeit remotely, in the Vilna Troupe's rise to fame. For years prior to the troupe's arrival in New York, American journalists were just as confused about the company as their European counterparts. As Pinkhas Katz, a Warsaw-based correspondent for the *Forverts*, told American readers in 1922,

> I have recently discovered that a single person can be in two cities at exactly the same time . . . and indeed, he can do the same thing, let's say, in New York at exactly the same moment that he is doing it in Toronto.
>
> What, do you think that's impossible?
>
> And if it is impossible—how can it be that this discovery is indeed true? It's a fact that the actors of the Vilna Troupe have demonstrated in black and white.[21]

Any Vilna Troupe production was virtually guaranteed to make international headlines. Members were thus able to assume that spectators—especially, but not only, Jewish spectators—would enter every Vilna Troupe production primed by years of accolades. Long before the curtain rose, audiences had already made up their minds that they were about to see something extraordinary.

The same multiplicity of companies, global presence, unified repertoire, and shared actors, directors, and designers that confounded spectators and critics was, in fact, the Vilna Troupe's greatest achievement. Through its multiplicity, the Vilna Troupe created an international brand that allowed each branch to have the same loyal audience and high art reputation no matter where it traveled.

Across the Ocean

The Yiddish press played a significant role in the dissemination of the Vilna Troupe brand. Interwar Yiddish newspapers regularly reviewed theater productions on other continents in keeping with the migratory patterns of their readers, who tended to keep their subscriptions even as they relocated. The Yiddish literary magazine *Literarishe Bleter* was published in Warsaw, but its readers lived around the world. By the mid-1930s, the magazine had major subscriber bases in London, Paris, Zurich, Lisbon, Milan, New York, San Francisco, Los Angeles, Montreal, Toronto, Mexico City, Rio de Janeiro, Montevideo, Buenos Aires, Santiago, Melbourne, Johannesburg, and dozens of other cities.[22] Similarly, the Yiddish daily *Haynt* was also published in Warsaw but maintained a circulation across Western Europe, the United States, Argentina, Venezuela, and British Mandate Palestine. Collections of Yiddish newspapers in libraries and archives often bear the address labels of local subscribers: a New Yorker with a subscription to a Buenos Aires Yiddish journal, an Australian who followed the Polish Yiddish press, or a Parisian Jew with a subscription to a Romanian Yiddish paper.[23] As one reader who moved from Warsaw to Tel Aviv wrote of his favorite Warsaw newspaper,

> *Haynt*, my beloved paper that I read as long as you existed. I was never able to part with you. Wherever I was and whenever I happened to be, you were there with me. I collected all of your issues and carried them across oceans, and when I arrived in our land, I collected you again.[24]

Just as advance praise had preceded the company's arrival in Western Europe in the early 1920s, so too was the Vilna Troupe's brand disseminated from one continent to another long before the actors ever set foot on a ship.

In 1919 Abraham Cahan, the editor in chief of New York's *Forverts*, had ventured across the Atlantic to find out if the Vilna Troupe was really as good as the Polish Yiddish press was reporting.[25] Cahan was a figure whose outsized influence on American Jewish culture was akin to Y. L. Peretz's role in turn-of-the-century Jewish Warsaw. He often traveled to report on foreign events of interest to the American Jewish community, and it was on such a trip to Warsaw that Cahan attended a Vilna Troupe production of Hirschbein's *Dem shmids tekhter* (*The Blacksmith's Daughters*). Impressed by the "seriousness and artistic collaboration" of the ensemble, Cahan wrote an enthusiastic review for the *Forverts*.[26] Over the next five years, he attended Vilna Troupe productions regularly on his trips to Europe until he was able to convince a few members to defect and bring a branch to New York City.

For a notoriously pedantic critic, Cahan's Vilna Troupe reviews were unusually effusive. Of Hirschbein's *The Abandoned Inn*, he confessed that while he had never liked the play before, the Vilna Troupe had reversed his opinion. Of the actors, Cahan gushed:

> His [Asro's] tone was just as people speak in real life and was absolutely correct—a characteristic that we have rarely seen in America, neither in Yiddish nor in English theater. . . . Her [Alomis's] acting overflowed with natural talent, like fresh water flows from a spring created by nature herself. These moments . . . could not have been the result of conscious thought, they could not have come from the mind. These moments were born in the soul, in a divine soul.[27]

The *Forverts* editor was notorious for his uncompromising theatrical tastes, and his reviews were known to make or break reputations. "He became the arbiter of the Yiddish stage," wrote a colleague, "and [he] could kill any play he disliked."[28] Indeed, in 1907 Cahan had turned against the playwright Jacob Gordin, publishing more than forty articles against him in a single year and almost single-handedly destroying his career.[29] But Cahan's Vilna Troupe reviews showed a softer side. He had panned Peretz Hirschbein's *Carcass* when it was first published, but watching the Vilna Troupe's production in London, he acknowledged that perhaps he had been mistaken. "I used to think," Cahan wrote, "that *Carcass* was one of Hirschbein's weakest plays. But after seeing [Sonia] Alomis perform it, I changed my mind . . . and recognized in the drama a spark I had not felt before."[30] Coming from a legendary curmudgeon, these enthusiastic reviews primed American Jews to expect that the Vilna Troupe would be better than any other Yiddish theater they had seen.

Under Cahan's editorship, the *Forverts* tracked the company's every move. Notices about the Vilna Troupe appeared on the *Forverts*'s theater page regularly throughout the 1920s. These articles enabled American Jews to participate, albeit remotely, in the Vilna Troupe's European rise to fame. Even the non-Jewish press reported occasionally on the Vilna Troupe's European performances. The entertainment magazine the *New York Clipper* told American readers of the Vilna Troupe's accolades in London and advised theatergoers to expect a Vilna Troupe production in New York soon. Amid coverage of major London theater happenings, the *Clipper* reported,

> [The Vilna Troupe] has met with a sensational success here, and have lived up to, in every way, the expectations had of them by the audiences, created by reputations already made in France, Germany, Holland, and Belgium. Their program doesn't contain a dull moment, even for the Gentile, for aside from the fact that the story of each offering is printed in English on the program, the act is so lively and interpretative that it is interesting to follow their performance, and everything is made obvious without the use of explanations.[31]

By the time a branch of the Vilna Troupe finally embarked for the United States, the company had already been metaphorically present on the American theater scene for years.

For the average New Yorker, January 11, 1924, was an uneventful day. There was a crackdown on police corruption in Philadelphia, the Prince of Wales had visited Paris, and an Austrian count who resembled Rudy Valentino was embroiled in yet another quarrel with his in-laws.[32] But for New York's nearly two million Jews, the news on the front page of the *Forverts* was a cause for celebration. "Yesterday morning, 7 o'clock A.M., at Pier 59 on 18th Street, the *Majestic* arrived and brought us the famous Vilna Troupe."[33] After years of anticipation, American theatergoers would finally glimpse the most famous Yiddish actors in the world.

A snapshot of Alexander Asro and Sonia Alomis on board the *Majestic* shows how the Vilner came ashore in style. Asro looks dapper in a long wool coat, cuffed pants, and bowler hat. Fine fitted gloves and patent leather shoes with white spats complete the classy ensemble. Alomis's fur coat features a fashionable wide collar, and she wears a jaunty boyish hat. Their coats and shoes look new. All in all, their attire is fashionable and of the moment, reflecting sartorial taste and garments acquired in Paris.[34] They look prosperous, comfortable, excited, and just a touch glamorous. They look like stars.

The Vilna Troupe's every move—its departure from London, the long transatlantic journey, the actors' first outings in New York—made front-page headlines in the American Yiddish press.[35] The excitement over the Vilna Troupe's arrival was not limited to Jewish theatergoers. The company's first U.S. productions were reviewed by major American papers, including the *New York Telegram and Evening Mail* and the *New York Times*.[36]

But the American public's romance with the Vilna Troupe was short-lived. As one journalist later quipped, New York was the Vilna Troupe's Waterloo.[37] Indeed, though New York City would eventually play host to five Vilna Troupe branches, none were ever able to achieve the level of success that had come so easily in Europe.[38]

This came as a surprise to the actors. By all indications, the Vilna Troupe ought to have been a hit in New York. In the early 1920s, American Jewish theatergoers were clamoring for the literary, high-minded Yiddish art theater sweeping Europe under the influence of the Vilna Troupe. These art theater aficionados were disproportionately young people who had emigrated from Europe. As Jacob Ben-Ami, a former Hirschbein Troupe actor who would later perform with a Vilna Troupe branch in 1928, recalled,

> They saw already theater in Europe and they . . . they were in the swing—and this [art theater] was already a movement there. And then they migrated here. . . . This was what they wanted.[39]

Meanwhile, producers had spent years trying to convince various factions of the Vilner to perform before an American public hungry for their arrival. What theater company had ever had a more promising setup for an American debut?

Yet the American Yiddish stage posed several challenges that were difficult for the Vilna Troupe to surmount. First, the troupe had stiff competition upon its 1924 arrival, including big-budget productions starring local celebrities like Aaron Lebedeff, Misha and Lucy German, Ludwig Zatz, Celia Adler, and Molly Picon.[40] In addition, the Vilna Troupe's American

Figure 9. Alexander Asro and Sonia Alomis on the *Majestic*, January 10, 1924. Sharon Asro and Alexander Zaloum.

reception was hindered by the company's success in Europe. Years of advance press had elevated audience expectations to unrealistic heights, and the company simply could not live up to its own hype. Spectators entered Vilna Troupe performances expecting to emerge transformed. Instead, they encountered all-too-human actors with only a few years of professional theater experience. Not only did the actors seem younger and less sophisticated than American audiences had anticipated, but their repertoire—groundbreaking in Europe—was already familiar to American audiences from New York's Yiddish art theaters. Audiences had already seen *The Dybbuk*, *Carcass*, *The Abandoned Inn*, *Yankl the Blacksmith*, and other signature Vilna Troupe plays performed by other companies, including Maurice Schwartz's Yiddish Art Theater and Jacob Ben-Ami's Jewish Art Theater. The Vilna Troupe's first American tour was thus subverted by the company's own success in inspiring other artists around the world to emulate it.

Still, though it failed to become a Second Avenue sensation, the Vilna Troupe's American debut demonstrates the global success of the brand. The anticipation that greeted the Vilna Troupe's arrival was unprecedented in the history of the Yiddish stage and shows how its reputation crossed continents long before it left Europe. Moreover, failure in America did not compromise this global reputation. If anything, the Vilna Troupe's American debut only expanded the company's influence.

The Courtship

When Asro and Alomis's branch returned to London in 1923, they were met by representatives from three New York Yiddish theaters: the National Theater, the Second Avenue Theater, and Boris Thomashefsky's Broadway Yiddish Theater. All three managers wanted to sponsor an American tour. They wooed the actors with fancy meals and promises of large dividends while gossiping about their colleagues. The quarrel was resolved only when the powerful Hebrew Actors' Union intervened and endorsed Thomashefsky's bid, citing his forty years of service to the American Jewish stage. In fact, Thomashefsky's company was on the brink of bankruptcy, and the union's support was a last-ditch effort to keep the aging actor's company alive.[41]

Boris Thomashefsky's role as American impresario for the Vilna Troupe was ironic. Of all the Yiddish actor-managers in New York, Thomashefsky was perhaps the least likely to be associated with high art idealism. As an actor, Thomashefsky was known for his sentimental heroes, larger-than-life personality, preening mannerisms, and for the women who swooned over his shapely stocking-clad legs.[42] As a manager, he gravitated toward melodramatic fare like *The Little Spark of Jewishness*, a musical comedy with a catchy number about the survival of the Jewish spirit against all odds.[43] By the early 1920s, Thomashefsky's theater was in dire financial straits as American Jewish theatergoers flocked to newer companies and their younger stars, like Molly Picon. As the Vilna Troupe's star was rising in Europe, Thomashefsky's was fading fast. In order to survive, he would need to get American Jews excited about his company again. The Vilna Troupe—with its young actors and trendy high art aesthetic—was his ticket to a fresh start.

The members of Asro and Alomis's Vilna Troupe, for their part, seemed uninformed about their new manager's *shund*ist reputation.[44] The actors spent their first night in New York attending a production of Avrom Shomer's comedy *Der griner milioner* (*The Green Millionaire*) at Thomashefsky's Broadway Yiddish Theater, starring their patron in the title role.[45] The play was the latest in a series of light entertainments about the comic blunders of American Jewish immigrants and was as far from "pure" art as anything. With journalists watching their every move, the actors clapped politely, told reporters how impressed they were by Thomashefsky's acting, and refused to comment further.[46]

The lesson for the Vilna Troupe was clear: art and *shund* in America were bedfellows. As a self-avowed "art theater," the Vilner would have to contend with the American public's fondness for melodrama suffused in high art rhetoric. Late at night in their hotel rooms, did the actors question the wisdom of accepting Thomashefsky's invitation? Face to face with the American Yiddish theater's appetite for *shund*, did they wonder how their work would fare?

For all of his faults, however, Thomashefsky was a competent theater manager who knew how to market a production. Upon returning from London, he convened a press conference to announce the Vilna Troupe's American tour, spurring a flurry of press attention. The *Forverts* crowed that the Vilna Troupe had "earned Jewish drama and Jewish acting a place in the world."[47] In *Morgn Zhurnal*, Alexander Mukdoni wrote glowing profiles of each actor.[48] Readers were also reminded about the Vilna Troupe's accolades in the European press. New York newspapers printed tongue-in-cheek articles from London writers complaining that the Americans had "kidnapped" the Vilna Troupe. London, wrote one, seemed "gray and workaday" without the Vilna Troupe's "holy" and "transformative" presence.[49]

Thomashefsky began running advertisements for *The Dybbuk* several weeks before the premiere: "The world famous *original* Vilna Troupe for only 5 weeks in New York!"[50] Of course, as Thomashefsky was aware, there was no such thing as an "original" troupe anymore. In fact, he had initially approached *Mazo*'s Vilna Troupe with his invitation for an American tour. It was only after Mazo declined the offer (reportedly replying, "What do we need America for?") that Thomashefsky turned his attention to Asro and Alomis's branch.[51] Thomashefsky designed the advertisements to counter any doubts that theatergoers might have about this branch's authenticity.

Thomashefsky also published his own version of the story of the managers' quarrel, in which he compared his victory to Morris Gest's achievement in bringing the Moscow Art Theater to American shores in 1923.[52] Indeed, the Moscow Art Theater's wildly successful New York debut just one year earlier was likely what inspired American Jewish theater managers to court the Vilna Troupe in the first place. Between January and June 1923, the Moscow Art Theater became an American stage sensation. The Moscow Art Theater's influence on American theater was so strong that by the mid-1920s, as Valleri Hohman has written, it was "difficult to imagine a modernist theater company in America without an interest in or connection to Russian theater."[53] The feeling was mutual—the American engagement reinvigorated the Russian company, which was on the brink of succumbing to internal disputes and external politics prior to its American tour.[54] As Stanislavsky wrote to a friend in Russia, "We never had such a success in Moscow or anywhere else."[55] If a Russian theater could achieve such success in America despite performing somewhat outdated productions in a foreign tongue, why not a Jewish theater with a similar approach?[56]

In fact, articles anticipating the Vilna Troupe's arrival frequently appeared alongside advertisements for the Moscow Art Theater's second American tour (November 23, 1923–May 24, 1924).[57] This was not the first time that the Vilna Troupe's travels corresponded to the movements of the Moscow Art Theater (MAT). When the MAT arrived in Berlin in October 1922, Asro and Alomis's Vilna Troupe had just departed the capital for other German cities.[58] When the MAT came to Paris in November 1922, this branch of the Vilna Troupe met them there a few weeks later.[59] The two companies shared a similar geographical pathway to international acclaim.

The Vilner, as long-time devotees of Stanislavsky and his company, were well aware that their travel plans ran parallel. Perhaps they planned trips with that in mind. For the Russian actors, the Vilna Troupe's nearby presence was probably less apparent. Still, the correlation between the touring schedules of the Vilna Troupe and the MAT reflects a shared understanding of the global geography of the art theater movement and its tour circuits—what Christopher Balme and Nic Leonhardt might call its "theatrical trade routes."[60] The MAT's success in Berlin drew upon an established interest in Eastern European theater among German theatergoers—the same context that had enabled the Vilna Troupe to captivate German audiences a few months earlier. Similarly, the Vilna Troupe's reception in Paris was enhanced by the "art theater" vogue inspired by the MAT's recent visit. Asro and Alomis's decision to embark for New York was once again in line with the trajectory of the global art theater movement, whose epicenter had now shifted from Russia to Western Europe to New York.

Celebrities in New York

Asro and Alomis's Vilna Troupe disembarked from the *Majestic* at seven o'clock in the morning on January 10, 1924, to find hundreds of fans and reporters waiting at the dock. Many had spent the entire night at the pier to secure their place in the throng. Asro greeted the crowd with an impromptu speech that was reprinted in the papers the next day.

> "We are arriving in a new world," announced Alexander Asro, speaking for the entire company. "We feel as though we are starting all over again. We have performed in Russia and in Poland, in France and in England. We have been highly praised and a hit everywhere we've gone. . . . "I know," stated the pale and charming actor, "that in America you have to sell yourself. I am, however, not yet an American, and I do not know how to do this, and thus I will not promote myself. Myself and my colleagues, we do not want to do this. It is not important what I say. What is important is how we perform."[61]

Sonia Alomis chimed in, echoing her husband's remarks. "We have come to conquer America. We have hearts that are full of love for theater art. We bring with us many years of experience, and an ideal that is holy to us. . . . But whether we will prevail or ourselves be conquered, that is something that America must judge for itself."[62] The crowd cheered.

Just as in Europe, the Vilna Troupe positioned itself as a company whose "holy" dedication to high art trumped commercial considerations. Of course, Asro and Alomis's insistence that they would not engage in American-style marketing stood in sharp contrast to Thomashefsky's sophisticated publicity maneuvers, the flood of preemptively laudatory articles, and the actors' own dealings with the press. Asro's disembarkment speech was decidedly self-promotional. He listed the Vilna Troupe's accomplishments in detail, making special mention of Cahan's approval, even as he vowed that the actors would never "sell themselves" to the American public. Asro's insistence on this point, which he repeated in dozens of interviews leading up to the premiere, was a marketing strategy that drew upon American Yiddish theatergoers' frustrations with decades of vicious competition and partisan politics. It worked. As one journalist, asked to summarize the history of the Vilna Troupe in a single sentence, proclaimed, "Everyone seeks bread, but a group of idealistic young people seeks art."[63]

Over the next two weeks, as the actors toured New York and rehearsed sporadically, a flurry of articles appeared describing the foreign celebrities. A lucky *Forverts* reporter lurking in the lobby of the Claridge Hotel was invited to join the actors for dinner, and he described their eating habits and dinner conversation in the next morning's paper (incidentally, this article appeared alongside a review of the Moscow Art Theater's production of *The Brothers Karamazov*). The members of the Vilna Troupe were "a completely different type of actor than we have ever seen before."[64] Indeed, the actors looked so young that the journalist initially thought they were local university students. At dinner they conversed like educated intellectuals. Other journalists detailed the actors' credentials: university attendance, advanced theatrical training, and in the case of Frida Vitalin, a brief stint in Russian dental school.[65]

Meanwhile, American Jewish actors and directors were getting nervous about their new competitors. But they were even more anxious about offending them. Maurice Schwartz, the founder of New York's Yiddish Art Theater, held exclusive rights to perform *The Dybbuk* in America and could have withheld his permission, thus preventing the Vilna Troupe from performing the most famous play in its repertoire. Instead, he granted the visiting actors the right to perform it.[66] As the director of the reigning high art Yiddish theater in America, it was Schwartz whose livelihood was most directly endangered by the Vilna Troupe's arrival. But Schwartz treated the Vilner with respect, even joining with the city's ten other professional Yiddish theater companies to send his actors to the Vilna Troupe's premiere.[67] As with Cahan's transformation from notoriously harsh critic to loyal Vilna Troupe supporter, American Jewish theater artists took journalistic proclamations that the Vilner were "a completely different type of actor" at face value.[68] For Schwartz and other directors, the arrival of the Vilna Troupe mandated exceptions to standard business practice.

Articles about the Vilner continued to be printed on a daily basis in the Yiddish press, though they had not yet begun to perform. "The politics of the American Yiddish theater today are all about the Vilna Troupe," wrote one journalist. "Everything centers around them."[69] Writing for *Di idishe velt*, Abraham Frumkin wondered if the Vilna Troupe's success would cause the downfall of the American Yiddish art theater. Could there possibly be enough art theater spectators to support another such company in New York? Or would the Vilna Troupe finally persuade *shund* audiences to improve their theatrical tastes? The Vilna Troupe's premiere might be a catastrophe for other art theater companies, Frumkin told his readers, but there was no reason to worry about the visiting artists themselves. The Vilna Troupe's success in New York seemed guaranteed.[70]

American Waterloo

On January 29, 1924, the crowd that gathered at Thomashefsky's theater included nearly every major Yiddish journalist, actor, and writer in New York. The entire American Jewish theater community put aside its differences and gathered together for a performance. Old Jacob P. Adler and his wife, Sarah, sat in the front row next to Thomashefsky and the German Jewish actor and director Rudolph Schildkraut. Maurice Schwartz sat alongside Jacob Ben-Ami. Younger Yiddish actors in the audience included stars like Molly Picon, Ludwig Satz, Leon Blank, Samuel Goldenberg, and Muni Vayzenfreund (who later became famous in American theater and film under the name Paul Muni). Reuven Guskin, head of the Hebrew Actors' Union, was there, as was Joseph Rumshinsky, Second Avenue's most important composer.[71] The audience represented a veritable cross-section of the American Jewish theater, from its founding fathers to its most popular contemporary artists.

Writers and intellectuals were also present. Peretz Hirschbein was there, as were the playwrights Dovid Pinski, Osip Dimov, and Leon Kobrin and prose writers and poets like Avrom Reyzen, Zishe Landau, and Mani Leyb. Critics at the premiere included Alexander Mukdoni, Hillel Rogoff, the theater historian B. Gorin, and of course, *Forverts*'s editor Abraham Cahan.[72] Word of the Vilna Troupe's American premiere had also spread beyond Yiddish-speaking circles. David Belasco ("the Reinhardt of the American stage!" Asro explained) had accepted their invitation.[73] According to the Yiddish press, Stanislavsky and some of the touring actors of the Moscow Art Theater were also present.[74]

After the first act ended, a tense atmosphere prevailed in the lobby and the smoking room. For a group that included some of the most opinionated members of the American Jewish community, the crowd was strangely silent. As one reporter described the scene,

> The lobby simmered like a covered pot. Each person wanted to hide his own opinions while finding out everyone else's. The conversations circled around and around the real topic, and everyone tried to figure out what everybody else thought, but as soon as somebody did say something, everyone else pounced with a counterargument.[75]

Entering the theater on opening night, the crowd expected what it had been promised: actors whose skills were beyond those of any other Jewish performers, an exceptionally high production value, and a communal experience akin to a religious rite. Instead, they encountered flesh-and-blood actors whose technique was imperfect. The set design was thoughtful but not revolutionary, the pacing seemed too slow, and the performances were uneven.

In short, the Vilna Troupe's *Dybbuk* was not all that different from what theatergoers could see on Second Avenue. The 1923–24 season included several high-quality productions with talented stars. In the same month that the Vilna Troupe held its American premiere, Ludwig Satz and Celia Adler played opposite one another in Kamanovitch's *Der meshugener* (*The Crazy Man*) and Aaron Lebedeff and Leon Blank costarred in *Dem tatns zundl* (*Father's Little Son*). Moreover, two other productions that premiered around the time of the Vilna Troupe's arrival were historical landmarks. The first, *Yankele*, was Molly Picon's Second Avenue debut, which catapulted the young actress to American fame. The second was Maurice Schwartz's production of Goldfaden's *Di tsvey kuni lemls* (*The Two Kuni-Lemls*) at the Yiddish Art Theater, a modernist adaptation of a classic.[76] By any measure, Second Avenue's Yiddish theaters were flourishing in 1924, leading audiences to question what the Vilna Troupe could add.

Not only did the Vilna Troupe face stiff competition from New York's Yiddish theaters, but it also had to contend with the presence of the most famous art theater of all. The Moscow Art Theater opened its highly acclaimed production of *Uncle Vanya* at the Jolson Theater just one night before the Vilna Troupe's New York *Dybbuk* premiere.[77] Americans with an interest in foreign-language art theater were more likely to attend the MAT than the Vilna Troupe.

While the Vilna Troupe's productions were attended by some English-language journalists, it was the Moscow Art Theater that the press flocked to see, just fifteen blocks north of Thomashefsky's theater. The few articles written about the Vilna Troupe's American tour in the English-language press, while vaguely positive, were not what the Vilner were accustomed to. American critics described the Vilna Troupe as mildly intriguing and exotic. The *New York Times* called *The Dybbuk* an "odd Yiddish drama" and "one of the strangest Yiddish novelties offered in New York City in a long time" and accorded more attention to the outpouring of enthusiasm among the American Jewish public than the performance itself.[78] The *New York Telegram and Evening Mail* described *The Dybbuk* as "an arresting performance" of a "strange occult drama."[79] The Vilna Troupe's subsequent productions of two Hirschbein dramas, *Carcass* and *Green Fields*, received similarly tepid reviews in the American press. Overshadowed by the famous Russian players up the road, the Vilna Troupe attracted scant attention.

Jewish journalists were also conflicted about the quality of the Vilna Troupe's productions. "I went to the Vilner premiere, to the *Dybbuk* production, with a predetermined verdict," confided Avrom Koralnik in *Der Tog*. "First, because of the play itself, but second—because the Vilna Troupe was too strongly heralded. They had become something of a legend."[80] Koralnik was surprised to find himself disappointed. The actors seemed nervous, their lines uttered too quickly to be understood ("not legendary enough!" charged Koralnik). He found the pacing inconsistent and the dance of death pretentious. Vladimir Grosman described for *Forverts* readers a disappointing *Dybbuk*. The tempo was too slow, and the actors seemed anxious about how they would be judged.[81] Others damned with faint praise. Another *Der Tog* journalist described the Vilna Troupe's *Green Fields* as "staged, as it was certain to be, in a new and interesting manner."[82] A curt description of the plot followed, with no mention of the direction, sets, costumes, or acting. After years of reading Vilna Troupe reviews, *Der Tog*'s readers were aware that this cursory review was not in keeping with the company's European reception.

Other Jewish journalists were less forgiving of the Vilna Troupe's faults. B. Y. Goldshteyn, also writing for *Der Tog*, attended *The Dybbuk* multiple times and was disappointed with the unevenness of the acting.[83] Morris Meyer, who wrote under the pen name Dr. Kritikus, was, as his pseudonym promised, especially harsh. In Europe, Meyer acknowledged, the Vilna

Troupe had been pioneers of a new mode of Yiddish theater. In America, however, the Vilna Troupe did not live up to the hype.

> They did not come to America as cultural ambassadors, as pioneers of a better Yiddish theater in Galicia and in Poland, but they instead arrived with pomp, with big announcements, as artists, and it is because of this that they had their "Waterloo" in America. When the Vilna Troupe first arrived we immediately said that many of the actors were not bad. But overall, in comparison with our [Maurice] Schwartzes, our [Muni] Weisenfreunds, our [Ludwig] Satzes, this was too strong [of an assessment]. They are simply a company with a good approach to theater.[84]

The Vilna Troupe was once a great theater company, concluded Meyer, but its work no longer compared to the achievements of the American Yiddish stage. While American Yiddish directors recruited new playwrights and experimented with adaptations of literary classics, the Vilna Troupe's repertoire had become static. Asro and Alomis presented the same plays that had earned them accolades in Europe, including An-sky's *Dybbuk*, Hirschbein's *Carcass* and *Green Fields*, Kobrin's *The Village Lad*, Asch's *The Compatriot*, and Pinski's *Yankl the Blacksmith*. Stylistic and repertoire choices that had been cutting edge nearly a decade earlier now seemed dated.

Even Cahan, who was largely responsible for the Vilna Troupe's presence in the United States, scrambled to reconcile his prior appraisals with the company's lackluster American debut. Instead of blaming the Vilna Troupe, he suggested that An-sky's *Dybbuk* was flawed and that the production failed only because the company did not adapt this play of "very little literary merit" enough. "If only the Vilna Troupe were not afraid to shorten An-sky's captivating play, this would have been one of the most remarkable and wonderful productions in the history of Yiddish theater in America," he lamented.[85] The acting was another disappointment. Perhaps the actors could learn about acting technique from their American colleagues, Cahan suggested. Still, he maintained that the Vilna Troupe had something unique to contribute.

> America is a land of technique. Technique is important. But when one puts too much emphasis on technique in art, it becomes just as destructive as it is useful. Let us not confuse technique with the real meaning of theater art. Too many theater people make that mis-

> take. A professional cook has more technique than a housewife, but a housewife's dinner has more flavor.[86]

The Vilna Troupe, Cahan argued, made up for what it lacked in technical sophistication with artistic merit. "They have a lot to learn from us," Cahan concluded, "But we also have much to learn from them."[87]

In spite of its failure to inspire enthusiasm among American theatergoers, the Vilna Troupe remained a crucial agent of transnational exchange between European and American theaters. "We may have good actors," lamented one journalist in the *Forverts*, "but the Vilna Troupe produces *good theater*."[88] If the Vilna Troupe's arrival in the United States showed New York audiences just how far American Yiddish theater had come, it also offered a poignant reminder of what American theatergoers were still missing.

Global Pioneers

By the spring of 1924, ticket sales in New York were down. The same Vilna Troupe that had sold out weeks in advance struggled to make enough to pay salaries. Cursory notices and brief reviews appeared occasionally, but the long-winded articles, special sections, photograph series, actor interviews, and lavish praise that had filled the pages of the American Yiddish press were nowhere to be found.

This was a tremendous disappointment for the performers, many of whom had hoped to settle down in New York. As Asro told a reporter before the *Dybbuk* premiere,

> We are searching for a home, a place of rest. Our work cannot progress because we are wandering. We remain artistically uncongealed, for all of our energy goes towards finding cities and countries where we can perform. . . . When we carry walking sticks in our hands, we cannot devote ourselves as we wish to our artistic development. Perhaps America will become our home, and we will once and for all do away with the bread problem.[89]

Just as Americans had imagined the Vilna Troupe as the savior of the American Yiddish stage, Asro and the actors had envisioned America as a place where they could finally stop traveling. While it was customary for American Yiddish actors to tour during the summer months, most were able to reside permanently in New York for the rest of the year. Thomashefsky and the other managers had promised stability and wealth in America; instead, the company found itself teetering on the edge of bankruptcy only three months in. Resourceful as always, Asro and Alomis returned to their standard operating strategy and declared that the Vilna Troupe would tour—this time, across the United States from Boston and Philadelphia to San Francisco and Los Angeles.

In New York, the Vilna Troupe's reputation for theatrical innovation had been compromised by not having a skilled director in residence. Dovid Herman, who had toured with Asro and Alomis's branch in Europe, had rejected Thomashefsky's offer and had opted to stay behind in Europe and rejoin Mazo's Vilna Troupe branch.[90] When American journalists accused the Vilna Troupe of being outmoded and stale, there was no director that Asro and Alomis could turn to for new stagings. But after leaving New York, Asro and Alomis managed to recruit the Vilna Troupe's other celebrated director, Leyb Kadison, away from Mazo's company. Kadison's primary motivation was personal: his sister was in America by herself and longed for the rest of the family to join her.[91] By the time the company returned to New York in September 1926, it could boast of an entirely new repertoire, primarily authored by non-Jewish European playwrights. There was a Yiddish version of Alexei Tolstoy and Pavel Shchegolev's historical Russian drama *Rasputin, or the Czarina's Plot*, alongside translations of plays by the German Jewish dramatist Gustav Kadelburg, the Dutch-Jewish writer Herman Heijermans, and the Russian Jewish playwright Semyon Yushkevich. In Chicago, Kadison even directed a restaged version of *The Dybbuk* that tried to address the critics' concerns about pacing.[92] He also introduced his own version of Goldfaden's *The Two Kuni-Lemls*, the operetta that had taken New York by storm in an adaptation by Schwartz's Yiddish Art Theater in January 1924.[93] Finally, Asro and Alomis hired an American business manager to take over the accounting.

In the archives of the Hebrew Actors' Union, months of meticulously kept ledger sheets document the company's efforts to stay afloat in America.[94] Between April 17 and July 3, 1924, Asro and Alomis's Vilna Troupe performed an average of 8.5 shows per week, with up to 11 in any given week. Even more ambitious, in a typical week the company performed in three cities and spent approximately $1,000 on travel. In today's dollars, this would be $14,000 per week on travel alone, a whopping 21 percent of the company's total expenses. In comparison, only 4 percent of the budget was allocated for sets, properties, costumes, and lighting combined.

In comparison, in the Ballet Russe de Monte Carlo, ostensibly a traveling company like the Vilna Troupe, travel costs accounted for only 0.05 percent of the operating budget.[95] Similarly, in the Moscow Art Theater's first season, the company spent 81 percent of its budget on salaries, production expenditures, and building rental.[96] The Vilna Troupe spent a greater percentage of its budget on travel alone than the Moscow Art Theater did on managerial staff, royalties, and publicity combined. The Moscow Art Theater spent significant sums on permanent design and technical staff. By 1900 the MAT included a professional stage crew of thirty-two. By 1908 the MAT had assembled a team of fifty designers (including "painters, paper-hangers, modelers, and wood and metal craftsmen"). By 1916 the MAT lighting department had fourteen technicians, and by 1918 the properties department had eighteen employees.[97]

The Vilna Troupe, in contrast, made do with a rotating series of designers, who rarely had assistants, and the most meager of stage crews. Nearly all of its income went to fund travel costs. In a single week in June, for example, the Vilna Troupe spent a whopping $3,462.79 on travel (over $47,000 in today's dollars). No wonder the Vilna Troupe struggled to stay afloat. And yet, remarkably, the box office receipts demonstrate that the company's investment in travel paid off.

The Vilna Troupe's rigorous travel schedule was unusual. A typical touring theater of the period might visit a city for a few weeks or months at a time. For example, when the Moscow Art Theater ventured out from New York during its first American tour in 1923, the company visited three cities (Chicago, Philadelphia, and Boston) in forty-six days, with an average stay of over two weeks in each city.[98] In contrast, the Vilna Troupe traveled on an almost daily basis during the three-month period documented in the ledger books. Even when the actors stayed in the same city, they frequently moved from one theater building to another, incurring sizable moving costs to cart set pieces across Manhattan. During the week of May 15, for example, Asro and Alomis's Vilna Troupe performed in five different theater buildings in New York City alone. This was extremely unusual—even among other Yiddish theaters in New York, which tended to secure building leases season by season—and speaks to the unique challenges the Vilna Troupe faced in securing performance spaces as it traveled.

But remarkably, all of this travel was what kept the company afloat. The more the Vilna Troupe traveled, the more it earned. The Vilna Troupe never learned how to make theater otherwise. And so they traveled, no matter the cost, performing in Bridgeport, Wilmington, New York City,

Paterson, Fall River, Worchester, Boston, Providence, Hartford, Rochester, Toronto, Buffalo, Cleveland, Detroit, St. Louis, Cincinnati, Pittsburgh, Philadelphia, Newark, New Haven, Brownsville (Pennsylvania), Youngstown, Chicago, and Montreal in 1924 alone, followed by a West Coast tour to San Francisco and Los Angeles in 1925.

Still, profits (and salaries) remained low, and one by one, the actors defected to more stable Yiddish companies, like Schwartz's Yiddish Art Theater. In mid-1926 Asro and Alomis's company folded. That fall Asro and Leyb Kadison tried to start a new branch of the Vilna Troupe featuring ten Vilna Troupe veterans and four seasoned American Yiddish actors who were members of the powerful Hebrew Actors' Union.[99] They opened in September 1926 with a Yiddish adaptation of Alexei Tolstoy and Pavel Shchegolev's 1925 play *Rasputin*, followed by a series of light comedies.[100] But ticket sales were not enough to sustain the company. By the end of 1926 this branch of the Vilna Troupe folded and the actors went their separate ways. Some returned to Europe, while others joined American Yiddish companies. The more stubborn performers set out on their own. Noah Nachbush maintained that without the Vilna Troupe, the entire American Yiddish theater was beneath him, and spent the next few decades giving solo performances around the country. Asro and Alomis traveled the world as a duo, performing dialogues and scenes from the Vilna Troupe's repertoire. When that work dried up, Asro turned to repairing watches and running a jewelry store in order to pay the bills.[101]

The Vilna Troupe had come to America hoping to find a permanent home. Instead, Asro and Alomis's company fell apart in less than two years. Yet, just as the failure of Y. L. Peretz's theater campaign laid the groundwork for the Vilna Troupe, the Vilna Troupe's failure to thrive in America also had an important historical impact. First, while individual Yiddish actors had been crossing the Atlantic for decades, the Vilna Troupe was the first full European Jewish theater *company* to travel to the United States. Second, it was uncommon for American Yiddish actors to attend each other's productions, as competition between New York's Yiddish theaters was fierce. The Vilna Troupe brought the entire American Yiddish theater community together for the first time and sparked important conversations among American Yiddish theater artists about style, repertoire, and standards.

Third, the Vilna Troupe attracted the attention of major figures from the American stage, most notably the American theater producer and director David Belasco. Belasco attended Vilna Troupe performances, met with the actors backstage after the curtain fell, and wrote them fan mail. When Belasco wrote a letter praising the company, Asro bought a large advertisement in the *Forverts* and reprinted it (translated into Yiddish) in its entirety.

> Dear friends,
>
> I had the pleasure to see you perform and I feel that it was an honor to have had this privilege. The sublimity of your artistic performance was a revelation for me. I hope that you will extend the duration of your stay with us, so that every true devotee of the best stage art will have the opportunity and pleasure to see your productions.
>
> Yours,
> David Belasco[102]

Finally, the Vilna Troupe's American tour inspired other Yiddish theater artists to develop their own cross-continental touring practices. After the Vilna Troupe's American debut, European Yiddish theater companies planned their own American tours and American Yiddish theater troupes began to dream of success in London, Paris, Berlin, and Warsaw.

"The *Vilner* in New York and the *Nyuyorkers* in London!"[103]

A headline in the *Forverts* proclaimed the above when Maurice Schwartz announced that he would bring his Yiddish Art Theater to Europe for the first time. Schwartz hoped to repeat the Vilna Troupe's triumphant march across Europe. In February 1924 Schwartz announced that his entire twenty-person troupe, including a stage manager, three carpenters, and a costumer, would sail to Europe. At last, an American Yiddish theater would join the ranks of internationally renowned ensembles like the Vilna Troupe and the Moscow Art Theater, crowed the *Forverts*.[104] In his speech announcing the tour, Schwartz credited the Vilna Troupe for inspiring his plans.[105]

While the Vilna Troupe had broken new ground by becoming the first Yiddish company to cross the Atlantic, Schwartz's tour of Europe was even more pioneering. American Jewish theatergoers had seen European Yiddish actors perform on their shores for decades. American Yiddish theater managers made frequents trips to Eastern Europe to search for new talent. Sigmund Mogulesco, David Kessler, Leon Blank, Regina

Prager, and Bertha Kalish were all recruited to the United States by traveling theater scouts.[106] Indeed, it was the rare American Jewish theater artist who was a native.

In contrast, European audiences saw American Jewish actors far less often. A few European-born theater artists who had spent significant time in America (like Clara and Boaz Young in the 1910s) returned to perform in Eastern Europe.[107] Other actors, like Yankev Spivakovski and Sam and Julius Adler, visited America briefly before returning to Europe.[108] Boris Thomashefsky performed occasionally in Europe, as did a handful of others like Molly Picon, whose European fame preceded her American breakthrough. Still, for many the 1924 tour of Schwartz's Yiddish Art Theater was the first time they had seen so many American Yiddish actors, let alone an entire American company.

The Yiddish Art Theater planned its European tour right after the most well received season in its history. The 1923–24 season had opened with a production of Zhulovsky's historical drama *Shabbatai Zvi* that featured a massive cast of thirty actors and dozens of extras. This production was cited by journalists as a turning point for the company, the first in a lineup of high art shows with sophisticated production values. Each of the next ten plays in the season received better reviews than the last.[109] By the time the Vilna Troupe arrived in 1924, the Yiddish Art Theater had become New York's Jewish center for intellectual productions.

When the Vilna Troupe had announced its American tour, many New York Jews feared it would be the death knell for Schwartz's company. The companies were similar, perhaps too similar, in their aesthetic and repertoire (journalists playfully referred to Schwartz's Yiddish Art Theater as "The American Vilna Troupe" and vice versa).[110] What if the Vilna Troupe's tour inadvertently caused the Yiddish Art Theater's demise? The Yiddish Art Theater, wrote one worried journalist prior to the Vilna Troupe's opening performance, was "the only place where an intelligent spectator can spend a few hours with true pleasure" and had "without a doubt, the best audience that one can find in New York, which is exactly the audience that is impatiently awaiting the productions of the Vilna Troupe."[111] It was widely anticipated that the Vilna Troupe's arrival would be catastrophic for Schwartz's company. Instead, the Yiddish Art Theater was more successful than ever.

The Yiddish Art Theater's European tour was likewise a hit. In England, members of the British government invited the actors to tea on the terrace of the Parliament building. In Austria, the Yiddish Art Theater performed at the Carltheater, Vienna's leading opera house, where it played to full houses for over a month.[112] Still, despite strong ticket sales, the Yiddish Art Theater struggled to meet its expenses abroad. Wages were higher in London than in New York, and moreover, the company had underestimated its travel expenses.[113]

Taken together, these two 1924 cross-continental tours (the Vilna Troupe in America and the Yiddish Art Theater in Western Europe) marked a new era of global travel for Yiddish theater. Inspired by these twin tours, journalists proclaimed that a new era of cosmopolitanism had dawned for Yiddish theater, in which Jews scattered around the world would share a single theatrical culture. Indeed, by the late 1920s, it was common for Yiddish theater artists and companies to embark on ambitious international tours. During the summer off-season, it became standard practice for New York actors to include South American cities like Buenos Aires and Montevideo along with the regular summer tour circuit of Boston, Philadelphia, Baltimore, Chicago, and Cincinnati.[114] Frequent travel brought Yiddish actors into contact with other theater practitioners around the globe, creating new transnational artistic networks that added to those already established by the Vilna Troupe.

Sixty Cities a Year

While Asro and Alomis's Vilna Troupe rose and fell in America and Maurice Schwartz's Yiddish Art Theater took over its vacated role as the new darlings of the Western European Yiddish stage, Mordechai Mazo's Vilna Troupe continued to plot an ambitious travel schedule across Eastern Europe. After its 1924 Bucharest hit *The Singer of His Sorrows*, the troupe traveled through the Romanian countryside, playing to packed houses in Jassy, Kishinev, Belz, Czernowitz, and elsewhere before returning to Bucharest by popular demand.[115]

At times, travel posed unexpected challenges. In Czernowitz in late 1924, local anti-Semitic authorities forbade the company from performing within the city limits. The Vilna Troupe spent weeks in Czernowitz unable to work, waiting for the proper permits to bring them back to Bucharest. Without an income, they hungered. Several members decided to leave the company, head west, and start a Vilna Troupe of their own. Finally, Mazo secured the permissions and the rest of the company returned to Bucharest.[116] One year later, Mazo's Vilna Troupe returned to Czernowitz to tremendous success. The one hundredth performance of *The Singer of*

His Sorrows was celebrated in the Czernowitz streets by a crowd so large that the Romanian police, fearing a mob, prohibited Mazo from giving his planned speech.[117]

In Transylvania in 1926, local Orthodox rabbis issued an edict that specifically forbade Jewish residents from attending Vilna Troupe performances.[118] Perhaps religious Jews were attending the Vilna Troupe's secular performances in such numbers that the rabbis felt they had to act. The Vilna Troupe stopped performing on Friday nights for the first time in its history, hoping to appease the rabbis, but the actors' efforts were in vain.[119] The ensuing controversy was reported in the international press.[120] When the Vilna Troupe returned to Transylvania one year later, it was no longer opposed by the rabbis but by locals. In Oradea, the actors were attacked by a group of stone-throwing anti-Semitic students during a performance. Several actors and audience members were injured.[121]

Czernowitz and Transylvania were not the only places where Mazo's Vilna Troupe encountered anti-Semitism. In Baden, Austria, in 1923, a Vilna Troupe performance was interrupted by anti-Semitic demonstrations carried out by members of a local affiliate of the Nazi Party. The disturbance received international coverage via the Jewish Telegraphic Agency. "So much noise was made that ultimately the curtain had to be rung down. The director of the theater appealed for quiet, but in vain, and ultimately the police had to be called in," reported the *Hebrew Standard of Australasia*. "About thirty demonstrators were arrested, but subsequently released. The actors had to be conducted to the railway station by the police."[122] In Lublin in 1927, the local municipal government was attacked by right-wing Polish political parties for renting the city's main theater to the Vilna Troupe. Again, this clash was widely reported in the Jewish press. "The anti-Jewish press and the Right parties denounced the Municipal Council for 'Jargonizing' the Municipal Theater, which they contend is intended solely for the production of Polish plays," reported one journalist for the *Sentinel*, a Chicago Jewish newspaper. "The Council contended that the theater had been standing idle for months, and they had not ejected any Polish company in order to make room for the Yiddish troupe."[123]

And still, Mazo's Vilna Troupe kept traveling, reporters around the world kept writing about its productions, and the glowing reviews kept on coming. In Lviv in 1927, the Yiddish writer Aaron Zeitlin, who had ventured to the city specifically to see the premiere and report on it for Warsaw fans, reviewed Yankev Preger's *Der nisoyen* (*The Temptation*). The play, wrote Zeitlin, was a "melo . . . melo . . . melodrama . . . no, I won't hold back," but somehow the Vilna Troupe managed to turn it into an excellent production.[124] The writer Eliezer Shteynbarg reported on the Vilna Troupe for *Di Frayhayt*. "The Messiah has come!" he wrote of one performance.[125]

As the company's reputation continued to grow, so did the pace of its travels. By 1930, according to Yiddish theater historian Nakhmen Mayzel, the company performed in approximately sixty cities each year.[126] Its tours followed a well-established trajectory across Eastern Europe, as the company returned to the same cities and towns again and again, often multiple times a year. When the Vilna Troupe left Lviv for Krakow and Warsaw in the summer of 1927, the actors knew they would return before winter. After years of wandering from one new place to another, Mazo's Vilna Troupe had settled into a comfortable routine.

But for many, Warsaw was the only place that felt like home. By 1927, 90 percent of Mazo's Vilna Troupe hailed from Warsaw, and many looked forward to spending time with relatives while visiting the Polish capital.[127] While the company continued to travel frequently, its tours during this period almost always started and ended in Warsaw.

Still, full stability continued to elude Mazo's Vilner. Membership turnover happened at a rapid pace. In a single year, it was not uncommon for Mazo to lose nearly all of his actors, who were replaced by eager newcomers. In the summer of 1927 in Lviv, for instance, the Vilna Troupe consisted of the following actors:

Chava Ayzn	Avrom Morevsky
Chaim Brakazsh	Naomi Natan
Dovid Herman (dir.)	Simkhe Natan
Rokhl Holtzer	Miriam Orleska
Yosef Kamien	Jacob Waislitz
Nadia Kareni	Yokheved Waislitz
Mordechai Mazo (mngr.)	Simkhe Vaynshtok[128]

Seven months later, Mazo's Vilna Troupe opened in Warsaw with the following members (* indicates individuals who were members in Lviv):

Dovid Birnboym	Naomi Natan*
Esther Goldenberg	Simkhe Natan*
Helena Gotlib	Miriam Orleska*
Zalmen Hirshfeld	Esther Rapel
Yosef Kamien*	Perl Ruth

Dina Kamien
Batsheva Kremer
Yankev Kurlender
Dovid Likht
Yankev Mansdorf
Mordechai Mazo* (manager)
Isaac Samberg
Shmuel Sheftel
Ruth Taru
Mikhl Weichert (dir.)
Jacob Waislitz*[129]

In just a few months, more than 75 percent of the actors had changed. These "new" actors, however, did not come from nowhere. More often than not, they had connections to current or past Vilna Troupe affiliates. Isaac Samberg, for example, had been a member of Mazo's Vilna Troupe in 1923–24 and had directed several productions, including Sholem Aleichem's *Dos groyse gevins* (*The Big Win*) and a Yiddish translation of Moliere's *The Miser*. After taking a break from the Vilna Troupe to perform with other companies, he returned in 1928, bringing along his actress wife, Helena Gotlib. Yankev Mansdorf had studied under Vilna Troupe director Dovid Herman before starting his career as an actor in Herman's experimental cabaret company Azazel. Dovid Likht had also been a Herman student before joining the Vilna Troupe, and Ruth Taru had worked under Herman in Azazel. Simkhe Natan had acted alongside Vilna Troupe regulars Avrom Morevsky, Alex Stein, Yosef Kamien, and Joseph Buloff before joining Mazo's Vilna Troupe in 1925. Shmuel Sheftel was a cousin of Vilna Troupe member Noah Nachbush, who had defected to Asro and Alomis's branch in America.

The constantly shifting roster of Vilna Troupe actors was augmented by the formation of several new branches in the late 1920s. In 1926 a quarrel led Jacob Waislitz, Khavel Buzgan, and Daniel Shapiro to form their own branch in Lviv. One year later, a contingent of defectors from this branch left for New York.[130] The year 1926 was also the point when a group of former Asro and Alomis company members started a new American Vilna Troupe in New York under Leyb Kadison's leadership. Neither of these branches lasted past 1927. Later, another group of actors formed a new Vilna Troupe in Antwerp in 1929 under Asro and Alomis's leadership. This group disbanded after a single season. A few months later, a group of former Vilner actors would start yet another Vilna Troupe branch in the Bronx.

The Vilna Troupe in the late 1920s was at once more influential and less stable than ever before. After the dissolution of Asro and Alomis's branch in 1926, the Vilna Troupe brand alone could no longer predict a company's success. Indeed, many folded during these years. By 1931 only Mazo's company was still standing from this roster, alongside several new branches.

Why did Mazo's Vilna Troupe last longer than the others? First, he brought in a constant influx of young talent to replace older members who left. Unlike their predecessors, most of these younger actors had completed formal theatrical training. While the other Vilna Troupes, with the exception of the Bronx-based company, were content to continue staging plays in the style of *The Dybbuk* and the other early 1920s productions, the younger actors in Mazo's company pushed the others to experiment with new repertoire and approaches. Thus, while other Vilna Troupes were struggling to compete with newer, younger, and more innovative Yiddish theater companies, Mazo's Troupe was flourishing.

A Grueling Schedule: The New Repertoire

Mazo's Vilna Troupe never stopped preparing new material. In 1924 Mazo developed seven new productions. From the European dramatic canon, the actors produced their own translations of Moliere's *The Miser*, Gogol's *Marriage*, Nikolai Yevreinov's *The Chief Thing* (a 1921 commedia dell'arte–inspired version of Gorky's *The Lower Depths*), and Russian poet Vasily Zhukovsky's drama about the would-be Jewish Messiah Shabbatai Zvi. From the Yiddish repertoire, they prepared two modernist productions of Yiddish plays, Alter Kacyzne's *Der dukus* (*The Duke*) and Osip Dimov's aforementioned *The Singer of His Sorrows*.

The constant preparation of new repertoire, combined with a robust travel and performance schedule, meant a grueling routine for the actors. A typical week included eight performances, seven days a week with matineé and evening shows on Saturdays, alongside hours of daily rehearsals. As members of a repertory company, the actors had to be prepared to play dozens of different roles in any given week. For example, during the week of April 23, 1926, Mazo's company performed *The Dybbuk*, *The Singer of His Sorrows*, *Motke the Thief*, *The Temptation*, and *The Underworld*.[131] With the premiere of an adaptation of Sholem Asch's novel *Kidush Hashem* (*Sanctification of the Holy Name*) scheduled for the following Wednesday, the actors rehearsed while presenting eight shows a week. There would be no time off before opening night—the company stopped performing for only two days in order to hold fifteen-hour dress rehearsals before nightly performances resumed. Indeed, between January and June 1926, Mazo's Vilna Troupe took only five days off: one long weekend in January, a Thursday night in February, and a Monday night in April to accommodate a lecture by *Kidush Hashem*'s director Mikhl Weichert, which the actors were required to attend. With the sole exception of those five evenings, the Vilna Troupe performed *and* rehearsed seven days a week for six months. This breakneck schedule continued even when the actors were on the road.

The frantic pace of performances, rehearsals, and travel may explain why so many performers spent only a short time in the Vilna Troupe. Mazo's ambitions were too great, the rehearsal schedule too stringent, the constant travel too exhausting. Only Miriam Orleska (who was rumored to be Mazo's lover) stayed by his side for decades (1919–35) without defecting to another branch.[132] A handful of others spent several years affiliated with Mazo's branch, but such multiyear engagements were unusual. Many, like Bela Daniel or Manya Bintus or Ida Kaminska or Sigmund Ree, were members for less than a year. To be an actor in the Vilna Troupe was to commit one's entire life to acting, to live and breathe theater twelve hours a day or more, to put aside personal desires, hobbies, and relationships for the collective good of the company. Few were able to sustain this pace for long.

One performer was even thought to have died from excessive travel. Yehudis Lares, a former professional Russian actress from Vilna, had joined the original Vilna Troupe in 1916. After learning Yiddish from scratch, she performed in the Vilna Troupe nonstop for the next ten years and was a loyal member of Mazo's branch who was known for playing mother and grandmother roles.[133] But the schedule proved too much for her health. In July 1926 in Arad, Transylvania, Lares collapsed and died at the age of forty-four.[134] The actors attributed her death to the exhaustion of constant travel.[135] Yet even in the face of tragedy, they could not stop moving for long. Unable to afford to cancel planned performances in the next town, the Vilna Troupe kept moving, leaving twenty-year-old Luba Kadison behind to tend to Lares on her deathbed and handle the funeral arrangements.[136]

Financial records also demonstrate the Vilna Troupe's success in attracting large audiences during the late 1920s. In a single week in April 1926, Mazo's branch performed before more than two thousand theatergoers. This was a typical week for the Vilna Troupe, which often attracted even more spectators to its newer productions. During the first three weeks of *Kidush Hashem*, for example, over twenty-five hundred people attended Vilna Troupe performances each week. In its final week in Warsaw, the Vilna Troupe sold 3,260 tickets. Government taxes, building rental fees, and massive production costs cut into the troupe's earnings significantly, and with fifteen to thirty actors in the company at any given time, there was rarely much money left over for each individual member. Still, it was enough to sustain the company, pay for travel costs, fund the development of new productions, and provide the company with a living wage. For many, this was enough—at least for a time. And when they were ready for a change, there was always a fresh crop of young actors eager to take their place.

Martyrs, O'Neill, Gargoyles, and Shakespeare: The 1928–29 Season

The 1928–29 season was the culmination of the development of Mazo's company. In a season full of hits, there were four productions that particularly captivated theatergoers: Sholem Asch's drama of martyrdom and massacre *Kidush Hashem*, a Yiddish translation of Eugene O'Neill's *Desire under the Elms*, Y. L. Peretz's symbolist verse drama *At Night in the Old Marketplace*, and *Shylock*, a Yiddish adaptation of Shakespeare's *Merchant of Venice*. These productions featured technical achievements on a scale that had previously been thought impossible for the Yiddish stage: dozens of sets, hundreds of costumes, a full orchestra, massive casts, and even projections.

For over a decade, the innovations introduced by the Vilna Troupe and other Yiddish art theaters had been mainly confined to modes of acting (i.e., an emphasis on ensemble) and directing (such as Herman's fusion aesthetic for *The Dybbuk* or Buloff's expressionist staging of *Singer*). Occasionally the Vilna Troupe had introduced design innovations, but these occurrences were almost always by accident, such as when the company ran out of money and jerry-rigged an eerie lighting effect to avoid paying for electricity. Intentional design innovation, on the other hand, was new for the Vilna Troupe. Since the Vilna Troupe's designers always had to develop portable sets, costumes, and lighting that could be transported cheaply and easily, they tended to favor simple, streamlined designs that worked in different spaces. In large cities, the Vilna Troupe often performed in grand proscenium theaters; in smaller towns, the company had to be prepared to work anywhere. Focusing on design required a measure of location-based stability that no branch of the company had ever had—until 1928. Indeed, the 1928–29 season was the only significant period of time that any Vilna Troupe ever remained in one place after the original company's departure from Vilna in 1918. From May 1928 to May 1929, Mazo's branch of the

Vilna Troupe performed almost exclusively in Warsaw at the same Elysium Theater where it had presented *The Dybbuk* back in 1920, with only a brief two-month hiatus when the actors took *Kidush Hashem* and *At Night in the Old Marketplace* on tour across Poland. Never again would the company be more stable; never again would its actors' schedules be more predictable. For a single year, this itinerant company had found a home.

Mazo's 1928–29 season represents an important counterpoint to the sustained itinerancy of the Vilna Troupe over two decades. On the surface, the company's record of innovation during this season might seem to suggest that its creativity had previously been hindered by travel. But the Vilna Troupe's achievements this season were actually the culmination of years of geographical mobility. As perpetual travelers, Mazo and his Vilna Troupe were well aware of new trends in constructivist set design and recent advances in lighting and projection technology; until now, however, they had had neither the means nor the stability with which to experiment with design. A yearlong residency at the Elysium Theater was the perfect platform for the actors to finally try out some of the new approaches they had encountered on their travels.

Ironically, the Vilna Troupe's turn to design innovation was initially an attempt to make its work more portable. Originally, Mazo did not foresee a Warsaw residency for the 1928–29 season. He expected a brief stay in the capital before continuing across Poland and Romania, as the company had done many times before. From Lviv, Mazo contacted Mikhl Weichert, a young Warsaw director who had studied avant-garde theater in Berlin under Max Reinhardt.[137] Weichert had first encountered the Vilna Troupe as a young man in Warsaw in 1918 when they were, as Weichert described in his memoirs, "at the center of theater culture."[138] He became friendly with the actors after being invited to a Vilna Troupe Passover seder at Leyb Kadison's home and directed briefly for the company before quitting after a quarrel with the actor Leonid Sniegov.[139] This was one of Weichert's first forays into directing for the professional Yiddish stage. Ten years later, Mazo invited a more seasoned Weichert to return to the Vilna Troupe to mount a production of his choice, and Weichert chose his own dramatization of Sholem Asch's novel *Kidush Hashem*.

Weichert had an ambitious vision: mass scenes with hundreds of extras, elaborate costumes, and a full original musical score composed by his friend Henekh Kon. Weichert also suggested that perhaps the troupe could employ new advances in projection technology to solve a recurring design problem. Because the Vilner never knew what kind of space they would be performing in next, their set designs often seemed ill-suited to the buildings that housed their productions. From friends in Berlin, Weichert probably knew that German directors like Reinhardt and Erwin Piscator had begun to experiment with a new optical device called the Linnebach projector. The Linnebach projector, a lensless system that projected shadows and simple shapes, had been invented at the turn of the century by the German lighting expert Adolph Linnebach, but it was not until the development of high-wattage filament lamps in the early 1920s that the Linnebach lantern could be used to project images onto a set or cloth.[140]

The Linnebach projector's simple design, which could be reproduced by anyone using inexpensive and readily available materials, coupled with its portability, made it an attractive choice for an itinerant theater company. Do-it-yourself instructions on how to build a Linnebach lantern out of plywood or scrap metal were widely circulated.[141] Cheap and portable, the Linnebach projector seemed tailor made to fit the needs of the Yiddish stage. A low-profile projector, Weichert explained to Mazo and the others, would be much easier to travel with than the bulky set pieces that the actors were accustomed to lugging on the train. With more storage space, the Vilna Troupe could also bring along more lighting equipment and costumes on its travels (Weichert suggested 150 individual costume pieces for *Kidush Hashem*, an unprecedented number for a Vilna Troupe production). More importantly, replacing static set pieces with dynamic projections would enable the company to tailor the scenery to fit whatever space it happened to find itself in. "We had to project them [the sets]," Weichert explained to reporters, "so that they would fit on every stage—even the most primitive ones—and so that they could change as quick as lightning."[142]

Asch's *Kidush Hashem* (1919) is a historical novel about violence against Jews during the seventeenth-century anti-Polish Chmielnicki Uprising in what is now Ukraine. The Vilna Troupe's adaptation followed the novel's plot faithfully, telling the story of a religious Jew, Mendl, and his family during tumultuous times. When a Polish noble discovers that Bogdan Chmielnicki disguised himself and hid in Mendl's attic, the entire Jewish community is driven away, then murdered at the hands of the Poles, who are then themselves murdered by Cossack revolutionaries. The action moves quickly between locales: from the steppes to the synagogue, from Chmielnicki's military fortress to a shtetl home. Projections, in addition to being more portable and economical than traditional set pieces, enabled the quick, seamless transitions that would make a play with so many settings a viable option.

Weichert recruited a team of visual artists and design specialists—professional painters, hairdressers, makeup artists, tailors, electricians, furriers, carpenters, and machinists—to collaborate on *Kidush Hashem*. Nearly half of the scenes depict military clashes and require large crowds. The Vilna Troupe contracted Warsaw's local Jewish choral group, nearly one hundred members strong, to perform as extras.[143] For the first time in the Vilna Troupe's history, the actors were also accompanied by a full orchestra. Between the actors, the chorus, and the musicians, there were over 150 artists involved in the production.[144] Four garment workshops of costumers worked day and night to outfit the enormous cast.[145]

Coordinating all of these people, many of whom had never acted on stage before, was a massive undertaking. The last dress rehearsal was reportedly such a disaster that Weichert kept the entire cast and crew working without a break from six in the evening until six the next morning.[146] But opening night was a success. The rush of ticket sales that followed enabled the company to cancel its travel plans and prepare instead for a full season in Warsaw. Ultimately, Mazo's Vilna Troupe would perform *Kidush Hashem* over 150 times in 1928 alone.[147]

Kidush Hashem was a massive spectacle on a scale that the Polish Yiddish theater had never seen. In New York, where companies like Schwartz's Yiddish Art Theater owned their own theater buildings, or in Russia, where the Moscow State Yiddish Theater (GOSET) was subsidized by the Soviet government, scenographic innovation had long been a component of the high art Yiddish stage.[148] But in Poland, where Yiddish companies tended to be more itinerant and shorter-lived, such design innovation was unprecedented. Journalists for the Polish-language Jewish press hailed the scenography as "perfect, first class, deeply poetic, and in perfect tune with the mood of the performance."[149] "An artistic achievement worthy of any European theater stage," wrote another.[150] Jewish critics compared *Kidush Hashem* favorably with Polish director Leon Schiller's acclaimed expressionist adaptation of Stefan Żeromski's *Dzieje grzechu* (*A Story of Sin*) at Teatr Polski in 1926.[151] *Kidush Hashem* adopted Schiller's methodology, which involved taking raw fragments of dialogue from the novel and reproducing them directly on stage rather than trying to rewrite the novel into a play. Yet while the production was a success with Jewish audiences, it attracted few Polish theatergoers. This was likely due to the subject matter. In scene after scene, *Kidush Hashem* depicts maniacal anti-Semites taking violent action against innocent Jewish families. There are no sympathetic Gentile characters in the entire play. Another Yiddish theater group might have taken the lack of Polish attendance in stride. But the Vilna Troupe had come to expect a certain level of attention from non-Jewish audiences, and Mazo and Weichert were disappointed that Polish theatergoers had failed to acknowledge the company's most technically innovative production yet.[152]

Still, *Kidush Hashem*'s impact was more wide-ranging than its producers initially realized. The Vilna Troupe's production premiered in May 1928; just four months later, Schwartz's Yiddish Art Theater in New York opened a production of the same play.[153] With just a four-month lag between productions of the same new play across continents, the Yiddish Art Theater must have started rehearsing almost as soon as the Vilna Troupe's reviews came out. Days after Schwartz's version opened in New York, Mikhl Weichert directed a second production with new actors and a different company in Riga.[154] Nineteen years later, Habima would stage its own Hebrew-language production.[155]

Kidush Hashem was followed in October 1928 by the very first production of a Eugene O'Neill play in Poland in any language: the Vilna Troupe's Yiddish translation of *Desire under the Elms* (*Di tayve unter di ulmer*), directed and translated by the longtime Vilna Troupe member Avrom Taytlboym.[156] During the mid- and late 1920s, O'Neill's work was frequently produced in Western Europe but remained virtually unknown east of Germany, outside of a handful of productions in Moscow.[157] Polish directors, who generally lived and worked in Warsaw full time, were unaware of O'Neill's growing reputation. Not so the itinerant Vilner. The Vilna Troupe thus became the first company to introduce Polish theatergoers to America's most famous playwright of the period.

The career of Avrom Taytlboym, *Desire*'s director, offers insight into how the Vilner became conduits for the dissemination of new repertoire. Taytlboym was born in 1889 to Hasidic parents in Warsaw. After embracing secularity as a teenager, Taytlboym became an avid attendee of Polish-language theater and learned acting in an amateur Yiddish theater company under the direction of Y. L. Peretz and Mark Arnshteyn. He began his professional career as a prompter for Sam Adler's traveling troupe before acting in various Yiddish companies in Paris, London, and Buenos Aires. After the war, Taytlboym directed an amateur theater club in New York and another in Minsk before joining the Vilna Troupe in 1918.[158] A year later, Taytlboym accepted Maurice Schwartz's invitation to join the Yiddish Art Theater in New York. Over the next nine years, he performed with several American Yiddish theater companies. Given O'Neill's growing

Figure 10. *Desire under the Elms*, Warsaw 1928. YIVO Institute for Jewish Research.

reputation and frequent presence in American theater during these years, it is likely that Taytlboym attended several O'Neill productions while living in New York. In 1928 he pitched a Yiddish version of *Desire under the Elms* to Mazo, who brought him to Warsaw to direct it.[159] Without Taytlboym's transcontinental migrancy, Mazo might not have been aware of theatrical trends happening an ocean away.

The Vilna Troupe's *Desire* was instrumental in inspiring Polish directors to produce O'Neill's work. When *Desire* premiered, Jewish journalists predicted that theatergoers would soon see O'Neill on the Polish stage—and they were correct.[160] Scarcely one year later, a production of *Anna Christie* opened at Warsaw's Teatr Nowy and was falsely billed by the Polish press as "O'Neill's first play in Poland." Polish productions of *Desire under the Elms* and *All God's Chillun Got Wings* soon followed.[161] Mazo's Vilna Troupe, in turn, translated *All God's Chillun* into Yiddish (under the title *Shvartse geto* [*Black Ghetto*]) and staged its own version in 1930. For a time, O'Neill flourished in translation on the Yiddish stage. After the Vilna Troupe's productions, other Yiddish theaters also began to produce O'Neill plays, including a second translation of *Desire* at the Warsaw Yiddish Art Theater under the direction of Zygmunt Turkow, a former Vilner.[162] In 1932 a

Yiddish translation of *Long Day's Journey into Night* (*Di lange rayze aheym*) premiered at the Misha and Lucy German Folks Theater in New York.[163]

Desire was not the first Vilna Troupe production to introduce new repertoire to the Polish stage. A Yiddish translation of Czech-Jewish playwright František Langer's 1925 drama *Periphery*, an expressionist play about a man who accidently kills another and seeks in vain to be convicted in order to absolve his guilt, was a hit in the Vilna Troupe's 1927–28 season. Just six months later, Warsaw's most prestigious Polish-language theater, Teatr Polski, presented a Polish translation of the same play.[164] The Vilna Troupe thus served as a major conduit for bringing new repertoire from Western Europe and the Americas to Eastern Europe.

As Mazo's branch prepared new plays, current and former members of other branches were paying close attention thousands of miles away. When Joseph Buloff read about Taytlboym's success with *Desire*, he wrote to his wife that the news made him "so moody" that he doubted whether he should tell her at all. Still, he continued,

> I know that Luba Kadison is no fool. She understands that even if such a second-rater as Teitlebaum [*sic*] can rise in this world, it is not impossible that we, too, can achieve success. But, dear God, do not send our salvation through the Vilna Troupes.[165]

At the time, Buloff was the artistic director of the Chicago Dramatishe Gezelshaft, a high art Yiddish theater inspired by the Vilna Troupe.[166] As he planned his season, he kept a close eye on productions happening nearly five thousand miles away and felt threatened by their successes. Long after Buloff had left the Vilna Troupe, he continued to write regularly to current members, eager for updates. "I want you to write me your impressions of the theaters and the actors with whom you are playing," he instructed Mordechai Mazo from the Catskills. "I wait impatiently for your letters."[167]

This was by no means unusual. During the 1920s, former Vilner stood at the helm of dozens of other Yiddish theater companies. Dovid Herman and Henekh Kon were among the organizers of Azazel in Warsaw. Avrom Morevsky directed for the Nayer Yidisher Teater in Riga and the Krokever Yidish Teater in Krakow. After leaving the Vilna Troupe, Zygmunt Turkow and Ida Kaminska founded the Warsaw Yiddish Art Theater (VYKT). Dovid Herman also directed for the company founded by Turkow's brother Yonas, the Warsaw New Yiddish Theater (VNIT). Beyond the Vilna Troupe branches themselves, former Vilner were heavily represented throughout the Yiddish theater world.

Meanwhile, Mazo's branch continued to stage one success after another. In the summer of 1928 Mazo reached out to former *Dybbuk* director Dovid Herman about developing a production that would highlight the Vilna Troupe's growing technical prowess. For years, Mazo had dreamed about staging Y. L. Peretz's 1907 symbolist drama *At Night in the Old Marketplace*, a nightmarish vision of the Jewish encounter with modernity. Herman agreed to take on the project.

At Night in the Old Marketplace is a panoramic chronicle of the modern Jewish experience told through a modernist lens.[168] The play takes place in a town marketplace over the course of a single night and features nearly one hundred distinct characters, including a wedding jester, a pair of lovers, a prostitute, musicians, wealthy Jews, impoverished Jews, revolutionaries, a cantor, shopkeepers, a perennial wanderer, a drunkard, a bishop, a night watchman, dead martyrs, and a hanged man. Halfway through the play, the dead rise up out of their graves and join the living in the marketplace, along with talking gargoyles, zombies, and dancing statues.

Yiddish theater artists are also represented. In a metatheatrical twist, the play opens with a director, a stage manager, a narrator, and a poet rehearsing a play that is proving difficult. The set is not finished, the script is unworkable, and the production team is behind schedule. Suddenly, a mysterious wanderer steps out from behind the curtain and the director leafs frantically through his script trying to figure out where he fits into the play. "I can't find him anyplace," he mutters, perturbed.[169] When the Wanderer falls asleep on stage, his dream becomes the action of the play.

A dizzying cast of characters takes turns expounding their philosophical observations on modern Jewish life in rhyming couplets. As they speak, characters sing and dance, they pray, they deny God's existence, they die and rise up from the dead and return to their graves. The Wedding Jester tries and fails to bring about the Messianic age. Political revolutions and religious reformers come and go. In the end, the Jester entreats the other characters to run to the synagogue ("Jews, / Go / to shul! Jews, go—") as the factory whistle drowns out his voice.[170] Modernity, in the guise of the factory, ultimately dissolves the dream.

At Night in the Old Marketplace was rarely ever produced because of its difficulty. Even with double- or triple-casting, dozens of actors would still be required (Herman heavily adapted the play for a cast of twenty-three).

Peretz also called for an enormous set that included eight shape-shifting buildings (stable enough for actors to climb upon), a hidden catapult, giant movable tombstones, a floating cemetery that emerges in midair, and a remote-control-operated mechanical rooster. The stage directions also call for ambitious lighting and sound effects: fully operational streetlights, a statue with blinking lights, and church bells whose chimes rhyme with specific lines.[171] *At Night* is remarkable in its refusal to conform to what seems physically possible to achieve onstage.

Many a young and ambitious Yiddish director had hoped to stage *At Night*, but these efforts had rarely made it past the planning stage. Back in 1921, Herman and Mazo had discussed a production of *At Night* as a follow-up to *The Dybbuk*, but they quickly abandoned this plan once they realized how difficult it would be to mount. The idea lay dormant until 1925, when the actors learned that GOSET was staging the play in Moscow. GOSET's version was heavily adapted by its director, Alexander Granovsky, who transformed Peretz's abstract poetic drama into a politicized attack on Jewish religious observance, in stylized grotesque.[172] GOSET's production of *At Night* was one of its most popular, and it received glowing accolades when the company took it on tour across Europe in 1928.[173] The members of the Vilna Troupe were paying close attention. But it was only after the technically sophisticated *Kidush Hashem* that Mazo and Herman decided to resume work on *At Night* in earnest. With the skilled design team that Weichert had assembled, they realized, a full-scale production might be possible, though Weichert himself had moved on. Unlike GOSET's production, which had adapted the play into a full-throated attack on shtetl culture, theirs would strive for loyalty to Peretz's abstract, mystical script.

Within the fragmented, plotless antinarrative of Peretz's play, there is no main character. Mazo and Herman decided to make the Wanderer the focus of their production. After all, it is the Wanderer who brings the marketplace and all of its inhabitants to life, and it is his dream, inspired by years of itinerancy, that enables the Poet to write the play. In the Vilna Troupe's version, as the Wanderer delivered his opening monologue, the lights gradually rose to reveal the set—a series of constructivist platforms, boxes, and arches that allowed characters to climb, jump, and scamper above the stage.

WANDERER: Where am I going to? Don't ask again.
Maybe Someone Up There knows,
But I myself

Have grown old but hardly wise
From seeing set and seeing rise
The sun that I've been following so long.
Nowhere a stranger and nowhere at home.[174]

The Wanderer is exhausted from his travels and seeks rest. "Hold on!" shouts the Poet. "I've just glimpsed one of his dreams: That's the play we'll put on!"[175]

Here was the traveler's dream—a technically sophisticated artistic fantasia—presented by some of the most itinerant performers of the Yiddish theater. In Herman's adaptation, the Wanderer invoked millennia of Jewish displacement. Unlike the traveler of Peretz's play, who dressed in modern attire, Herman's Wanderer wore biblical robes and spoke in an old-fashioned manner. While the rest of the characters congregated in the marketplace, the Wanderer stood off to the side in a dimly lit corner, seeming to hover several inches above the stage as he stood upon one of the platforms scattered about the set.[176] As the only character that adopted premodern clothing and speech, the Wanderer stood out in every scene. Just as the "between two worlds" theme of *The Dybbuk* had seemed poignant in a production that brought together an audience of unprecedented diversity, so too did *At Night*'s glorification of travel as the engine of Jewish creativity resonate with the Vilna Troupe's own itinerancy.

This time, Polish intellectuals turned out in droves, intrigued by Herman's boasts that *At Night* was more technically sophisticated than anything yet seen on the Polish stage. Moreover, with GOSET touring the same play in Vienna just weeks earlier, many in Warsaw were eager to see the play that was attracting so much attention in Western Europe.[177] Among the prominent critics at the premiere was Tadeusz Boy-Żeleński, a Polish playwright, translator, and theater critic and the enfant terrible of the Polish literary and theater scene.[178] Back in 1920, Boy had attended a Vilna Troupe performance of *The Dybbuk* in Warsaw and had been impressed. But it was the Vilna Troupe's production of *At Night*, Boy argued, that proved that Yiddish theater was at the forefront of theatrical innovation in Poland.

> From a technical point of view, the Vilna Troupe ranks very high. There are various innovative solutions that are being discussed in the Polish theaters—in the Jewish theater they have all already been introduced and they seem to have grown organically into its very

Figure 11. *At Night in the Old Marketplace*, Warsaw 1928. YIVO Institute for Jewish Research.

> fabric. Perhaps it is its closeness to Russian theater that makes Jewish theater so progressive? The innovations are: stylized gestures, working with groups of actors on the stage, and musical and scenographic elements that are in perfect sync with the action on the stage. All of these seem to function quite organically on the Jewish stage, and—what's more important—they do not in any way hinder the pace of the play.[179]

After the production, Boy visited Mazo backstage and discussed his impressions. Their conversation touched upon broader questions of Jewish-Polish cultural interaction. "Could the play possibly have been influenced by Wyspiański?" he asked. "Absolutely," answered Mazo, explaining that Peretz had admired the great Polish playwright. "The cult of Wyspiański among the Jews is something that refutes many narrow-minded racial theories," Boy explained to readers. "How is it possible that two nations living next to each other, side by side, so close together, know so little of each other? Does it make any sense not to know thy neighbor at all?"[180]

Tadeusz Boy-Żeleński was one of the architects of modernist Polish theater. In 1906 he had cofounded the Zielony Balonik ("Green Balloon") cabaret, where many prominent writers, scenic artists, and actors of the modernist Polish stage began their careers.[181] Boy's proclamation that the Vilna Troupe's productions were more technically sophisticated than those of any other theater in Poland was a remarkable coup for the Vilna Troupe. Indeed, at the end of the review Boy explicitly called for Polish artists and intellectuals to engage with Yiddish theater.[182] Boy's review was translated into Yiddish and widely circulated and commented upon in the Yiddish press.[183] A glowing review from such a highly regarded member of the Polish intelligentsia influenced not only Poles but also assimilated Polish Jews who did not regularly attend Yiddish theater productions.[184]

Boy did not speak any Yiddish, and as such, his review focused on visual elements and staging. His review offers a glimpse into the pacing, imagery, and emotional resonance of this production from a spectator with no knowledge of the language or the original play:

> The shadows appear out of darkness one by one, the action flows as if it was a musical phrase with continuously changing rhythm. And then suddenly something happens, something big, the tension is growing and finally the spectacle reaches the pinnacle of pathos, with the poet shouting something out in vain while the ghosts dance around him in a dream fashion, until they finally freeze to the sound of a sarcastic rant of the jester.[185]

Like many non-Jewish critics, the language barrier did not seem to bother him. "I understood only a few words originating from German," Boy admitted, "but the play was so expressive, and the actors performed with such zeal, that there was almost no need for translation."[186]

The Yiddish critics were harder on the production.[187] Some thought that Herman's adaptation veered too far from the original. In *Literarishe Bleter*, Nakhmen Mayzel criticized Herman's direction as too "episodic," the lighting too dark, and the interpretation ill suited to Peretz's masterpiece. "Why try to 'improve' upon Peretz?" he wondered.[188] Zalmen Zylbercweig also accused Herman of failing to capture the essence of Peretz's poetry and suggested that perhaps *At Night* did not belong on the stage. "It has nothing to do with theater," wrote Zylbercweig. "The play is full of such allusions that one must study it, and a theater is not a studyhouse."[189] Others simply disagreed with Herman's stylistic choices. The Yiddish humor writer Der Tunkeler published a scathing review in *Moment*. "And the actors, how do they perform? What do you mean? They perform? They don't act, they just do what people tell them to do," he complained. "And the dead characters? They're really dead."[190]

Still, for many the very attempt to stage such an ambitious play made the production a success. While some debated the merits of staging the most bizarre and difficult play in the Yiddish dramatic canon, most rallied behind *At Night* as a triumph. Many commented on the fact that the Vilna Troupe's *At Night* premiered in the same week that GOSET's production of the same play was performed to critical acclaim in Berlin. "If Peretz had only lived to see this! In Berlin and in Warsaw, in one week—*At Night in the Old Marketplace*!" rejoiced Ber Karlinski.[191] Yehezkel-Moyshe Nayman commented that several scenes reminded him of Herman's directorial prowess in *The Dybbuk*. "Anyone who is part of the intellectual community and has a connection to Jewish culture must see this production not just once but twice or more," he told readers, echoing critics' assessments of *The Dybbuk* in 1920. "For this is more than just theater. It is the spark of a religious experience."[192]

The 1928–29 season concluded with a new Yiddish version of *The Merchant of Venice*, translated by Yisroel Shtern and Mark Rakovski and retitled *Shylock*.[193] Directed by Weichert, the production featured original music and a modernist set design. The translation scarcely changed a single line. But Weichert's direction recast Shylock as the drama's central character.[194] Most productions strive to remain true to the author's original intent, Weichert wrote in an article published the day after the play's premiere. This production would be different:

> There is no doubt that with his *Merchant of Venice* Shakespeare's goal was to amuse his theater audience with the comic figure of a Jew, as was the fantasy of our people in his time. . . . Today we find in Shylock's pathetic heroism nothing but noise, just a comic play, full of cheap amusement. We must find our own approach. . . . we see two worlds in a bloody struggle. On the one hand, fortunate Venice, on the other, the Jewish ghetto. And between them a struggle for life and death.[195]

The production team used visual elements and costuming to carefully distinguish the Jewish world from the non-Jewish world. The acts alternated between milieus—act 1 was set in Antonio's Venice, act 2 in Shylock's

Jewish ghetto, act 3 in the palace, and act 4 (the trial and verdict) in the courtroom. Not only was Shylock (played by Isaac Samberg) clothed in traditional Jewish garb, but the design team also employed distinctive set pieces, costume designs, and lighting cues to evoke the cultural vibrancy of his Venetian ghetto.[196]

The production was a box-office success and attracted critical acclaim.[197] Nakhmen Mayzel praised Weichert for bringing Shylock's Jewish world (unknown to Shakespeare) to light.[198] *Shylock*'s fans also included Alexander Granovsky, the former director of GOSET who had recently defected from the company and was working at the Deutsches Theater in Berlin, who came to Warsaw to see a performance.

> They found the courage and the power to bring out the artistry of Shylock in a new, clearer, more artistic form, with the guiding principle of Jewish dignity. . . . It is a great triumph! We are all very fortunate and proud. Weichert, the Vilna Troupe, and the Jewish audience have accredited themselves as a European theater, and thus they deserve a *mazl tov*.[199]

Granovsky's claim that the Vilna Troupe had become "accredited" as a "European theater" with this production carried special significance because he had played the role of Shylock in several German productions in the early 1920s.[200]

A few reviewers were more critical. Yehezkel-Moyshe Nayman, a journalist who had praised the Vilna Troupe's productions earlier in the season, was disappointed. The actors were not good enough to play Shakespeare, he argued.[201] Mazo was so furious about this review that he wrote a letter to the editor of *Literarishe Bleter* contesting Nayman's claims point by point.[202] The controversy soon petered out, and the production continued.

Wandering Cosmopolitans: Itinerancy as Survival Strategy

The 1928–29 season represented the culmination of the Vilna Troupe's artistic development. With skilled avant-garde directors and designers at its helm, Mazo's Vilna Troupe presented four technically and dramaturgically innovative productions that attracted widespread critical acclaim. "Theater is our fulcrum, our partner in the fight for Yiddish and for Yiddish culture," wrote Nakhmen Mayzel of the Vilna Troupe's achievements at the season's close.[203]

After more than a decade of traveling, Mazo hoped that the yearlong residency at the Elysium would establish his Vilna Troupe as a local Warsaw institution, like other Yiddish art theaters of the period (the Warsaw Yiddish Art Theater, the GOSET, or Schwartz's Yiddish Art Theater in New York) that had a home. Of course, none of these theaters was as financially solvent as the Vilner might have imagined: the Warsaw Yiddish Art Theater disbanded and reformed multiple times when it ran out of money, GOSET relied upon subsidies from the Soviet government, and Schwartz took out multiple mortgages on his house, produced plays he disliked, and ultimately gave up ownership of the theater building he had built for his company in order to keep his Yiddish Art Theater afloat.[204]

As a resident company in Warsaw, the Vilna Troupe suffered from the same onerous taxes that had long plagued its competitors. Warsaw's draconian theater tax system imposed special tariffs on Yiddish theaters. While producers of Polish plays paid a 5 percent tax, the city imposed a 10 percent tax on plays by "foreign" writers, which included all plays written in Yiddish. Mazo was thus forced to pay a steep tax of 40,000 złotys on the box office receipts for *A Night*, even though Peretz was a Polish Jew who wrote the play in Warsaw.[205] Due to these steep taxes, the Vilna Troupe teetered on the edge of bankruptcy all year long. Meanwhile, the actors were also responsible for paying income taxes to a government that subsidized only the city's Polish-language theaters. Warsaw's Yiddish theaters were on their own.

In May 1929 Mazo announced that the Vilna Troupe had no choice but to leave Warsaw. Between the high taxes and the lack of financial investment from Warsaw's Jewish community, the company could no longer pay its bills.[206] On tour in Krakow, Lodz, Radom, Lublin, Vilna, and Bialystok, the troupe was able to recoup its losses. Never again would this branch of the Vilna Troupe find another home. Ever the consummate theater manager, Mazo, had seen the writing on the wall. Had the Vilna Troupe remained in Warsaw, it would not have survived another season. Mazo's decision to return to the road, however painful it must have been, ensured the company's survival.

This was the eternal dilemma of the high art Yiddish stage. To survive without compromising their principles, the actors had to remain perennial wanderers. As Joseph Buloff wrote to a friend, there was no such thing as home for a Yiddish actor.

> You ask me where my home is now. Empirically, I just live in the wide world without a place, without a purpose. Realistically, I live

> out of a suitcase. In it, I carry around the few goods that I own in the world, which consists of several hundred crazy scripts and some dozens of souvenirs of past triumphs. A few times, I almost caught Pushkin's Golden Fish. A few times, I almost acquired a home and a position. But my cursed ambition, and my seven times cursed fate as a Yiddish actor always bring me back to my poor, broken bowl.[207]

Or in a later letter to fellow Vilner Khane Braz: "You write that Russia is good but that you long for home. I don't know what you mean by home. Does a Jewish actor even have a home?"[208]

In the 1920s the Vilna Troupe traveled farther and more consistently than any Jewish theater company ever before. Faced with the dilemma of wandering or dissolution, the Vilna Troupe chose the road again and again. Like the weary Wanderer of *At Night in the Old Marketplace*, the Vilna Troupe's incessant travel was the engine of its creativity.

INTERLUDE III

A Family Affair

It wasn't just actors, directors, and designers who traveled with the Vilna Troupe. There were also spouses and children, nephews and nieces, cousins and grandchildren. Many joined their relatives onstage, first as extras, then as actors themselves. The Vilna Troupe was just as much a group of families as it was a group of performers. Out of the 290 members of the Vilna Troupe, 73 (more than one-quarter) were related.

As a company of traveling actors, the Vilner found that children posed particular challenges. For some, having children interrupted their careers. When Luba Kadison gave birth to a daughter in 1941, she took a long break from acting. "A role comes and role goes, but a child is a child," she later told interviewers."[1] Instead, she helped her husband translate and adapt dozens of plays and traveled with him. Others did not stop for anything. Vilner Ida Kaminska was literally born into the life of a traveling Yiddish theater artist. Her mother, the legendary Yiddish actress Esther Rokhl Kaminska, gave birth to her at the Theatrical Hotel in Odessa while on tour.[2] Ida grew up backstage and began her theater career when she was just five years old.

Often, traveling Yiddish actors had to make difficult choices between their personal and professional lives. Chaim Shniur and Bella Bellarina argued about only one subject: children. Shniur desperately wanted a child, but Bellarina feared the impact that motherhood would have on her career. During the first few years of their marriage, Bella had several abortions.[3] Finally, in 1920, she acquiesced to her husband's wishes and decided to continue a pregnancy. After the baby was born, she hired a Polish wet-nurse and returned to the stage almost immediately. Chaim and Bella sent their infant son, Theodore, to live with Chaim's recently widowed mother so they could resume traveling.[4]

At first, their absences were intermittent. But in 1924 Chaim and Bella left Theodore behind in Europe when they joined Maurice Schwartz's Yiddish Art Theater in the United States. America would give them temporary visas as foreign performers, but the immigration laws did not allow them to bring dependents.[5] When Chaim and Bella arrived, they found out that they needed five years of uninterrupted residence in the United States to acquire American citizenship. So Theodore did not see his parents at all from the age of four until he was nine. Gradually, he forgot what they looked like.[6] "Being good parents is much more difficult for people who are in show business than for those who are not," he later reflected.[7]

Alexander Asro and Sonia Alomis had similar problems. They also immigrated to America in 1924, leaving their six-month-old baby behind in Eastern Europe. Like Chaim and Bella, Alexander and Sonia wanted to become U.S. citizens and could not leave the country. Joseph Asro did not see his parents for six years. Unlike Theodore, he didn't have a grandmother willing to take him in. Instead, he was sent from governess to governess and from one boarding school to another across Germany and England.[8] Later in life, Joseph Asro wanted to become an actor. His parents dissuaded him.[9]

Life in the Yiddish theater required personal sacrifices so great that many Vilner discouraged their children from following in their footsteps. Jeanne Cojocaru, the niece of Vilner Zygmunt Turkow and Ida Kaminska, grew up doing her homework backstage. Her mother, however, was emphatic that she not become an actor. When Jeanne's mother found out that her ballet teacher was planning to cast her in a traveling dance show, she promptly withdrew her daughter from the school.[10] Even a minor association with the stage was suspect.

Still, the next generation was often captivated with the romance of their parents' lifestyles. Some actors thought it was important to pass down hard-won information. "I knew about Stanislavsky when I was ten years old," Noah Nachbush's nephew told me.[11] Baruch Lumet cast both of his children in his radio plays; his daughter didn't take to it but his son did. Soon young Sidney Lumet was a Yiddish radio and stage star. Playwright and Group Theater member Sidney Kingsley heard the boy on the radio and auditioned him for a Broadway role in his new play *Dead End*.[12] That was the beginning of Lumet's illustrious stage and screen career.

Others inspired their children to become actors even when they weren't around. Sasha Lipovski, the illegitimate son of Vilner Leyzer Zhelazo and Ester Lipovska, was raised by his maternal grandmother. "How can you raise a child while shlepping yourself around from town to town?" she argued to her daughter. "You can't simply leave an infant by the side of the road!"[13] So Ester continued performing and traveling and her mother brought the baby to see her whenever she was in town. When theater director Nokhum Lipovski married Ester, he formally adopted five-year-old Sasha and gave the boy his last name. Still, Nokhum and Ester continued to travel and Sasha continued to live with his grandmother.

When war broke out in 1914, Nokhum and Ester set out for Siberia with their troupe to get away from the war. But nine-year-old Sasha was so attached to his grandmother that just as the wagon was pulling away, he leapt out of it and ran to her. Sasha would not see his mother and stepfather again until they returned six years later.[14] Upon their arrival back in Poland, Sasha decided to become an actor and joined their company. Soon he would leave and join the same branch of the Vilna Troupe that his biological father had just recently left.[15] Like so many Vilner children, he would follow in his parents' footsteps.

CHAPTER 5

The Vilna Troupe Nexus

> In order to embrace it and understand what Jewish theater meant, you know, it was a world theater. But who has the patience for it, who the hell needs it? It's all forgotten in the past.
> —Joseph Buloff

What happened to the Vilna Troupe? Why did it come to an end prior to World War II? And perhaps more importantly, why did it disappear so thoroughly from the historical record?

In the 1930s the Vilna Troupe was subject to the same fate as every other Yiddish theater of the period: linguistic assimilation and the transfer of its audience to non-Jewish theaters, the aging of the idealists whose vision had fueled a movement, the specter of rising anti-Semitism around the world, the growing leverage of modern Hebrew culture, and the financial pressures of the Great Depression, which stretched already paper-thin budgets. But this chapter is not merely about the decline of the Vilna Troupe, though that is part of the story.

This chapter is also not about the almost unilaterally depressing fates of individual Vilner. Some actors struggled to reinvent themselves in middle age as their careers became obsolete. Some learned new trades, a few succeeded in transitioning to acting in another language, and others became destitute. Worse still were the fates of those who were murdered during the Holocaust, like Mordechai Mazo and Isaac Sheftel, who perished during the Warsaw Ghetto uprising, or Miriam Orleska, Khane Braz, and Shloyme Kon, all of whom died in Treblinka. The Vilna Troupe's critical acclaim provided no protection against the Final Solution.

Instead, this chapter examines the Vilna Troupe's final years through the lens of its legacy. In fact, the 1930s marked both the end of the Vilna Troupe and the expansion of its influence. Even as new incarnations of the Vilna Troupe arose and disintegrated in rapid succession, a tightly interconnected network of former Vilner was expanding the Yiddish art theater movement to new frontiers. During these years, the hundreds of theater artists who had once performed with the Vilna Troupe became seminal figures in a wide range of other theatrical endeavors around the world.

The Vilna Troupe was the entry point for hundreds of actors, directors, and designers to begin their theatrical careers; as such, it cultivated the talent pool for Yiddish theater worldwide. In Poland, former Vilner were at the helm of dozens of professional and amateur Yiddish theater companies, including the Warsaw Yiddish Art Theater, Yung Teater, the Ida Kaminska Theater, the Warsaw Nayer Idisher Teater, the Studio of the Yiddish Drama School, the New Yiddish Theater, Azazel, Ararat, Khad Gadyo, Teater Far Yugnt, Balaganeydn, and Nay Azazel. In Latvia, a group of Vilna Troupe affiliates founded the Nayer Idisher Teater. In the United States, Vilner performed in and directed for the Jewish Art Theater, Maurice Schwartz's Yiddish Art Theater, the Folksbiene, Artef, the Second Avenue Theater, Unzer Teater, the Chicago Dramatishe Gezelshaft, and the Yiddish Theater Unit of the Federal Theater Project, among others. In Paris, a group of former Vilner founded the Parizer Yidisher Arbeter Teater. In Belgium, a team of Vilner ran the Yiddish Folk Theater of Brussels. In Russia, half a dozen former Vilner performed with the Moscow State Yiddish Art Theater. In Brazil, Yankev Kurlender directed the São Paulo Dramatic Circle. In South Africa, Vilna Troupe members led five different Yiddish theater companies. In Mexico City, Alexander Asro and Sonia Alomis ran a Yiddish drama school. In Australia, former Vilna Troupe affiliates were among the founding members of the Kadimah Art Theater and its long-lived successor, the Dovid Herman Theater. In Argentina, the Yiddish Folk Theater (IFT) was developed by one-time Vilner. In Johannesburg, Natan Breitman and Hertz Grosbard performed with the Breitner-Teffner Yiddish Theater. Indeed, it was the rare Yiddish theater anywhere in the world that did not have a former Vilna Troupe member involved.

But Yiddish theater was not the only field where the Vilner made contributions. Others left the Yiddish stage behind to pursue careers in theater and film in other languages. In New York, former Vilner Wolfe Barzell and Jacob Ben-Ami performed in several Theater Guild productions. In the 1930s, 1940s, and 1950s Barzell also acted on Broadway under the direction of Sanford Meisner, Lee Strasberg, and Tyrone Guthrie and performed in major roles alongside Ethel Barrymore and John Garfield.[1] Alexander Asro acted on Broadway with Gene Kelly, Martin Martin, Jack Lemmon, and Sophie Tucker and had a briefly successful Hollywood film career starring in the Marx Brothers' 1938 film *Room Service* alongside Lucille Ball.[2] Joseph Buloff also became a Broadway and Hollywood star, performing alongside Paul Newman, Rita Hayworth, Edgar G. Ulmer, Fred Astaire, Cyd Charisse, Warren Beatty, Jack Nicholson, Gene Hackman, Diane Keaton, Harold Clurman, Sanford Meisner, Uta Hagen, Agnes de Mille, Helen Hayes, and others.[3] In Dallas, former Vilner Baruch Lumet directed the Knox Street Theater and was the founder of the Dallas Institute for the Performing Arts.[4] Andrzej Pronaszko, who designed sets for the Vilna Troupe in Poland between 1932 and 1934, subsequently designed sets for the National Theater in Warsaw, Krakow's Narodowy Stary Teatr, and the Słowacki Theater, among others. Pronaszko also became an important Polish painter and scenic design teacher.[5] Szymon Syrkus, who designed sets for the Vilna Troupe in the early 1930s, was an influential Polish architect and architecture teacher.[6] Gertrud Kraus, who choreographed for a branch of the Vilna Troupe in the early 1930s, choreographed and performed with Habima and the Israel Ballet Company, and shaped the first generation of Israeli dancers through her teaching.[7] In the 1940s and 1950s, other Vilner also played a seminal role in shaping the nascent Israeli theater. Zygmunt Turkow directed the Tel Aviv–based company Zuta, Zalmen Hirshfeld acted in Habima, Dovid Likht directed for Habima, Josef Kaminski composed music for Habima, and Reuven Rubin designed sets for Habima and the Ohel Theater.[8]

Paradoxically, it is only in examining the disintegration of the Vilna Troupe and the dispersal of its members that the full measure of its impact comes into focus. As members left the struggling company for brighter horizons in the 1930s, they brought their distinctive training, repertoire, and style to new enterprises around the world.

Part One: The End of the Vilna Troupe

The story of the decline of Yiddish culture in the 1930s is familiar, so much so that we tend to ascribe a false sense of inescapability to Jewish life during these years. As Michael André Bernstein has argued, the natural inclination when writing about a historical catastrophe is to engage in "backshadowing"—a kind of "retroactive foreshadowing" that imposes linearity and inevitability on the past. By engaging with the past through the biased lens of knowledge of the present, the writer deprives historical figures of agency so that they become caricatures of themselves—"victims-in-waiting," in Bernstein's terms.[9]

Historical accounts of Yiddish theater in the 1930s tend to be dominated by motifs of imminent catastrophe. But this belies the true position of Yiddish theater artists in the years leading up to the Second World War. The Yiddish actors of the 1930s may have worried about their future, but they were by no means convinced that it was coming to an end. In the fall of 1938 the Yiddish theater union in Poland published a detailed agenda for its next annual meeting; in 1939 Gimpel's Garden Theater in Lemberg opened a beautiful new building that no Yiddish actor would ever use.[10] To understand what happened to the Vilna Troupe in the 1930s, we must try to put ourselves in the mind-set of these artists, who imagined that their theater had a long future ahead.

At the beginning of the 1930s, the Vilna Troupe was larger and more famous than ever before. What had begun as a company of fifteen actors had ballooned into seven Vilna Troupes employing hundreds of artists. But the dawn of a new decade brought fresh challenges that threatened to undermine all that the Vilna Troupe had achieved. Yiddish theater had never been able to guarantee steady employment, living wages, or adequate performance venues. Virtually the only thing that Jewish actors could count upon in the 1920s was an audience. But in the 1930s, even that started to disappear. The next generation of Jewish youth never quite took to the Vilna Troupe like their parents had. This was not a local problem, nor was it only the Vilna Troupe's. Around the globe, Yiddish theaters struggled to attract young people, who tended to be more assimilated than their parents. The growth of the film industry also contributed to the Yiddish theater's audience problems. The 1930s and 1940s were the first golden age of cinema. In the United States, movie theater attendance steadily rose each year between 1934 and 1948, and movies accounted for 80 percent of American entertainment spending.[11] Theaters in every language struggled to compete, and Yiddish was no exception.

In New York, the reigning world capital of Yiddish theater, companies were shutting down one after another. In the first few months of 1930, the manager of the National Theater committed suicide after his company went under, the Public Theater was bought out by a movie theater conglomerate, ticket sales for Maurice Schwartz's Yiddish Art Theater were so poor that the company was forced to end its season several months prematurely, and two minor Yiddish theaters, the Liberty Theater in Brooklyn and the McKinley Square Theater in the Bronx, shut down permanently.[12] The rapid worsening of the economic situation for American Yiddish theater was a result of the Immigration Act of 1924, which severely restricted Eastern European immigration and cut the Yiddish theaters off from a steady influx of new immigrant spectators. Without them, there were no longer enough Yiddish theatergoers to support thirteen professional companies in New York. "Now that immigration has halted, Yiddish theater has faded," wrote Joseph Buloff to a friend in the USSR in 1932. "We play mostly for old folks who are too old to learn English."[13] The Vilna Troupe's vision of a Yiddish theater that would be the central institution of modern Jewish life no longer had the same resonance in an era of rapid linguistic and cultural assimilation.

For the Vilna Troupe actors, the 1930s was a period of steadily increasing anxiety. Joseph Buloff's description of the Vilna Troupe's precarious position captures the frustrations felt by many:

> The Vilner are cursed by God, like the Eternal Jew. May they live forever, as he does. They were drowned so many times, but each time the water rejected them. They were burned again and again, and did not go up in smoke. So often it looked as if they already had departed for the next world, but when a testing feather brushed against their nose, they sneezed and lived again.[14]

Many had been wandering for decades and were desperate for stability. The creation of each new branch dangled the tantalizing prospect of geographical permanence. But this dream of a permanent home receded again and again as one company after another dissolved, sending its members back on the road once more.

And yet, in spite of these challenges, the Vilna Troupe continued even as dozens of other Yiddish theater companies succumbed to the pressures of the period. By 1931 the Vilna Troupe had been performing—in one incarnation or another—for fifteen years without interruption. No other Yiddish theater company to date could claim such a feat. The Vilna Troupe had survived far worse than declining audiences: starvation, typhoid epidemics, expulsions, anti-Semitic protests, bankruptcy, and internal splits. Perhaps, as Buloff suggested, the Vilna Troupe was condemned to roam the earth forever like the Wandering Jew of Christian lore, simultaneously blessed with eternal life and cursed with permanent itinerancy.

The case of the Bronx Vilna Troupe demonstrates the new challenges that would-be Vilna Troupe founders encountered. In 1929 a group of Vilner—including Leyb Kadison, his wife, Khane, his daughter Luba and son-in-law Joseph Buloff, along with Noah Nachbush, Leah Naomi, Shmuel Tanin, Reuven Vendorf, and some new talents—decided to start a Vilna Troupe in the Bronx.[15] The location was, in part, an attempt to distance themselves from the crowded Yiddish theater scene on Second Avenue and in part due to financial constraints. Vilna Troupe actors who had been in high demand just a few years earlier now found themselves unemployed for long stretches. Leasing a grand theater on Second Avenue was simply not an option. Kadison and the others could barely scrape together enough money to rent the America Theater, an outdated turn-of-the-century vaudeville venue in the heart of the Bronx on 149th Street. The theater's inconvenient distance from Jewish spectators on the Lower East Side was a significant concern, but the actors had few choices.[16]

Location was only the beginning of the Bronx Vilna Troupe's troubles. After paying rent to their new landlord, the actors could not afford to hire union stagehands. Instead, the company imported amateur stagehands from Chicago who were willing to work for a pittance. Infuriated, the powerful Yiddish stagehands' union staged protests outside of the theater and set off stink bombs during performances.[17] The actors tried to ignore these disturbances as much as possible, throwing open the stage doors to ventilate the theater, but spectators were less willing to withstand the picket lines and the stench.[18]

The Bronx Vilna Troupe's first production, Czech playwright František Langer's *Periphery*, produced under the title *Mord* (*Murder*), opened on November 1, 1929 (Mazo's branch had staged its own translation of the same play in Poland a year and a half earlier—a testament to the continuation of a shared Vilna Troupe repertoire). Three more productions and scarcely four months later, the company folded. Audiences were sparse, save for a dwindling group of loyal fans. The fact that the America Theater had a large house only made the pitiful size of the audiences more apparent. "A long journey to the Bronx through the seven halls of hell, and after that long march is nothing more than a large, empty, cold, uncomfortable theater where after all that, you sit among a thousand empty seats, which glare at you with their emptiness," critic Alexander Mukdoni told readers.[19] An empty seat in a theater, Mukdoni continued, is like having a hole in your clothing. The rest of the cloth might be whole, but the missing piece ruins the outfit.

The situation worsened as even the most loyal fans grew weary of the long trek to the Bronx, the stink bombs, and the picket lines. A thousand unsold tickets on *Periphery*'s opening night became fifteen hundred empty seats at every show.[20] Mukdoni tried to put a positive spin on the situation, hailing the actors for their "bravery" for continuing in spite of the unsold tickets. "What a tremendous artistic effort is required to be able to perform before a thousand empty seats!" he extolled. "This is the only theater that has, in this dark season, created something new; the only theater that has not been demoralized by the poverty and despair [of today's Yiddish theater], but quite the opposite—the poverty and despair have actually enhanced their theater."[21] These sentiments, however, did little to raise morale as the weeks wore on and the audience failed to materialize.

Only two weeks into *Periphery*'s run, the Bronx Vilna Troupe was already facing financial ruin. The actors pleaded with prominent writers to urge their readers to buy tickets and save the Bronx Vilna Troupe before it was too late. A few took up the cause. Yiddish poet Aaron Glants-Leyeles railed against the American Jewish community for failing to adequately fund the Vilna Troupe.

> Listen up—in a humble theater, almost entirely without help, without means, and without any sort of commotion, a thoroughly interesting and fine production took place. What might have been possible if they had had all that they required? . . . Support the Vilna Troupe. Help them—and yourselves—to create a true Jewish artistic stage.[22]

These efforts had little effect.

For the Bronx Vilna Troupe's second production, Buloff adapted, under the title *Ger tsedek* (*The Righteous Convert*), Alter Kacyzne's play *The Duke*, a drama based on the legend of the eighteenth-century Polish Count Valentine Potocki, who converted to Judaism and was martyred.[23] Buloff had originally performed in the play as a member of Mazo's Vilna Troupe in Romania in 1925, where it had been a success. In the Bronx, however, the critics were less than enthusiastic. "It's hard to say what is wrong with the play," grumbled one reviewer.[24] Alexander Mukdoni was more critical, calling the production *shund* in artsy disguise. "The production itself, if you plug up your ears and don't hear how it grates, is well done. . . . But they took a *treyf* [nonkosher] bit of *shund* and snuck it in like an *etrog* [citron fruit] in a fine, filigreed box."[25]

By the time the Bronx Vilna Troupe opened its third production, a Yiddish translation of a German comedy by Ludwig Fulda, even the company's most loyal defenders concluded that the actors were trying to "drown their sorrows in comedy."[26] But the lighthearted spirit of the play was ill suited to the desperation of the actors. The jokes fell flat, the jovial tone seemed forced, and their demeanor seemed more appropriate for a tragedy. "The Vilna Troupe artists . . . make a serious attempt to bring the necessary levity into their playing . . . but it is not successful in the slightest," wrote one Yiddish journalist who had always sung the Vilna Troupe's praises in the past.[27] Reviewers also expressed concern about the Bronx Vilna Troupe's repertoire, which drew equally from European, American, and Yiddish dramas. To be fair, this merging of Jewish and non-Jewish repertoire had always been part of the Vilna Troupe's approach. But in the highly charged political and social atmosphere of the 1930s, the Vilna Troupe's repertoire was more problematic. The Vilna Troupe had a responsibility to support Jewish playwrights, critics wrote, by producing their work—exclusively.

Perhaps influenced by these critiques, the Bronx Vilna Troupe chose for its fourth and final production a musical revue that wove together traditional Yiddish folksongs with improvised scenes based on Jewish folklore. *Der regnboygn* (*The Rainbow*) received strong reviews, and the small audiences that gathered at the America Theater were mostly enthusiastic, though some quibbled that not all of the actors were equally good singers.[28] But there were still hundreds of empty seats in the theater each night. After only a few performances, the Bronx Vilna Troupe accepted defeat. Once again, the actors said their goodbyes and dispersed to other Yiddish theater companies: some to Buenos Aires, others to Paris and London, and a few back to Second Avenue. Noah Nachbush, who once originated the role of the Messenger in *The Dybbuk*, decided to quit the professional Yiddish stage altogether. For the rest of his life, Nachbush would travel on his own giving solo recitals of material from the Vilna Troupe's repertoire, first in small theaters in the United States, later in displaced persons' camps across Europe, and finally, as those who fondly remembered the Vilna Troupe continued to age, in senior centers and retirement homes.[29]

Other branches were hardly faring better. Alex Stein's Vilna Troupe (1930–33) did well for a few years in Berlin, Vienna, and Prague but eventually ran out of money. Stein was an actor and director who had been involved with the Vilna Troupe on and off since 1917. After the original Vilna Troupe split, Stein had bounced back and forth between Mazo's branch and Asro and Alomis's. In 1930 he decided to strike out on his own in Vienna.

Like many Vilna Troupe offshoots, Stein's company included people from many branches of the company. Personal connections often motivated the decision to join a new branch. Among Stein's first recruits were his brother and sister-in-law, Yosef Kamen and Dina Koenig. Sonia Altboym and Adam Domb, another couple, defected together from Mazo's Vilna Troupe to join Stein's. So did Jacob and Yokheved Waislitz, their daughter Mila, and her husband, Moyshe Potashinski. Shmuel Sheftel, who had first joined the original Vilna Troupe in 1916 and had been a continuous member of Mazo's company since the split, brought his wife, Franya, who made her Vilna Troupe debut with Stein's company. Jacob Shigorin came from Asro and Alomis's short-lived Belgium Vilna Troupe (1929–30), where he had met Moyshe Potashinski, Mila Waislitz, and others. Leon Kolker came from the Bronx Vilna Troupe. Others, like Stein, had been involved with multiple Vilna Troupe branches over the years. Matisyahu Kovalski and Pola Valter had performed with the original Vilna Troupe, Mazo's branch, Asro and Alomis's original branch, Leyb Kadison's first American revival branch, and Asro and Alomis's Belgium branch before joining Stein's Vilna Troupe. Others were newcomers. More than half of the members of Stein's company had never been involved with a Vilna Troupe before. There was the Viennese dancer and choreographer Gertrud Kraus, the German painter Eric Isenburger and his dancer wife, Jula (he designed sets, she choreographed), and dozens of Yiddish actors.[30]

In Vienna, Stein's company presented Vilna Troupe classics like *The Dybbuk* and *The Singer of His Sorrows* to acclaim, despite a less than ideal stage space. "They created a legendary miracle world for us, conjuring belief and soulfulness," wrote a reviewer for the *Neues Wiener Tagblatt* of their production of *The Dybbuk*. "To accomplish this on such a small and primitive stage was difficult. Alex Stein dealt with this problem masterfully."[31] Indeed, Stein's Vilna Troupe attracted significant attention from Austrian journalists, who often framed their reviews as letting readers in on a secret. In *Österreichs Ilustrierte Zeitung*, a reviewer wrote, "Only a few people in Vienna know that on Brater Street, the most brilliant theater is being performed."[32]

After a successful few months in Vienna, Stein brought his Vilna Troupe to Brno in what is now the Czech Republic, en route to Prague.[33] They opened with An-sky's *Day and Night*, a play first introduced into the Vilna Troupe repertoire by Mazo's company in 1921. "Even if one does not understand every word," noted a reviewer for the *Brünner Tagesboten*, "one quickly overlooked any shortcomings due to the masterful sculpting of gesture and facial expressions."[34] *Day and Night* was followed by *Hard to Be a*

Jew, *The Singer of His Sorrows*, and *Periphery*.[35] Brno critics were particularly impressed with *Singer*. "To not have seen it and its reproduction by the Vilna Troupe would be an embarrassing gap in the intellectual and artistic assets of any friend of the theater," wrote one reviewer who hoped that the Vilna Troupe would bring *Singer* back for a return engagement.[36]

The following year, Stein's branch went to Berlin, where they once again received glowing reviews from the German-language press.[37] In Vienna, flush with success, Stein's Vilna Troupe even presented its own ambitious version of *At Night in the Old Marketplace* in 1931.[38] Several of the actors had performed in Mazo's 1928 production in Warsaw, including Jacob and Yokheved Waislitz and Dina Koenig.[39] Like Asro and Alomis's Western European *Dybbuk* in 1921, this second production of *At Night* was a virtual replica of the first.

For a few years, Stein's Vilna Troupe did well in Western Europe, so much so that by 1933 the company had temporarily settled in Prague under the auspices of the local Maccabi Association.[40] Local reviewers were also charmed. The Vilna Troupe's performances, wrote one reporter for the *Prager Presse*, were unlike anything local theatergoers had seen. "Their priestly movements, their rhythmic delivery, which frequently sounds like a style of psalmody singing, is so profoundly different from anything else that the modern theater movement has produced on stage, that such an evening can awaken deep feelings."[41] But in spite of the enthusiasm of audiences and of the press, Stein's branch dissolved—like so many of its predecessors—in 1933, and its members scattered to other theater companies around the world.

Even Mordechai Mazo's branch was struggling. For well over a decade, Mazo's company had been largely insulated from the difficulties faced by other branches because it had never ventured west of Vienna. By remaining in Eastern Europe while the others traveled widely, Mazo's Vilna Troupe had benefitted from the brand's global reputation while remaining safely ensconced within the most densely populated Yiddish-speaking territory in the world. But just as young American Jews were increasingly choosing to attend the English-language theaters of their peers rather than the Yiddish-language theaters of their parents, linguistic assimilation was also rampant among Polish Jewish youth.[42]

In 1931 the Lodz Jewish community published a booklet in honor of the fifteenth anniversary of the Vilna Troupe that included appeals for financial support. Writer Moyshe Broderzon urged readers to remember that the Vilna Troupe was special.

> Currently, the Vilna Troupe is the one and only place of refuge in Jewish Poland. . . . The Jewish community in Poland needs to think about a trousseau for its only successful daughter, about a dowry, and especially about a practical apartment—its own building. Because one cannot be a wanderer forever. . . . How long can one wander in the desert? Support them, defend your honor, give at least a small portion. Show the nations of the world that the Vilner are worthy.[43]

Broderzon likened the Vilna Troupe to a daughter about to get married who needs her family's support. The Vilna Troupe was like the only child of the Jewish community, Broderzon chided: support it like you would support your daughter. The booklets sold to loyal fans, but financial support did not follow. Mazo and his actors continued to have trouble paying the bills.

Like many theaters of the period, Mazo's Vilna Troupe turned away from aesthetic experimentation and toward politically conscious social realism in the early 1930s. In 1929 Mazo hired a young director named Jacob Rotbaum. Rotbaum had studied in Moscow with Meyerhold, Stanislavsky, and Tairov; upon his return to Poland in 1929, he traveled around the country giving lectures on "Theatrical Culture in the Soviet Union." Mazo attended such a lecture in Warsaw and decided to hire Rotbaum on the spot.[44] Rotbaum would go on to direct productions for Mazo's Vilna Troupe for the next six years.

Inspired by a Russian production he had seen, Rotbaum staged his own Yiddish translation of Eugene O'Neill's *All God's Chillun Got Wings*, a play about relations between blacks and whites in the United States, under the title *Shvartse geto* (*Black Ghetto*).[45] The Vilna Troupe's production of *Black Ghetto* marked the first—and last—time that Vilna Troupe actors would perform in blackface. O'Neill's drama about a doomed romance between a white woman and a black man in a racist community was a timely choice. The primarily Jewish audiences that attended *Black Ghetto* readily understood that while O'Neill was writing about racial tensions in the United States, the Vilna Troupe's version was just as much about deteriorating relations between Jews and non-Jews in Europe. The Vilner were not immune to rising anti-Semitic tensions. One day while walking home from a rehearsal for *Black Ghetto*, Rotbaum recalled, he and Miriam Orleska were attacked by a group of students carrying canes covered in razor blades.[46] Orleska was badly hurt but still managed to perform in the scheduled opening.

Rotbaum continued to direct politically oriented productions for Mazo's Vilna Troupe, to critical acclaim. But audiences were dwindling and the bills remained high. In March 1931 Rotbaum found himself stranded on the road. He wrote in his diary,

> We owe Palast Hotel a month's rent. We have an invitation to go to Lodz, but no money [with which] to go. . . . This morning everybody left the hotel. They escaped and left me as a pledge for payment. . . . I have no money. What can I do? Three days later, Mr. Marek Juwiler, the secretary of the Jewish Actors' Union, came from Warsaw to bail me out. In seven days I have to present the premiere in Lodz.[47]

In spite of these political and economic challenges, major figures in Polish theater continued to take an interest in Mazo's Vilna Troupe and regularly attended productions. Alexander Zelwerowicz was a frequent attendee, as was Leon Schiller.[48]

In 1933 Rotbaum and Schiller even got into a highly publicized conflict about a Vilna Troupe premiere. The production in question was a Yiddish translation of Russian playwright Sergei Tretiakov's *Roar, China!*, a political drama critiquing European imperialism. The play was inspired by a historical incident in which a captain of a British gunboat ordered two innocent Chinese men put to death after a conflict arose between the British navy and the local inhabitants.[49] *Roar, China!*, according to one theater historian, was "the most successful of all revolutionary plays," and it became wildly popular across Europe and the United States after the Meyerhold Theater's international tour in 1929.[50] When the Vilna Troupe, under Rotbaum's direction, produced a Yiddish translation of *Roar, China!* in Warsaw, Schiller published a letter to the editor of the influential Polish literary journal *Wiadomości Literackie* accusing Rotbaum of plagiarizing his Lodz production of the play a few months earlier. The "so-called Vilna Troupe, dissolved a long time ago," Schiller charged, was led by "a beginner Jewish director," "a con man" engaged in "theatrical trickery."[51] Moreover, Schiller accused the Vilna Troupe of producing the play illegally and claimed that he alone had the rights to produce the play in Poland. Rotbaum, who had long admired Schiller, was horrified and retorted that there was no plagiarism and that the Vilna Troupe had full rights to stage *Roar, China!*[52] Yiddish theater reviewers fumed. "Leon Schiller did not discover *Roar,*

China!," wrote Nakhmen Mayzel. "The whole affair has an anti-Semitic aftertaste."[53]

Roar, China! was a moderate success for the Vilna Troupe, though because of the controversy, it attracted fewer Polish intellectuals than Rotbaum had hoped.[54] Did Rotbaum plagiarize Schiller's production? Perhaps. The Vilna Troupe had a long tradition of borrowing amply from other theater makers. The evidence is inconclusive. But what the controversy between Schiller and Rotbaum does attest to is the extent to which the Vilna Troupe was integrated into mainstream Polish theater. When Schiller penned his letter for *Wiadomości Literackie*, he was preparing his own Warsaw production of *Roar, China!*, which opened at the Ateneum Theater a few weeks after the Vilna Troupe's. Predictably, Yiddish theater critics accused Schiller of plagiarizing from the Vilna Troupe. "The Polish director Leon Schiller is a great student of the Jewish director Jacob Rotbaum," observed one critic wryly.[55] Schiller responded to Rotbaum and others' counterattacks by writing more letters to newspapers and literary journals. Clearly, the famous Polish director was concerned that the Vilna Troupe's Yiddish production, the first to bring *Roar, China!* to Warsaw, would impinge upon the success of his Polish-language production. Despite the linguistic divide, the Vilna Troupe's audience base overlapped enough with Schiller's that a production of the same play would attract comparison, and Schiller wanted his *Roar, China!* to be seen as the original. Schiller's letters and his anxiety over Rotbaum's production are a testament to the Vilna Troupe's theatrical import in 1930s Poland.

Still, financially, Mazo's company continued to struggle. *Roar, China!* was not the hit that the Vilna Troupe had hoped for. The company's finances were dire, Mazo told reporters in a press conference. In 1932 the company nearly fell apart in the southern Polish city of Będzin because they lacked 200 guilden to travel to Sosnowiec (less than five miles away), even though they had already sold 600 guilden worth of tickets there.[56] The Vilna Troupe was not alone; Jewish theaters were struggling across Poland in the face of dwindling audiences, heavy tax burdens, and discriminatory rental agreements with theater landlords. "Every step of the way Jewish theater encounters solid walls," wrote the Polish Jewish author Wilhelm Fallek in an article entitled "The Dire Situation of the Jewish Theater" in 1932. "Directors of Jewish theaters are at the mercy of landlords and subletters, who are pocketing the lion's share of gross incomes while the actors are forced to starve."[57]

Conditions for Yiddish theater may have been deteriorating in Poland but, Mazo reminded his actors, the other Vilna Troupes had always found enthusiastic non-Jewish audiences farther afield. And so in October 1933 Mazo's Vilna Troupe set off on its first Western European tour. "The First World Tour of the Vilna Troupe!" proclaimed the company's programs in bold type, disregarding the fact that Asro and Alomis's Vilna Troupe had toured in most of the same cities a decade earlier.[58] Mazo's branch began in Paris, then traveled to Strasbourg, Antwerp, Brussels, the Netherlands, Switzerland, and London with their greatest hits: *The Dybbuk*, *At Night in the Old Marketplace*, *Kidush Hashem*, Sholem Aleichem's *200,000*, and *Roar, China!*.

The tour was not without its triumphs. The queen of Belgium attended *Kidush Hashem* in Brussels and personally congratulated Mazo and the actors backstage after the performance; the visit was intended to demonstrate Belgian solidarity with Europe's Jews in the face of rising German anti-Semitism.[59] In London, members of Parliament attended the Vilna Troupe's opening production of *200,000*.[60]

But overall, the company's 1933 "world tour" was less successful than Mazo had hoped. The non-Jewish Europeans who had flocked to see Asro and Alomis's *Dybbuk* a decade earlier were no longer quite so eager to attend Yiddish theater. Going to see Jewish theater had held few negative consequences for non-Jews in the 1920s, when cosmopolitanism was trendy. But it was something else altogether to enter a Yiddish theater fifteen years later, when anti-Semitic rhetoric, legislation, and acts of violence were on the rise. In 1933 alone, anti-Semitic acts in Great Britain, France, Germany, Italy, and Romania more than quadrupled.[61] In this climate, going to a Yiddish play was no longer an innocuous act. The devoted non-Jewish following that previous Vilna Troupes had come to expect in Western Europe was virtually nonexistent for Mazo's branch.

Worse still, Asro and Alomis wrote letters to theater managers and reviewers across Western Europe arguing that Mazo's company was a new group with no connection to the "original" company.[62] Ticket sales slowed. Midway through the tour, Mazo made drastic changes to the playbills and publicity materials, translating everything and eliminating Hebrew characters entirely in hopes of attracting more non-Jews. It made little difference. With debts mounting and not enough cash on hand to cover the actors' salaries, Mazo was forced to ask everyone to perform without pay for a few weeks so that the company could afford its return fare back to Warsaw. A group of actors defied Mazo's orders, returned to Poland at their own expense, and started a new branch. Others performed without pay and finished out the tour as Mazo had requested. When there was finally enough cash to book train tickets, another argument erupted over the company's next step. Some sided with Mazo and returned to Eastern Europe while others defected.

Nearly bankrupt, the actors returned to Warsaw, where they begged the local Jewish community to save them from bankruptcy. We are the last Vilna Troupe in the world, Mazo told leaders. This was true; all of the other branches had folded by 1935. Surely Warsaw would not want to go down in history as responsible for its end? A subsidy of 3,000 złotys enabled Mazo to make good on his promise to pay the actors' back salaries while also funding the preparation of two new productions: Israel Aksenfeld's *Rekrutn* (*Recruits*) and humorist Der Tunkeler's comedy *Gots ganovim* (*God's Thieves*). Both were flops.[63]

After twenty years of working continuously for the Vilna Troupe, Mazo gathered the actors and formally disbanded the company. He had accepted a long-standing offer from Maurice Schwartz to join his Yiddish Art Theater in New York. Like many before him, Mazo would discover that his art theater idealism was no match for Second Avenue's commercialism or Schwartz's notorious egotism; after just a few months, he would return to Warsaw.[64] The dream was over, and a darker challenge was approaching. The same month that Mazo's Vilna Troupe dissolved also brought the passage of Hitler's Nuremberg Laws.

The Vilna Troupe's last gasp was a production of—what else?—*The Dybbuk* in 1936, directed by Dovid Herman in honor of the twentieth anniversary of the first performance. The 1936 *Dybbuk* featured an all-star cast of the most famous Vilna Troupe performers from every branch of the company: Alexander Asro, Sonia Alomis, Pola Valter, Noah Nachbush, Sholem Tanin, Luba Kadison, Chaim Shniur, Bella Bellarina, Joseph Buloff, Leah Naomi, Leyb Kadison, and others. These actors were no longer the young firebrands whose idealism had propelled them to the forefront of the international art theater scene two decades earlier. Asro and Alomis, starring as the young lovers, were in their midforties, Leyb and Khane Kadison were well into their fifties, and many had children and even grandchildren of their own.

Ten years earlier, a New York production of *The Dybbuk* with this cast would have likely sold out. But times had changed, and the Vilna Troupe was no longer the unassailable brand it had once been. The 1936 *Dybbuk* was not exactly the commemorative event honoring the Vilna Troupe's accomplishments that was advertised. It was a last-ditch effort to revive a company that had all but vanished in a bleak new economic landscape.

Herman had also aged; at sixty, he was overweight, with tired eyes and a wild tangle of graying hair. His rehearsals were no longer the grueling all-night affairs that the actors remembered from the first productions of *The Dybbuk*. Once notoriously stubborn and demanding, Herman had softened with time. By 1936 he was sometimes willing to compromise on high-minded ideals if it paid the bills. But the aging director found the American Yiddish theater more frustrating than he had imagined. Established directors saw Herman as competition and shunned him; younger Yiddish actors, many of whom hoped to leave Second Avenue for the bright lights of Broadway, did not know who he was; and worst of all, American producers were unwilling to invest in his productions. Cahan was horrified. After years of trying to lure Herman to New York, the *Forverts* editor was forced to acknowledge that perhaps Yiddish art theater did not belong there after all.[65]

But in spite of Cahan's entreaties, and a deft publicity campaign that featured old Vilna Troupe endorsements from George Bernard Shaw, Israel Zangwill, and Albert Einstein, the "twentieth anniversary" production of *The Dybbuk* was a flop.[66] Few even bothered to review the production, and those who did were underwhelmed. The performance was "not as fluid as it should be," wrote Olin Downes for the *New York Times*.[67] In 1920 and 1921 the Vilna Troupe's dual Eastern and Western European premiere of *The Dybbuk* had dazzled audiences. A decade and a half later, it was the aging actors of the Vilna Troupe who could no longer live up to *The Dybbuk*.

The play itself was not the problem. Less than three months after the Vilna Troupe's anniversary production closed, Italian composer Lodovico Rocca's *Dybbuk* opera opened at Carnegie Hall to glowing reviews.[68] Rocca's *Dybbuk* opera, performed in English translation by a cast of non-Jewish singers, was worthy of Carnegie Hall. The Vilna Troupe's Yiddish version, on the other hand, could not even attract a large enough audience to justify a second week of performances. The 1936 revival of *The Dybbuk* closed after only six performances. It was also Dovid Herman's last theatrical endeavor. A few months later, Herman died suddenly at the age of sixty-one. He was shattered in his last few months, his wife told reporters, and he died from a broken heart.[69]

The 1936 *Dybbuk* was the Vilna Troupe's swan song. After the failure of this production and Herman's death, the company that had dominated Yiddish theater for two decades was gone. Never again would another group of actors call themselves "the Vilna Troupe," never again would theatergoers quarrel about which branch was the real one. With the dissolution of the last Vilna Troupe and the overall decline of the Yiddish theater, the Vilner had to find new ways of making a living. Some crossed over to the English-language stage—most famously Joseph Buloff, who built a career on Broadway in the 1940s and in Hollywood in the 1950s. In letters to friends, Buloff called New York "a cemetery of Yiddish theater" where "only the tombstones increase."[70] Others tried to reinvent themselves by forming new Yiddish companies, which rarely lasted for long. Still others left the theater altogether. Vilna Troupe composer Henekh Kon became dependent on checks from benefactors; his archive at YIVO is filled with desperate letters to friends begging for money in his final years.[71] Actor Avrom Bell became a door-to-door Fuller brush salesman. "He didn't leave the theater," Bell's grandson Michael Levy told me. "Basically, the theater escaped him."[72] The same could be said for most of the Vilner.

The Vilna Troupe brand had once conveyed an aura of near invincibility. Against the backdrop of an explosion of Jewish cultural creativity in the 1920s, the Vilna Troupe had signified a bright future for a Yiddish culture that was at last gaining recognition. By 1936, however, the Vilna Troupe brand evoked only aging actors and dwindling audiences.

For the most part, young Jewish actors who might once have dreamed of running away with the Vilna Troupe no longer sought to enter the Yiddish theater. In Warsaw, the Polish stage beckoned. In New York, young Jewish intellectuals with a theatrical bent dreamed of joining companies like the Group Theater, which was largely populated by first-generation American Jews who grew up attending Yiddish theater with their parents. Eleven of the Group Theater's members were first-generation American Jews: Harold Clurman, Lee Strasberg, Stella Adler, John Garfield, Howard Da Silva, John Randolph, Clifford Odets, Morris Carnovsky, Sanford Meisner, Anna Sokolow, and Lee J. Cobb. Two of the Group Theater's founders, Clurman and Strasberg, grew up in Yiddish-speaking homes where they first experienced theater in Yiddish. Had they been born a decade earlier, these two visionaries might just as likely have started a Yiddish-language experimental theater. But by the time that Clurman, Strasberg, and Cheryl Crawford founded the Group Theater in 1931, the audience for Yiddish theater had aged. Young Jewish actors sought to emulate new idols like Paul Muni, who left the Yiddish theater behind—along with his given name, Meshulem Vayzenfreund—and was amply rewarded in Hollywood.

The disintegration of the last branch of the Vilna Troupe was hardly surprising to anyone who had been following the company's gradual slide from international sensation to yesterday's news. That the end of the Vilna Troupe elicited so little comment was emblematic of the brand's overall depreciation.

Back in 1930, when Mazo's Vilna Troupe had first decided to leave Warsaw and never return (though of course they did), the company had held a press conference. A visibly distraught Mazo leveled with the press. The Vilna Troupe, Mazo told reporters, was more successful than any other Yiddish theater company in history, earning approximately 1,100 złotys per performance. But its expenses were also greater than any other Yiddish theater company in history. Mazo estimated that his performers had to transport about six thousand kilos (or 13,227 pounds—the same weight as a large African elephant or a Tyrannosaurus Rex) of sets, costumes, lights, and props everywhere that they traveled. With an average cost of 900 złotys per day to cover production costs and travel expenses, the Vilna Troupe was left with only 200 złotys each day to pay its fifteen to thirty actors, along with dozens of musicians and the stage crew. It was a Catch-22: the company could barely afford to continue traveling but it could not afford to stay in one place either. And so the wandering actors would take to the road once again. For a time, constant travel enabled Mazo's Vilna Troupe to hold on in spite of its precarious economic position. But by 1936, against the backdrop of worsening conditions for European Jews, tightening borders, and rising anti-Semitism, the transnational strategy that had enabled the Vilna Troupe to thrive for two decades was no longer enough. "This summer we were supposed to travel to Poland," Joseph Buloff wrote to friends in 1933, "but Hitler has put all such plans on hold. With the mounting panic among the Jews there, no talk of theater or raising money for plays is possible."[73] Fearing the outbreak of war, Buloff concluded, he and Luba would stay in America and stick to radio plays for a time. The art of itinerancy had no place in a world where all of the borders had hardened.

Part Two: The Vilna Troupe Network

The Vilna Troupe's influence did not vanish with the dissolution of its branches. Instead, like Théâtre Libre after 1896 or the Group Theater after 1941, echoes of the ideology, aesthetic, and repertoire developed by the Vilna Troupe continued to linger long after the company's demise. Without the Vilna Troupe, we might never have had a Eugene Ionesco or a Harold Clurman, or at the very least, their careers would have unfolded differently. An entire generation of groundbreaking scenic designers—including Mordecai Gorelik, Sam Leve, and Boris Aronson in the United States and Szymon Syrkus and Andrzej Pronaszko in Poland—cut their teeth working in Yiddish art theaters alongside Vilner. Without the Vilna Troupe, the world might have never known *The Dybbuk*. The Vilna Troupe was a pivotal node in a vast global network that included many of the leading figures of the interwar stage, a network that forged pathways for the circulation of theatrical ideas across borders.

The Vilna Troupe's role at the nexus of the interwar stage has long remained invisible to theater historians. Details of the company's connections to other theater artists and companies have remained buried in actors' archives and in never-translated Yiddish books, letters, and theatrical ephemera. The Vilna Troupe's size, multiplicity, and geographical instability add further challenges. There are dozens of well-documented Yiddish-language studies of other Yiddish theaters of the period. But to the great consternation of the Vilner, nobody ever wrote a book about them. This has been a frequent topic of conversation among Jewish theater historians, who have lamented the paucity of scholarship on the subject without ever attempting a book-length study of the Vilna Troupe themselves.

Even those who were most closely involved with the company were reluctant to take up the task. For example, the critic Nakhmen Mayzel would have been a perfect candidate. Mayzel had a uniquely accurate sense of the Vilna Troupe's scope and structure because he had often embedded himself in different branches of the company to conduct research for his reviews. But even Mayzel believed that writing a book about the company was beyond him. In his otherwise comprehensive book about Polish Jewish cultural life between the two world wars, Mayzel explained the absence of the Vilna Troupe thus:

> Yes, we have long needed [a history] about that very Vilna Troupe. . . . It has long needed to be written, and more than once somebody decided to write the history of the Vilner and solemnly vowed as much before the open graves of former Vilna Troupe members, swearing to complete it. But it seems that there is not the right person who will do it, nor is there the organization to subsidize such an important cultural and historical monograph.[74]

Similarly, Vilna Troupe actor Joseph Buloff often remarked that in order to pen a history of the Vilna Troupe, a writer would need to know Yiddish, German, Polish, Romanian, Hebrew, French, Dutch, Russian, English,

Lithuanian, Spanish, and other languages just to be able to read the company's multilingual reviews. "The trouble is the languages, who is going to read all these languages, you know?" Buloff told Jack Garfein. "There'll always be people who part of me they wouldn't know because it's in Romanian, or South African, or American, or Yiddish."[75]

Moreover, the Vilna Troupe's complex organizational structure made writing about it a contentious career move. In a theatrical landscape in which the livelihoods of hundreds depended upon a fluid definition of the term *Vilner*, any attempt to specifically situate "the Vilna Troupe" was bound to spark controversy. No Yiddish writer, no matter how accomplished, was immune. When Alexander Mukdoni wrote a brief profile of the Vilna Troupe that focused primarily (though not exclusively) on Asro and Alomis's company, he received a flurry of letters from furious actors claiming that he had gotten it all wrong. Mukdoni may have been a renowned writer who had more or less invented the field of Yiddish theater criticism, but his reputation did not prevent angry Vilner and their fans from calling him a fraud.[76] And so Mukdoni, like many of his colleagues, turned his attention elsewhere—continuing to review occasional Vilna Troupe productions without ever again trying to analyze the company's broader contours. One must always be careful when mentioning the Vilna Troupe in public, Mukdoni cautioned readers, for even the most casual conversations almost always end in heated argument.[77]

The erstwhile Vilna Troupe historian may no longer have to contend with angry letters from outraged Vilner, but Mayzel, Buloff, and Mukdoni's warnings still ring true decades later. The actors' ever-fluctuating relationships with multiple branches of the Vilna Troupe present a complex historical puzzle. Like the famous joke about a lone Jew stranded on a desert island who builds two synagogues just so he can reject one of them, one of the most salient characteristics of the Vilna Troupe was the staunch refusal of its members to publicly acknowledge the existence of other branches.[78] Compounding the problem is the Vilner's tendency to treat their individual pathways through a myriad of companies as though it were a single "Vilna Troupe" affiliation. For example, Leyb Kadison wrote in his memoirs that he performed with the Vilna Troupe for fifteen years.[79] In truth, Kadison's fifteen-year career with "the Vilna Troupe" actually included work with three different Vilna Troupe branches. For Kadison, "the Vilna Troupe" was shorthand for the overall trajectory of his career during this period. If we judge by the actors' memoirs, the real Vilna Troupe was simply whichever branch the writer happened to be working with at that moment.

The Vilna Troupe's historical impact is even more difficult to pin down. As Yiddish actors entered non-Jewish theater culture, many shed their Jewish identities by changing their names and rewriting the narratives of their careers. In the process, the role that Yiddish theater played in their emergence was often willfully obscured. The Jewish actors and directors who were most successful at entering mainstream theater culture were often those who were most skilled at these acts of erasure, like Paul Muni. Those who were less skilled assimilators—like Alexander Asro, who, try as he might, could not shake the thick Yiddish accent that doomed his brief Hollywood career—rarely achieved mainstream success and were largely forgotten in the annals of theater history.

But the Vilna Troupe historian of the twenty-first century has access to digital methodologies that offer new ways to account for the artistic networks of the Vilner. In the beginning, based on the extant historical record, I initially believed that the Vilna Troupe was a small company with a core group of performers. But I soon realized that this was not the case. Who was in the Vilna Troupe? Every artist had a different answer that said more about their own relationships with other actors than the company as a whole. Where did the Vilna Troupe perform? Why, everywhere, it seemed. How many Vilna Troupes were there? Each source had a different answer. The more I learned about the Vilna Troupe, the more riddles I encountered. In seeking to understand the Vilna Troupe as a discrete theater company, I was asking all the wrong questions. It was only when I began to think of the Vilna Troupe as a cultural phenomenon that it began to come into focus.

This shift in my thinking was inspired and enabled by digital tools. Initially, I began to explore digital humanities tools for data management. My roster of Vilna Troupe actors had grown to include nearly three hundred names; my list of locales where Vilna Troupe branches performed had turned into a massive collection of geographical data points; my hand-drawn network map of how Vilna Troupe actors were connected to other theater artists had so many names that it was illegible. Digital tools enabled me to compress the data drawn from archives and actors' memoirs into visual forms that I could analyze. First I plotted the geographical data onto digital maps. Next I created data visualizations to explore the relationships between members of the Vilna Troupe and other artists. This material is available online at www.vilnatroupe.com.

My data visualization project offers a distant reading (as opposed to a close reading) of the Vilna Troupe that takes all 290 of the individual

Vilner into account. I began by compiling a dataset about the personal and professional relationships of the 290 Yiddish theater artists I was able to identify who worked on at least one Vilna Troupe production between 1915 and 1936. The first step was to identify which artists were involved in the Vilna Troupe and the roles that they played (actor, designer, director, musician, etc.). Most of these people were obscure even within Yiddish theater history. Some had no mentions in secondary sources in any language. Interviews that I conducted with descendants of Vilna Troupe members, along with theater reviews and memoirs, helped to fill in some, but not all, of these gaps. Even so, there were still dozens of individuals for whom I was never able to find even the most schematic biographical details, and many whose names appeared nowhere outside of theater programs. This problem, of course, is not limited to Yiddish theater. Traditional scholarship requires that scholars manually identify figures of significance; as such, theater historians have tended to write about artists who attained major acting, directing, and design roles. Those who remained in the chorus or spent their entire careers as assistants or stagehands tend to recede into the background of theater historiography. My project offers a model for using the data contained in theater programs to recover the role of the "minor" theater artist.

I drew data from Zalmen Zylbercweig's seven-volume reference work *Leksikon fun yidishn teater* (Encyclopedia of the Yiddish theater) and from listings of names, dates, plays, and locations from hundreds of Vilna Troupe programs found in the archival collections of individual actors at the YIVO Institute for Jewish Research, the Harvard Library Judaica Division, the Billy Rose Theater Division and the Dorot Jewish Division of the New York Public Library, and the Columbia University Jewish Studies Collection. I also collected data from the Internet Broadway Database and the Internet Movie Database and from interviews that I conducted with living descendants of Vilna Troupe members.

Next I traced the personal and professional relationships developed by each artist over the course of his or her lifetime: the actors, directors, and designers with whom they worked; their families; their marriages, affairs, and divorces; their teachers and students; their friendships; and the artists they inspired. My goal was to capture every social connection that I could document in order to build a database that accounted for the social networks of these artists.

For the purposes of this project, I considered any individual who ever worked with the Vilna Troupe—even if only for a single production—to be a member of the company, regardless of his or her specific role or the length of his or her tenure. Leading actors and assistant stage managers, set designers and build crews, producers and extras were all accorded equal attention in the dataset. Some of the artists on my list, like Millie Alter, were involved with the Vilna Troupe for only one production, while others, like Joseph Buloff, performed with the company for decades. Because members tended to cycle in and out of the Vilna Troupe frequently and because many continued to leverage their Vilna Troupe credentials to market their work long after leaving the company, I considered all 290 artists as equal parts of the same phenomenon.

I also built a second linked dataset of non–Vilna Troupe members who were connected to more than one Vilna Troupe member. This dataset of second- and third-degree Vilna Troupe connections included type of connection, biographical information, and fields of influence. Taken together, these two datasets offer an account of how the members of the Vilna Troupe were connected to one another *and* to other artists, writers, and thinkers.

Finally, I worked with a data visualization programmer to create an online tool (www.vilnatroupe.com) that demonstrates how these Yiddish performers were connected to each other and to other artists.[80] This visualization, built in D3 (a Javascript library), allows users to interact with the data I collected using responsive filters. My visualization animates the social relationships that shaped the careers of the Vilna Troupe members and brings the broader social context of the interwar Yiddish stage to light.

Relationships in the visualization are expressed as colored lines, with each color signifying a different type of connection. Viewers can manipulate the filters to choose which relationships they see in order to compare how different types of social connections shaped the Vilna Troupe and contributed to its impact. For example, a user interested in how gender impacted the formation of friendships in Yiddish theater could choose to view only friendships and compare the results by gender.

The filters organize the data into five types of connections. Family connections include kinship, marriages, and romantic relationships. Study connections document relationships between teachers and their students. Professional connections reflect people who worked together on theater productions and/or films. The friendship category includes close friendships. Finally, the "inspired" category shows how Vilna Troupe members influenced each other and other artists. For each of these categories, I included only relationships that were well documented in the sources. For example, for the friendship category I included only those who engaged in frequent correspondence over a period of at least five years and/or described close friendships in letters or memoirs. For the "inspired" category, I included only instances where one artist claimed to have been directly inspired by another. A sidebar on the left side of the screen allows viewers to see more information about the specific relationships between individuals.

Connection lines between Vilna Troupe members represent professional connections outside of the company. For example, Hanoch Mayer is listed as performing with Yankev Mestel. This means that Mayer and Mestel worked together on at least one non–Vilna Troupe production (they may have worked together in the Vilna Troupe as well, but the visualization is designed to document how the company fostered artistic networks beyond itself). The connections between Vilna Troupe members thus document how the relationships that people formed within this single company influenced Yiddish theater at large between the world wars.

Vilna Troupe members worked with one another in productions by at least seventy-five other theater companies, including groups performing in Yiddish, English, German, Hebrew, and Polish in Warsaw, Lodz, Bialystok, Moscow, Odessa, Kharkov, Lemberg, Krakow, Kishinev, Riga, Vilna, Brussels, Paris, Berlin, New York City, Philadelphia, Chicago, Buenos Aires, Johannesburg, and beyond. In addition, the 290 Vilna Troupe members worked with a total of 132 theater companies over the course of their careers. This data offers insight into how the Vilna Troupe members were connected, socially and professionally, to other theater companies.

Users can also filter which Vilna Troupe members are shown in the center circle by gender, branch membership, and role. A second set of filters allows users to sort individuals who had second-degree connections to the Vilna Troupe by gender, field of influence (theater, film, literature, television, dance, etc.), and an impact rating that I assigned to track how famous these figures were. I assigned each second-degree connection artist a numerical rating on a scale from 1 (low) to 5 (high). The "high impact" category (impact rating of 4–5) includes those who made significant contributions to their fields that are well documented by historians. Most "high impact" individuals have merited numerous entries in other encyclopedias and reference works and all have met the notability criteria for inclusion in *Wikipedia*. For example, Stella Adler, Cary Grant, Eugene Ionesco, and Sanford Meisner all were assigned "high" impact ratings. "Low impact" individuals (impact rating 1–2) are either lesser known or have made smaller contributions to their fields. Most "low impact" individuals have neither encyclopedia entries nor *Wikipedia* pages. In my dataset, this category includes figures like Max Wiskind, Liza Schlossberg, and Paul Breitman. Those in the "medium impact" category received impact ratings of 3 and their names may be somewhat familiar to viewers. "Impact," in this schema, refers to historiographic impact, not necessarily historical impact; indeed, as I have argued in this book, these do not always line up. I assigned impact ratings simply to enable users to filter the visualization for names that are likely to already be familiar.

My visualization suggests that the Vilna Troupe was a central node in a vibrant artistic network that connected hundreds of influential artists around the world and across the twentieth century. The visualization also reveals how the members of the Vilna Troupe were transnational cultural conduits, connecting theater artists in Russia and Eastern Europe with their counterparts in North and South America, and vice versa. Stanislavsky, Meyerhold, Stella Adler, Leon Schiller, Max Reinhardt, David Belasco, Harold Clurman, Eugene Ionesco, and hundreds of other key figures worked alongside, were related to, were friends with, or were directly inspired by encounters with Vilna Troupe members. For example, director Dovid Herman maintained close friendships with many leading Yiddish writers of the day, including Peretz Hirschbein and Sholem Asch, as well as with Alexander Zelwerowicz, a major Polish actor and director of the period. Director Mikhl Weichert's friendships were firmly concentrated in the Polish avant-garde, including Juliusz Osterwa, Arnold Szyfman, and Leon Schiller.

Like all theater companies, the Vilna Troupe did not create in isolation. It was part of a complex web of entangled artistic collaborations, interpersonal relationships, romances, and networks of influence. Visualizing the Vilna Troupe at the center of a network of personal and professional connections reveals previously invisible relationships between theater practitioners who otherwise might have had little connection with one another.

For example, Stella Adler began her career performing in Yiddish with Maurice Schwartz's Yiddish Art Theater, alongside many Vilna Troupe members. A few years later, she enrolled in the Theater Arts Institute of the American Laboratory Theater, run by former Moscow Art Theater actors Richard Boleslavsky and Maria Ouspenskaya. It was there that Adler first encountered the Method acting techniques that became the foundation for her actor-training methods. It was also there that Adler met Lee Strasberg, her future Group Theater collaborator, and Harold Clurman, her future colleague and husband. Like Stella Adler, Clurman's first encounter with the stage had also been via the Yiddish theater, and he remained fascinated with the tradition for his entire life.[81] Helen Krich Chinoy has suggested that a shared love of Yiddish theater was what first brought Stella Adler and Harold Clurman together and helped spark their ideas for the Group Theater.[82] Meanwhile, Adler's career continued to intersect with the Vilna Troupe. In 1928 Adler starred opposite Luba Kadison in a production of Sholem Asch's *Di kishefmakherin fun Castille* (*The Witch of Castille*) at the Yiddish Art Theater. They became friends, and for years Kadison would meet Adler and Harold Clurman at the Café Royal on Second Avenue for coffee, dinner, and gossip.

Richard Boleslavsky, a former Moscow Art Theater actor and Adler's first acting teacher, had Vilna Troupe connections of his own. In 1923 Boleslavsky was a founding member of America's first Yiddish drama school, where he taught acting alongside former Vilna Troupe director Mendl Elkin and playwrights Peretz Hirschbein, Dovid Pinski, and H. Leivick.[83] A year later, the teachers and pupils of this Yiddish drama school formed their own Yiddish art theater called Unzer Teater (Our Theater).

Nearly everyone in the company was connected to the Vilna Troupe in one way or another: besides Elkin and the playwrights from the short-lived drama school, the founding members of Unzer Teater also included Vilner husband-and-wife acting team Chaim Shniur and Bella Bellarina and Egon Brecher, Dovid Herman's director friend from Vienna. Other members included an unknown but talented stage designer who had just immigrated to the United States named Boris Aronson. In an explicit nod to the Vilna Troupe, Unzer Teater opened with a production of one of its most successful plays: An-sky's *Day and Night*. The directors gave Boris Aronson free reign to experiment with the set, costumes, and lighting. None of them quite understood his strange ideas about design anyway.

When *Day and Night* opened in 1924, Aronson's designs catapulted him to instant fame. After designing for Maurice Schwartz's Yiddish Art Theater, the Artef Theater, and the Schildkraut Theater to steady acclaim, Aronson moved on to the English-language stage in 1932, working first for the Group Theater and then on Broadway, where he would go on to win six Tony Awards for designing hit musicals like *Cabaret*, *Company*, *Follies*, and *Pacific Overtures*. Aronson also famously designed the sets for the Broadway production of *Fiddler on the Roof*.

Aronson's designs were instrumental in bringing abstract sets to the mainstream American stage.[84] Robert Brustein called Aronson "the leader of a national movement."[85] Aronson was also responsible for training some of the American theater's most important designers.

In the 1950s, one of his Broadway apprentices was a young unknown named Ming Cho Lee. It was Aronson who first introduced Lee to the constructivist aesthetics of the Russian and German stage; years later, Lee would describe Aronson as "an outside comet that fell into the Western world."[86] Today, Lee is a Tony Award–winning designer and Yale professor. The American Theater Wing considers Lee to have exerted "a greater influence on American scenography than any other contemporary designer," and his former students include scenic designers Tony Straiges, Santo Loquasto, and John Lee Beatty.[87] Without the Vilna Troupe, there would likely have been no Unzer Teater to give Aronson his big break. Perhaps he never would have brought his unconventional ideas to American scenic design.

Aronson's approach to theatrical design was developed during his early career in the Yiddish theater, working alongside former Vilner in a company modeled after the Vilna Troupe. Aronson's conception of the stage as an artistic laboratory, his transnational aesthetic that drew equally upon Russian, Jewish, Polish, and German material for inspiration, his interest in visual abstraction, his technical prowess and ability to make beautiful sets regardless of budget—all came from the Yiddish art theater movement. The contemporary American stage thus owes significant debts to the Vilna Troupe for incubating Stella Adler's early acting training and for its influence on a young Boris Aronson.

A network model of the interwar stage that takes the Vilna Troupe as its starting point reveals whole centers of activity that were concentrated around particular individuals like Dovid Herman, who not only personally trained nearly every major Yiddish director of the interwar period but also maintained close professional ties to key figures in the Polish, Russian, and German theatrical avant-garde, or Yankev Blayfer. The members of the Vilna Troupe were global theatrical conduits, connecting theater artists in Russia and Eastern Europe with work that was happening in North and South America, and vice versa.

Other kinds of connections happened outside of the theater. Vilna Troupe actor Baruch Lumet, father of American film director Sidney Lumet, worked briefly at Camp Kindervelt, a Jewish overnight camp outside of New York City. One of the kids enrolled in his drama class was a young Martin Ritt, who drove his teacher crazy when he kept skipping rehearsal to play baseball. Years later, when the elder Lumet (who went by the nickname "Bulu") saw a Group Theater play, he was shocked to see Martin's name in the program.

> I pick up a program, I see "Martin Ritt." I said, "What in the devil is he doing there? That boy, he should be a ball player." I couldn't believe it, it's the same Martin Ritt. I go backstage. I said, "Martin, what in the devil are you doing here?" He said, "Bulu, you poisoned me."[88]

For Martin Ritt, those rehearsals that he laughed off at Camp Kindervelt stayed with him and set the direction of his future theater career.

There are many such stories of Vilner inspiring talented young people to enter the theater. For Judy Graubart and Manny Azenberg, it was seeing their uncle Wolfe Barzell, a former Vilna Troupe actor, perform on Second Avenue. Wearing his signature purple pants and a black beret, Barzell would take his niece and nephew backstage; inspired by their uncle's bohemian lifestyle, the siblings pursued theatrical careers as a comedian and a producer, respectively. Judy Graubart went on to star in the *The Electric Company* with Morgan Freeman, Rita Moreno, and Bill Cosby and to marry actor Bob Dishy. Manny Azenberg became a legendary producer who has produced almost every Neil Simon play since 1972, along with dozens of other Broadway plays and musicals.[89] In 2012 Azenberg received a lifetime achievement Tony Award for his contributions to the American stage. "Wolfie was the inspiration for everyone in the family to go into the entertainment business," Azenberg told me, "because who would have thought of it otherwise?"[90] The Vilna Troupe was the connective tissue that bound hundreds of important figures in the theater together, across language, geography, and time.

Part Three: Microhistory Redux

Over the course of its twenty-one-year tenure, nearly three hundred theater artists worked for the Vilna Troupe. Many performed with multiple branches of the company, frequently switching affiliations to suit personal or geographical preferences. Most also worked for other theater companies. It was highly unusual for a Vilner to work exclusively for the Vilna Troupe.

By and large, the Vilner thought of their affiliation with the company as a portable artistic identity. This Vilna Trope identity could follow an actor wherever he or she went, regardless of where or with whom or even in what language one was performing. The extreme geographical instability of Ashkenazic Jewry in this period made it nearly impossible for a Jewish actor to remain with a single company for long. Actors had to reevaluate their circumstances month by month and season by season. With only a handful of exceptions, even the most loyal Vilner cycled in and out of various Vilna Troupe branches while also performing variously for other Yiddish and Hebrew theater companies or on the non-Jewish stage.

Any reading of the Vilna Troupe that does not take the idiosyncratic movements of its individual artists into account would exclude a crucial dimension of its history. In fact, the rapid cycling of individual performers in and out of various Vilna Troupe branches was a primary way that the company forged connections with other theater artists. It was through individual defections that the company built a global network to disseminate its reputation worldwide.

Following the pathways of individual actors brings the full global dimensions of the Vilna Troupe's impact into focus. Though they traveled widely, the Vilna Troupe branches stayed within three geographical regions: Eastern Europe, Western Europe, and North America. Technically speaking, no Vilna Troupe ever performed east of Odessa, south of Bucharest, north of Vilna, or west of San Francisco. Yet individual Vilner frequently used the brand across a much larger terrain. It was not uncommon for a Vilner in São Paulo, Bulawayo, or Auckland to publicize his or her independent projects using the Vilna Troupe brand. When Alexander Asro and Sonia Alomis did a solo show in Glasgow in 1935 or in Buenos Aires or Mexico City in 1942, they billed themselves as "Founders and Principals of the World Famous Original Vilna Troupe" and prominently displayed the company's logo.[91] Husband-and-wife acting team Nokhum Melnick and Devorah Rosenblum did the same when they traveled through Argentina and Brazil, and local newspapers thanked the couple for bringing "the masterpieces of 'Vilner' theater art to the Jewish communities of South America."[92] These appropriations of the Vilna Troupe brand by former members may have been unofficial, but they were also a key way that the company built its reputation.

A series of maps at www.vilnatroupe.com depict the differences between the geographical pathways of Vilna Troupe branches and the individual travels of its actors. The first set of maps depict the pathways of the ten "official" Vilna Troupe branches:

- the original Vilna Troupe (1915–18)
- Alexander Asro and Sonia Alomis's Vilna Troupe (1918–26)
- Mordechai Mazo's Vilna Troupe (1918–35)
- American Revival Vilna Troupe #1 (1926–27)

- Waislitz, Buzgan, and Shapiro's Vilna Troupe (1926–27)
- the Bronx Vilna Troupe (1928–30)
- the Belgium Vilna Troupe (1929–30)
- Alex Stein's Vilna Troupe (1930–33)
- American Revival Vilna Troupe #2 (1932–33)
- American Revival Vilna Troupe #3 (1936)

But it is only when we add the performances of individual Vilner that we can see the full scope of the company's reach. The second set of maps shows how five individual actors navigated through the transnational artistic networks established by the company: Joseph Buloff and Luba Kadison, Shmuel Iris, Avrom Taytlboym, and Jacob Waislitz. Each was a longtime member of the Vilna Troupe who frequently used the company's name, logo, and repertoire to advertise solo performances and individual projects. Though unofficial, these activities were also part of the Vilna Troupe's geographical reach.

Mapping the career of Joseph Buloff, for instance, expands the territory of the Vilna Troupe's influence to include Argentina, Brazil, and Israel. If we add the trajectory of Jacob Waislitz, the territory expands again to include Sweden, South Africa, Zimbabwe, Australia, and New Zealand. Adding the travels of actor Avrom Taytlboym to the mix demonstrates how Vilner migrated back and forth between Eastern Europe, Western Europe, and the United States while performing with different branches of the company. Though no official branch was ever active in South America, Africa, or Australia, affiliated actors like Buloff, Taytlboym, and Waislitz traveled to these countries and staged classics from the Vilna Troupe repertoire, advertised their connection to the company, and displayed the Vilna Troupe logo in their posters and programs.

Let us briefly trace the career of one exceptional family of Vilna Troupe members: husband-and-wife team Jacob and Yokheved Waislitz, their actor son David Waislitz, their daughter Mila, and their son-in-law Moyshe Potashinski, all of whom performed together in Mazo's branch. The Waislitzes were not representative of the typical or "average" Vilna Troupe actor. Yet their careers offer important insight into how the Vilna Troupe went global through the travels of its individual artists. A microhistorical focus on this single family reconciles the gap between the collective phenomenon of the Vilna Troupe, as detailed in the previous chapters, and the idiosyncratic experiences of its individual artists.

Jacob Waislitz (1891–1966) and his family were among the most well-traveled members of the Vilna Troupe. The Waislitzes performed across Eastern and Western Europe, North and South America, sub-Saharan Africa, Israel, and Australasia, bringing a Vilna Troupe–inspired repertoire, methodology, and aesthetic to audiences across the globe. While most other Vilner were content to stick to the standard Eastern Europe–Western Europe–North America tour circuits (with the occasional southward foray), the dissolution of Mordechai Mazo's Vilna Troupe in 1935 inspired Waislitz and his family to seek new audiences in far-flung locales. And so, while their colleagues struggled to resurrect the Vilna Troupe in New York or tried unsuccessfully to relive the Vilna Troupe's "triumph march" across Western Europe, Waislitz's Vilner family made the Southern Hemisphere their home. In doing so, the Waislitzes brought new sectors of the Jewish world into conversation with the European-born Yiddish art theater movement. While the career trajectories of these actors were atypical for their extreme mobility, examining the Waislitz family demonstrates how the Vilna Troupe continued to exert a global presence even—and perhaps especially—after the company's official demise.

Born Avrom-Yankev Vayslits in a provincial Polish shtetl around the turn of the century, the young man who would become known as Jacob Waislitz was among the thousands of Jews who attended Y. L. Peretz's Yiddish theater symposium at the Warsaw Philharmonia in January 1910. At the time, Waislitz was nineteen, an impressionable young man who had just finished his secondary schooling and was unsure of his next step. Peretz, Nomberg, Vayter, and Mukdoni's speeches calling for the creation of a "better" Yiddish theater had a profound impact on Waislitz, who swore that from that moment forward he would "dedicate his life to the Yiddish stage."[93] When Peretz founded a short-lived Yiddish drama academy with the future Vilna Troupe director Dovid Herman, Waislitz was one of the first to join. After two years of study under Herman, Waislitz graduated the school in May 1915, just one month after Peretz's death. Unbeknownst to Waislitz and his classmates at the time, their graduation also coincided with the first stirrings of the Vilna Troupe.

In 1915 there was still not a single professional Yiddish theater company in Warsaw that Jewish intellectuals considered respectable. For a student of Peretz or Herman to join a *shund* theater was unthinkable, since such a move would have been perceived as a rejection of his or her training. Waislitz and his peers thus found themselves in professional limbo upon graduation. They dreamed of becoming Yiddish actors but there was no practical way to do so without horrifying their mentors. The students had been trained for a career that did not yet exist. Instead, Waislitz joined an amateur Yiddish drama club and took on various day jobs to pay his bills.

The First World War brought an end to Waislitz's ability to make a living wage working odd jobs. The young actor set out on the road performing one-man shows and staged readings across Eastern Europe. It was while traveling in 1916 that Waislitz first heard of the Vilna Troupe.[94] Little is known about Waislitz's activities during this period, but it is not inconceivable to imagine that rumors of a "better Yiddish theater" could have brought the itinerant young actor to Vilna, where he might have ventured over to the Circus Theater. Or perhaps he first encountered the company during its 1917 tour of the Polish countryside. On the road during the years of the Vilna Troupe's emergence, Waislitz was uniquely positioned to witness the rapid growth of the company's reputation firsthand.

Perhaps Waislitz even tried to join the Vilna Troupe and was rebuffed; early on, the company took few new members. But when Asro and Alomis founded their own Vilna Troupe in 1919 and took nearly half of the company's members with them, those who stayed behind under Mazo's leadership had to recruit dozens of new members to replace their departed colleagues. Jacob Waislitz was invited to join along with his actress wife Yokheved. At twenty-eight and thirty, respectively, Jacob and Yokheved Waislitz were nearly a decade older than most of their new colleagues, and they were among the few who were married. When Yokheved became pregnant with their first child, the Waislitzes became the first in the company to bear and raise children. For the adult members of the Vilna Troupe, the work and travel schedule was grueling. They would rehearse one play in the morning and another in the afternoon, then perform a different show each night. But for the children, it was paradise. Mila and David Waislitz would play hide-and-seek in the train cars that carried the costumes, sets, and props from one town to the next. While their parents rehearsed, they tried on costumes backstage and put on their own plays.[95] The members of the Vilna Troupe were their extended family; the stage and the train were their home, their school, and their playground.

The Waislitzes were also unusual in another way: they were among the few Vilner who remained loyal to a single branch. For sixteen years, between 1919 and 1935, Jacob, Yokheved, Mila, and David Waislitz traveled exclusively with Mazo's Vilna Troupe. Other actors came and went, but the Waislitzes stayed. The only other members of a Vilna Troupe company to remain with a single branch longer than a decade were Mazo and the actress rumored to be his lover, Miriam Orleska. As Jacob and Yokheved's children grew up, they too became Vilna Troupe actors. When eighteen-year-old Mila Waislitz fell in love with a fellow actor, Moyshe Potashinski, who was temporarily performing with Mazo's branch in the early 1930s, she convinced him to marry her and stay.[96] The Waislitzes continued to perform with Mazo's Vilna Troupe until the last curtain call of the final performance in 1935.

Still, the Waislitzes' loyalty did not stop Jacob from continuing to perform as a solo artist. Every summer during the Vilna Troupe's off-season, Jacob would leave his wife and children behind and set out on his own. On makeshift stages in taverns, lecture halls, restaurants, synagogues, barns, and private homes, Jacob would perform material drawn from the Vilna Troupe's repertoire in which he played all of the parts himself (of the fifteen plays he listed as his "recitation repertoire," thirteen had been staged by the Vilna Troupe, including *The Dybbuk*, *Carcass*, *Shylock*, *Day and Night*, *Kidush Hashem*, and *The Singer of His Sorrows*).[97] These off-season performances by itinerant Vilner like Waislitz were yet another way that the Vilna Troupe brand gained transnational currency.

The collapse of the Vilna Troupe infrastructure was by no means the end of the Vilna Troupe for the Waislitzes. Their Vilna Troupe identity was just as alive as ever. After the last performance of Mazo's branch in 1935, Jacob Waislitz became a professional Vilna Troupe solo performer. In a way, the dissolution of Mazo's company brought Waislitz newfound freedom; without having to plan his solo tours around the Vilna Troupe, he could travel anywhere that suited him so long as he could find an audience. In the two years immediately following the dissolution of Mazo's branch, Jacob Waislitz performed material from the company's repertoire in Poland, Austria, Czechoslovakia, France, Belgium, Holland, Denmark, Sweden, South Africa, Rhodesia, Canada, Brazil, and Australia.[98] In South Africa, Waislitz met up with fellow former Vilner Simkhe Natan and tried unsuccessfully to start a Yiddish drama school there; in 1933 Natan would start a Johannesburg Yiddish drama studio on his own. Waislitz returned in 1936 and started a second experimental theater studio in Johannesburg.[99] His work never stopped being inspired by the Vilna Troupe. "The people here will appreciate the creations of Jewish genius," he told reporters in South Africa, "if I should succeed in presenting them in the best tradition of the Wilno [*sic*] Troupe."[100] In Sydney, he billed himself as "Jacob Waislitz, Great Jewish Dramatic Artist—Star of the Vilna Troupe."[101] Meanwhile, Jacob's daughter Mila and son-in-law Moyshe Potashinski took their own two-actor revue across Poland, France, Norway, Denmark, Sweden, and Belgium, while Yokheved and David stopped performing temporarily and moved to Vilna.

In addition to these independent performances, Waislitz and his daughter each created a new theater company of their own modeled upon the Vilna Troupe. In Melbourne, Jacob Waislitz united the best talents of the Australian Yiddish theater scene in the Kadimah Art Theater, which he would later rename the Dovid Herman Theater after his lifelong mentor. When Waislitz's new company presented *The Dybbuk*, the director reminded spectators that the play was to be presented "according to the Vilna Troupe tradition."[102]

Mila and Moyshe founded their own company in Brussels, the short-lived Yiddish Folk Theater. Like the Kadimah Theater, the Yiddish Folk Theater adopted virtually the same repertoire, rehearsal methods, and aesthetic that Yiddish theatergoers had come to expect from the Vilna Troupe. The Dovid Herman Theater and the Yiddish Folk Theater, like many companies founded by former Vilner, were essentially new branches of the Vilna Troupe, virtually indistinguishable from the others except in name. In this way, the Vilna Troupe brand continued to exert a strong presence long after its dissolution.

Jacob, Yokheved, and Mila Waislitz continued to tour right up until the Nazi invasion of Poland. When the war broke out, the Waislitzes—like so many Vilner—found themselves stranded along the theatrical tour circuits that had been their home for decades. Stuck in Melbourne while on a solo performance tour, Jacob Waislitz was the luckiest of the clan. Together with another former Vilna Troupe colleague, Rokhl Holtzer, who was also stranded midtour in Australia during the war, Waislitz worked to build the Dovid Herman Theater. Meanwhile, his wife and son were stranded in Vilna with the German army fast approaching. In a daring attempt to reunite her family, Yokheved Waislitz and her son smuggled themselves to Moscow, where they boarded the Trans-Siberian Railroad and eventually made their way to Australia via Japan.[103] Her daughter Mila and son-in-law Moyshe, however, would not escape Nazi Europe unscathed. Mila and Moyshe continued performing in Brussels with the Yiddish Folk Theater right up until the Nazi invasion of Belgium in May 1940, at which point they went into hiding together with their fellow actors. Three years later, a neighbor betrayed them, and Mila and Moyshe were sent to Auschwitz. They both managed to survive and reunite with their family in Melbourne after the war.

Just as they had performed together with the Vilna Troupe in the 1920s and 1930s, the members of the Waislitz family continued to act together in the 1950s, 1960s, and 1970s in the Dovid Herman Theater. With Melbourne as their new home, the Waislitzes also continued to travel over the next few decades, keeping the Vilna Troupe's style and repertoire alive as they traveled across Australia, New Zealand, South Africa, Canada, the United States, Brazil, Argentina, and Israel. Under their influence, Melbourne became a major center of Yiddish theatrical activity in the postwar period, attracting dozens of Yiddish performers to the Dovid Herman Theater. More often than not, these visiting artists were also former Vilna Troupe members like Zygmunt Turkow, Ida Kaminska, and Jacob Rotbaum. Others, like Shmuel Dzigan and Yisroel Shumacher, knew the Waislitzes before the war from their professional connections to other Vilner colleagues. Decades after its demise, the Vilna Troupe remained instrumental in establishing Melbourne as a Yiddish theater center.

Rokhl Holtzer, Waislitz's colleague at the Dovid Herman Theater and a former Vilner herself, maintained active correspondence with her former Vilna Troupe colleagues around the world. Holtzer, writing from Melbourne, and former Vilna Troupe director Mikhl Weichert in Ramat Aviv, Israel, were especially close. Throughout the 1950s and 1960s, Holtzer and Weichert sent each other dozens of letters reminiscing about their Vilna Troupe past and commiserating about personal and professional problems. Holtzer and Weichert were so close that, judging from the letters, a reader might imagine that they were related. They talk about the birth of each other's grandchildren as "our grandchildren."[104] Most importantly, Holtzer and Weichert kept each other apprised about theater in their respective countries. Weichert provided Holtzer with detailed accounts of the Israeli theaters and their major productions, and Holtzer replied with information about every Yiddish production in Australia. Waislitz and Holtzer also kept each other updated about their mutual friends who had survived the war. Buloff was a successful Broadway actor in America. Reuven Rubin, their old set designer in Romania, had become one of Israel's most celebrated painters. Leyb Kadison and Dovid Likht continued directing for the Folksbiene in New York. Khavel Buzgan performed in the Ida Kaminska Theater in Warsaw. Even decades after the end of the last Vilna Troupe branch, the old Vilner networks were still making world theater.

Encompassing both the collective activities of multiple companies and the careers of hundreds of independent theater artists, the Vilna Troupe did not end in 1936 with the failure of Dovid Herman's New York *Dybbuk* production, or with postwar linguistic assimilation in America, or with

Hitler's annihilation of Eastern European Jewry. It was only with the death of its last surviving member (Luba Kadison, who died in 2006 at the age of ninety-nine) that the Vilna Troupe finally vanished as a living theater tradition, leaving behind a legacy of echoes that can still be felt today in the work of the countless actors, designers, and theater artists who fell under its spell.[105]

INTERLUDE IV

The Dybbuk in Auschwitz

In the fall of 1939 hundreds of Vilner lived in countries that would soon come under Nazi rule. Of the 290 Vilna Troupe members, at least 45 were murdered during the Holocaust. They died in the Warsaw Ghetto and the Lviv Ghetto, in Ponar and Majdanek, in Belzec and Auschwitz. Shmuel Sheftel perished in the Warsaw Ghetto. Khane Braz was killed in Treblinka. Alex Stein died in a Soviet prison. Yosef Kamen died during the war in Uzbekistan, probably of starvation.[1] Shloyme Kon was killed in Treblinka. Mordechai Mazo was killed in the Warsaw Ghetto uprising of April 1943. Miriam Orleska perished in Treblinka. Many others probably died alongside them, their fates unrecorded. I could not find any information about what happened to nearly a hundred Vilner during the war. Most likely, this was because they did not survive it.

Isaac "The Tsar" Samberg stayed in Warsaw in 1939 because his wife, fellow Vilner Helena Gotlib, was wounded by a German bomb. Samberg was convinced that the Russians would soon liberate Warsaw. In the meantime, he and Gotlib performed in the Warsaw Ghetto's Yiddish theater company Nay Azazel. Samberg, who had fought bitterly over billing order in the past, was listed second in the posters and programs. When a fellow actor asked him how he felt about having second billing, Samberg replied, "The era of the Tsars is over. . . . If only the war should end—and this will surely happen soon . . . I will make an effort to play with the best Yiddish artists, and everyone, with no exceptions, will be listed according to the alphabet."[2] Samberg never got the chance. He was killed in Majdanek in 1943.

Some Vilna Troupe actors were spared by the nomadic lifestyle that had given their theater its global reputation. It just so happened that Hertz

Grosbard went on tour with his wife, Vilner Frida Blumental, to Buenos Aires three weeks before the outbreak of the war. A well-timed trip saved their lives. Grosbard performed in Brazil, Chile, Argentina, Uruguay, and Bolivia during the war, then moved to the United States, Canada, and finally, Israel.[3]

Those who survived did not escape unscathed. At least seven surviving Vilner lost children in the Holocaust. At least two Vilner survived the war but died shortly thereafter of heartbreak. Adam Domb fled to Astrakhan, Russia, only to learn that his wife and only child had perished in the Lviv Ghetto. He had met his wife, actress Sonia Altboym, when they were traveling together with the Vilna Troupe; their daughter had been attending theater school in Lviv while Domb traveled as a solo performer. Domb had survived a perilous flight across Europe by foot, but he had a heart attack and died when he heard the news about his family.[4]

Simkhe Natan suffered a similar fate. When the Germans invaded Warsaw, Simkhe, his wife, Naomi, and their two children, Ida and Misha, fled to Lviv and became performers in the local Yiddish theater. When the Nazis took Lviv, Simkhe and his son, Misha, fled farther east to Rovne. But Ida had just given birth to a newborn baby, and it was not yet safe for her to travel. Naomi decided to stay behind to help her daughter and the baby escape. Miraculously, the two women and the infant slipped through German clutches and made it back to Warsaw, where they hoped friends would be able to help them get farther west. But it was no use. All three died in Treblinka.

Meanwhile, Simkhe and Misha fled to Russia and kept going east to evade the war. Simkhe performed in Kazakhstan, while Misha went back to Poland to fight the Germans as a partisan. Both survived. But in 1946 Simkhe finally learned that his wife, daughter, and grandchild had perished at the hands of the Nazis. He died shortly thereafter, reportedly of a broken heart, at the age of fifty-four.[5] Misha Natan was the only family member to survive.

In 1939 Mila Waislitz and her Vilner husband, Moyshe Potashinski, were a young married couple running a theater company in Belgium. When the Nazis invaded in May 1940, Mila and Moyshe went into hiding, joined the resistance, and kept performing, albeit underground in private homes. Three years later, they were betrayed and sent to Auschwitz.[6]

Still, they kept performing. They organized concerts in barracks at the transit camps. Upon her arrival in Auschwitz, Mila was recognized by her fellow inmates as a famous actress. Many of the women who slept beside her in the barracks had seen her on stage in the Vilna Troupe.[7] They begged her to perform, and perform she did, night after night, her shaved head wrapped with a scarf.[8] Her performances were so popular that the other inmates helped her hide during selections.[9]

A few months later, Mila was sent to Dr. Carl Clauberg's Block 10 as a subject for medical experimentation. Clauberg was trying to find a method for mass sterilization and injected acids in the uteruses of the women in Block 10 that caused severe pain and sometimes even death.[10] But still, Mila Waislitz performed. As Rebecca Rovit has documented, Mila even organized cabaret evenings in Block 10's operating room:

> Some of the women made gowns from bed sheets; they eventually staged a production so popular that it was repeated. Dr. Clauberg discovered the cabarets and the word spread to SS officers who attended the evenings. Waislitz gained protection and a reputation as a star.[11]

Meanwhile, Mila's husband, Moyshe Potashinski, was performing for the men on the other side of the camp. One day while hauling bricks, Moyshe began to chant the openings lines to *The Dybbuk*.[12] Soon he too began performing cabaret style every night in the barracks.[13] Somehow, Mila and Moyshe both survived, though Mila was never able to bear children as a result of the experiments conducted on her. After the war, they reunited with Mila's parents in Australia and kept on performing. When steady work in the Yiddish theater dried up, Moyshe became a dressmaker and a rag picker to make ends meet.[14] But still they performed—in cabarets and concerts, wherever they could, despite the circumstances. After all, what else was a Yiddish actor to do?

Epilogue

Jewish Theater, World Theater

In the archives of Vilna Troupe cofounder Alexander Asro, there is a pile of handwritten notes marked "Plan for the History of the Vilna Troupe." It is an outline for a book that Asro never wrote. The chapter outline is as follows:

> Foundations of the Troupe
> Instead of the horses is us
> No money, hunger. We put up our own posters.
> What is this Yiddish?
> First exam
> Success
> Kovne
> Grodne
> Warsaw
> Lodz tour
> Influence—disappearance of *shund*
> Berlin
> Leipzig
> Holland
> Antwerp
> Paris
> London
> America[1]

The first few chapters of Asro's book would have covered the Vilna Troupe's emergence during World War I, with a focus on the obstacles faced by the actors. (I imagine that the "Instead of horses is us" chapter might have included a detailed description of how they painstakingly cleaned the horse dung from between the boards of the circus-turned-stable-turned-theater). But then Asro's book would have followed the places where his Vilna Troupe performed, one after another. Looking back on his career toward the end of his life, Asro believed that the best way to demonstrate the Vilna Troupe's significance was to describe the scope of its geographical presence.

Writing these reflections in the 1960s, Asro was well aware that his life's work had already been mostly forgotten. Still, he believed that history would someday vindicate the Vilna Troupe.

> The Vilna Troupe was dissolved, but its soul, its spirit, lives and will continue to live. *It will awaken and demand its due*. For the Vilna Troupe was no mere episode, no mere flash in the history of Yiddish theater, but the beginning of a new epoch, a new era.[2]

With any luck, Asro concluded, future historians would someday "with reverence and love, restore the Golden Era of the Vilna Troupe," returning its "soul" to theater history, just like Khonen's spirit refuses to be parted from his predestined bride in *The Dybbuk*.[3]

The Vilna Troupe was a world theater whose influence touched virtually every corner of the globe where Jews lived between the wars. As Joseph Buloff quipped, interwar Yiddish theater was like the British Empire. Both were global powers that, as Chaim Shniur proclaimed of the Vilna Troupe, once had a "triumph march" across the globe.[4] Without a nation or a military to call their own, the itinerant artists of the Yiddish stage nevertheless laid claim to the grandest theaters of one country after another. Offstage, Jewish theater artists were subject to discrimination, forced eviction, and legal powerlessness. But on the grand proscenium stages where the Vilna Troupe performed to adoring fans who included some of the most influential artists and thinkers of the century, Jews had agency. In the theater, a Jew could be anybody he or she wanted to be. Offstage, Yiddish was illegitimate; onstage, Yiddish had a home. Yiddish culture may not have had a country of its own, but—for a brief moment in time—the Vilna Troupe's theatrical empire had the world at its feet.

Through the Vilna Troupe, Yiddish theater transcended the national, cultural, and religious divides of the period. For the first time in history, theater artists around the globe learned to accept Jewish theater as an important tradition and a welcome influence. The Vilner, as Luba Kadison told interviewers, did not simply want to make theater. They wanted "to have a theater in the Yiddish language," a theater "that would be very cosmopolitan but in Yiddish, with Yiddish plays, but also of the world repertory."[5] In short, they wanted a theater in their vernacular that would garner respect. In this they succeeded beyond their wildest dreams.

And yet, in the end, the Vilner vanished from history. At the end of their lives, most could no longer afford to be actors. They were door-to-door-salesmen and store owners and garment district workers. Only a few were able to make a career in the theater after the rapid demise of Yiddish culture after the Second World War.

Above all, the actors wanted their Vilna Troupe to be remembered. They inscribed odes to the company on their gravestones: "Vilner trupe! Mayn sheyner kholem" ("Vilna Troupe! My beautiful dream") reads Alexander Asro's, while Sonia Alomis asked her children to ensure that "Beloved Star of the Vilna Troupe" would appear as her epitaph.[6] They left handwritten instructions for future historians in their personal archives. They preserved every Vilna Troupe program, review, letter, and photograph in meticulously organized scrapbooks. They kept detailed records of tour schedules, repertoire, ticket sales, and production expenses. Others painstakingly copied every letter they wrote or received by hand. The Vilner firmly believed that their theater company had profound significance. They were not wrong. Still, I found many of their archives uncataloged and dusty, hardly touched since their original owners donated them. Bella Bellarina's archive at the YIVO Institute for Jewish Research, for example, was full of taped-up boxes that had never once been opened. Inside, amid dust, rusty paperclips, and disintegrating newspaper clippings, I found a treasure trove of reviews.

Others had no archives at all. I searched their names on Google and Ancestry.com and found relatives who graciously invited me into their homes and told me their grandparents' stories. Other descendants turned up in the most unlikely places. The great-grandson of Alexander Asro and Sonia Alomis—the spitting image of his great-grandfather and his namesake—just happened to be a student in an undergraduate course that I taught at Harvard. The material preserved by his family rivaled what I had found in any archive.

At the end of their lives, historical vindication eluded the Vilner. Still, they never stopped trying. Long after audiences and critics had turned their attention elsewhere, the Vilner were still fighting for a "better" Yiddish theater. Even after Sidney Lumet's film career took off, Baruch Lumet still dreamed of starting "a group of players to produce and put on plays based on Jewish literature."[7] In 1963 Joseph Buloff and playwright-screenwriter Irv Bauer tried to start a Jewish art theater in New York. Their proposal to potential funders included a list of plays of which half were from the Vilna Troupe's repertoire.[8] "We believe that there is a need for a special JEWISH THEATER CENTER in New York City," they wrote.[9] The venture failed, but Buloff still continued to espouse his vision of a Yiddish art theater revival. In one of his last recorded interviews, the eighty-year-old Buloff insisted to actor and director Jack Garfein that the Yiddish art theater "shouldn't get lost."

> BULOFF: If it's possible, if there are the people who have the energy and dedicate themselves to it—let me tell you something, it could bring about a tremendous response.
>
> GARFEIN: And it should be a Yiddish art theater.
>
> BULOFF: Yes, not the cheap—
>
> GARFEIN: Inspired by the Vilna Troupe.
>
> BULOFF: Yes. Not anything else. On this basis. And if we are presenting a play, maybe a little bit more advanced, as the theater is now. But basically, *on that principle*.[10]

Cosmopolitan and national, naturalist and modernist, local and global, literary and theatrical, simultaneously embracing and rejecting tradition—the Vilna Troupe negotiated between the seemingly irreconcilable tensions that tugged at modern Jewish life. The Vilna Troupe drew equally from two different ideas about the theater: eighteenth- and nineteenth-century notions of theater as an instrument of national cohesion and the cosmopolitanism of the twentieth-century art theater movement. The company never resolved the tension between these competing paradigms; instead it embraced both in tandem.

Like Lessing and Schiller, the eighteenth-century German architects of national theater ideology, the Vilna Troupe envisioned theater as a crucial site for nation building. This was, after all, the period when Jews began "to debate the parameters of Jewish nationhood" in earnest.[11] Performers and critics often invoked the Vilna Troupe as a symbol of Jewish national emergence. As one critic wrote in 1922,

> The theater of the Vilner is a part of our national art. . . . Today, when we will see the Vilner on our Vilna stage for the last time, we must proclaim: we wish the theater that they have built all the best, not only from one relative to another or from one Vilna resident to another, but as an ancient center of Jewish culture to the new flower in the flourishing garden of our national spirit.[12]

The Vilna Troupe symbolized the revivification of a national Jewish culture dormant since antiquity. As another journalist described the first performance of Mazo's Vilna Troupe in Antwerp,

> You walk into a Yiddish theater. And yet, one has the impression, one hundred percent, that you are sitting in a real theater—in a European theater that is Jewish, in a Jewish theater that is European. Here you are sitting in a theater where your face does not burn from shame but only from excitement. This is a Yiddish theater where we can open the doors wide and invite in cultured people, Jewish or non-Jewish. We have nothing to be ashamed of. We can be proud of this.[13]

The Vilna Troupe suggested that Jewish culture was just as rich and vibrant as the national cultures of other Europeans—a radical assertion at the time. The Vilna Troupe did not just perform Yiddish plays, it performed Jewish nationhood.

The Vilner may have subscribed to eighteenth-century ideas about the theater as a nation-building institution, but they were also thoroughly cosmopolitan. As a traveling theater company with an international fan base, the Vilna Troupe offered a prototype for spectators to imagine what kinds of global theater might be possible in an age of rapid travel and technological innovation.

When asked to describe what made the Vilna Troupe so important, Joseph Buloff replied, "The Vilna Troupe in its conflicting complexity reflects the Jewish community in its entirety."[14] Torn between nation building and cosmopolitan impulses, the Jews of Eastern Europe created a thriving modern Yiddish culture predicated upon this very in-betweenness. As Y. L. Peretz instructed his disciples in 1910,

> Ghetto means impotence. Interchange of cultures is the only hope for human growth. Man, the complete man, will be the synthesis of all the varied forms of national culture and experience.[15]

But he also wrote,

> Leave the ghetto, see the world—yes, but with Jewish eyes. He [the Yiddish writer] should consider his problem from a point of view that's Jewish. The ethical light in which he sees it must be Jewish. To have Jewish art, you need Jewish artists.[16]

A theater company like the Vilna Troupe could have emerged only within the idiosyncratic context of modern Jewish culture. It was this merging together of the national voice of a diasporic people with repertoire, acting techniques, directing styles, and design innovations culled from theater artists around the globe that propelled the Vilna Troupe to the forefront of the international theater scene.

What differentiated the Vilna Troupe from other theater companies of the period was not always what was on stage. Rather, it was how these artists approached theater making that set them apart. The Vilner envisioned theater as a kind of spiritual calling. Journalists loved to describe how every Vilna Troupe production occasioned "elaborate ritual preparations, like the Kohanim [high priests in the ancient Temple] preparing for their holy work."[17] In the estimation of another contemporary, it was this quasi-religious orientation that distinguished the company from all others:

> In the Vilna Troupe, a tremendous reverence for theater work prevailed. For them, theater frequently took on the character of religious service. This approach elicited tremendous reverence among audiences for their work. Their productions were sleek and refined. And this was crucial in creating the proper atmosphere around theater.[18]

The Vilner treated theater as secular holy work with national implications. To them, quality theater was a crucial step in the development of a fully fledged modern Jewish culture, which would, in turn, legitimize Jews in the eyes of other nations. Jewish intellectuals had long sought precisely this sort of public acceptance, but the genius of the Vilna Troupe was that it dramatized the struggle for Jewish cultural legitimacy in a public forum. Why was theater so important to Yiddish cultural activists of the interwar period? Because, as Vilna Troupe director Dovid Herman later reflected, theater offered Jews a rare opportunity to perform their national identity before a global jury of artistic peers:

> If theater is for all other peoples one of the most important national-cultural factors, it is for us, in our situation, the most important factor. A whole complete system of visible and invisible factors influence other peoples. The characteristics specific to that nation are expressed everywhere, even in the streets, not to mention museums, schools, theaters, and so on. . . . But we Jews live everywhere among foreign communities that influence us every day, every minute, consciously and subconsciously. And therefore, the theater question must be a matter of the utmost concern for us. Our theater ought to be a kind of smithy, where Jewish individuality can come into being. The better Yiddish theater ought to become for the modern Jewish community that which the synagogue was for the pious Jew in the past, its place of rest and refuge.[19]

The Vilna Troupe was not simply a campaign to reform Jewish theater. Rather, it represented the cultural, intellectual, and national aspirations of Eastern European Jewry between the two world wars. The central question that motivated the Vilna Troupe was the same question that haunted modern Jewish culture during this period: What ought to be the place of the Jew in the modern world? The Vilna Troupe suggested a compelling answer to this dilemma. It is possible to fuse together the past with the future, the religious with the secular, Jewish with European, folk traditions with high ideals, the Vilner told their audiences. In the world theater of the Vilna Troupe, one could be both Jewish and modern at the same time. This was the promise of the Vilna Troupe's theatrical revolution.

Notes

Prologue

Epigraph: Eleanore Lester, "Buloff Sees a 'Miracle' in Future of Yiddish Theatre," *Sentinel*, March 25, 1976, 48.

1. Max Weinreich, *History of the Yiddish Language*, trans. Shlomo Noble (New Haven, CT: Yale University Press 2008), 1:247–314.

2. Dr. Alexander Mukdoni, "Zikhroynes fun a yidishn teater-kritiker: Yidisher teater in Poyln fun 1909 biz 1915," in *Arkhiv far der geshikhte fun yidishn teater un drame*, ed. Jacob Shatzky (Vilna: YIVO, 1930), 341–421, at 354. All translations are my own unless otherwise indicated.

3. See Luba Kadison, Joseph Buloff, and Irving Genn, *On Stage Off Stage: Memories of a Lifetime in the Yiddish Theatre* (Cambridge, MA: Harvard University Library Judaica Division, 1992), 43–44; and Lisa Silverman, "Max Reinhardt between Yiddish Theatre and the Salzburg Festival," in *Jews and the Making of Modern German Theatre*, ed. Jeanette R. Malkin and Freddie Rokem (Iowa City: University of Iowa Press, 2010), 197–218.

4. See "Dovid Belasko shraybt tsu der 'Vilner trupe,'" *Forverts*, March 7, 1924, 7.

5. Dovid Lerner, "Di Vilner trupe in Brisl," *Literarishe Bleter* 7 (February 16, 1934): 97–98.

6. Shaw wrote, "In the name of art, I wish the Vilna Troupe every success." Israel Zangwill was also an admirer: "I took a very experienced English manager to see the Vilna Troupe. He was as full of admiration as of envy. 'If only I could get such actors,' he said, 'for the British drama.'" Program, *The Dybbuk* (1936), Program 175267A/4298, Box 60, RG 8, YIVO. On Ionesco's relationship to the Vilna Troupe, see Joseph Buloff, "How the Yiddish Theatre Invented Theatre of the Absurd," Folder BG22, Papers: Collection 5, Buloff Collection, Harvard Judaica Division. On Yiddish writers' support of the Vilna Troupe, see Moyshe Broderzon, "Der zinger fun unzer freyd iz 'Der zinger fun zayn troyer' bay der Vilner trupe," *Getseylte Verter*, September 13, 1929, 3–4; Yehoshua Perle, "Yidish teater," *Der Moment*,

February 7, 1933, 6; Itzik Manger, "Vilner trupe: Shabsay tsvi," *Unzer Vort*, March 9, 1926, 2–3; Itzik Manger, "Di beyde kuni-lemls: An epizod mit a komentar in azoy fil un azoy fil paragrafn," *Getseylte Verter*, August 23, 1929, 2–3; and Eliezer Shteynbarg, "Moshiakh iz gekumen: Tsur oyffirung funem *Mabul* fun Berger, *Di Frayhayt*, April 15, 1924, 2. On Max Nordau's interest in the Vilna Troupe, see "Maks Nordau vegn Dibek," *Teater un Kino*, November 10, 1922, 6. For Albert Einstein's thoughts on the Vilna Troupe, see "To the Directors of the Jewish Theater, Berlin," in *The Collected Papers of Albert Einstein*, vol. 12, *The Berlin Years*, ed. Diana Kormos Buchwald et al., trans. Ann M. Hentschel (Princeton, NJ: Princeton University Press, 2009), 158.

7. For example, in a single eight-year period (1914–22), Vilna changed hands nine times. Israel Cohen, *Vilna* (1943; repr. Philadelphia: Jewish Publication Society, 1992), 358–88; and Alfred E. Senn, *The Great Powers: Lithuania, and the Vilna Question, 1920–1928* (Leiden: E. J. Brill, 1966).

8. Jeffrey Shandler defines Yiddishland as "a virtual locus construed in terms of the use of the Yiddish language, especially, though not exclusively, in its spoken form." Shandler, *Adventures in Yiddishland: Postvernacular Language and Culture* (Berkeley: University of California Press, 2008), 33.

9. See S. E. Wilmer, "The Development of National Theatres in Europe in the Eighteenth and Nineteenth Centuries," in *National Theatres in a Changing Europe*, ed. S. E. Wilmer (New York: Palgrave Macmillan, 2008), 9–20.

10. See Luis Eduardo Guarnizo and Michael Peter Smith, "The Locations of Transnationalism," in *Transnationalism from Below*, ed. Michael Peter Smith and Luis Eduardo Guarnizo (New Brunswick, NJ: Transaction, 1998), 3–34 and Steven Vertovec, "Conceiving and Researching Transnationalism," *Ethnic and Racial Studies* 22.2 (1999): 447–62.

11. Christopher Balme, "Maurice E. Bandmann and the Beginnings of a Global Theatre Trade," *Journal of Global Theatre History* 1.1 (2016): 36.

12. Ibid., 43.

13. Ibid., 39.

14. See Marlis Schweitzer, *Transatlantic Broadway: The Infrastructural Politics of Global Performance* (New York, Palgrave Macmillan, 2015); and Leigh Woods, *Transatlantic Stage Stars in Vaudeville and Variety* (New York: Palgrave Macmillan, 2006).

15. Robert Gottlieb, *Sarah: The Life of Sarah Bernhardt* (New Haven, CT: Yale University Press, 2010).

16. Laurence Senelick and Sergei Ostrovsky, eds., *The Soviet Theater: A Documentary History* (New Haven, CT: Yale University Press, 2014), 203–4, 341–42.

17. Occasionally, the Moscow Art Theater was absent Moscow for an extended period, such as between September 1922 and May 1924. See Jean Benedetti, *The Moscow Art Theatre Letters* (New York: Routledge, 1991), 316. Between 1924 and 1956, however, the Moscow Art Theater only made one trip abroad, to Paris in 1937. See Nick Worrall, *The Moscow Art Theatre* (New York: Routledge, 1996), 4.

18. Emanuel Levy, *The Habima, Israel's National Theater, 1917–1977: A Study of Cultural Nationalism* (New York: Columbia University Press, 1979).

19. Shelly Zer-Zion, "The Birth of Habima and the Yiddish Art Theatre Move-

ment," in *Jewish Theatre: Tradition in Transition and Intercultural Vistas*, ed. Ahuva Belkin (Tel Aviv: Tel Aviv University, 2008), 73–88.

20. On Sergei Diaghilev's Ballets Russes, see Lynn Garafola, *Diaghilev's Ballets Russes* (Boston: Da Capo Press, 1998); Davinia Caddy, *The Ballets Russes and Beyond: Music and Dance in Belle-Èpoque Paris* (Cambridge: Cambridge University Press, 2012); and Juliet Bellow, *Modernism on Stage: The Ballets Russes and the Parisian Avant-Garde* (Burlington, VT: Ashgate, 2012). On the Ballets Russes de Monte Carlo and the Original Ballets Russes, see Victoria Tennant, *Irina Baronova and the Ballets Russes de Monte Carlo* (Chicago: University of Chicago Press, 2014); Vincente Garcia-Marquez, *The Ballets Russes: Colonel de Basil's Ballets Russes de Monte Carlo, 1932–1952* (New York: Knopf, 1990); and Katharine Sorley Walker, *De Basil's Ballets Russes* (New York: Atheneum, 1983).

21. Diaghilev's Ballets Russes never once performed in Russia and had no ties with St. Petersburg after 1909. Garafola, *Diaghilev's Ballets Russes*, vii.

22. Lynn Garafola, "Introduction: The Legacy of Diaghilev's Ballets Russes" in *The Ballets Russes and its World*, ed. Lynn Garafola and Nancy Van Norman Bear (New Haven, CT: Yale University Press, 1999), 7.

23. David Savran, "Trafficking in Transnational Brands: The New 'Broadway-Style' Musical," *Theatre Survey* 55.3 (September 2014): 318.

24. Ibid., 319 and 337.

25. Rebecca Kobrin, *Jewish Bialystok and Its Diaspora* (Bloomington: Indiana University Press, 2010), 5–6.

26. "Rekhtlozikayt un negishes fartrayben di Vilner trupe fun Varshe," *Haynt*, May 10, 1929, 10.

27. Roger Waldinger and David Fitzgerald, "Transnationalism in Question," *American Journal of Sociology* 109.5 (2004): 1177–95.

28. Solomon A. Birnbaum, *Yiddish: A Survey and a Grammar* (Toronto: University of Toronto Press, 1979), 41.

29. See Savran, "Trafficking in Transnational Brands," 318; and Laura MacDonald and Myrte Halman, "*Geen Grenzen Meer*: An American Musical's Unlimited Border Crossing," *Theatre Research International* 39.3 (October 2014): 198–216.

30. Oscar G. Brockett and Franklin J. Hildy, *History of the Theater*, 10th ed. (Boston: Pearson, 2008); John Russell Brown, *The Oxford Illustrated History of Theatre* (Oxford: Oxford University Press, 2001); David Wiles and Christine Dymkowski, *The Cambridge Companion to Theatre History* (Cambridge: Cambridge University Press, 2013); Phillip B. Zarrilli et al., *Theatre Histories: An Introduction*, 2nd ed. (New York: Routledge, 2010).

31. For example, see Don B. Wilmeth and Christopher Bigsby, eds., *The Cambridge History of American Theatre* (Cambridge: Cambridge University Press, 2000), 3:134, 498.

32. Margaret Werry, "'The Greatest Show on Earth': Political Spectacle, Spectacular Politics, and the American Pacific," *Theatre Journal* 57.3 (Oct. 2005), 357.

33. Edna Nahshon, "Overture: From the Bowery to Broadway," in *New York's Yiddish Theater: From the Bowery to Broadway*, ed. Edna Nahshon (New York: Columbia University Press, 2016), 28–30.

34. Judith Thissen, "Reconsidering the Decline of the New York Yiddish Theatre in the Early 1900s," *Theatre Survey* 44.2 (November 2003): 174.

35. See Michael C. Steinlauf, "Fear of Purim: Y. L. Peretz and the Canonization of Yiddish Theater," *Jewish Social Studies* 1.3 (Spring 1995): 44–65; and Barbara J. Henry, *Rewriting Russia: Jacob Gordin's Yiddish Drama* (Seattle: University of Washington Press, 2011).

36. Agnieszka Legutko, "Possessed by the Other: Dybbuk Possession and Modern Jewish Identity in Twentieth-Century Jewish Literature and Beyond" (PhD diss., Columbia University, 2012), 248–81.

37. Levy, *Habimah*, 290–92.

38. Worrall, *Moscow Art Theatre*, 58.

39. Joseph Buloff, Luba Kadison, Reuven Vendorf, Avrom Morevsky, Jacob Rotbaum, Bella Bellarina, Avrom Taytlboym, Jacob Ben-Ami, Leah Naomi, Noah Nachbush, Yankev Mestel, Chaim Shniur, Joseph Green, Mordechai Mazo, Alex Stein, Ida Garber, Mordechai Yachson, Ester Orzevskaya, Leonid Sniegov, Rivka Shiller, Moyshe Feder, Fela Biro, Yankev Kurlender, Dovid Likht, Ester Neroslavska, Leola Vendorf, Molly Pickus, Isaac Samberg, Helen Zelinskaya, Wolf Zilberberg, and Shloyme Krause.

40. Moyshe Feder, Yankev Gertner, Morits Norvid, Sara Rotbaum, Yosef Shayn, Lea Rotbaum, and Yankev Shidlo.

41. See David George, *The Modern Brazilian Stage* (Austin: University of Texas Press, 1992), 14–15 and Armando Sérgio da Silva, ed., *J. Guinsburg: Diàlogos sobre theatro* (São Paulo: Edusp, 1992), 70–72, 77, 95–106.

42. Former Vilner Josef Kaminski, Reuven Rubin, and Zalmen Hirshfeld worked with Habima; Hirshfeld also performed with Zavit. Zygmunt Turkow and Dovid Likht were guest directors for the Cameri Theater. Reuven Rubin designed for the Ohel Theater. Gertrud Kraus founded the Israel Ballet Company. Josef Kaminski was the concertmaster first violinist of the Israel Philharmonic Orchestra.

43. Monika Mokrzycka-Pokora, "Andrzej Pronaszko," Culture.pl, http://culture.pl/pl/tworca/andrzej-pronaszko

44. In London, a large number of theaters were built between 1866 and 1900. See Michael R. Booth, *Theatre in the Victorian Age* (Cambridge: Cambridge University Press, 1991), 7. In New York there was an unprecedented boom in theater building between 1900 and 1928. See Mary C. Henderson, "New York City Theatres" in *The Cambridge Guide to Theatre*, edited by Martin Banham (Cambridge: Cambridge University Press, 1995), 788.

45. For example, see the Vilna Troupe's program for *The Dybbuk* in Berlin in 1921, which featured a lengthy German synopsis. Folder 11, RG 729, YIVO.

46. Zalmen Zylbercweig, ed. *Leksikon fun yidishn teater*, 6 vols. (New York: Farlag Elisheva, 1931–69).

47. Marek Web, "Yiddish Actors Union," in, *The YIVO Encyclopedia of Jews in Eastern Europe*, ed. Gershon David Hundert (New Haven, CT: Yale University Press, 2008), 2:2058–9.

48. Correspondence with the International Union of Theatre Artists, 1927–1929, Box 1, Folder 240, RG 26, YIVO. I have found no other references to the International Union of Theatre Artists (IUTA) and it is unclear whether this cor-

respondence, which includes letters from the IUTA on official union letterhead, reflects a fully operational union or simply plans for a union that never came to fruition.

49. Finding Aid, RG 26, YIVO.

50. Ibid.

51. "Di Vilner in Nyuyork un di Nyuyorker in London," *Forverts*, February 22, 1924, 3; my emphasis.

Chapter 1

Epigraph: Jacob Ben-Ami, interview by Nahma Sandrow, December 1973, William E. Wiener Oral History Library of the American Jewish Committee, New York Public Library (hereafter NYPL).

1. Baruch Lumet, interview by Anita M. Wincelberg, December 12–20, 1976, Wiener Library, NYPL.

2. Ibid. The year was 1905.

3. Ibid.

4. Ibid.

5. See Nathaniel Buchwald, *Teater* (New York: Farlag Komitet Teater, 1943), 305–18; and Steinlauf, "Fear of Purim," 45.

6. Everett C. Hughes, *On Work, Race, and the Sociological Imagination* (Chicago: University of Chicago Press, 1994), 192–99.

7. Avrom Goldfaden's company is widely considered to be the first professional modern Yiddish theater, though some cite evidence of earlier efforts. See Nahma Sandrow, *Vagabond Stars: A World History of Yiddish Theater* (Syracuse, NY: Syracuse University Press, 1996), 40–69; and Jeffrey Veidlinger, *Jewish Public Culture in the Late Russian Empire* (Bloomington: Indiana University Press, 2009), 169. On early Hebrew theater, see Freddie Rokem, "Hebrew Theater from 1889 to 1948," in *Theater in Israel*, ed. Linda Ben-Zvi (Ann Arbor: University of Michigan Press, 1996), 51–84.

8. Alexander Mukdoni, *Teater* (New York: A. Mukdoni yuviley komitet, 1927), 10.

9. Cecile Esther Kuznitz, *YIVO and the Making of Modern Jewish Culture* (Cambridge: Cambridge University Press, 2014), 3.

10. Benjamin Harshav, *The Meaning of Yiddish* (Berkeley: University of California Press, 1990), 28.

11. David E. Fishman, *The Rise of Modern Yiddish Culture* (Pittsburgh: University of Pittsburgh Press, 2005), 6–8 and 18–19.

12. Sandrow, *Vagabond Stars*, 16.

13. See Baruch David Schreiber, "The Woman's Voice in the Synagogue," *Journal of Jewish Music and Liturgy* 7 (January 1984): 27–32; and Andrea Most, *Theatrical Liberalism: Jews and Popular Entertainment in America* (New York: NYU Press, 2013), 18–20.

14. See Evi Bützer, *Die Anfänge der jüddischen purim shpiln in ihrem literarischen und kulturgeschichtlichen Kontext* (Hamburg: Helmut Buske Verlag, 2003); and Ahuva Belkin, *Ha-purim-shpil: Iyunim ha-te'atron ha-yehudi ha-amami* (Jerusalem: Mosad Bialik, 2002).

15. See Joel Berkowitz and Jeremy Dauber, foreword to *Landmark Yiddish Plays: A Critical Anthology* (Albany: State University of New York Press, 2006), 9–10.

16. John Klier, "'Exit, Pursued by a Bear': The Ban on Yiddish Theatre in Imperial Russia," in *Yiddish Theatre: New Approaches*, ed. Joel Berkowitz (Oxford: Littman Library of Jewish Civilization, 2003), 168–70.

17. Mukdoni, "Zikhroynes," 341.

18. Sandrow, *Vagabond Stars*, 57.

19. See Veronica Belling, *Yiddish Theatre in South Africa: A History from the Late Nineteenth Century to 1960* (Cape Town: Isaac and Jessie Kaplan Centre for Jewish Studies and Research, 2008); and Irena Vladimirsky, "The Jews of Kyrgyzstan," Beit Hatfutsot, http://www.bh.org.il/jews-kyrgyzstan/

20. Klier, "Exit, Pursued by a Bear," 172–73.

21. N. Buchwald, *Teater*, 386–87.

22. Michael C. Steinlauf, "Polish-Jewish Theater: The Case of Mark Arnshteyn. A Study of the Interplay among Yiddish, Polish, and Polish-Language Jewish Culture in the Modern Period" (PhD diss., Brandeis University, 1988), 149.

23. Ruth R. Wisse, *I. L. Peretz and the Making of Modern Yiddish Culture* (Seattle: University of Washington Press, 1991), xiii–xvi.

24. Among these teenagers was a young Jacob Waislitz, who would later become a member of the Vilna Troupe. Yitzkhak Kahan, "Yankev Waislitz—The Veteran of the Yiddish Stage (to His 50 Years of Theatrical Activities)," Yiddish Melbourne, Monash University, http://future.arts.monash.edu/yiddish-melbourne/download/--documents/almanac-3-yankev-waislitz.pdf

25. Yitzkhok Turkow-Grudberg, *Varshe, dos vigele fun yidishn teater* (Warsaw: Yidish Bukh, 1956), 15–16.

26. See N. Buchwald, *Teater*, 305–18; and Steinlauf, "Fear of Purim," 45.

27. Dovid Pinski, *Dos idishe drama: Eyn iberblik iber ir entviklung* (New York: S. Drukerman, 1909), 56.

28. Henry, *Rewriting Russia*, 154.

29. Quoted in Steinlauf, "Fear of Purim," 49–50.

30. See, for example, Y. L. Peretz, "Oy, dales, dales!: Teater-felyeton" and "Dovid in der midber," in Peretz, *Ale verk* (New York, 1947), 7:174–77, 190–91.

31. Yitskhok Turkow-Grudberg, *Y. L. Perets—der veker: Tsu der 50-ter yortsayt* (Tel Aviv: Farlag Y. L. Peretz, 1965), 31–32.

32. Dr. Alexander Mukdoni, *Yitskhok Leybush Perets un dos yidishe teater* (New York: IKUF, 1949), 142.

33. Turkow-Grudberg, *Y. L. Perets*, 36–37.

34. Boaz Young, *Mayn lebn in teater* (New York: Ikuf farlag, 1950), 220.

35. Sandrow, *Vagabond Stars*, 209–10.

36. Young, *Mayn lebn in teater*, 222.

37. Mukdoni, "Zikhroynes," 347.

38. Ibid., 353.

39. Ibid., 353–54.

40. Turkow-Grudberg, *Varshe, dos vigele*, 15–16.

41. Ibid., 15.

42. Sheldon Cheney, *The Art Theatre: A Discussion of Its Ideals, Its Organization,*

and Its Promise as a Corrective for Present Evils in the Commercial Theatre (New York: Alfred A. Knopf, 1917), 56.

43. Mukdoni, "Fun yidishn teater," *Der Fraynd*, January 1, 1910, 4.

44. Turkow-Grudberg, *Y. L. Perets*, 54.

45. Mukdoni, "Fun yidishn teater," 4.

46. See Loren Kruger, *The National Stage: Theatre and Cultural Legitimation in England, France, and America* (Chicago: University of Chicago Press, 1992).

47. See Robert Welch, *The Abbey Theater 1899–1999: Form and Pressure* (Oxford: Oxford University Press, 1999).

48. T. Artsishevska, "Y. L. Peretz mont zayn teater," in *Dos amolike Yidishe Varshe biz der shvel fun dritn khurbn, 1414–1939*, ed. Melekh Ravitsh (Montreal: Farband fun Varshever yidn in Montreal, 1967), 100.

49. Steinlauf, "Fear of Purim," 46–47.

50. Turkow-Grudberg, *Y. L. Perets*, 29.

51. Steinlauf, "Fear of Purim," 50.

52. Zylbercweig, *Leksikon fun yidishn teater*, 6:5259–60.

53. Ibid., 3:1911.

54. Quoted in a letter from Stanislavsky to Vladimir Alekseiev, February–March 1906, Berlin, in Benedetti, *Moscow Art Theatre Letters*, 238.

55. There is some disagreement about whether Kaminski was actually involved with *Temptation*. Zylbercweig's *Leksikon* names Fishzon as the sole director ("Fishzon," in Zylbercweig, *Leksikon fun yidishn teater*, 4:3284). Similarly, Elinor Rubel claims that Fishzon and Kaminski broke off their partnership prior to the production. See Rubel, "Fishzon's Theater and the Premiere of Peretz's *Nisojen (Temptation)* in Warsaw (1906)," in *Teatr żydowski w Polsce: Materiały z międzynarodowej konferencji naukowej, Warszawa, 18–21 października 1993 roku*, ed. Anna Kuligowska-Korzeniewska and Małgorzata Leyko (Łódź: Uniwersytetu Łódzkiego, 1998), 113–26. Other sources, however, suggest that Kaminski did work on the production. Shmuel Niger wrote of Kaminski's involvement in his biography of Peretz. Peretz himself also wrote of Kaminski's involvement in the *Temptation* production. Nakhmen Mayzel, ed., *Briv un redes fun Y. L. Perets* (New York: IKUF, 1944), 248. Since Peretz and his main biographer ascribe a directorial role to Kaminski, I have chosen to follow their lead.

56. Zylbercweig, *Leksikon fun yidishn teater*, 3:1912.

57. Aron Albek, "Zikhroynes vegn Y. L. Peretsn," *Shtern* 16.10 (October 1940): 35.

58. Zylbercweig, *Leksikon fun yidishn teater*, 3:1916.

59. Bal-Makhshoves, "Der nisoyen: Drame in fir aktn fun Y. L. Perets," *Dos Yudishe Folk* 1.1 (May 15, 1906): 21.

60. Ibid., 22.

61. *Temptation* was never published and I have not been able to locate a manuscript of the version that was produced in Warsaw. My analysis of *Temptation* is based on its immediate antecedent, the Hebrew-language *Khurban beit tsadik* (The Ruin of the Sage's House), which was published serially in *Hashiloakh* between May 1903 and December 1903. By all accounts, Peretz's Yiddish *Temptation* was a translation of the Hebrew version with some modifications. Y. L. Peretz, *Khurban beit*

tsadik: Hashiloakh 11 (May 1903, June 1903): 471–74; 12 (December 1903): 566–70, 529–43.

62. Peretz, *Khurban*, 542.

63. Zylbercweig, *Leksikon fun yidishn teater*, 3:1913.

64. "Perets Hirshbayn (biografye)," in *Perets Hirshbayn (tsu zayn zekhtsikstn geboyrntog)*, ed. Shmuel Niger (New York: CYCO, 1948), 5.

65. Berkowitz and Dauber, *Landmark Yiddish Plays*, 52.

66. Shelly Zer-Zion, "Theater: Hebrew Theater," 2010, *YIVO Encyclopedia of Jews in Eastern Europe*, http://www.yivoencyclopedia.org/article.aspx/Theater/Hebrew_Theater

67. Quoted in Berkowitz and Dauber, *Landmark Yiddish Plays*, 55.

68. Peretz Hirschbein, *In gang fun lebn: Zikhroynes* (New York: Tsiko, 1948), 29–35.

69. Ibid., 45.

70. Eisig Silberschlag, "Hebrew Literature, Modern" in *Encyclopedia Judaica*, 2nd ed. (Detroit: Macmillan Reference USA, 2007), 8:718.

71. Hirschbein, *In gang*, 105.

72. Ibid.

73. See Peretz's letter dated January 30, 1907, to Kaminski in Mayzel, *Briv un redes*, 248.

74. Peretz Hirschbein, "In kamf far a besern teater," *Literarishe Bleter*, October 24, 1930, 800.

75. Dan Miron, foreword to *Tales of Mendele the Book Peddler: Fishke the Lame and Benjamin the Third* (New York: Schocken Books, 1996), xxii–xxiii.

76. See Joshua Fishman, "Czernowitz Conference" in Hundert, *YIVO Encyclopedia*, 1:384–85; and Kalman Weiser, introduction to Keith Ian Weiser and Joshua A. Fogel, eds., *Czernowitz at 100: The First Yiddish Language Conference in Historical Perspective* (Lanham, MD: Lexington Books, 2010), 1–10.

77. Quoted in Marie Schumacher-Brunhes, "Peretz's Commitment to Yiddish in Czernowitz: A National Caprice?" in Weiser and Fogel, *Czernowitz at 100*, 48.

78. See Max Weinreich, Zalmen Reyzen, and Khayim Broyde, eds., *Di ershte yidishe shprakh-konferets: Barikhtn, dokumentn un opklangen fun der Tsernovitser konferents, 1908* (Vilna: VIVO, 1931).

79. Hirschbein, "In kamf," 801.

80. Veidlinger, *Jewish Public Culture*, 187.

81. See David S. Lifson, *The Yiddish Theater in America* (New York: T. Yoseloff, 1965), 252–53.

82. Peretz Hirschbein, "Dos literarishe teater: Likoved dem finf un tsvantsikstn yubiley fun der Folksbine," 1940, RG 833, Folder 109, 24, YIVO.

83. Ibid., 24–25.

84. Veidlinger, *Jewish Public Culture*, 187. Veidlinger counts fourteen plays but does not include *Shadkhonim*.

85. Yankev Mestel, *Literatur un teater* (New York: IKUF, 1962), 95.

86. See Nokhem Oyslender, *Yidisher teater, 1887–1917* (Moscow: Der emes, 1940), 240–42.

87. For example, see Y. Korohodski, "Peretz Hirshbayns literarish-kinstlerishe drame in Yekaterinoslav," *Idishe Tsaytung*, June 24, 1909, 2; and M. K., "Dos yidishe teater in Yekaterinoslav," *Idishe Tsaytung*, May 19, 1909, 3.

88. Steinlauf, "Fear of Purim," 45.

89. Mukdoni, "Zikhroynes," 371.

90. Ibid., 151–152.

91. Sandrow, *Vagabond Stars*, 203.

92. See the front-page advertisement for the symposium that appeared in *Fraynd* on January 5, 1910.

93. "A groyse farzamlung vegn yidishn teater," *Fraynd*, January 10, 1910, 1.

94. Turkow-Grudberg, *Y. L. Perets*, 30.

95. Ibid.

96. Quoted in Leyb Kadison, "A bisl zikhroynes," *Literarishe Bleter* 36 (September 4, 1931): 692.

97. Bal-Makhshoves, "Shtrikhn un gedanken—Perets Hirshbayns trupe," *Fraynd*, February 25, 1910, 2.

98. Avrom Reyzen, "Di vanderndike yidishe trupe," in Niger, *Perets Hirshbayn*, 205.

99. Mukdoni, *Yitskhok Leybush Perets*, 168.

100. Ibid., 381.

101. Zylbercweig, *Leksikon fun yidishn teater*, 3:2020.

102. Mukdoni, "Zikhroynes," 381–2.

103. Mukdoni, *Yitskhok Leybush Perets*, 171.

104. See, for example, Mukdoni, "Fun yidishn teater: Peretz Hirschbayn's trupe," *Der Fraynd*, March 5, 1910, 4; Mukdoni, "Der sakhakol vegn Perets Hirshbayn's trupe," *Der Fraynd*, March 10, 1910, 4; and Iks [Noah Prilutski, pseud.], "Fun yidishn teater," *Unzer Lebn*, March 3, 1910, 3.

105. Hirschbein, *In gang*, 389.

106. See Peretz Hirschbein, "Varshe: der letster akt fun mayn teater-trupe" in Ravitsh, *Dos amolike Yidishe Varshe*, 236–39.

107. Mukdoni, "Zikhroynes," 380.

108. "Oyfgehert tsu ekzistirn Hirshbayns trupe," *Gut Morgen* (Odessa), July 12, 1910, 3.

109. Mukdoni, "Zikhroynes," 379.

110. N. Buchwald, *Teater*, 387.

111. Peretz Hirschbein, "Eliyahu hanovi, oder der letster etap," unpublished manuscript, September 1930, RG 833, Folder 116, YIVO; my emphasis.

112. Mukdoni, *Yitskhok Leybush Perets*, 176.

113. Noyekh Prilutski, *Yidish teater: 1905–1912* (Bialystok: A. Albek, 1921), 63; original emphasis.

114. These fundraising trips were supported by an existing network of Jewish literary societies. See Veidlinger, *Jewish Public Culture*, 192–94.

115. Sandrow, *Vagabond Stars*, 207.

116. Shmuel Niger, *Y. L. Perets: Zayn lebn, zayn firndikn perzenlekhkayt* (Buenos Aires: Congress for Jewish Culture, 1952), 429.

117. Ibid.
118. On the "American Period" in Polish Yiddish theater between 1910 and 1913, see Mukdoni, *Yitskhok Leybush Perets*, 178.
119. On *Dos pintele yid* in Warsaw, see Nina Warnke, "Going East: The Impact of American Yiddish Plays and Players on the Yiddish Stage in Czarist Russia, 1890–1914," *American Jewish History* 92.1 (March 2004): 20–25. On *Dos pintele yid* in the American Yiddish theater, see Nina Warnke, "Theater as Educational Institution: Jewish Immigrant Intellectuals and Yiddish Theater Reform" in *The Art of Being Jewish in Modern Times*, eds. Barbara Kirshenblatt-Gimblett and Jonathan Karp (Philadelphia: University of Pennsylvania Press, 2008.), 23–41.
120. Mukdoni, *Yitskhok Leybush Perets*, 201.
121. Ibid., 199–200.
122. Ibid., 225.
123. Chone Shmeruk, "Aspects of the History of Warsaw as a Yiddish Literary Center," *Polin* 3 (1988): 152.
124. See Niger, Y. L. *Perets*, 432; and Turkow-Grudberg, *Y. L. Perets*, 27.
125. Martin Puchner, *Poetry of the Revolution: Marx, Manifestos, and the Avant-Gardes* (Princeton, NJ: Princeton University Press, 2006), 196–97.
126. Turkow-Grudberg, *Y. L. Perets*, 33.
127. Veidlinger, *Jewish Public Culture*, 181. The Pale of Settlement refers to "the territory between the Black and Baltic Seas to which a majority of Russia's Jews had been legally restricted since the time of Catherine the Great." Nathanial Deutsch, *The Jewish Dark Continent: Life and Death in the Russian Pale of Settlement* (Cambridge, MA: Harvard University Press, 2011), 1.
128. On efforts to reform the Yiddish theater in New York, see Nina Warnke, "Reforming the New York Yiddish Theater: The Cultural Politics of Immigrant Intellectuals and the Yiddish Press, 1887–1910" (PhD diss., Columbia University, 2001).
129. Leyb Kadison, "A bisl zikhroynes," *Literarishe Bleter* 36 (September 4, 1931): 692.
130. A. H. Bialin, *Moris Shvarts un der idisher kunst teater* (New York: Biderman, 1934), 10.

Chapter 2

Epigraph: Joseph Buloff, interview by Jack Garfein, June 30, 1980, tape recording JSCRC 236 (10), Joseph Buloff Jewish Theater Archive, Harvard Judaica Division.

1. Luba Kadison, interview by Louise Cleveland, 1980, tape recording JSCRC 236 (4–6). Buloff Archive, Harvard Judaica Division.
2. Ibid.
3. Kadison, Buloff, and Genn, *On Stage Off Stage*, 3.
4. Luba Kadison, interview by Clifford Chanin, October 29 and November 8, 1978, Wiener Library, NYPL.
5. David S. Lifson, "The History of the Yiddish Art Theatre Movement in New York from 1918 to 1940" (PhD diss., New York University, 1962), 281.

6. Sandrow, *Vagabond Stars*, 211. Joseph Lateiner (1853–1935), ("Professor") Moyshe Ha-Levi Ish Hurwitz (d. 1910), and Shomer [Nokhem Meyer Shaikevitch, pseud.; 1849–1905] were three of the most popular Yiddish playwrights of the nineteenth century and were associated with *shund* by Peretz. Sandrow, *Vagabond Stars*, 104–7.

7. "Because there were no Jewish drama schools," Vilna Troupe director Mikhl Weichert wrote in his memoirs, "the dramatic societies were the only reservoir of young talent for the professional stage." Weichert also noted that only wealthy Jews could afford to study in Russian or Polish drama academies. The Yiddish drama societies, on the other hand, offered a free theatrical education. Mikhl Weichert, *Zikhroynes* (Tel Aviv: Farlag Menorah, 1961), 2:26.

8. Dovid Ber Tirkel, *Di yugntlekhe bine: Geshikhte fun di idish-hebreishe dramatishe gezelshaftn, 1890–1940* (Philadelphia: Hebrew Literature Society, 1940), 38.

9. Halina Chybowska, "Dovid Herman and the Jewish Theatre in Poland," *Polish Review* 4.19 (May 17, 1944): 11–12; and Zylbercweig, *Leksikon fun yidishn teater*, 1:634–35.

10. Zylbercweig, *Leksikon fun yidishn teater*, 1:184.

11. Leyb Kadison, "Amatorn un profesioneln" in *Finf un tsvantsik yor folksbiene*, ed. Yankev Fishman, B. Levin, and B. Stabinovitsh (New York: Posy-Shoulson Press, 1940), 47–48.

12. Tens of thousands of Jews were expelled from Kovne, Grondo, Suvalk, and other towns. Most came to Vilna. Cohen, *Vilna*, 362.

13. Luba Kadison, interview by Louise Cleveland, 1980, tape recording JSCRC 236 (4–6), Buloff Archive, Harvard Judaica Division.

14. Cohen, *Vilna*, 362.

15. Luba Kadison, interview with Chanin, Wiener Library, NYPL.

16. Leyb Kadison, "A bisl zikhroynes," *Literarishe Bleter* 36 (September 4, 1931):, 693.

17. See Mendl Elkin, "Di Vilner," *Tealit* 4 (February 1924), 16; and Shane Baker, "Beginnings of the Vilna Troupe: Jewish and German Politics in the Formation of a Yiddish Art Theater" (MA thesis, University of Texas at Austin, 2002), 10–11.

18. Mendl Elkin, "FADA: Tsum tsvantsik yorikn yovl fun der Vilner trupe," *Bodn* 3.1 (Spring/Summer 1936), 111.

19. Leyb Kadison, "A bisl zikhroynes," *Literarishe Bleter* 36 (September 4, 1931): 693.

20. Cohen, *Vilna*, 360–64.

21. Jacob Wygodski, *In shturem: Zikhroynes fun di okupatsye tsaytn* (Vilna: B. Kletskin, 1926), 39–40.

22. Ibid.

23 Ibid., 36–41.

24. Leyb Kadison, "A bisl zikhroynes," *Literarishe Bleter* 38 (September 18, 1931): 733.

25. Ibid., *Literarishe Bleter* 36 (September 4, 1931), 693.

26. Leyzer Ran, *Vilna, Jerusalem of Lithuania*, Fourth Annual Avrom-Nokhem Stencl Lecture in Yiddish Studies (Oxford: Oxford Centre for Postgraduate He-

brew Studies, 1987). On Vilna's literary reputation, see Shmuel Rozshanski, ed., *Vilne in der yidisher literatur* (Buenos Aires: YIVO in Argentina, 1980); and Justin Cammy, foreword to *Vilna, My Vilna: Stories*, by Abraham Karpinowitz (Syracuse: Syracuse University Press, 2015), xi–xvii.

27. Baker, "Beginnings of the Vilna Troupe," 3–4

28. Wygodski, *In shturem*, 43.

29. Chaim Shniur, "Zikhroynes vegn der Vilner trupe," RG 574, Box 4, 8, YIVO.

30. Leyb Kadison, "A bisl zikhroynes," *Literarishe Bleter*, 38 (September 18, 1931): 733.

31. Baker, "Beginnings of the Vilna Troupe," 46–51.

32. Luba Kadison, untitled lecture on the Vilna Troupe, Papers Collection 3, Folder LK/Lecture/Vilna Troupe, July 2, 1985, 4, Buloff Archive, Harvard Judaica Division.

33. Zylbercweig, *Leksikon fun yidishn teater*, 1:704–17.

34. Luba Kadison, interview by Chanin, Wiener Library, NYPL.

35. Luba Kadison, interview by Cleveland, Buloff Archive, Harvard Judaica Division.

36. Leyb Kadison, "A bisl zikhroynes," *Literarishe Bleter* 36 (September 18, 1931): 732.

37. Luba Kadison, interview with Chanin, Wiener Library, NYPL.

38. Chaim Shniur, "On a nomen: A bintl zikhroynes vegn der Vilner trupe," *Literarishe Bleter*, August 25, 1929, 661.

39. Luba Kadison, interview by Lea Shlanger, 1987, tape recording JSCRC 236 (1), Buloff Archive, Judaica Division.

40. Leyb Kadison, "A bisl zikhroynes," *Literarishe Bleter* 36 (September 18, 1931): 732.

41. Ibid., 733.

42. Ibid., 732.

43. Shniur, "Zikhroynes," 17, YIVO.

44. See, for example, Zalmen Reyzen, "Der yidisher teater in Vilna," in *Vilner zamelbukh*, ed. Tsemakh Shabad (Vilna: M. Rosental, 1918), 2:165.

45. Kadison, Buloff, and Genn, *On Stage Off Stage*, 8.

46. Leyb Kadison, "A bisl zikhroynes," *Literarishe Bleter* 39 (October 2, 1931): 772.

47. Ibid.

48. Alexander Asro, "Der onheyb," in *Yidisher teater in Eyrope tsvishn beyde velt milkhomes: Poyln*, ed. Itzik Manger, Yonas Turkow, and Moyshe Perenson (New York: Congress for Jewish Culture, 1968), 24.

49. Leyb Kadison, "A bisl zikhroynes," *Literarishe Bleter* 39 (October 2, 1931): 772.

50. Ibid.

51. Ibid.

52. Cohen, *Vilna*, 363–64.

53. Ibid., 363.

54. Ibid., 369.

55. Leyb Kadison, "A bisl zikhroynes," *Literarishe Bleter* 42 (October 16, 1931): 800–801.

56. Ibid., 801.

57. Asro, "Der onheyb," 24.

58. The original program for *Der landsman* at the Circus Theater is preserved as Program 175345 in Box 41, RG 8, YIVO.

59. Quoted in Baker, "Beginnings of the Vilna Troupe," 17.

60. Leyb Kadison, "A bisl zikhroynes," *Literarishe Bleter* 42 (October 16, 1931): 801.

61. Sammy Gronemann, *Hawdoloh und Zapfenstreich: Erinnerungen an die ostjüdische etappe, 1916–18* (Berlin: Jüdischer Verlag, 1924), 77. On Gronemann's travelogue in the context of German Jewish travel writing of the period, see Wesley Todd Jackson, "Where Do We Go from Here?: Tortured Expressions of Solidarity in the German Jewish Travelogues of the Weimar Republic" (PhD diss., University of Cincinnati, 2015), 234–300.

62. Gronemann, *Hawdoloh und Zapfenstreich*, 80.

63. Ibid., 198–99.

64. Ibid.

65. On these writers and their impressions of Eastern European Jewry, see David Midgley, "The Romance of the East: Encounters of German-Jewish Writers with Yiddish-Speaking Communities, 1916–27," in *The Yiddish Presence in European Literature: Inspiration and Interaction*, ed. Ritchie Robertson and Joseph Sherman (London: European Humanities Research Centre, 2005), 87–98.

66. Gronemann, *Hawdoloh und Zapfenstreich*, 198–99.

67. Ibid., 80; and Elkin, "FADA," 111.

68. See "Appendix D: Partial Production History" in Baker, "Beginnings of the Vilna Troupe," 57–60; and S. Gelbart, ed., *15 yor Vilner trupe: Zamlung lekoved 15 yorikn yoyvl fun der "Vilner trupe"* (Lodz, 1931), 21–23. FADA's initial repertoire included plays by Sholem Asch (*Der landsman*, *Got fun nekome*, *Mitn shtrom*, *Yikhes*), Peretz Hirschbein (*Farvorfene vinkl*), H. D. Nomberg (*Di mishpokhe*), Mark Arnshteyn (*Der vilner balebesl*, *Dos eybike lid*), Leon Kobrin (*Der dorfsyung*), Jacob Gordin (*Got, mentsh un tayvl*, *Der umbakanter*), Dovid Pinski (*Di gliks-fargesene*), Y. L. Peretz (*Din toyre mitn vint*), and others.

69. Elkin, "FADA," 111.

70. Baker, "Beginnings of the Vilna Troupe," 18.

71. Oscar Wilde, *Complete Works of Oscar Wilde*, 3rd ed. (Glasgow: HarperCollins, 1994), 47–48.

72. The Vilna Troupe's founding coincided with German expressionism's emergence as a theater movement. See David F. Kuhns, *German Expressionist Theatre: The Actor and the Stage* (Cambridge: Cambridge University Press, 1997), 4.

73. Leyb Kadison, set design for act 2 of *Got fun nekome*, RG 729, Box 2, Folder "Scenic Projects," YIVO.

74. The first mention in a German newspaper I was able to find is an announcement that appeared in *Zeitung der 10. Armee* on February 17, 1916 ("Eröffnung des jüdischen Theaters"), 3.

75. Curt Winter, "Jüdisches Theater," *Zeitung der 10. Armee*, February 22, 1916, 8.

76. Curt Pabst, "Jüdisches Theater," *Zeitung der 10. Armee*, March 7, 1916, 8.

77. For additional articles in army newspapers and magazines, see Hermann Struck, "Das Jüdische Theater in Wilna," *Korrespondenz B*, November 8, 1916; Erich Weferling, "Jüdisches Theater in Subat," *Zeitung der 10. Armee*, February 21, 1918, 4; and Erich Weferling, "Jüdisches Theater in Subat," *Zeitung der 10. Armee*, February 22, 1918, 4.

78. Hans Goslar, "Das Jüdische Theater in Wilna," *Zeitbilder*, October 7, 1917, AR 2371, Folder 3, Leo Baeck Institute, digitized at http://www.archive.org/stream/jewishtheaterf003#page/n2/mode/1up

79. Vejas G. Liulevicius, *War Land on the Eastern Front: Culture, National Identity, and German Occupation in World War I* (Cambridge: Cambridge University Press, 2000), 139.

80. Ibid., 138; and *Das land Ober Ost: Deutsche Arbeit in den Verwaltungsgebieten Kurland, Litauen, und Bialystok-Grodno* (Berlin: Presseabteilung Ober Ost, 1917), 423–24.

81. Herbert Eulenberg, "Jüdisches Theater," *Vossische Zeitung*, April 22, 1917.

82. Freidrich von Wilpert for the *Wilnaer Zeitung*, quoted in Joachim Hemmerle, "Jiddisches Theater im Spiegel Deutschsprachtiger Kritik von der Jahrhundertwende bis 1928—eine Dokumentation," in *Beter und Rebellen: Aus 1000 Jahren Judentum in Polen*, ed. Michael Brock (Frankfurt am Main: Deutscher Koordinierungsrat der Gesellschaften für Christlich-Jüdische Zusammenarbeit, 1983), 289.

83. "Gastspiel des Wilnaer jiddischen Theaters in Berlin," *Tageblatt*, February 2, 1918.

84. Leyb Kadison, "A bisl zikhroynes," *Literarishe Bleter* 45 (November 6, 1931): 853–54.

85. Gennady Estraikh, "Vilna on the Spree: Yiddish in Weimar Berlin," *Aschkenas* 16 (2006), 107.

86. Jackson, "Where Do We Go from Here?," 239.

87. Cohen, *Vilna*, 364–68.

88. Ibid., 368.

89. Ibid., 369.

90. Leyb Kadison, "A bisl zikhroynes," *Literarishe Bleter* 45 (November 6, 1931): 853.

91. Asro, "Der onheyb," 4.

92. See David J. Fine, *Jewish Integration in the German Army in the First World War* (Boston: De Gruyter, 2012), 95–128.

93. Gronemann, *Hawdoloh und Zapfenstreich*, 199–200.

94. Y. Honig, "Alomis un Asro (a vort tsu zeyer kumen keyn London)," printed in the program for the Vilna Troupe's 1921-22 production of *The Dybbuk* at the Kommandantenstrasse Theater in Berlin, RG 729, Folder 11, YIVO.

95. Ibid., 2.

96. Y. Shulman, "Yidishe gezelshaft vu bistu?," in *15 yor "Vilner trupe": Zamlung lekoved 15 yorikn yoyvl fun der "Vilner trupe,"* ed. S. Gelbart (Lodz, 1931), 18.

97. Kadison, Buloff, and Genn, *On Stage Off Stage*, 26.

98. Shmeruk, "Aspects of the History of Warsaw," 140–55.

99. Piotr Wróbel, "The First World War—The Twilight of Jewish Warsaw," in

The Jews in Warsaw: A History, ed. Władysław T. Bartoszewski and Antony Polonsky (Oxford: Basil Blackwell, 1991), 278–90.

100. Shmeruk, "Aspects of the History of Warsaw," 151.

101. Ibid.

102. Ida Kaminska, *My Life, My Theater* (New York: Macmillan, 1973), 27.

103. Yitskhok Turkow-Grudberg, *Yidish teater in Poyln* (Warsaw: Yidish Bukh, 1951), 46; and Gronemann, *Hawdoloh und Zapfenstreich*, 201–2.

104. Alexander Asro, "Dray Septembers . . . (Teater-zikhroynes un gedanken)," September 1944, RG 729, Box 1, Folder 5, YIVO.

105. Leyb Kadison, "A bisl zikhroynes," *Literarishe Bleter* 43 (October 23, 1931): 818.

106. See Shniur, "On a nomen," 662; and Asro, "Der onheyb," 29. There is a slight discrepancy between Asro and Shniur about the date of Nomberg's visit.

107. Waislitz, "Der gang in der velt," in *Yidisher teater in Eyrope tsvishn beyde velt milkhomes: Polyn*, ed. Itzik Manger, Yonas Turkow, and Moyshe Perenson (New York: Congress for Jewish Culture, 1968), 37.

108. Asro, "Der onheyb," 29–30.

109. Ibid.

110. Ibid., 30.

111. Gronemann, *Hawdoloh und Zapfenstreich*, 202.

112. Asro, "Dray Septembers," 3, YIVO.

113. H. D. Nomberg, "Vokhedike shmuesn: Di Vilner trupe," *Der Moment*, October 5, 1917, 3.

114. Ibid.

115. Ibid.

116. Justin Cammy, "Yung-Vilne: A Cultural History of a Yiddish Literary Group in Interwar Poland" (PhD diss., Harvard University, 2003), 5.

117. For example, see the 1920 program for Andreyev's *Der vos krigt di petsh*, directed by Leyb Kadison, RG 8, Vilna Troupe Programs, Box 41, Program 175199, YIVO.

118. Gronemann, *Hawdoloh und Zapfenstreich*, 203.

119. For example, see Asro, "Dray Septembers," 2–4, YIVO; Shniur, "On a nomen," 662; and Sandrow, *Vagabond Stars*, 216.

120. D. Druk, "Di tsveyte forshtelung fun der Vilner trupe," *Der Moment*, October 7, 1917, 5.

121. Waislitz, "Der gang in der velt," 38.

122. Luba Kadison, interview by Cleveland, Buloff Archive, Harvard Judaica Division.

123. Shniur, "Zikhroynes," 11, YIVO.

124. M. Vagvild, "Guts un shlekhts vegn di Vilner," *Dos Folk* (Warsaw), 1918, RG 574, Box 2, Scrapbook, YIVO.

125. Anonymous, "Bay di Vilner," *Arbeter Tsaytung* (Warsaw), 1918, RG 574, Box 2, Scrapbook, YIVO.

126. Yankev Vaserman, "Unzer teater un zayne kritiker," *Dos Folk* (Warsaw), 1918, RG 574, Box 2, Scrapbook, YIVO.

127. See Elkin, "FADA," 116; Elkin, "Di Vilner," 18; and Turkow-Grudberg, *Yidish teater in Poyln*, 47.

128. These new members included director Dovid Herman and actors Moritz Norvid, Yankev Shidlo, Yankev Gertner, Henrik Tarlo, Miriam Veyde, and Miriam Shik. Waislitz, "Der gang in der velt," 40.

129. Sandrow, *Vagabond Stars*, 216.

130. Lazar Kahan, "*Der dorfsyung*," in *Di Vilner in Lodz: Literarish zamelheft*, RG 574, Box 2, YIVO, 5.

131. Zvi Cahan, "Di Vilner: Eynike shtrikhn," in *Di Vilner in Lodz*, YIVO, 10.

132. Fuks, *Di Vilner in Lodz*, YIVO, 7.

133. Adolf Kargel, "Die Wilnaer," in *Di Vilner in Lodz*, YIVO, 29.

134. Y. Uger, "Der ershter debyut," in *Di Vilner in Lodz*, YIVO, 4.

135. Lazar Kahan, "Brukhim haboim," in *Di Vilner in Lodz*, YIVO, 3.

136. Sh. Y. Stupnitski, "Di Vilner trupe," *Lubliner Togblat*, 1918, RG 574, Box 2, Scrapbook, YIVO.

137. Heinreich Tsimerman, "Di yudishe dramatishe kunst," in *Di Vilner in Lodz*, YIVO, 8.

138. Fuks, *Di Vilner in Lodz*, YIVO, 7.

139. Luba Kadison, interview by Cleveland, Buloff Archive, Harvard Judaica Division.

140. Leyb Kadison, "A bisl zikhroynes," *Literarishe Bleter* 38 (September 18, 1931): 732.

141. Shniur, "On a nomen," 661.

142. Armin A. Wallas, "Jiddisches Theater: Das Gastspiel der Wilnaer Truppe in Wien 1922/23," in *Das Jüdische Echo: Zeitscrift fur Kultur und Politik* 44 (1995): 179–92.

143. See W. Gareth Jones, "Tolstoy Staged in Paris, Berlin, and London," in *The Cambridge Companion to Tolstoy*, ed. Donna Tussing Orwin (Cambridge: Cambridge University Press, 2002), 145; and Maxim D. Shrayer, *An Anthology of Jewish-Russian Literature: Two Centuries of Dual Identity in Prose and Poetry* (New York: Routledge, 2015), 134.

144. See "Chirikov, Evgenii Nikolaevich (1864–1932)," in *Historical Dictionary of Russian Theatre*, by Laurence Senelick, 2nd ed. (Lanham, MD: Rowman and Littlefield, 2015), 96; Georg Witkowski, *The German Drama of the Nineteenth Century*, trans. L. E. Horning (New York: Henry Holt and Company, 1909), 152–61; and John Osborne, *Gerhart Hauptmann and the Naturalist Drama* (New York: Routledge, 2005), 206.

145. Peretz Hirschbein, *Gezamlte dramen* (New York: Literarish-dramatish faraynen in Amerike), 4:99.

146. Arno Nadel, "Newejle," quoted in Hemmerle, "Jiddisches Theater," 294.

147. See Osborne, *Gerhart Hauptmann*, 205; and Worrall, *Moscow Art Theatre*, 143–47.

148. Fritz Engel, "Jargonkunst," *Berliner Tageblatt*, September 2, 1921, 2.

149. Jerry Bock, Joseph Stein, Sheldon Harnick, *Fiddler on the Roof: Based on Sholem Aleichem's Stories* (New York: Limelight Editions, 1964), 67.

Interlude I

1. Michael S. Levy, phone interview by the author, July 11, 2014.
2. Ben-Ami, interview by Sandrow, Wiener Library, NYPL.
3. Ibid.
4. Ibid.
5. Ibid.
6. Ibid.
7. Joseph Buloff, *From the Old Marketplace: A Memoir of Laughter, Survival, and Coming of Age* (Cambridge, MA: Harvard University Press, 1991), 121.
8. Tova Reich, "Once Upon a Time in Vilnius," *Washington Post*, March 3, 1991, https://www.washingtonpost.com/archive/entertainment/books/1991/03/03/once-upon-a-time-in-vilnius/9453dd44-a103-475f-b94a-64156b6f1b37/
9. Baruch Lumet, interview by Anita M. Wincelberg, Wiener Library, NYPL.
10. Ibid.
11. Yonas Turkow, *Farloshene shtern* (Buenos Aires: Tsentral-farband fun Poylishe yidn in Argentine, 1953), 209–11.
12. Ibid., 212.
13. Ibid.
14. Ibid.
15. Ibid., 19.
16. Ibid., 22–23.
17. Hersh Poznanski questionnaire, RG 26, Box 33, Folder 797, YIVO.

Chapter 3

1. Noah Nachbush, *Gems of Yiddish Poetry and Folklore* (Brooklyn: N. Nachbush).
2. Mark Kligman, "Jewish Liturgical Music," in *The Cambridge Companion to Jewish Music*, ed. Joshua S. Walden (Cambridge: Cambridge University Press, 2015), 90–91.
3. Judah Cohen, email to the author, December 20, 2012.
4. Indeed, the Vilna Troupe's first performance had taken place on Friday night, February 18, 1916. "Eröffnung des jüdischen Theaters."
5. Waislitz, "Der gang in der velt," 41.
6. Legutko, "Possessed by the Other," 248–81.
7. Waislitz, "Der gang in der velt," 40.
8. Gedalyah Nigal, *Magic, Mysticism, and Hasidism: The Supernatural in Jewish Thought* (Northvale, NJ: Jason Aronson, 1994), 100–101. See also J. H. Chajes, *Between Worlds: Dybbuks, Exorcists, and Early Modern Judaism* (Philadelphia: University of Pennsylvania Press, 2003); and Legutko, "Possessed by the Other."
9. See Gabriella Safran, *Wandering Soul: The Dybbuk's Creator, S. An-sky* (Cambridge, MA: Harvard University Press, 2010), 186–205.
10. Deutsch, *Jewish Dark Continent*, 11.
11. Ibid., 12–13.

12. S. Ansky, "From The Ethnographic Expedition: Questionnaire," in *The Dybbuk and the Yiddish Imagination: A Haunted Reader*, ed. Joachim Neugroschel (Syracuse, NY: Syracuse University Press, 2000), 56.

13. See H. Kremer, "Freydke R. Noach's from Olyka Tells Ansky the Story of a Dybbuk," in *Pinkas ha-Kehilah Olyka: Sefer Yizkor* (Tel Aviv: Hotsaat Irgun Yotsey Olyka be-Yisrael, 1972), 69–72.

14. In 1916 Stanislavsky reviewed An-sky's original Russian script for *The Dybbuk* and offered suggestions, including a request for the character of the Messenger, who was not in the original. An-sky complied, and the play was accepted for production by the First Studio of the Moscow Art Theater. A director was named, roles were cast (including Mikhail Chekhov in the role of Reb Azriel), and rehearsals were well underway when Stanislavsky abruptly canceled the production, concerned that the play was too dark to produce after the Russian Revolution. See Wolitz, "Inscribing An-sky's *Dybbuk* in Russian and Jewish Letters" and Vladislav Ivanov, "An-sky, Evgeny Vakhtangov, and *The Dybbuk*," in *The Worlds of S. An-sky*, ed. Gabriella Safran and Steven J. Zipperstein (Stanford, CA: Stanford University Press, 2006), 164–202, 252–65.

15. See Safran, *Wandering Soul*, 214.

16. Ibid.

17. Avrom Morevsky, *Ahin un tsurik: Zikhroynes un rayoynes fun a yid, an aktyor* (Warsaw: Yidish Bukh, 1960), 3:481–86.

18. Safran, *Wandering Soul*, 285, 287.

19. "Funerals in this era," notes Gabriella Safran, "were mass events, occasions for political statements on a grand scale." Safran, *Wandering Soul*, 291.

20. Avrom Morevsky, "Sh. An-ski's levaye" in Ravitsh, *Dos amolike Yidishe Varshe*, 429–30.

21. On Herman's life and career, see Zylbercweig, *Leksikon fun yidishn teater*, 1:634–35; Chybowska, "Dovid Herman," 11–12; and Nakhmen Mayzel, "Dovid Herman," *Literarishe Bleter*, May 21, 1937, 329–31.

22. Zylbercweig, *Leksikon fun yidishn teater*, 1:634; and Chybowska, "Dovid Herman," 11.

23. W.E. Yates, *Theater in Vienna: A Critical History (1776–1995)* (Cambridge: Cambridge University Press, 1996), 178–218.

24. Zylbercweig, *Leksikon fun yidishn teater*, 1:635; and Chybowska, "Dovid Herman," 11.

25. See Morevsky, *Ahin un tsurik*, 82; and Yonas Turkow, "Dovid Herman," *Literarishe Bleter*, May 21, 1937, 333.

26. Waislitz, "Der gang in der velt," 41.

27. J. Hoberman, *Bridge of Light: Yiddish Film between Two Worlds* (Philadelphia: Temple University Press, 1995). See also Elżbieta Ostrowska, "Der Dibuk / The Dybbuk," in *The Cinema of Central Europe*, ed. Peter Hames (New York: Wallflower Press, 2004), 31.

28. Joseph Rumshinsky, *Klangen fun mayn lebn* (New York: A. Biderman, 1944), 637–38.

29. Kazimierz Braun, "Religious Theatre in a Totalitarian Atheistic State: The

Polish Experience," in *Theatre and Holy Script*, ed. Shimon Levy (Brighton: Sussex Academic Press, 1999), 115.

30. Y. A-Ki, "Shtarker farn toyt: Tsu der oyffirung fun An-skis 'Dibek,'" December 1920, RG 8, Folder 24, YIVO.

31. Ibid.

32. Braun, "Religious Theatre in a Totalitarian Atheistic State," 115.

33. Ibid.

34. See Michael C. Steinlauf, "'Fardibekt!': An-sky's Polish Legacy," in *The Worlds of S. An-sky*, ed. Gabriella Safran and Steven J. Zipperstein (Stanford, CA: Stanford University Press, 2006), 234–35; and Marian Melman, "Teatr Żydowski w Warszawi w latach międzywojennych," in *Warszawa II Rzeczypospolitej* (Warsaw: Państwowe Wydawn. Naukowe, 1968), 1:383.

35. Monika Mokrzycka-Pokora, "Stanisława Wysocka," Culture.pl, http://culture.pl/pl/tworca/stanislawa-wysocka

36. Luba Kadison, interview by Cleveland, Buloff Archive, Harvard Judaica Division.

37. Juliusz Osterwa, "O *Dybuku* Trupy Wileńskiej (1925)," *Pamiętnik Teatralny* 41.1 (1992): 494; trans. Katarzyna Sitkiewicz. This reprints an interview conducted by the journalist Lezki at *Nasz Przegląd*, A Yiddish translation of this article appeared in the Yiddish press as "Yuliush Osterva vegn yidishn teater," *Vilner Tog*, February 3, 1925, 3.

38. Osterwa, "O *Dybuku* Trupy Wileńskiej," 493.

39. Ibid.

40. Ibid.

41. See Maya Peretz, "Jewish Theatre in Poland before the Second World War: Its Audiences and Its Critics," *Polin: Studies in Polish Jewry* 13 (2000): 359; and Tadeusz Boy-Żeleński, "Ze sceny żydowskiej," *Kurjer Poranny*, October 24, 1928, 7; trans. Zosia Sochanska.

42. Rumshinsky, *Klangen fun mayn lebn*, 640.

43. Ibid., 637.

44. Ibid., 638.

45. Ibid., 639–40.

46. Osterwa, "O *Dybuku* Trupy Wileńskiej," 493.

47. Wilm Stein, "Verborgene Kunst in Warschau," *Berliner Tageblatt*, February 16, 1921, 2.

48. *Fardibekt* is a Yiddish neologism that emerged out of the publicity surrounding the Vilna Troupe's production and suggests being "shot through with dybbuks, dybbuks all around." Steinlauf, "Fardibekt!," 234.

49. On Jewish literary modernism, see Allison Schachter, *Diasporic Modernisms: Hebrew and Yiddish Literature in the Twentieth Century* (Oxford: Oxford University Press, 2011); and Shachar Pinsker, *Literary Passports: The Making of Modernist Hebrew Fiction in Europe* (Stanford, CA: Stanford University Press, 2010).

50. Morevsky, *Ahin un tsurik*, 36.

51. Ibid., 82–83.

52. *Moment*'s coverage of *The Dybbuk* during its first month of performances

was slightly more thorough than *Haynt*'s. In addition to the reviews described in this chapter, *Moment* also published a humor piece by Yiddish author Der Tunkeler, entitled "*Der Dibek*: A heymisher shpas" [*The Dybbuk*: A down-to-earth joke"], December 20, 1920, 2, parodying the extreme devotion that the play inspired among audiences.

53. Eyner [Aron Aynhorn, pseud.], "Teatrale notitsn: Tsvishn tsvey veltn," *Haynt*, December 17, 1920, 6.

54. A. Foygl [Yehezkel-Moyshe Nayman, pseud.], "Nokhamol vegn Anskis Dibek: A por bamerkungen tsu H. Eyner's retsenzye," *Haynt*, December 24, 1920, 5.

55. Ibid; original emphasis.

56. Eyner [Aron Aynhorn, pseud.], "Un take nokhamol," *Haynt*, December 24, 1920, 6.

57. Ibid.

58. A-Ki, "Shtarker farn toyt," original emphasis.

59. Appenszlak, Jakób "Scena Żydowska: Teatr trupy wileńskiej," *Nasz Kurier*, December 14, 1920; trans. Christopher M. Peterson.

60. Ber Karlinski, "Dos ekho: Tsum 50-ter offirung fun dibek," *Der Moment*, January 28, 1921, 6.

61. Ben Levi [Avrom Levinson, pseud.], "Shmuesn: Dibek, haftke, un politikmakheray," *Haynt*, January 19, 1921, 4.

62. B. Khilinovitsh [Ben Zion, pseud.], "Der dibek in a nayer geshtalt . . ." *Der Moment*, January 18, 1921, 2.

63. Khad Gadyo, "Der dibek un 'Fankoni,'" *Der Moment*, March 6, 1921, 4.

64. M. Kipnis, "An emeser dibek . . . (A varshever felieton)," *Haynt*, January 3, 1921, 3.

65. See Steinlauf, "Fardibekt!," 235–36.

66. Nakhmen Mayzel, *Geven a mol a lebn: Dos yidishe kultur-lebn in Poyln tsvishn beyde velt milkhomes* (Buenos Aires: Tsentral-farband fun Poylishe yidn in Argentine, 1951), 122.

67. Avrom Morevsky, "Tsvishn tsvey dibukim," *Ringen* 3–4 (1921): 165.

68. Mayzel, *Geven a mol a leb*, 118–19.

69. The program for *The Dybbuk* is undated. However, given its contents, which include a review published on December 24, 1920, it is clear that the booklet was produced after the first few weeks of performances.

70. See, for example, the Vilna Troupe's program for *Eyferzukht* (175308/4305), RG 8, YIVO.

71. *The Dybbuk* program, Alef section, Programs Collection 1, Europe Programs folder, Buloff Archive, Harvard Judaica Division.

72. See Peter Bürger, *Theory of the Avant-Garde*, trans. Michael Shaw (Minneapolis: University of Minnesota Press, 1984), 52.

73. *The Dybbuk* program, Gimel section, Buloff Archive, Harvard Judaica Division.

74. Herman's direction in this final scene positioned Leah and Khonen's reunion as a happy ending, but in An-sky's play the reader is left uncertain as to how to respond to their death/reconciliation. Having defied all of the authorities, have Leah and Khonen at last achieved peace or are their souls doomed to eternal suf-

fering? An-sky is anything but clear on this point.

75. *The Dybbuk* program, Hey section, Buloff Archive, Harvard Judaica Division.

76. Ibid., Daled section.

77. Ibid., Hey section.

78. Ibid., Vov section.

79. On *taytsh* as a Yiddish linguistic feature, see Neil G. Jacobs, *Yiddish: A Linguistic Introduction* (Cambridge: Cambridge University Press, 2005), 295–96. On *taytsh* as an alternative name for the Yiddish language, see Weinreich, *History of the Yiddish Language*, 1:316–17.

80. Luba Kadison, interview by Shlanger, Buloff Archive, Harvard Judaica Division.

81. See the repertoire list published in *Komödie: Wochenrevue für Bühne und Film*, nos. 37/38 ("Sonderheft: Wilnaer Truppe"), November 11, 1922, AR 2371, S43/2, Folder 1, Leo Baeck Institute; digitized at http://www.archive.org/stream/jewishtheaterf002#page/n13/mode/1up

82. Lisa Silverman, *Becoming Austrians: Jews and Culture between the World Wars* (Oxford: Oxford University Press, 2012), 152.

83. See Kadison, Buloff, and Genn, *On Stage Off Stage*, 43–44; and Silverman, "Max Reinhardt." Silverman situates Reinhardt's comments to the Vilna Troupe in light of his recent involvement in Catholically inflected theatrical productions (197–99).

84. "Der Erfolg des Wilnner jüdischen Künstlertheaters in Wien," *Jüdische Rundschau*, November 24, 1922, 613; and Elkin, "Di Vilner," 20.

85. Soma Morgenstern, "Zur Entstehung der Oper Lulu," in *Alban Berg und seine Idole: Erinnerungen und Briefe* (Berlin: Aufbau, 1999), 130–33. See also Silverman, *Becoming Austrians*, 288.

86. Silverman, *Becoming Austrians*, 266.

87. Otto Abeles, theater critic for the *Wiener Morgenzeitung*, quoted in Wallas, "Jiddisches Theater," 183.

88. From Ben-Gavriel's diary, November 1, 1922, quoted in ibid., 183–84.

89. Moshe Yaacov Ben-Gavriel, *Tagebücher 1915 bis 1927* (Vienna: Böhlau Verlag Wien, 1999), 163. This entry is dated February 15, 1923.

90. Eugen Hoeflich, "Di Wilnaer (anmerkungen gelegntlich ihres Wiener Gastspiels)," *Neue Freie Presse*, November 10, 1922, 7.

91. Silverman, *Becoming Austrians*, 152.

92. Ibid., 149.

93. Robert Musil, *Sämtliche Werke: Vollständige Ausgaben* (Berlin: e-artnow, 2013), e-book, http://www.beam-ebooks.de/ebook/78705

94. "Kunst und Wissen," *Arbeter-Zeitung*, November 2, 1922, 5.

95. For example, in addition to the reviews quoted above, see "Bühne und Kunst," *Wiener Morgenzeitung*, June 28, 1921, 3; "Die Geshichte der Wilnaer: Ein Gesprach mit Direktor M. Mazo," *Wiener Morgenzeitung*, October 13, 1922, 5–6; "Jüdisches Theater," *Der Nachmittag*, November 16, 1922, 3; and "Kunst und Wissen," *Arbeter-Zeitung*, November 30, 1922, 6.

96. *Komödie*, 1–7, Leo Baeck Institute.

97. Ibid., 4–5.

98. See Senn, *Great Powers*; and Alfonsas Eidintas, Vytautas Žalys, and Alfred Erich Senn, *Lithuania in European Politics: The Years of the First Republic, 1918–1940* (New York: St. Martin's Press, 1998).

99. Elkin, "Di vilner," 19. The other late defectors from Mazo's company who joined Asro and Alomis's Vilna Troupe in 1920 were Chaim Shniur, Morits Norvid, Yankev Shidlo, and Yankev Gertner. Together with the original defectors Asro, Alomis, Roza Birnboym, Leyzer Zhelazo, Avrom Taytlboym, Shloyme Kon, Yankev Sherman, Leah Naomi, and Leonid Sniegov, this was the makeup of Asro and Alomis's branch.

100. Upon leaving Vilna, Herman convinced local Vilna actor Avrom Morevsky (unaffiliated with either Vilna Troupe at this point) to join Mazo's company. Herman and Morevsky would both later become famous for their collaboration on *The Dybbuk*. Zylbercweig, *Leksikon fun yidishn teater*, 1:708.

101. Ibid. There are competing explanations for why these actors went to Moscow, but Zylbercweig suggests that the three actors in question (Shidlo, Gertner, and Norvid) may have been drafted into the Bolshevik army.

102. Elkin, "Di Vilner," 19.

103. See Michael Brenner, *The Renaissance of Jewish Culture in Weimar Germany* (New Haven, CT: Yale University Press, 1998), 1–8; and Estraikh, "Vilna on the Spree."

104. See Brenner, *Renaissance of Jewish Culture*, 192; Gronemann, *Hawdoloh und Zapfenstreich*, 203; and Elkin, "Di Vilner," 20.

105. On the Herrnfeld Theater's reputation as a venue for Jewish theater, see Steven E. Aschheim, "Reflections on Theatricality, Identity, and the Modern Jewish Experience," in *Jews and the Making of Modern German Theatre*, ed. Jeanette Malkin and Freddie Rokem (Iowa City: University of Iowa Press, 2010), 31–32.

106. Former members of the Asro and Alomis company who came to Berlin included Chaim Shniur, Leyzer Zhelazo, Bella Bellarina, Frida Blumental, Hertz Grosbard, and Moyshe Feder. From Mazo's company they acquired Roza Birnboym and Dovid Herman.

107. Asro's business card reads: "Alexander Asro, Jüdisches Künstler Theater, Wilnaer Truppe." Box 1, Folder 2, RG 729, YIVO.

108. Ruth Apter-Gabriel, *Tradition and Revolution: The Jewish Renaissance in Russian Avant-Garde Art, 1912–1928* (Jerusalem: Israel Museum, 1987), 99. Steinhardt's set design for *The Dybbuk* was reprinted in Hans Tietze, *Jakub Steinhardt* (Berlin: J. J. Ottens-Verlag).

109. For an overview of the Vilna Troupe's initial reception in Berlin, see Delphine Bechtel, "Yiddish Theatre and Its Impact on the German and Austrian Stage" in *Jews and the Making of Modern German Theatre*, ed. Jeanette R. Malkin and Freddie Rokem (Iowa City: University of Iowa Press, 2010),77–98; and Heidelore Riss, *Ansätze zu einer Geschichte des jüdischen Theaters in Berlin 1889–1936* (Frankfurt am Main: Peter Lang, 2000), 98–107.

110. A.S. Lirik, "Der 'Dibek' in Berlin iz a durkhfal," *Der Tog*, December 16, 1921, 3.

111. Dr. Anzelm Klaynman, "Der Dibek in Nyu York un in Berlin: A por farglaykhende batrakhtungen." *Yidish Teater* 4–5 (March/April 1922): 31.

112. Ibid., 31–32.

113. These quotes are from two reviews: Alfred Kerr, "S. Anski: Der dybuk," *Berliner Tageblatt*, September 27, 1921, Folder 3, AR 2371, Leo Baeck Institute; digitized at http://www.archive.org/stream/jewishtheaterf003#page/n10/mode/1up; and Alfred Kerr, "Ein koscherer Exl? Schlierseer aus Tarnopol . . . der Rickudl," in *So liegt der Fall: Theaterkritiken 1919–1933 und im Exil*, ed. Günther Rühle (Frankfurt am Main: S. Fischer Verlag, 2001), 143. On Kerr as "Kulturpapst," see Inge Moossen, *Theater als Kunst: Sinn und Unsinn des Stanislawski-Systems* (Frankfurt am Main: Haag und Herchen, 1993), 16.

114. Felix Stössinger, "Vom unbekannten Judentum: *Dybuk* im Jüdischen Künstlertheater," *Die Freiheit*, October 28, 1921; trans. William Boletta.

115. Norbert Falk, "Der dybuk," *Berliner Zeitung*, undated (probably 1921), Folder 3, AR 2371, Leo Baeck Institute; digitized at http://www.archive.org/stream/jewishtheaterf003#page/n22/mode/1up

116. "Das Jüdische Theater," 1922, Folder 3, AR 2371, Leo Baeck Institute; digitized at http://www.archive.org/stream/jewishtheaterf003#page/n49/mode/1up

117. Alfred Döblin, *Kleine Schriften* (Olten: Walter-Verlag, 1985), 1:366–67.

118. Ibid.

119. "Das Jüdische Theater," Leo Baeck Institute.

120. Shelly Zer-Zion, "*The Dybbuk* Reconsidered—The Emergence of a Modern Jewish Symbol Between East and West," *Leipziger Beiträge zur jüdischen Geschichte und Kultur* 3 (2005): 185.

121. "*Der dybuk*: Dramatische legend in 3 bedrijven," *Het Vaderland*, November 26, 1921, 1. See also "Tooneel te Berlin: Jüdisches Künstlertheater: S. Anski: *Der Dybuk*," *Algemeen Handelsblad*, December 15, 1921, 7.

122. Stössinger, "Vom unbekannten Judentum."

123. Fechter, "Anski: Der dybuk," *Berliner Lokalanzeiger*, undated clipping, RG 8, Box 61, YIVO.

124. Otto Abeles, "Der sechste Abend der 'Wilnaer,'" unidentified review clipping, RG 8, Box 61, YIVO.

125. Engel, "Jargonkunst," 2.

126. Riss, *Ansätze*, 98.

127. Ibid., 101–2.

128. "Hamburger Kammerspiele: Gastspiel des Jüdischen Künstlertheaters, Berlin, Der Dybuk," *Hamburger Fremden-Blatt*, May 14, 1922; trans. William Boletta.

129. Paul Ahrend, "Die Jüdischen Künstler: Gastspiel im Thalia-Theater," *Chemnitzer Tageblatt*, April 18, 1922.

130. Julius Hart, "Grüne Felder: Dorfidyll von Peretz Hirschbein," *Der Tag*, February 18, 1922.

131. Max Alexander Meumann, "Hamburger Kammerspiele: Gastspiel des Jüdischen Künstlertheaters, Berlin, Newejle" *Hamburger Fremden-Blatt*, May 8, 1922; trans. William Boletta.

132. Brenner, *Renaissance of Jewish Culture*, 190.

133. Ibid., 190–91.

134. Einstein, "To the Directors of the Jewish Theater in Berlin," September 16, 1921, in Buchwald et. al, eds., *The Collected Papers of Albert Einstein*, 158.

135. See, for example, Baruch Krupnik, "Jüdisches Künstlertheater," *Jüdische Rundschau*, October 7, 1921, 586–87.

136. Riss, *Ansätze*, 107.

137. "Das Jüdische Theater," Leo Baeck Institute.

138. Ibid.

139. Morris Meyer, *Idish Teater in London 1902–1942* (London: M. Meyer, 1943), 282–83.

140. "Plays in Yiddish," *Era*, November 2, 1922, 18.

141. N. Frank, "Di 'Vilner' trupe in Pariz," *Di Tsayt*, October 17, 1922, 2.

142. Ibid.

143. "Das Jüdische Theater," Leo Baeck Institute.

144. For a representative sampling of Dutch reviews, see Jan Fabricius, "Het Jüdische Künstlertheater," *Het Vaderland*, June 17, 1922, 2; Arno Nadel, "Dybuk," *Het Vaderland*, June 17, 1922, 2; "Kunst en letteren," *Haagsche Courant*, June 23, 1922, 2; "Kunst," *Algemeen Handelsblad*, June 24, 1922, 2; "Kunst en letteren," *Haagsche Courant*, June 26, 1922, 2; H. B., "Jüdisches Künstlertheater Eeravond," *Het Vaderland*, June 20, 1922, 3; "Haagsche Briewen," *Arnhemsche Courant*, July 1, 1922, n.p.; Jan Fabricius, "Dybbuk . . . en nog iets," *Het Vaderland*, July 8, 1922, 2; A. M. DeJong, "Hollandse Schouwburg: Dybuk," *Het Volk*, July 12, 1922, n.p.; W. B., "Jüdisches Künstlertheater: Neweijle," *De Telegraaf*, July 20, 1922, 9; S. D., "Als Figurant en interviewer het Jüdisches Künstlertheater," *Het Vaderland*, August 30, 1922, 4; "Jüdisches Künstlertheater: Dybuk," *Rotterdamsch Nieuwblad*, July 28, 1923, n.p.; "Jüdisches Künstlertheater," *Niuwe Rotterdamsche Courant*, June 29, 1923, 5; and "Afscheid Jüdische Künstlertheater," *Het Vaderland*, July 10, 1922, 6.

145. "Das Jüdische Theater," Leo Baeck Institute.

146. David Hermann, "Iets over de regie van 'Dybuk,'" *Het Masker*, special issue on Jewish theater, July 1922, 152–55.

147. "Ven Khayim Shniur un Bela Belarina hobn geshpilt dem *Dibek* in Pariz," *Lodzer Togblat*, January 17, 1930, RG 574, Box 2, YIVO.

148. Ibid. See also "Maks Nordau vegn Dibek."

149. Ibid.

150. "Plays in Yiddish," 18.

151. Augustus John, *Augustus John: Finishing Touches* (London: Jonathan Cape, 1964), 93.

152. "Kingsway Theatre: Yiddish Players in 'The Knacker,'" *Star*, October 28, 1922, RG 574, Box 2, YIVO.

153. "Some London Press Opinions," publicity sheet printed to advertise the Vilna Troupe's London residency, 1922, RG 574, Box 2, YIVO.

154. Max Alexander Meumann, "Newejle," clipping from unidentified Hamburg newspaper, May 3, 1922, RG 8, Box 61, YIVO; trans. William Boletta.

155. See, for instance, "The Play in Paris," *Era*, October 19, 1922, 18.

156. H. Fa, "Great Acting: The Vilna Players in 'The Knacker' at the Kingsway," *Daily Herald*, October 28, 1922, RG 574, Box 2, YIVO.

157. Simon Koster, "Het 'Spel' van de 'Wilnaërs,'" *Het Masker*, July 1922, 157; Translated by Dorrine Oz.

158. Jan Fabricius, "De Handen Ineen!," *Het Masker*, July 1922, 147–48.

159. "Some London Press Opinions," YIVO.

160. "A Lesson in Acting: What the Vilna Troupe Could Teach Our Players," *Daily News*, November 4, 1922.

161. *New Statesman*, reprinted in "Some London Press Opinions," YIVO.

162. "Vet di Vilner trupe blaybn in London?," RG 8, Box 60, YIVO.

163. L. Blumenfeld, "Di barimte Vilner trupe shpilt itst in Pariz," *Forverts*, November 3, 1922, 3.

164. *Westminster Gazette*, October 27, 1922, reprinted in "Some London Press Opinions," YIVO.

165. "Di Grine Felder: Jewish Arts Theatre Players," *Sunday Times*, November 19, 1922, RG 8, Box 61, YIVO.

166. Habitue, "Newejle: Het Jüdisches Küstlertheater. Een Geweldig Tooneelgebeuren," *Haagsche Post*, July 1, 1922, RG 8, Box 60, YIVO; trans. Lena Vanelslander.

167. Hemmerle, ""Jiddisches Theater," 296. Originally published in the *Berliner Allgemeine Zeitung*, February 18, 1922.

168. Ibid., 294.

169. Zylbercweig, *Leksikon fun yidishn teater*, 1: 709–10.

170. See Martin Boris, *Once a Kingdom: The Life of Maurice Schwartz and the Yiddish Art Theatre* (New York, 2002); and Sandrow, *Vagabond Stars*, 261–67.

171. Sandrow, *Vagabond Stars*, 267–70.

172. See Mirosława Bulat, "Warsaw Yiddish Art Theater," in Hundert, *YIVO Encyclopedia*, 2:2004–5; Mordkhe Shner (Shinar), "Varshever yidisher kunst-teater ('VYKT')," in *Yidisher teater in Eyrope tsvishn beyde velt milkhomes: Polyn*, ed. Itzik Manger, Yonas Turkow, and Moyshe Perenson (New York: Congress for Jewish Culture, 1968), 53–72; and Zygmunt Turkow, *Di ibergerisene tkufe* (Buenos Aires: Tsentral-farband fun Poylishe yidn in Argentine 1961).

173. Lifson, "History of the Yiddish Art Theater Movement," 645–46.

174. See Boris, *Once a Kingdom*, 71–180.

175. Mayzel, *Geven a mol a lebn*, 123.

176. See Jeffrey Veidlinger, *The Moscow State Yiddish Theater: Jewish Culture on the Soviet Stage* (Bloomington: Indiana University Press, 2000); Béatrice Picon-Vallin, *Le théâtre juif soviétique pendant les années vingt* (Lausanne, Switzerland: La Cité, 1973); Mordechai Altshuler, ed., *Ha-Teatron ha-yehudi bi-Verit ha-Mo'atsot* (Jerusalem: Hebrew University, 1996); and Benjamin Harshav, ed. and trans., *The Moscow Yiddish Theater: Art on Stage in the Time of Revolution* (New Haven, CT: Yale University Press, 2008).

177. See Veidlinger, *Moscow State Yiddish Theater* and Veidlinger, *Jewish Public Culture*, 36, 129, 139.

178. Lifson, "History of the Yiddish Art Theater Movement," 48.

179. When historian David Lifson asked Jacob Ben-Ami about where the idea for "Yiddish art theater" came from, Ben-Ami replied, "Yiddish theatres or troupes in New York assumed the word 'art' in their name to identify their efforts with the objectives of the Moscow Art Theatre." Ibid., 34.

180. Ibid., 57.
181. S. Niger, "Di rezshi fun Dibek in Shvarts's Kunst teater," *Der Tog*, September 12, 1921.
182. See Khayim Zhitlovski, "A por verter vegn Anskis Dibek," *Unzer Teater* 1.1 (September 1921), 5–10; and Y. Vitkin, "Anskis 'Dibek' bay di 'Vilner,'" *Unzer Lebn*, RG 8, Box 60, YIVO.
183. Vitkin, "Anskis 'Dibek,'" YIVO.
184. Zhitlovski, "A por verter vegn Anskis Dibek," 5–10.
185. Maurice Schwartz, "Impresionizm un realizm: Velkhe fun di tsvey metodn darf ongevendet vern in der oyffirung fun Anskis dramatishe legende *Der dibek*?" *Unzer Teater* 1.1 (September 1921), 10–12.
186. Schwartz, "Impresionizm un realism,"10–11.
187. Ibid., 11.
188. Quoted in Boris, *Once a Kingdom*, 111. Originally published in *Forverts*, January 14, 1942.
189. "Yiddish Art Theatre: 'The Dibbuk,' a Strange and Imaginative Folk Play, Acted," *New York Times*, September 2, 1921, 15.
190. Klaynman, "Der Dibek in Nyu York," 32.
191. Boris, *Once a Kingdom*, 114–18.
192. Maurice Schwartz, "Theatre in a Democracy: The Yiddish Art Theatre's Director States a Case and Points a Warning," *New York Times*, December 1, 1940, X1.
193. Levy, *Habimah*, 7.
194. See Zer-Zion, "Birth of Habima."
195. Shelly Zer-Zion, "Ha-'Vilner trupe'—prolog la-historiyah shel 'Habima,'" *Bikoret ve-Parshanut* 41 (2009): 65–92.
196. Ibid., 92.
197. Ivanov, "An-sky, Evegeny Vakhtangov, and *The Dybbuk*," 258–59.
198. Ibid.
199. Ibid., 254.
200. See Giora Manor, "Extending the Traditional Wedding Dance: Inbal's *Yemenite Wedding* and the Beggar's Dance in Habima's *The Dybbuk*," *Dance Research Journal* 17.2/18.1 (Autumn 1985–Spring 1986): 71–75.
201. Zer-Zion, "Ha-'Vilner trupe,'" 92.
202. Turkow-Grudberg, *Yidish teater in Poyln*, 50–51.
203. On Shternberg's career as a poet and theater director prior to his involvement with the Vilna Troupe, see Israel Berkovitsh, *Hundert yor yidish teater in Rumenye, 1876–1976* (Bucharest: Farlag kriteryon, 1976), 147; and Moyshe Lemster, "Shternberg, Yankev," 2010, *YIVO Encyclopedia of Jews in Eastern Europe*, www.yivo encyclopedia.org/article.aspx/Shternberg_Yankev
204. See Y. Botoshansky, "Di Vilner trupe in Rumenye," *Yidish Teater* 1 (January, February, March 1927), 65–66; and Berkovitsh, *Hundert yor yidish teater*, 149.
205. "Jubiloul de 25 reprezentatii al piesei *Cântărețul tristței sale*," Scrapbook 2, 134, Buloff Archive, Harvard Judaica Division; trans. Ioana Costache.
206. Kadison, Buloff, and Genn, 5 *On Stage Off Stage*, 3.
207. Ibid., 97–98.

208. Victor Eftimiu, untitled letter to the editor, Scrapbook 2, 136, Buloff Archive, Harvard Judaica Division; trans. Ioana Costache.

209. Berkovitsh, *Hundert yor yidish teater*, 153.

210. A. Dominic, untitled article, Scrapbook 2, 138, Buloff Archive, Harvard Judaica Division; trans. Ioana Costache.

211. I. P., untitled article, Scrapbook 2, 138, Buloff Archive, Harvard Judaica Division; trans. Ioana Costache; original emphasis.

212. Fulmen [Ecaterina I. Raicoviceanu], "Ioşke eu vioara," *Dimineaţa*, Scrapbook 2, 141, Buloff Archive, Harvard Judaica Division; trans. Ioana Costache. Casa Capşa was a Bucharest restaurant, hotel, and coffee shop that was frequented by the city's political and intellectual elite.

213. Review in *Gazeta Sorturilor*, Scrapbook 2, 174, Buloff Archive, Harvard Judaica Division; trans. Ioana Costache.

214. Review by Scarlat Froda [Solomon Weitzendorf, pseud.], Scrapbook 2, 144, Buloff Archive, Harvard Judaica Division; trans. Ioana Costache.

215. Review by Isac Peltz, Scrapbook 2, 169, Buloff Archive, Harvard Judaica Division; trans. Ioana Costache.

216. Khayim Geler, "Briv fun Rumenie: der dervayliker sof funem shayres-hapleyte 'Vilner' in Rumenie," *Literarishe Bleter*, November 7, 1924, 6.

217. F. Aderca, "*Cântăreţul trisţei ştiri*," Scrapbook 2, 140, Buloff Archive, Harvard Judaica Division.

218. Berkovitsh, *Hundert yor yidish teater*, 153.

219. Review in *Gazeta Sporturilor*, Scrapbook 2, 174, Buloff Archive, Harvard Judaica Division.

220. "Jubiloul de 25 reprezentatii al piesei *Cântăreţul trisţei sale*," Buloff Archive, Harvard Judaica Division.

221. "Teatrul Cenţral—Trupa din Vilna: A 50eac reprezentaţia a *Cântăreţului tristeţel sale*," Scrapbook 2, 142, Buloff Archive, Harvard Judaica Division.

222. Kadison, Buloff, and Genn, *On Stage Off Stage*, 53; and William Schack, "Introducing Joseph Buloff of Russia," *New York Times*, November 23, 1930, 112.

223. Joseph Buloff, "A briv vegn der Vilner trupe in Rumenien," *Literarishe Bleter* 59 (June 19, 1925), 5.

224. Berkovitsh, *Hundert yor yidish teater*, 150.

225. Broderzon, "Der zinger fun unzer freyd," 4.

226. Luba Kadison, interview by Shlanger; Scrapbook 2, 21 and 24, Buloff Archive, Harvard Judaica Division; and Schack, "Introducing Joseph Buloff," 112.

227. Botoshansky, "Di Vilner trupe in Rumenye," 66; and Buloff, "How the Yiddish Theatre Invented Theatre of the Absurd," Buloff Archive, Harvard Judaica Division. On Ionesco in Bucharest, see Claude Bonnefoy, *Conversations with Eugene Ionesco* (New York: Holt, Rinehart, and Winston, 1970), 21. Ionesco had many Jewish friends, and he may indeed have attended a production of *Singer*, as Buloff and Botoshansky claim. Around the same time as *The Singer of His Sorrows* was selling out in Bucharest, Ionesco's father accused him of "siding with the Jews," and Ionesco retorted, "It is better to be on the side of the Jews than to be a stupid idiot."

Eugene Ionesco, *Present Past, Past Present: A Personal Memoir*, trans. Helen R. Lane (New York: Da Capo Press, 1971), 18–19.

228. Buloff, "How the Yiddish Theatre Invented Theatre of the Absurd," Buloff Archive, Harvard Judaica Division.

Interlude II

1. Luba Kadison, interview by Cleveland, Buloff Archive, Harvard Judaica Division.
2. Michael Taub, "Bella Bellarina," Jewish Women's Archive, http://jwa.org/encyclopedia/article/bellarina-bella
3. Theodore S. Hamerow, *Remembering a Vanished World: A Jewish Childhood in Interwar Poland* (New York: Berghahn Books, 2001), 58.
4. Taub, "Bella Ballerina."
5. Ibid.
6. Hamerow, *Remembering a Vanished World*, 39–41.
7. Ibid., 44.
8. Ibid., 60.
9. Ibid., 61.
10. Zylbercweig, *Leksikon fun yidishn teater*, 5:3817–8.
11. Ibid.
12. RG 803, YIVO.
13. Zalmen Zylbercweig, unpublished seventh volume of his *Leksikon fun yidishn teater*, 6240–41, RG 662, YIVO.
14. Alexander Asro, memoir fragment, RG 729, Folder 5, YIVO.
15. Sharon Asro, interview with the author, Arlington, VA, November 28, 2014.
16. Sharon Asro with Joseph Asro, interview by Alexander Zaloum, Florida, 2010, video provided by Sharon Asro and Alexander Zaloum.
17. Michael H. Hutchins, "Leave It to Me," The Cole Porter Reference Guide, http://www.sondheimguide.com/porter/leave.html
18. Sharon Asro, interview with the author.
19. Luba Kadison, interview by Shlanger, Buloff Archive, Harvard Judaica Division.
20. Ibid.
21. Ibid.

Chapter 4

1. Buloff, "How the Yiddish Theatre Invented Theatre of the Absurd," Buloff Collection, Harvard.
2. Ibid. Judging from Buloff's notes, the production was probably an evening of three Beckett plays (*Ohio Impromptu*, *Catastrophe*, and *What Where*) at the Harold Clurman Theatre in 1983 or 1984 (Buloff's essay is undated, but the production ran from June 1983 through April 1984).
3. Luba Kadison, interview by Cleveland, Buloff Archive, Harvard Judaica Division.

4. *Forverts*, January 6, 1924, 1.

5. B. Botvinik, "Epes gor anander sort idishe aktyorn zaynen zey," *Forverts*, January 11, 1924, 3.

6. Liliput, "Kunst kohanim in der fremd," *Frayhayt*, January 18, 1924, 5.

7. Pinkhas Katz, "Ir zayt a Vilner?: Oyb ye, vet ir hobn parnose in Varshe," *Forverts*, March 7, 1924, 3.

8. Information about actors, branches, and locations collected from the Vilna Troupe programs contained in RG 8, Boxes 41, 60, and 61, YIVO.

9. Mikhl Weichert, "Di shefe fun Vilner trupes," *Literarishe Bleter*, July 25, 1930, 560.

10. Pinkhas Katz, "Di barimte Vilner teater trupe—oder beyde kuni-lemels," *Forverts*, December 30, 1922, 3.

11. "Meisterwerke der Jiddishen Literatur," Menorah Society, Mexico City, July 7–14, 1944, Judaica Ephemera Collection, Series B, Collection 3, Harvard Judaica Division.

12. Program for Asro and Alomis performance, Lyric Theater, Glasgow, February 11, 1935. Judaica Ephemera Collection, Series B, Collection 3, Harvard Judaica Division.

13. Poster advertising Asro and Alomis's performance at Teatro del Pueblo, Buenos Aires, July 11, 1942. Judaica Ephemera Collection, Series B, Collection 3, Harvard Judaica Division.

14. Melnick and Rosenblum scrapbook of newspaper clippings, Box 5, Folder 35, RG 1147, YIVO.

15. "Di 'Vilner' tsugast in redaktsiye fun 'San Pauler Idisher Tsaytung,' *San Pauler Idisher Tsaytung*, February 7, 1939. Melnick and Rosenblum Scrapbook, RG 1147, Box 5, Folder 35, YIVO.

16. Ibid.

17. Douglas B. Holt, *How Brands Become Icons: The Principles of Cultural Branding* (Cambridge, MA: Harvard Business Review Press, 2004), 2.

18. Yitskhok Katznelson, "Der koyekh fun di Vilner," *Literarishe Bleter*, February 20, 1931, 15.

19. Ibid.

20. Weichert, "Di shefe fun Vilner trupes," 560.

21. Katz, "Di barimte," 3.

22. "Di hoypt-punktn in gor der velt vuhin es dergeyen tsu 'Literarishe Bleter,'" *Literarishe Bleter*, December 8, 1933, 789.

23. See Kobrin, *Jewish Bialystok*, 180–90; and D. Fishman, *Rise of Modern Yiddish Culture*, 21–24.

24. Letter from Mordkhe-Yosif Huberman, quoted in Chaim Finkelstein, *Haynt: A tsaytung bay yidn, 1908–1939* (Tel Aviv: I. L. Peretz Publishing House, 1978), 5.

25. See Cahan's description of his 1919 encounter with the troupe in Ab. Cahan, "Di shoyshpiler fun der barimter Vilner trupe," *Forverts*, November 16, 1923, 3.

26. Ibid.

27. Ibid.

28. Melech Epstein, *Profiles of Eleven* (Detroit: Wayne State University Press, 1965), 94–95.

29. Ibid., 151–57.

30. Cahan, "Di shoyshpiler," 3.

31. "Yiddish Players Score," *New York Clipper*, November 29, 1922, 14.

32. Summary of front-page headlines in the *New York Times*, January 11, 1924.

33. "Vilner aktyorn dertseyln vi azoy zeyer barimte trupe iz organizirt gevorn," *Forverts*, January 11, 1924, 1.

34. Costume designer Orli Nativ, email message to author, September 11, 2015.

35. See, for example, Ab. Cahan, "Der geyeg nokh di aktiorn fun der 'Vilner trupe,'" *Forverts*, December 3, 1923, 5.

36. Robert Gilbert Welsh, "Spirit Control in Yiddish Play: *The Dibuk* by the Vilna Troupe Is Strange Occult Drama," *New York Telegram and Evening Mail*, February 15, 1924, 17; "Vilna Troupe Give Odd Yiddish Drama: Throng Greets Their First Appearance Here in 'The Dibbuk' at Thomashefsky's Theatre," *New York Times*, January 29, 1924, 17.

37. Dr. Y. Kritikus, "Di 'Vilner' vern Amerikaner," *Der Amerikaner*, April 16, 1926, 10.

38. These branches included Asro and Alomis's Vilna Troupe (1924–26), Leyb Kadison's American revival branch (1926–27), the Bronx Vilna Troupe (1928–30), Joseph Buloff's American revival branch (1932–33), and Dovid Herman's final Vilna Troupe (1936).

39. Ben-Ami, interview by Sandrow, Wiener Library, NYPL.

40. Productions advertised in *Der Tog* in January 1924 included Aaron Lebedeff and Leon Blank in *Dem tatns zundl* at the National Theater, Misha and Lucy German in *Shlekht on gelt* at Orchestra Hall, Ludwig Zatz and Celia Adler in *Der meshugener* at the Shubert Michigan Theater, and Molly Picon in *Yankele* at Kessler's Theater.

41. A. Frumkin, "Di Vilner in Nyu York," *Di Idishe Velt*, January 22, 1924, 4.

42. See Stefanie Halpern, "Boris Thomashefsky: Matinee Idol of the Yiddish Stage," in *New York's Yiddish Theater: From the Bowery to Broadway*, ed. Edna Nahshon (New York: Columbia University Press, 2016), 118–27.

43. Henry, *Rewriting Russia*, 162–63.

44. B. Bronz, "Di Vilner trupe in Nyu York," *Forverts*, January 12, 1924, 8.

45. "Vilner teater politik in Amerika," *Forverts*, January 18, 1924, 3.

46. Ibid.

47. "'Di makhsheyfim fun der dramatisher kunst'—di originele Vilner trupe afn vegn keyn Nyu York," *Forverts*, January 6, 1924, 9.

48. A. Mukdoni, "Alte bakantn tsvishn di Vilner: Tsum onkumen fun der Vilner trupe," *Morgn Zhurnal*, January 11, 1924, 7.

49. Y. L. Fayn, "Londoner yidn hobn faribl afn 'Forverts' farvos er hot gekidnept di Vilner trupe," *Forverts*, January 6, 1924, 5.

50. For example, *Frayhayt*, January 29, 1924, 3; and *Forverts*, January 2, 1924, 2.

51. Luba Kadison, interview by Shlanger, Buloff Archive, Harvard Judaica Division.

52. Boris Thomashefsky, "Thomashevski dertseylt vos es hot zikh ongeton in teater velt mit der Vilner trupe," *Forverts*, December 12, 1923, 3. On Gest's career

as an impresario, see Valleri J. Hohman, *Russian Culture and Theatrical Performance in America, 1891–1933* (New York: Palgrave MacMillan, 2011), 75–100.

53. Hohman, *Russian Culture and Theatrical*, 58.

54. Anatoly Smeliansky, "In Search of El Dorado: America in the Fate of the Moscow Art Theatre" in *Wandering Stars: Russian Emigré Theatre, 1905–1940*, ed. Laurence Senelick (Iowa City: University of Iowa Press, 1992), 44–68.

55. Paul Grey, "From Russia to America: A Critical Chronology," in *Stanislavski and America*, ed. Erika Munk (New York: Hill and Wang, 1964), 144.

56. See Elena Poliakova, "In Time, Out of Time: The Moscow Art Theatre's American Tours," in Senelick, *Wandering Stars*, 32–43.

57. Advertisements for the Moscow Art Theater's American tours appeared regularly in the Yiddish press. See, for example, advertisements printed in *Der Tog* on January 1, 1924, 2, and January 4, 1924, 2.

58. On the MAT in Berlin, see H. A. L., "The Moscow Art Theatre," *Broom: An International Magazine of the Arts* 4.1 (December 1922), 66–67; and Cyril Brown, "News of the Russians," *New York Times*, October 22, 1922, 97.

59. See Mark Evans, *Jacques Copeau* (New York: Routledge, 2006), 29–30.

60. Christopher Balme and Nic Leonhardt, "Introduction: Theatrical Trade Routes," *Global Theatre Histories* 1.1 (2016): 1–9.

61. "Vilner aktyorn dertseyln."

62. Ibid.

63. B. Botvinik, "Di Vilner trupe iz geboyrn in a tsayt fun shrek, hunger, un fartsveyflung," *Forverts*, January 24, 1924, 4.

64. Botvinik, "Epes gor anander," 3.

65. See "Vilner aktyorn dertseyln"; and Zylbercweig, *Leksikon fun yidishn teater*, 5:3781–83.

66. "Vilner teater politik," 3.

67. Ibid.

68. Botvinik, "Epes gor anander," 3.

69. Ibid.

70. Frumkin, "Di Vilner in Nyu York," 4.

71. Led Pensil, "Vos es hot zikh opgeton in teater bay der ershter forshtelung fun di Vilner," *Forverts*, February 1, 1924, 3.

72. Asro, "Der onheyb," 33.

73. Ibid. The opening night performance of *The Dybbuk* on January 29, 1924, was an invitation-only event.

74. Led Pensil, "Vos es hot zikh opgeton," 3. I have found no other mentions of their presence at the premiere.

75. Ibid.

76. See Joel Berkowitz, "The *Tallis* or the Cross?: Reviving Goldfaden at the Yiddish Art Theatre," *Journal of Jewish Studies* 50 (Spring 1999): 120–38.

77. "Di Moskver fangen on tsu shpiln a naye Tshekhov pyese," *Forverts*, January 25, 1924, 3.

78. "Vilna Troupe Give Odd Yiddish Drama," 17.

79. Welsh, 17.

80. Dr. A. Koralnik, "Der Vilner 'Dibek,'" *Der Tog*, January 30, 1924, 5.
81. Vladimir Grosman, "Der dibek bay di Vilner: Etlekhe bamerkungen vegn der ershter forshtelung," *Forverts*, February 1, 1924, 3.
82. *Der Tog*, February 22, 1924, 3.
83. B.Y. Goldshteyn, "Bay di Vilner un in kunst-teater," *Der Tog*, February 22, 1924, 3.
84. Kritikus, 10.
85. Ab. Cahan, "Di ershte Amerikaner forshtelung fun der Vilner trupe: Ir 'simbol-shpil' fun Anskis 'Dibek,'" *Forverts*, January 30, 1924, 4.
86. Ibid.
87. Ibid.
88. B. Botvinik, "Far vos ken men nit makhn in Amerika aza teater vi di Vilner trupe?," *Forverts*, March 9, 1924, 5.
89. Alef Alef, "Dos naye in der Vilner trupe," *Morgn Zhurnal*, January 18, 1924, 6.
90. Zylbercweig, *Leksikon fun yidishn teater*, 1:635; and Chybowska, "Dovid Herman," 12.
91. Luba Kadison, interview by Shlanger, Buloff Archive, Harvard Judaica Division.
92. Program for *The Dybbuk* in Chicago, Buloff Archive, Harvard Judaica Division.
93. Zylbercweig, *Leksikon fun yidishn teater*, 1:709.
94. Vilna Troupe Accounts, RG 1843, Folder 1925. YIVO.
95. Ballet Russes de Monte Carlo Records, Folder 12, Harvard Theatre Collection, Houghton Library.
96. Worrall, *Moscow Art Theatre*, 49.
97. Ibid., 60.
98. See Bokshanskaya's March 23, 1923 letter to Nemirovich outlining the Moscow Art Theatre's performance schedule in Benedetti, *Moscow Art Theatre Letters*, 317–19.
99. Annie Shapiro, Yitzkhok Blifeld, Moyshe Zilbershteyn, and Itzik Hershkovitsh. Zylbercweig, *Leksikon fun yidishn teater*, 1:710. A program for this branch's performance of *Shver tsu zayn a yid* in October 1926 is in the YIVO Archives (17033A / 4755, RG 8).
100. Zylbercweig, *Leksikon fun yidishn teater*, 1:710.
101. Kadison, Buloff, and Genn, *On Stage Off Stage*, 160; and Sharon Asro, interview by the author.
102. I have not been able to locate Belasco's original letter, which was dated March 3, 1924. This is my translation of the Yiddish translation printed in the *Forverts*. "Dovid Belasko shraybt," 7.
103. "Di Vilner in Nyuyork," 3.
104. Ibid.
105. Ibid.
106. Warnke, "Going East," 7–8.
107. Ibid., 26–28.

108. Ibid., 8–12.

109. Boris, *Once a Kingdom*, 129–30.

110. See, for example, Led Pensil, "Vos es hot zikh opgeton," 3 and Frumkin, "Di Vilner in Nyu York," 4.

111. Frumkin, "Di Vilner in Nyu York," 4.

112. Boris, *Once a Kingdom*, 137–42.

113. Ibid.; and Hershel Zohn, *The Story of the Yiddish Theatre* (Las Cruces, NM: Zohn, 1979), 174–76.

114. For example, Schwartz took his adaptation of I. J. Singer's *Yoshe Kalb* on tour to Buenos Aires in 1933. Boris, *Once a Kingdom*, 219.

115. Berkovitsh, *Hundert yor yidish teater*, 149; and "Theater und Kunst," *Czernowitzer Allgemeine Zeitung*, November 4, 1923, 7. On the Vilna Troupe in Czernowitz, see also Elena Viorel, "Deutsches und Jüdisches Theater im Czernowitz der Zwanziger Jahre" in *Teatru şi politică: Teatre minoritare de limba gemană din sudestul Europei în secolul al 20-lea / Theater und Politik: deutschsprachige Minderheitentheater in Südosteuropa im 20. Jahrhundert*, edited by Horst Fassel (Cluj-Napoca: Presa Universitară Clujeană, 2001), 117–34.

116. Geler, "Briv fun Rumenie," 6.

117. Khayim Geler, "Di 'Vilner' in Yerusholayim d'Rumenie," *Literarishe Bleter*, August 7, 1925, 9.

118. "Orthodox Rabbis Condemn Theatre," *Sentinel*, July 30, 1926, 20.

119. Berkovitsh, *Hundert yor yidish teater*, 160.

120. "Orthodox Rabbis Condemn Theatre."

121. "Transylvania Sees New Anti-Jewish Excesses," *Jewish Telegraphic Agency*, May 24, 1927.

122. "Austrian Anti-Semites Raid Theatre," *Hebrew Standard of Australasia*, May 18, 1923, 12.

123. "Polish Parties Object to Play," *Sentinel*, August 19, 1927, 6.

124. Aron Tsaytlin, "Bay di Vilner in Lemberg," *Literarishe Bleter*, August 26, 1927, 659.

125. Shteynbarg, "Moshiakh iz gekumen," 2. Shteynbarg also reviewed *The Village Lad* for *Di Frayhayt* on March 1, 1924.

126. Nakhmen Mayzel, "Fuftsn yor Vilner trupe," *Literarishe Bleter*, February 20, 1931, 138.

127. Turkow-Grudberg, *Varshe, dos vigele*, 19–20.

128. Members of Mazo's Vilna Troupe as of August 12, 1927. Zylbercweig, *Leksikon fun yidishn teater*, 1:711

129. Members of Mazo's Vilna Troupe as of March 28, 1928. Ibid.

130. Waislitz, "Der gang in der velt," 44.

131. "Vokhn barikht fun 23 April biz 30 April, Vilner trupe," RG 26, Box 12, Folder 269, YIVO.

132. Kadison, Buloff, and Genn, *On Stage Off Stage*, 26.

133. Luba Kadison, interview by Cleveland, Buloff Archive, Harvard Judaica Division.

134. Berkovitsh, *Hundert yor yidish teater*, 156.

135. See Dovid Likht, "Baym keyver fun Yehudis Lares," *Literarishe Bleter*, December 12, 1929, 983–84; and Avrom Morevsky, "Lares—in shotn fun fargangenhayt," *Unzer Veg*, August 13, 1926, 3.

136. Luba Kadison, interview by Cleveland, Buloff Archive, Harvard Judaica Division.

137. Mikhl Weichert, "Mayn oyffirung fun Sholem Ash's Kidush Hashem," in Ravitsh, *Dos amolike Yidishe Varshe*, 257. On Weichert's biography, see Mirosława M. Bułat, "Michał Weichert," 2010, *YIVO Encyclopedia of Jews in Eastern Europe*, http://www.yivoencyclopedia.org/article.aspx/Weichert_Micha%C5%82

138. Weichert, *Zikhroynes*, 2;25.

139. Ibid., 2:25–38.

140. See Max Keller, *Light Fantastic: The Art and Design of Stage Lighting* (New York: Prestel, 2010), 156–57; Gwendolyn Waltz, "Filmed Scenery on the Live Stage," *Theatre Journal* 58.4 (December 2006): 547–73; Thomas Wilfred, "The Projected Setting," *Educational Theatre Journal* 6.2 (May 1954): 136–44; and "New Stagecraft Lifts Scenes through Floor and Paints Them with Light," *Popular Science* 102.2 (February 1923): 38–39.

141. See, for example, Harold Helvenston, *Scenery: A Manual of Scene Design* (Stanford, CA: Stanford University Press, 1931), 41–43; Theodore Fuchs, *Home-Built Lighting Equipment for the Small Stage* (New York: Samuel French, 1939), 18–19; and Theodore Fuchs, *Stage Lighting* (Boston: Little, Brown, 1929), 198–200.

142. Y. B., "Hinter di kulisn fun der *Kidush-hashem* oyffirung: A shmues mit Mikhl Vaykhert," *Literarishe Bleter*, May 25, 1928, 410.

143. Weichert, *Zikhroynes*, 2:259.

144. *Kidush hashem* program (1928), 175368A / 4308, RG 8, YIVO.

145. Y. B., "Hinter di kulisn," 410.

146. Ibid.; and Weichert, *Zikhroynes*, 2:260.

147. "Di Vilner trupe heybt on donershtik dem vinter-sezon," *Naye Folkstsaytung*, October 9, 1928.

148. For example, GOSET's 1922 production of Goldfaden's *Di kishefmakherin* (*The Sorceress*) was staged on a constructivist set of scaffolding where the actors performed on different levels. Veidlinger, *Moscow State Yiddish Theater*, 46–47.

149. "Gdzie byłam, co widziałam," *Ewa: Pismo Tygodniowe*, May 13, 1928, 6; trans. Zosia Sochanska.

150. Jakób Appenszlak, "Scena Żydowska," *Nasz Przegląd*, May 4, 1928, 5; trans. Zosia Sochanska.

151. Ibid.

152. "Przed nowym sezonem trupy wileńskiej: Rozmowa z dyrektorem Mazo," *Nasz Przegląd*, October 10, 1928, 5; trans. Zosia Sochanska.

153. Zylbercweig, *Leksikon fun yidishn teater*, 1:108.

154. Ibid.

155. Habima's production premiered on December 23, 1947. Levy, *Habimah*, 297.

156. See the program (175224 / 4297) in RG 8, Box 41, YIVO.

157. The first known European production of an O'Neill play was *Anna Christie*

in Berlin in 1923. Productions in Paris (*The Hairy Ape*, 1924), London (*All God's Chillun Have Wings*, 1926) and Moscow (*Desire under the Elms*, directed by Alexander Tairov, 1926) soon followed. See Horst Frenz and Susan Tuck, eds., *Eugene O'Neill's Critics: Voices from Abroad* (Carbondale: Southern Illinois University Press, 1984).

158. Zylbercweig, *Leksikon fun yidishn teater*, 2:876.

159. Ibid.

160. "Święto teatru żydowskiego," *Ewa: Pismo Tygodniowe*, October 21, 1928, 4; trans. Zosia Sochanska.

161. Halina Filipowicz-Findlay, "O'Neill's Plays in Poland," *Eugene O'Neill Newsletter* 3.1 (May 1979), http://www.eoneill.com/library/newsletter/iii_1/iii-1e.htm

162. Program 175226 / 4297, RG 8, Box 61, YIVO.

163. Program 175224 / 4297, RG 8, Box 61, YIVO.

164. Helena Griess, "Święto teatru żydowskiego," *Ewa: Pismo Tygodniowe*, October 21, 1928, 4.

165 Joseph Buloff to Luba Kadison, Chicago, August 1928, Letter 33, Joseph Buloff Papers, Billy Rose Theater Collection, NYPL.

166. See my article "*Heymish* Modernism: Joseph Buloff's Chicago Revaluation of the American Yiddish Theater," *New England Theater Journal* 23 (2012): 111–31.

167. Joseph Buloff to Mordechai Mazo, Kerhonkson, NY, 1930, Letter 52, Buloff Papers, NYPL.

168. See Abraham Novershtern, "Between Dust and Dance: Peretz's Drama and the Rise of Yiddish Modernism," *Prooftexts* 12 (1992): 71–90.

169. Y. L. Peretz, *A Night in the Old Marketplace*, trans. Hillel Halkin, in *The I. L. Peretz Reader*, ed. Ruth R. Wisse (New Haven, CT: Yale University Press, 2002), 371.

170. Ibid., 431–32.

171. Hilel Halkin, afterword to Wisse, *I.L. Peretz Reader*, 439.

172. See Veidlinger, *Moscow State Yiddish Theater*, 61–63.

173. Ala Zuskin Perelman, *The Travels of Benjamin Zuskin* (Syracuse, NY: Syracuse University Press, 2015), 61–62. While the production received enthusiastic reviews in Western Europe and was popular with audiences, it had a more ambivalent reception back home in Moscow. See Veidlinger, *Moscow State Yiddish Theater*, 64. For Yiddish press on GOSET's European tour and *At Night in the Old Marketplace*, see Nakhmen Mayzel, "Peretzs *Bay nakht afn altn mark* in Moskver yidishn melukheteater, gastshpiln in Berlin," *Literarishe Bleter*, November 9, 1928, 881–82.

174. Peretz, *A Night*, 371–72.

175. Ibid., 373.

176. Mayzel, "Peretzs *Baynakht*," 818–20.

177. See Shmuel-Yankev Dorfszohn, "Unter a sotsialn forhang: Tsu di gastshpiln funem yidishn-akademishn teater in Vin," *Ilustrirte Vokh*, October 5, 1928, 9.

178. See "Tadeusz Boy-Żeleński," Culture.pl, http://culture.pl/en/artist/tadeusz-boy-zelenski; and F. L. Schoell, "L'Enfant terrible de la Pologne," *La Pologne*, 1931, 580–600.

179. Boy-Żeleński, "Ze sceny żydowskiej," 7; trans. Zosia Sochanska.

180. Ibid.

181. See Harold B. Segel, *Turn-of-the-Century Cabaret* (New York: Columbia University Press, 1987), 221–53.

182. Boy-Żeleński, "Ze sceny żydowskiej," 7; trans. Zosia Sochanska.

183. See Tadeusz Boy-Żeleński, "Mayn nisiye tsu di Vilner af Karove gas," *Ilustrirte Vokh*, November 2, 1928, 18–19; and "Goyim kumen shoyn in yidishn teater," *Ilustrirte Vokh*, November 2, 1928, 21.

184. Zylbercweig, *Leksikon fun yidishn teater*, 3:1967.

185. Boy-Żeleński, "Ze sceny żydowskiej," 7.

186. Ibid.

187. See Maks Erik, "Bay nakht afn altn mark bay di Vilner," *Vilner Tog*, December 12, 1928, 3; Alter Kacyzne, "Tsu der oyffirung fun Bay nakht afn altn mark bay di Vilner," *Literarishe Bleter*, November 2, 1928, 869–71; and Nakhmen Mayzel, "Di ershte Perets-oyffirung in Varshe," *Haynt*, October 26, 1928, 7.

188. Mayzel, "Peretzs *Baynakht*," 820.

189. Zylbercweig, *Leksikon fun yidishn teater*, 3:1966.

190. Der Tunkeler, "Nisht dos un nisht yents: Baynakht afn altn mark," *Der Moment*, October 21, 1928, 5.

191. Ber Karlinski, "Baynakht afn altn mark: Tsu der oyffirung fun der Vilner trupe (teater elezium)," *Der Moment*, October 19, 1928, 7.

192. Yehezkel-Moyshe Nayman, "Bay nakht afn altn mark fun Y. L. Peretsn," *Haynt*, October 19, 1928, 8.

193. Program for *Shylock*, Program 177242-A, RG 8, YIVO.

194. Weichert, *Zikhroynes*, 2:145–64.

195. Mikhl Weichert, "Shaylok," *Literarishe Bleter*, March 8, 1929, 197–98.

196. Nakhmen Mayzel, "Der 'Soykher fun Venedik' bay der Vilner trupe," *Literarishe Bleter*, March 8, 1929, 199–200.

197. Nakhmen Mayzel, "Tsu der oyffirung fun Shaylok bay di Vilner," *Literarishe Bleter*, March 1, 1929, 172.

198. Mayzel, "Der 'Soykher fun Venedik,'" 199.

199. Aleksander Granakh, *Ot geyt a mentsh* (New York: IKUF, 1948), 363.

200. See the list of productions in Irene R. Makaryk and Marissa McHugh, eds., *Shakespeare and the Second World War: Memory, Culture, Identity* (Toronto: University of Toronto Press, 2012), 312.

201. Yehezkel-Moyshe Nayman, "Shaylok bay di Vilner," *Haynt*, March 7, 1929, 3; and Nayman, "Dos ergste fun der gantser geshikhte: Tsu der shaylok-debate," *Haynt*, April 19, 1929, 321.

202. M. Mazo, "S'volt geven dos ergste," *Literarishe Bleter*, April 24, 1929, 345.

203. Nakhmen Mayzel, "Di Vilner trupe in Varshe," *Literarishe Bleter*, March 30, 1928, 270.

204. Boris, *Once a Kingdom*, 166–73.

205. "Rekhtlozikayt un negishes," 10. See also "Special Taxes for Jewish Theatre Productions," *Jewish Telegraphic Agency*, May 14, 1929.

206. Ibid.

207. Joseph Buloff to unnamed recipient, n.d., Letter 41, Buloff Papers, NYPL.

208. Joseph Buloff to Khane Braz, New York, September 7, 1930, Letter 56, Buloff Papers, NYPL.

Interlude III

1. Luba Kadison, interview by Shlanger, Buloff Archive, Harvard Judaica Division.
2. Michael C. Steinlauf, "Kaminski Family," 2010, *YIVO Encyclopedia of Jews in Eastern Europe*. http://www.yivoencyclopedia.org/article.aspx/Kaminski_Family
3. Hamerow, *Remembering a Vanished World*, 61.
4. Ibid., 64–65.
5. Ibid., 86.
6. Ibid., 89–90.
7. Ibid., 62.
8. Joseph Asro, interview by Alexander Zaloum and Sharon Asro.
9. Sharon Asro, interview by the author.
10. Jeanne Cojocaru, interview by the author, New York, July 30, 2014.
11. Dan Ben-Amos, interview by the author, Mt. Airy, PA, September 30, 2012.
12. Baurch Lumet, interview by Wincelberg, Wiener Library, NYPL.
13. Zylbercweig, *Leksikon fun yidishn teater*, 5:3817.
14. Ibid.
15. Ibid.

Chapter 5

Epigraph: Buloff, interview by Garfein, Buloff Archive, Harvard Judaica Division.

1. "Wolfe Barzell," Internet Broadway Database, https://www.ibdb.com/broadway-cast-staff/wolfe-barzell-31219
2. "Alexander Asro," Internet Broadway Database, https://www.ibdb.com/broadway-cast-staff/alexander-asro-30279; and "Alexander Asro," Internet Movie Database, http://www.imdb.com/name/nm0039729/
3. "Joseph Buloff," Internet Broadway Database, https://www.ibdb.com/broadway-cast-staff/joseph-buloff-14313; and "Joseph Buloff," Internet Movie Database, http://gb.imdb.com/name/nm0120233/?ref_=filmo_li_st_3
4. D. Troy Sherrod, *Historic Dallas Theatres* (Charleston, SC: Arcadia, 2014), 111; and finding aid, Baruch Lumet Papers, UCLA Library, http://www.oac.cdlib.org/findaid/ark:/13030/kt2199p8q5/
5. Mokrzycka-Pokora, "Andrzej Pronaszko."
6. "Szymon and Helena Syrkus," Culture.pl, http://culture.pl/en/artist/szymon-and-helena-syrkus
7. Judith Brin Ingber, "Identity Peddlers and the Influence of Gertrud Kraus," *Congress on Research in Dance Conference Proceedings* 39 (January 2007), 100–105.
8. Mirosława Bułat, "Turkow Family," 2010 *YIVO Encyclopedia of Jews in Eastern Europe*, http://www.yivoencyclopedia.org/article.aspx/Turkow_Family; "Zalmen Hirshfeld," HaBait, http://www.habait.co.il/document/80,62,29.aspx; Donny

Inbar, "No Raisins and Almonds in the Land of Israel," in *Inventing the Modern Yiddish Stage*, edited by Joel Berkowitz and Barbara Henry (Detroit: Wayne State University Press, 2012), 314; Reuven Rubin, *Rubin: My Life, My Art* (New York: Sabra Books, 1974), 12

9. Michael André Bernstein, *Foregone Conclusions: Against Apocalyptic History* (Berkeley: University of California Press, 1994), 16.

10. Sandrow, *Vagabond Stars*, 335.

11. Richard Butsch, "American Movie Audiences of the 1930s," *International Labor and Working Class History* 59 (April 2001), 107.

12. William Schack, "The Yiddish Theatre in Travail," *New York Times*, March 30, 1930, X2.

13. Joseph Buloff, Letter 69, New York, 1932, Buloff Papers, NYPL.

14. Kadison, Buloff, and Genn, *On Stage Off Stage*, 87.

15. Zylbercweig, *Leksikon fun yidishn teater*, 1:709–710.

16. Kadison, Buloff, and Genn, *On Stage Off Stage*, 90–91; and A. Leyeles, "Arum teater: 'Mord' bay di Vilner in Amerike teater," *Di Vokh*, November 15, 1929, 19.

17. Luba Kadison, interview by Cleveland, Buloff Archive, Harvard Judaica Division; Lifson, "History of the Yiddish Art Theater Movement," 641; and Hoberman, *Bridge of Light*, 157.

18. Kadison, Buloff, and Genn, *On Stage Off Stage*, 93.

19. A. Mukdoni, "In oremkayt," Scrapbook 2, 109–10, Buloff Archive, Harvard Judaica Division.

20. Ibid.

21. Ibid.

22. Leyeles, "Arum teater," 19.

23. Berkowitz and Dauber, *Landmark Yiddish Plays*, 65.

24. A. Les, "Arum teater: Alter Kacyzne's *Ger tsedek* bay di Vilner," *Di Vokh*, January 3, 1930, 18.

25. Alexander Mukdoni in *Morgn Zhurnal*, January 3, 1930, clipping from Joseph Buloff's Scrapbook, SB2, 109, Buloff Archive, Harvard.

26. William Edlin, "Di Vilner trupe in 'alte bokherim' in Amerike teater," *Der Tog*, February 7, 1930.

27. Ibid.

28. I. G., "The Vilna Troupe in Different Ways: With 'The Rainbow' for Review with Yiddish Flavors," *Boston Evening Transcript*, May 28, 1930, Box 5, Folder 17, Buloff Archive, Harvard Judaica Division.

29. Samuel D. Kassow, *Who Will Write Our History: Emanuel Ringelblum, the Warsaw Ghetto, and the Oyneg Shabes Archive* (Bloomington: Indiana University Press, 2007), 101–2.

30. For biographies of Eric and Jula Isenburger, see the Isenburger Gesellschaft website, http://www.isenburger.org/

31. "Theater und Art," *Neues Wiener Tagblatt*, February 25, 1930, 9.

32. "Theater, Kabaret, und Film," *Österreichs Illustrirte Zeitung* 52 (December 28, 1930), 14–15.

33. Ursula Stamberg, "Das Theaterlebn der jüdischen Bevölkerung Brünns," *Maske und Kothurn* 47.3–4 (December 2001), 74.

34. "Wilnaer Künstlertruppe 'Tag und Nacht' von An-skie," *Brünner Tagesboten*, June 12, 1930, 3.

35. Stamberg, "Das Theaterlebn," 75–77. For German-language reviews from these productions, see "Wilnaer 'Shver zu sein ein Jud' Scholem Alejchem," *Brünner Tagesboten*, June 13, 1930, 3; "Der Sänger seiner Trauer," *Brünner Tagesboten*, June 16, 1930, 3; Dr. Epstein, "Getto Künstler," *Brünner Tagesboten*, June 14, 1930, 7.

36. "Der Sänger," 3.

37. See reviews from *Berliner Tageblatt*, *Montagspost*, *Vossische Zeitung*, and *Vorwärts* quoted in "Das Berliner Gastspiel der Wilnaer Truppe," *Jewish Telegraphic Agency*, February 10, 1931.

38. Program for *Bay nakht afn altn mark*, Vienna, 1931, MS #1685, Yiddish Theatre Collection, Rare Book and Manuscript Library, Columbia University Library.

39. Program for *Baynakht afn altn mark*, Warsaw, May 22, 1929, 176616, RG 8, Box 41, YIVO.

40. Doris Karner, "Jüdische Identitäten in der Prager Theaterszene zwischen 1910 und 1939," *Maske und Kothurn*, 40.2–4 (December 1994), 122. On the international Maccabi organization, see Diethelm Blecking, "Maccabi Movement," 2010, *YIVO Encyclopedia of Jews in Eastern Europe*, http://www.yivoencyclopedia.org/article.aspx/Maccabi_Movement

41. "Kulturchronik," *Prager Presse*, June 22, 1933, 6; trans. Daniel Dinsenbacher.

42. On the linguistic assimilation of Jews in Poland in the interwar period, see Eugenia Prokop-Janiec, *Polish-Jewish Literature in the Interwar Years*, trans. Abe Shenitzer (Syracuse, NY: Syracuse University Press, 2003), 55–56.

43. Moyshe Broderzon, "Fun getselt tsu templ," in S. Gelbart, ed., *15 yor Vilner trupe*, 11-12.

44. Anna Hannowa, "The Vilna Years of Jakub Rotbaum," trans. Gwido Zlatkes, in *Polin: Studies in Polish Jewry*, vol. 14, *Jews in the Polish Borderlands*, ed. Anthony Polonsky (Oxford: Littman Library of Jewish Civilization, 2001), 157.

45. Ibid.

46. Ibid., 159.

47. Ibid., 163.

48. Ibid., 158, 165.

49. Walter Meserve and Ruth Meserve, "The Stage History of *Roar, China!*: Documentary Drama as Propaganda," *Theatre Survey* 21.1 (May 1980), 1–2.

50. Robert Leach, *Revolutionary Theatre* (New York: Routledge, 1994), 167. See also Steven S. Lee, *The Ethnic Avant-Garde: Minority Cultures and World Revolution* (New York: Columbia University Press, 2015), 83–118.

51. Leon Schiller, "'Krzyczcie Chiny!' Na Dzielnej," *Wiadomości Literackie*, March 19, 1933, 6; trans. Katarzyna Sitkiewicz.

52. Schiller and Rotbaum both published several letters to the editors of literary magazines and newspapers (including *Literarishe Bleter*, *Nasz Przegląd*, and *Wiadomości Literackie*) about the conflict. These letters are collected in Leon Schiller, *Droga Przez Teatr* (Warsaw: J. Timoszewicz, 1984), 169–80.

53. Nakhmen Mayzel, "Mayne-loshn funem Poylishn rezshiser Leon Shiler," *Literarishe Bleter*, March 24, 1933, 209.

54. See Nakhmen Mayzel, "'Shray, khine' in der Vilner trupe," *Literarishe Bleter*, March 24, 1933, 207; S. Kon, "'Shray khine' bay di Vilner," *Vokhnshrift*, March 31, 1933, 6; "'Shray khine' in Skala-teater," *Unzer Ekspres*, May 8, 1933, 2; Avrom-Yitzkhok Grofman, "Hundert mol 'Shray, khine,'" *Der Moment*, May 26, 1933, 7; and "Letste teg fun 'Shray khine' in Skala-teater," *Unzer Ekspres*, May 29, 1933, 2.

55. Vladimir Grosman, "Shray, khine!," *Haynt*, April 14, 1933, 7.

56. Nakhmen Mayzel, "Vilner trupe in kamf far ir kiyum," *Literarishe Bleter*, February 17, 1933, 126.

57. Reprinted in Małgorzata Leyko, ed., *Lódzkie sceny żydowskie* (Łódz: Wydawnictwo Uniwersytetu Łódzkiego, 2000), 227–28.

58. "Première tournée mondiale du théâtre artistique Juif 'Trupa Wilenska' sur la direction de M. Mazo," 1933, Theater Series B, Collection 3, Box 16292: Netherlands, Belgium, France Folder, Judaica Ephemera Collection, Harvard Judaica Division.

59. "Belgian Queen Visits Yiddish Theatre to Express Sympathies with Jews," *Jewish Telegraphic Agency*, November 29, 1933.

60. Program for *200,000* in London, April 19, 1934, RG 1147, Box 3, Folder 28, YIVO.

61. See William Brustein, *Roots of Hate: Anti-Semitism in Europe before the Holocaust* (Cambridge: Cambridge University Press, 2003), 15–16.

62. For a mention of one of these letters, see Leslie Rees, "This Week at the Playhouse," *Era*, April 4, 1934, 4.

63. Waislitz, "Der gang in der velt," 49.

64. Turkow-Grudberg, *Yidish teater in Poyln*, 56.

65. Ab. Cahan, "A por spetsiele verter vegn der Vilner trupe," *Forverts*, February 19, 1936, 3.

66. *The Dybbuk* program (1936), RG 8, Box 60, Program 175267A/4298, YIVO.

67. Olin Downes, "Vilna Troupe Revived: On the 20th Anniversary of Its Founding 'Dybbuk' Is Given," *New York Times*, February 24, 1937, 18.

68. "New York 'Dybbuk' Premiere," *New York Times*, May 10, 1936, X5.

69. Chybowska, "Dovid Herman," 12.

70. Letter 70, March 8, 1932, Buloff Papers, NYPL.

71. RG 1102, YIVO.

72. Levy, interview.

73. Kadison, Buloff, and Genn, *On Stage Off Stage*, 116.

74. Mayzel, *Geven a mol a lebn*, 120.

75. Buloff, interview by Garfein, Buloff Archive, Harvard Judaica Division.

76. Mukdoni, "Alte bakantn," 7.

77. Ibid.

78. Joseph Telushkin, *Jewish Humor: What the Best Jewish Jokes Say about the Jews* (New York: William Morrow, 1992), 19–20.

79. Leyb Kadison, "A bisl zikhroynes," *Literarishe Bleter* 36 (September 4, 1931), 692.

80. D3 programming by Jessica Hamel. Support for this project was provided

by a PSC-CUNY Award, jointly funded by the Professional Staff Congress and the City University of New York.

81. Harold Clurman, "Ida Kaminska and the Yiddish Theater," *Midstream: A Monthly Jewish Review* 14.1 (January 1968): 53–57.

82. Helen Krich Chinoy, *The Group Theatre: Passion, Politics, and Performance in the Depression Era*, ed. Don B. Wilmeth and Milly S. Barranger (New York: Palgrave, 2013), 22.

83. Sandrow, *Vagabond Stars*, 276.

84. See June Mamana, "From the Pale of Settlement to *Pacific Overtures*: The Evolution of Boris Aronson's Visual Aesthetic" (PhD diss., Tufts University, 1997), 1–2.

85. Robert Brustein, "Design for Living Rooms (The Theatre of Boris Aronson)," in *Reimagining American Theatre* (New York: Macmillan, 2003), 232.

86. Mamana, "From the Pale of Settlement to *Pacific Overtures*," 2.

87. "Ming Cho Lee," 2008, American Theatre Wing, http://americantheatrewing.org/biography/detail/ming_cho_lee

88. Baruch Lumet, interview by Wincelberg, Wiener Library, NYPL.

89. See Azenberg's Internet Broadway Database page, http://www.ibdb.com/Person/View/21830.

90. Manny Azenberg, interview by the author, New York, February 7, 2014.

91. These programs can be found in the Theater Series B, Collection 3, Eastern Europe Box 16292, Judaica Ephemera Collection, Harvard Judaica Division.

92. "Di 'Vilner' tsugast in redaktsiye fun 'San Pauler idisher tsaytung,'" *San Pauler Idishe Tsaytung*, February 7, 1939, Box 5, Folder 35, RG 1147, YIVO.

93. Arnold Zable, *Wanderers and Dreamers: Tales of the David Herman Theater* (Melbourne: Hyland, 1998), 14.

94. Ibid.

95. Ibid.

96. Ibid., 25.

97. Recitation repertoire, RG 633, Box 1, Folder 3, YIVO.

98. Diaries, RG 633, Box 1, Folders 1–2, YIVO.

99. Belling, *Yiddish Theatre in South Africa*, 67–78.

100. "Socialities," *South African Jewish Times*, October 16, 1936.

101. Advertisement for Jacob Waislitz solo performance, *Hebrew Standard of Australasia*, August 18, 1938, 4.

102. Linda Phillips, "The Dybuk as Seen through Australian Eyes: Its Unique Aspects," *Australian Jewish Herald*, RG 633, Box 1, Folder 3, YIVO.

103. Zable, *Wanderers*, 25.

104. These letters are preserved in RG 535, Box 1, YIVO.

105. Caraid O'Brien, "Luba Kadison Buloff, 99, Last Survivor of Yiddish Theater Company," *Jewish Daily Forward*, May 12, 2006, http://forward.com/articles/1388/luba-kadison-buloff—last-survivor-of-yiddish-th/; and Dennis Hevesi, "Luba Kadison, 99, an Actress in Yiddish Theater's Heyday," *New York Times*, May 9, 2006, B7.

Interlude IV

1. See Peter Lande, "Jewish Refugees in Tashkent," April 2007, JewishGen, http://www.jewishgen.org/databases/Holocaust/0136_uzbek.html

2. Y. Turkow, *Farloshene shtern*, 23–25.

3. M. Tsanin, *Herts Grosbard* (Tel Aviv, 1995).

4. Zylbercweig, *Leksikon fun yidishn teater*, 5:4164, 5:4047.

5. Y. Turkow, *Farloshene shtern*, 213–15.

6. Arnold Zable, *The Fig Tree* (Melbourne: Text Publishing Company, 2002), Kindle ed.

7. Ibid.

8. Rebecca Rovit, "Theatrical Performance at Auschwitz: A Concert of Words," in *The Last Expression: Art and Auschwitz*, ed. David Mickenberg, Corrine Granof, and Peter Hayes (Chicago: Northwestern University Press, 2003), 110.

9. Ibid.

10. United States Holocaust Memorial Museum, "Carl Clauberg," *Holocaust Encyclopedia*, http://www.ushmm.org/wlc/en/article.php?ModuleId=10007061

11. Rovit, "Theatrical Performance," 110.

12. Ibid., 106–7.

13. Ibid. 110.

14. Zable, *Fig Tree*.

Epilogue

1. Alexander Asro, "Plan tsu der geshikhte fun der Vilner trupe," RG 729, Box 1, Folder 4, YIVO.

2. Asro, "Der onheyb," 34.

3. Ibid.

4. "Ven Khayim Shniur un Bela Belarina hobn geshpilt," YIVO.

5. Luba Kadison, interview with Chanin, Wiener Library, NYPL.

6. Sharon Asro and Alexander Zaloum, interview by the author, Cambridge, MA, March 3, 2013.

7. Baruch Lumet, interview by Wincelberg, Wiener Library, NYPL.

8. Joseph Buloff and Irv Bauer, "Project for a Jewish Theater Center in New York City," September 1963, Papers Collection 1, Folder BG 4, Buloff Archive, Harvard Judaica Division.

9. Ibid; original emphasis.

10. Buloff, interview by Garfein, Buloff Archive, Harvard Judaica Division.

11. Simon Rabinovitch, ed., *Jews and Diaspora Nationalism: Writings on Jewish Peoplehood in Europe and the United States* (Waltham, MA: Brandeis University Press, 2012), xxvi.

12. Falk Heylperin, "Nit nor vi kroyvim: Tsum gezegnen mit der Vilner trupe," March 28, 1922, RG 8, Box 60, Folder 24, YIVO.

13. Kh. Ts., "Der derfolg fun der 'Vilner trupe,'" *Yidishe Prese* (Antwerp), 1933, RG 1147, Box 5, Folder 36, YIVO.

14. Quoted in Lifson, "History of the Yiddish Art Theater Movement," 642.

15. Ibid.

16. I. L. Peretz, "What Our Literature Needs," trans. Nathan Halper, in *Voices from the Yiddish: Essays, Memoirs, Diaries*, ed. Irving Howe and Eliezer Greenberg (Ann Arbor: University of Michigan Press, 1972), 25–31.

17. Katznelson, "Der koyekh fun di Vilner," 16.

18. Turkow-Grudberg, *Yidish teater in Poyln*, 46.

19. Mayzel, "Dovid Herman," 330.

Bibliography

Manuscripts and Archival Collections

Columbia University Rare Book and Manuscript Library, New York
MS 1685, Yiddish Theatre Collection
Harvard University Libraries, Cambridge, MA
Harvard Theatre Collection, Houghton Library
Ballet Russe de Monte Carlo Records
Judaica Division, Widener Library
Joseph Buloff Jewish Theater Archive
Judaica Ephemera Collection
Leo Baeck Institute, New York
AR 2371, Jewish Theater Collection
New York Public Library
Billy Rose Theatre Collection
Joseph Buloff Papers
Dorot Jewish Division
William E. Wiener Oral History Library of the American Jewish Committee
University of California, Los Angeles Library
Baruch Lumet Papers
YIVO Institute for Jewish Research, New York
RG 8, Esther Rokhl Kaminska Theater Collection
RG 26, Yidisher Artistn Fareyn Records
RG 209, David Herman Papers
RG 453, Mendl Elkin Papers
RG 535, Rokhl Holtzer Collection
RG 574, Bella Bellarina Papers
RG 633, Jacob Weislitz Collection
RG 662, Zalmen Zylbercweig Papers
RG 729, Alexander Asro and Sonia Alomis Papers

RG 803, Morris Feder, Eliezer and Rose Zhelazo Collection
RG 833, Peretz Hirschbein Papers
RG 1100, Leib Kadison Papers
RG 1102, Henekh Kon Papers
RG 1147, Nachum Melnick and Devorah Rosenblum Collection
RG 1843, Records of the Hebrew Actors' Union

Interviews

Asro, Sharon, and Alexander Zaloum. Interview by the author. Cambridge, MA. March 3, 2013.

Asro, Sharon, and Alexander Zaloum. Interview by the author. Arlington, VA. November 28, 2014.

Azenberg, Manny. Interview by the author. New York. February 7, 2014.

Ben-Amos, Dan. Interview by the author. Mt. Airy, PA. September 30, 2012.

Cojocaru, Jeanne. Interview by the author. New York. July 30, 2014.

Levy, Michael S. Phone interview by the author. July 11, 2014.

Published Material

"Afscheid Jüdische Künstlertheater." *Het Vaderland*, July 10, 1922, 6.

Ahrend, Paul. "Die Jüdischen Künstler: Gastspiel im Thalia-Theater." *Chemnitzer Tageblatt*, April 18, 1922.

Albek, Aron. "Zikhroynes vegn Y. L. Peretsn." *Shtern* 16.10 (October 1940): 32–38.

Alef Alef. "Dos naye in der Vilner trupe." *Morgn Zhurnal*, January 18, 1924, 6.

"Alexander Asro." Internet Broadway Database, https://www.ibdb.com/broadway-cast-staff/alexander-asro-30279

"Alexander Asro." Internet Movie Database, http://www.imdb.com/name/nm0039729/

Altshuler, Mordechai, ed. *Ha-Teatron ha-yehudi bi-Verit ha-Mo'atsot*. Jerusalem: Hebrew University, 1996.

Ansky, S. *"The Dybbuk" and Other Writings*. Edited and introduced by David Roskies. New York: Schocken Books, 1992.

Ansky, S. "From the Ethnographic Expedition: Questionnaire." In *"The Dybbuk" and the Yiddish Imagination: A Haunted Reader*, edited by Joachim Neugroschel, 53–58. Syracuse, NY: Syracuse University Press, 2000.

Antoine, André. *Mes souvenirs sur le Théâtre-Libre*. Paris: A. Fayard, 1921.

Appenszlak, Jakób. "*Nocą na starym rynku* Peretza w wykonaniu Trupy Wileńskiej." *Nasz Przegląd*, October 13, 1928, 5.

Appenszlak, Jakób. "Scena Żydowska." *Nasz Przegląd*, May 4, 1928, 5.

Appenszlak, Jakób. "Scena Żydowska: Teatr trupy wileńskiej." *Nasz Kurier*, December 14, 1920.

Apter-Gabriel, Ruth. *Tradition and Revolution: The Jewish Renaissance in Russian Avant-Garde Art, 1912–1928*. Jerusalem: Israel Museum, 1987.

Aschheim, Steven E. "Reflections on Theatricality, Identity, and the Modern Jewish

Experience." In *Jews and the Making of Modern German Theatre*, edited by Jeanette Malkin and Freddie Rokem, 21–38. Iowa City: University of Iowa Press, 2010.

Asro, Alexander. "Der onheyb." In *Yidisher teater in Eyrope tsvishn beyde velt milkhomes: Polyn*, edited by Itzik Manger, Yonas Turkow, and Moyshe Perenson, 23–34. New York: Congress for Jewish Culture, 1968.

"Austrian Anti-Semites Raid Theatre." *Hebrew Standard of Australasia*, May 18, 1923, 12.

Baker, Shane. "Beginnings of the Vilna Troupe: Jewish and German Politics in the Formation of a Yiddish Art Theater." MA thesis, University of Texas at Austin, 2002.

Bal-Makhshoves. "Der nisoyen: Drame in fir aktn fun Y. L. Perets." *Dos Yudishe Folk* 1.1 (May 15, 1906): 21–23.

Bal-Makhshoves. "Shtrikhn un gedanken—Perets Hirshbayns trupe." *Fraynd*, February 25, 1910, 2.

Balme, Christopher. "Maurice E. Bandmann and the Beginnings of a Global Theatre Trade." *Journal of Global Theatre History* 1.1 (2016): 34–45.

Balme, Christopher. *Pacific Performances: Theatricality and Cross-Cultural Encounter in the South Seas*. New York: Palgrave Macmillan, 2007.

Balme, Christopher, and Nic Leonhardt. "Introduction: Theatrical Trade Routes." *Global Theatre Histories* 1.1 (2016): 1–9.

Bechtel, Delphine. "Yiddish Theatre and Its Impact on the German and Austrian Stage." In *Jews and the Making of Modern German Theatre*, edited by Jeanette R. Malkin and Freddie Rokem, 77–98. Iowa City: University of Iowa Press, 2010.

"Belgian Queen Visits Yiddish Theatre to Express Sympathies with Jews." *Jewish Telegraphic Agency*, November 29, 1933.

Belkin, Ahuva. *Ha-purim-shpil: Iyunim ha-teatron ha-yehudi ha-amami*. Jerusalem: Mosad Byalik, 2002.

Belling, Veronica. *Yiddish Theatre in South Africa: A History from the Late Nineteenth Century to 1960*. Cape Town: Isaac and Jessie Kaplan Centre for Jewish Studies and Research, 2008.

Bellow, Juliet. *Modernism on Stage: The Ballets Russes and the Parisian Avant-Garde*. Burlington, VT: Ashgate, 2012.

Benedetti, Jean. *The Moscow Art Theatre Letters*. New York: Routledge, 1991.

Ben-Gavriel, Moshe Yaacov. *Tagebücher 1915 bis 1927*. Vienna: Böhlau Verlag Wien, 1999.

Ben Levi [Avrom Levinson, pseud.]. "Shmuesn: Dibek, haftke, un politik-makheray." *Haynt*, January 19, 1921, 4.

Berkovitsh, Israel. *Hundert yor yidish teater in Rumenye, 1876–1976*. Bucharest: Farlag kriteryon, 1976.

Berkowitz, Joel. "The Tallis or the Cross?: Reviving Goldfaden at the Yiddish Art Theatre." *Journal of Jewish Studies* 50 (Spring 1999): 120–38.

Berkowitz, Joel, ed. *Yiddish Theatre: New Approaches*. Oxford: Littman Library of Jewish Civilization, 2003.

Berkowitz, Joel, and Jeremy Dauber. *Landmark Yiddish Plays: A Critical Anthology*. Albany: State University of New York Press, 2006.

Bernstein, Michael André. *Foregone Conclusions: Against Apocalyptic History*. Berkeley: University of California Press, 1994.

Bialin, A. H. *Moris Shvarts un der idisher kunst teater*. New York: Biderman, 1934.

Birnbaum, Solomon A. "Victims-in-Waiting: Backshadowing and the Representation of European Jewry." *New Literary History* 29.4 (Autumn 1998): 625–51.

Birnbaum, Solomon A. *Yiddish: A Survey and a Grammar*. Toronto: University of Toronto Press, 1979.

Blecking, Diethelm. "Maccabi Movement." 2010. *YIVO Encyclopedia of Jews in Eastern Europe*. http://www.yivoencyclopedia.org/article.aspx/Maccabi_Movement

Bloom, Cecil. "*The Dybbuk* and George Gershwin." *Midstream* 54.5 (September-October 2008): 20–22.

Blumenfeld, L. "Di barimte Vilner trupe shpilt itst in Pariz." *Forverts*, November 3, 1922, 3.

Bock, Jerry, Joseph Stein, and Sheldon Harnick. *Fiddler on the Roof: Based on Sholem Aleichem's Stories*. New York: Limelight Editions, 1964.

Bohrn, Patricia. *André Antoine und sein Théâtre Libre: Eine spezifische Ausformung des naturalistischen Theaters*. New York: Peter Lang, 2000.

Bonnefoy, Claude. *Conversations with Eugene Ionesco*. New York: Holt, Rinehart, and Winston, 1970.

Booth, Michael R. *Theatre in the Victorian Age*. Cambridge: Cambridge University Press, 1991.

Boris, Martin. "The Life and Death of a Yiddish Art Theatre." Museum of Family History. http://www.museumoffamilyhistory.com/yt-lad-yat.htm

Boris, Martin. *Once a Kingdom: The Life of Maurice Schwartz and the Yiddish Art Theatre*. New York: Author, 2002.

Botoshansky, Y. "Di Vilner trupe in Rumenye." *Yidish Teater* 1 (January, February, March 1927): 61–70.

Botvinik, B. "Epes gor anander sort idishe aktyorn zaynen zey." *Forverts*, January 11, 1924, 3.

Botvinik, B. "Far vos ken men nit makhn in Amerika aza teater vi di Vilner trupe?" *Forverts*, March 9, 1924, 4–5.

Botvinik, B. "Di Vilner trupe iz geboyrn in a tsayt fun shrek, hunger, un fartsveyflung." *Forverts*, January 24, 1924, 4.

Boy-Żeleński, Tadeusz. "Mayn nisiye tsu di Vilner af Karove gas." *Ilustrirte Vokh*, November 2, 1928, 18–19.

Boy-Żeleński, Tadeusz. "Ze sceny żydowskiej." *Kurjer Poranny*, October 24, 1928, 7.

Braun, Kazimierz. "Religious Theatre in a Totalitarian Atheistic State: The Polish Experience." In *Theatre and Holy Script*, edited by Shimon Levy, 115–27. Brighton: Sussex Academic Press, 1999.

Brenner, Michael. *The Renaissance of Jewish Culture in Weimar Germany*. New Haven, CT: Yale University Press, 1998.

Brockett, Oscar G., and Franklin J. Hildy. *History of the Theater*. 10th ed. Boston: Pearson, 2008.

Broderzon, Moyshe. "Der zinger fun unzer freyd iz 'der zinger fun zayn troyer' bay der Vilner trupe." *Getseylte Verter*, September 13, 1929, 3–4.

Bronz, B. "Di Vilner trupe in Nyu York." *Forverts*, January 12, 1924, 8.

Brown, Cyril. "News of the Russians." *New York Times*, October 22, 1922, 97.
Brown, John Russell. *The Oxford Illustrated History of Theatre*. Oxford: Oxford University Press, 2001.
Brustein, Robert. "Design for Living Rooms (The Theatre of Boris Aronson)." In *Reimagining American Theatre*, 230–34. New York: Macmillan, 2003.
Brustein, William. *Roots of Hate: Anti-Semitism in Europe before the Holocaust*. Cambridge: Cambridge University Press, 2003.
Buchwald, Diana Kormos, Ze'ev Rosenkranz, Tilman Sauer, Jözsef Illy, and Virginia Iris Holmes. *The Collected Papers of Albert Einstein*. Vol. 12, *The Berlin Years*. Translated by Ann M. Hentschel. Princeton, NJ: Princeton University Press, 2009.
Buchwald, Nathaniel. *Teater*. New York: Farlag Komitet Teater, 1943.
"Bühne und Kunst." *Wiener Morgenzeitung*, June 28, 1921. 3.
Bułat, Mirosława. "Michał Weichert." 2010. *YIVO Encyclopedia of Jews in Eastern Europe*, http://www.yivoencyclopedia.org/article.aspx/Weichert_Micha%C5%82
Bułat, Mirosława. "Turkow Family." 2010. *YIVO Encyclopedia of Jews in Eastern Europe*, http://www.yivoencyclopedia.org/article.aspx/Turkow_Family
Bułat, Mirosława. "Warsaw Yiddish Art Theater." In *The YIVO Encyclopedia of Jews in Eastern Europe*, edited by Gershon David Hundert, 2:2004–5. New Haven, CT: Yale University Press, 2008.
Buloff, Joseph. "A briv vegn der Vilner trupe in Rumenien." *Literarishe Bleter*, June 19, 1925, 5.
Buloff, Joseph. *From the Old Marketplace: A Memoir of Laughter, Survival, and Coming of Age*. Cambridge, MA: Harvard University Press, 1991.
Bürger, Peter. *Theory of the Avant-Garde*. Translated by Michael Shaw. Minneapolis: University of Minnesota Press, 1984.
Butsch, Richard. "American Movie Audiences of the 1930s." *International Labor and Working Class History* 59 (April 2001): 106–20.
Bützer, Evi. *Die Anfänge der jüddischen purim shpiln in ihrem literarischen und kulturgeschichtlichen Kontext*. Hamburg: Helmut Buske Verlag, 2003.
Caddy, Davinia. *The Ballets Russes and Beyond: Music and Dance in Belle-Èpoque Paris*. Cambridge: Cambridge University Press, 2012.
Cahan, Ab. "Di ershte Amerikaner forshtelung fun der Vilner trupe: Ir 'simbolshpil' fun Anskis 'Dibek.'" *Forverts*, January 30, 1924, 4.
Cahan, Ab. "Der geyeg nokh di aktiorn fun der 'Vilner trupe.'" *Forverts*, December 3, 1923, 5.
Cahan, Ab. "A por spetsiele verter vegn der Vilner trupe." *Forverts*, February 19, 1937, 3.
Cahan, Ab. "Di shoyshpiler fun der barimter Vilner trupe." *Forverts*, November 16, 1923, 3.
Cammy, Justin. Foreword to *Vilna, My Vilna: Stories*, by Abraham Karpinowitz, ix–xxiii. Syracuse, NY: Syracuse University Press, 2015.
Cammy, Justin. "Yung-Vilne: A Cultural History of a Yiddish Literary Group in Interwar Poland." PhD diss., Harvard University, 2003.
Caplan, Debra. "*Heymish* Modernism: Joseph Buloff's Chicago Revaluation of the American Yiddish Theatre." *New England Theatre Journal* 23 (2012): 111–31.

Caplan, Debra. "Nomadic Chutzpah: The Vilna Troupe's Transnational Yiddish Theater Paradigm, 1915–1935." *Theater Survey* 55.3 (September 2014): 296–317.

Caplan, Marc. *How Strange the Change: Language, Temporality, and Narrative Form in Peripheral Modernisms*. Stanford, CA: Stanford University Press, 2011.

Carlson, Marvin. *The Haunted Stage: The Theatre as Memory Machine*. Ann Arbor: University of Michigan Press, 2003.

Chajes, J. H. *Between Worlds: Dybbuks, Exorcists, and Early Modern Judaism*. Philadelphia: University of Pennsylvania Press, 2003.

Cheney, Sheldon. *The Art Theatre: A Discussion of Its Ideals, Its Organization, and Its Promise as a Corrective for Present Evils in the Commercial Theatre*. New York: Alfred A. Knopf, 1917.

Chinoy, Helen Krich. *The Group Theatre: Passion, Politics, and Performance in the Depression Era*. Edited by Don B. Wilmeth and Milly S. Barranger. New York: Palgrave, 2013.

Chybowska, Halina. "Dovid Herman and the Jewish Theatre in Poland." *Polish Review* 4.19 (May 17, 1944): 11–12.

Clurman, Harold. "Ida Kaminska and the Yiddish Theater." *Midstream: A Monthly Jewish Review* 14.1 (January 1968): 53–57.

Cohen, Israel. *Vilna*. 1943. Reprint, Philadelphia: Jewish Publication Society, 1992.

"Das Berliner Gastspiel der Wilnaer Truppe." *Jewish Telegraphic Agency*, February 10, 1931.

Da Silva, Armando Sérgio, ed. *J. Guinsburg: Diàlogos sobre teatro*. São Paulo: Edusp, 1992.

Das land Ober Ost: Deutsche Arbeit in den Verwaltungsgebieten Kurland, Litauen, und Bialystok-Grodno. Berlin: Presseabteilung Ober Ost, 1917.

DeJong, A. M. "Hollandse Schouwburg: Dybuk." *Het Volk*, July 12, 1922.

"*Der dybuk*: Dramatische legend in 3 bedrijven." *Het Vaderland*, November 26, 1921, 1.

"Der Erfolg des Wilnner jüdischen Künstlertheaters in Wien." *Jüdische Rundschau*, November 24, 1922, 613.

"Der Sänger seiner Trauer." *Brünner Tagesboten*, June 16, 1930, 3.

Der Tunkeler. "*Der Dibek*: A heymisher shpas." *Der Moment*, December 20, 1920, 2.

Der Tunkeler. "Nisht dos un nisht yents: Baynakht afn altn mark," *Der Moment*, October 21, 1928, 5.

Deutsch, Nathaniel. *The Jewish Dark Continent: Life and Death in the Russian Pale of Settlement*. Cambridge, MA: Harvard University Press, 2011.

Dharwadker, Aparna. "Modernism, 'Tradition,' and History in the Postcolony Vijay Tendulkar's *Ghashiram kotwal* (1972)." *Theatre Journal* 65.3 (December 2013), 467–87.

"Die Geshichte der Wilnaer: Ein Gesprach mit Direktor M. Mazo." *Wiener Morgenzeitung*, October 13, 1922, 5–6.

"Di hoypt-punktn in gor der velt vuhin es dergeyen tsu 'Literarishe bleter.'" *Literarishe Bleter*, December 8, 1933, 789.

"'Di makhsheyfim fun der dramatisher kunst'—di originele Vilner trupe afn vegn keyn Nyu York." *Forverts*, January 6, 1924, 9.

"Di Moskver fangen on tsu shpiln a naye Tsekhov pyese." *Forverts*, January 25, 1924, 3.

"Di Vilner in Nyuyork un di Nyuyorker in London." *Forverts*, February 22, 1924, 3.

"Di Vilner trupe heybt on donershtik dem vinter-sezon." *Naye Folkstsaytung*, October 9, 1928.

Döblin, Alfred. *Kleine Schriften*. Olten: Walter-Verlag, 1985.

Dorfszohn, Shmuel-Yankev. "Unter a sotsialn forhang: Tsu di gastshpiln funem yidishn-akademishn teater in Vin." *Ilustrirte vokh*, October 5, 1928, 9.

"Dovid Belasko shraybt tsu der 'Vilner trupe.'" *Forverts*, March 7, 1924, 7.

Downes, Olin. "Vilna Troupe Revived: On the 20th Anniversary of Its Founding 'Dybbuk' Is Given." *New York Times*, February 24, 1937, 18.

Druk, D. "Di tsveyte forshtelung fun der Vilner trupe." *Der Moment*, October 7, 1917, 5.

Edlin, William. "Di Vilner trupe in 'alte bokherim' in Amerike teater." *Der Tog*, February 7, 1930.

Eidintas, Alfonsas, Vytautas Žalys, and Alfred Erich Senn. *Lithuania in European Politics: The Years of the First Republic, 1918–1940*. New York: St. Martin's Press, 1998.

Elkin, Mendl. "Di Vilner." *Tealit* 4 (February 1924): 16–24.

Elkin, Mendl. "FADA : Tsum tsvantsik yorikn yovl fun der Vilner trupe." *Bodn* 3.1 (Spring/Summer 1936): 105–32.

Engel, Fritz. "Jargonkunst." *Berliner Tageblatt*, September 2, 1921, 2–3.

Epstein, Dr. "Getto Künstler." *Brünner Tagesboten*, June 14, 1930, 7.

Epstein, Melech. *Profiles of Eleven*. Detroit: Wayne State University Press, 1965.

Eric and Jula Isenburger Gesselschaft. http://www.isenburger.org/

Erik, Maks. "Bay nakht afn altn mark bay di Vilner." *Vilner Tog*, December 12, 1928, 3.

"Eröffnung des jüdischen Theaters." *Zeitung der 10. Armee*, February 17, 1916, 3.

Estraikh, Gennady. "Vilna on the Spree: Yiddish in Weimar Berlin," *Aschkenas* 16 (2006), 103–27.

Eulenberg, Herbert. "Jüdisches Theater." *Vossische Zeitung*, April 22, 1917.

Evans, Mark. *Jacques Copeau*. New York: Routledge, 2006.

Eyner [Aron Aynhorn, pseud.]. "Teatrale notitsn: Tsvishn tsvey veltn." *Haynt*, December 17, 1920, 6.

Eyner [Aron Aynhorn, pseud.]. "Un take nokhamol." *Haynt*, December 24, 1920, 6.

Fabricius, Jan. "De Handen Ineen!" *Het Masker*, July 1922, 147–50.

Fabricius, Jan. "Dybbuk . . . en nog iets." *Het Vaderland*, July 8, 1922, 2.

Fabricius, Jan. "Het Jüdische Künstlertheater." *Het Vaderland*, June 17, 1922, 2.

Fayn, Y. L. "Londoner yidn hobn faribl afn 'Forverts' farvos er hot gekidnept di Vilner trupe." *Forverts*, January 6, 1924, 5.

Filipowicz-Findlay, Halina. "O'Neill's Plays in Poland." *Eugene O'Neill Newsletter* 3.1 (May 1979). http://www.eoneill.com/library/newsletter/iii_1/iii-1e.htm.

Fine, David J. *Jewish Integration in the German Army in the First World War*. Boston: De Gruyter, 2012.

Finkelstein, Chaim. *Haynt: A tsaytung bay yidn, 1908–1939*. Tel Aviv: I. L. Peretz Publishing House, 1978.

Fishman, David E. *The Rise of Modern Yiddish Culture*. Pittsburgh: University of Pittsburgh Press, 2005.

Fishman, Joshua. "Czernowitz Conference." In *The YIVO Encyclopedia of Jews in Eastern Europe*, edited by Gershon David Hundert, 1:384–85. New Haven, CT: Yale University Press, 2008.

Fowler, Mayhill C. "'A Theatrical Mecca': The Stages of Kyiv in 1907." In *Modernism in Kyiv: Jubilant Experimentation*, edited by Irena R. Makaryk and Virlana Tkacz, 29–34. Toronto: University of Toronto Press, 2010.

Foygl, A. [Yehezkel-Moyshe Nayman, pseud.]. "'Das ist der Dibuk,' oder der 'Dibek' in Berlin." *Haynt*, November 7, 1921, 2.

Foygl, A. [Yehezkel-Moyshe Nayman, pseud.]. "Nokhamol vegn Anskis Dibek: A por bamerkerungen tsu H. Eyner's retsenzye." *Haynt*, December 24, 1920, 5–6.

Frank, N. "Di 'Vilner' trupe in Pariz." *Di Tsayt*, October 17, 1922, 2.

Frenz, Horst, and Susan Tuck, eds. *Eugene O'Neill's Critics: Voices from Abroad*. Carbondale: Southern Illinois University Press, 1984.

Frumkin, A. "Di Vilner in Nyu York." *Di Idishe Velt*, January 22, 1924, 4.

Fuchs, Theodor. *Home-Built Lighting Equipment for the Small Stage*. New York: Samuel French, 1939.

Fuchs, Theodor. *Stage Lighting*. Boston: Little, Brown, 1929.

Garafola, Lynn. *Diaghilev's Ballets Russes*. Boston: Da Capo Press, 1998.

Garafola, Lynn. "Introduction: The Legacy of Diaghilev's Ballets Russes." In *The Ballets Russes and Its World*, edited by Lynn Garafola and Nancy Van Norman Bear, 1–12. New Haven, CT: Yale University Press, 1999.

Garcia-Marquez, Vincente. *The Ballets Russes: Colonel de Basil's Ballets Russes de Monte Carlo, 1932–1952*. New York: Knopf, 1990.

"Gastspiel des Wilnaer jiddischen Theaters in Berlin." *Tageblatt*, February 2, 1918.

"Gdzie byłam, co widziałam." *Ewa: Pismo Tygodniowe*, May 13, 1928, 6.

Gelbart, S, ed. *15 yor "Vilner trupe": Zamlung lekoved 15 yorikn yoyvl fun der "Vilner trupe."* Lodz, 1931.

Geler, Khayim. "Briv fun Rumenie: Der dervayliker sof funem shayres-hapleyte 'Vilner' in Rumenie." *Literarishe Bleter*, November 7, 1924, 6.

Geler, Khayim. "Di 'Vilner' in Yerusholayim d'Rumenie." *Literarishe Bleter*, August 7, 1925, 9.

George, David. *The Modern Brazilian Stage*. Austin: University of Texas Press, 1992.

Goldshteyn, B. Y. "Bay di Vilner un in kunst-teater." *Der Tog*, February 22, 1924, 3.

Gottlieb, Robert. *Sarah: The Life of Sarah Bernhardt*. New Haven, CT: Yale University Press, 2010.

"Goyim kumen shoyn in yidishn teater." *Ilustrirte Vokh*, November 2, 1928, 21.

Granakh, Aleksander. *Ot geyt a mentsh*. New York: IKUF, 1948.

Grey, Paul. "From Russia to America: A Critical Chronology." In *Stanislavski and America*, ed. Erika Munk, 137–77. New York: Hill and Wang, 1964.

Griess, Helena. "Święto teatru żydowskiego." *Ewa: Pismo Tygodniowe*, October 21, 1928, 4.

Grofman, Avrom-Yitzkhok. "Hundert mol 'Shray, khine.'" *Der Moment*, May 26, 1933, 7.

Gronemann, Sammy. *Hawdoloh und Zapfenstreich: Erinnerungen an die ostjüdische etappe, 1916–18*. Berlin: Jüdischer Verlag, 1924.

Grosman, Vladimir. "Der dibek bay di Vilner: Etlekhe bamerkungen vegn der ershter forshtelung." *Forverts*, February 1, 1924, 3.

Grosman, Vladimir. "Der groyser shprung fun dem 'dibek' biz tsu der 'neveyle.'" *Der Tog*, February 6, 1924, 5.

Grosman, Vladimir. "Shray, khine!" *Haynt*, April 14, 1933, 7.

"A groyse farzamlung vegn yidishn teater." *Fraynd*, January 10, 1910, 1.

Guarnizo, Luis Eduardo, and Michael Peter Smith. "The Locations of Transnationalism." In *Transnationalism from Below*, edited by Michael Peter Smith and Luis Eduardo Guarnizo, 3–34. New Brunswick, NJ: Transaction, 1998.

"Haagsche Briewen." *Arnhemsche Courant*, July 1, 1922.

H. A. L. "The Moscow Art Theatre." *Broom: An International Magazine of the Arts* 4.1 (December 1922): 66–67.

Halkin, Hilel. Afterword to *The I. L. Peretz Reader*, edited by Ruth R. Wisse, 433-440. New Haven, CT: Yale University Press, 2002.

Halpern, Stefanie. "Boris Thomashefsky: Matinee Idol of the Yiddish Stage." In *New York's Yiddish Theater: From the Bowery to Broadway*, edited by Edna Nahshon, 118–27. New York: Columbia University Press, 2016.

"Hamburger Kammerspiele: Gastspiel des Jüdischen Künstlertheaters, Berlin, Der Dybuk." *Hamburger Fremden-Blatt*, May 14, 1922.

Hamerow, Theodore S. *Remembering a Vanished World: A Jewish Childhood in Interwar Poland*. New York: Berghahn Books, 2001.

Hannowa, Anna. "The Vilna Years of Jakub Rotbaum." Translated by Gwido Zlatkes. In *Polin: Studies in Polish Jewry*, vol. 14, *Jews in the Polish Borderlands*, edited by Anthony Polonsky, 156–69. Oxford: Littman Library of Jewish Civilization, 2001.

Harshav, Benjamin. *The Meaning of Yiddish*. Berkeley: University of California Press, 1990.

Harshav, Benjamin, ed. and trans. *The Moscow Yiddish Theater: Art on Stage in the Time of Revolution*. New Haven, CT: Yale University Press, 2008.

Hart, Julius. "Grüne Felder: Dorfidyll von Peretz Hirschbein." *Der Tag*, February 18, 1922.

H. B. "Jüdisches Künstlertheater Eeravond." *Het Vaderland*, June 20, 1922, 3.

Helvenston, Harold. *Scenery: A Manual of Scene Design*. Stanford, CA: Stanford University Press, 1931.

Hemmerle, Joachim. "Jiddisches Theater im Spiegel Deutschsprachtiger Kritik von der Jahrhundertwende bis 1928—eine Dokumentation." In *Beter und Rebellen: Aus 1000 Jahren Judentum in Polen*, edited by Michael Brock, 277–312. Frankfurt am Main: Deutscher Koordinierungsrat der Gesellschaften für Christlich-Jüdische Zusammenarbeit, 1983.

Henderson, Mary C. "New York City Theatres." In *The Cambridge Guide to Theatre*, edited by Martin Banham, 787–88. Cambridge: Cambridge University Press, 1995.

Henry, Barbara J. *Rewriting Russia: Jacob Gordin's Yiddish Drama*. Seattle: University of Washington Press, 2011.

Hermann, David. "Iets over de regie van 'Dybuk.'" *Het Masker*, July 1922, 152–55.

Hevesi, Dennis. "Luba Kadison, 99, an Actress in Yiddish Theater's Heyday." *New York Times*, May 9, 2006, B7.

Hirschbein, Peretz. *Gezamlte dramen*. Vols. 1–5. New York: Literarish-Dramatish Faraynen in Amerike, 1916.

Hirschbein, Peretz. *In gang fun lebn: Zikhroynes*. New York: Tsiko, 1948.

Hirschbein, Peretz. "In kamf far a besern teater." *Literarishe Bleter*, October 24, 1930, 800–802.

Hoberman, J. *Bridge of Light: Yiddish Film between Two Worlds*. Philadelphia: Temple University Press, 1995.

Hoeflich, Eugen. "Di Wilnaer (anmerkungen gelegntlich ihres Wiener Gastspiels)." *Neue Freie Presse*, November 10, 1922, 7.

Hohman, Valleri J. *Russian Culture and Theatrical Performance in America*. New York: Palgrave Macmillan, 2011.

Holdsworth, Nadine. *Theatre & Nation*. New York: Palgrave Macmillan, 2010.

Holt, Douglas B. *How Brands Become Icons: The Principles of Cultural Branding*. Cambridge, MA: Harvard Business Review Press, 2004.

Howe, Irving. *World of Our Fathers: The Journey of the Eastern European Jews to America and the Life They Found and Made*. 30th anniversary ed. New York: New York University Press, 2005.

Hughes, Everett C. *On Work, Race, and the Sociological Imagination*. Chicago: University of Chicago Press, 1994.

Hutchins, Michael H. "Leave It to Me." The Cole Porter Reference Guide, http://www.sondheimguide.com/porter/leave.html

Inbar, Donny. "No Raisins and Almonds in the Land of Israel." In *Inventing the Modern Yiddish Stage*, edited by Joel Berkowitz and Barbara Henry, 295–320. Detroit: Wayne State University Press, 2012.

Ingber, Judith Brin. "Identity Peddlers and the Influence of Gertrud Kraus." *Congress on Research in Dance Conference Proceedings* 39 (January 2007): 100–105.

Ionesco, Eugene. *Present Past, Past Present: A Personal Memoir*. Translated by Helen R. Lane. New York: Da Capo Press, 1971.

Ivanov, Vladislav. "An-sky, Evgeny Vakhtangov, and *The Dybbuk*." In *The Worlds of S. An-sky*, edited by Gabriella Safran and Steven J. Zipperstein, 252–65. Stanford, CA: Stanford University Press, 2006.

Jackson, Wesley Todd. "Where Do We Go from Here?: Tortured Expressions of Solidarity in the German Jewish Travelogues of the Weimar Republic." PhD diss., University of Cincinnati, 2015.

Jacobs, Neil G. *Yiddish: A Linguistic Introduction*. Cambridge: Cambridge University Press, 2005.

John, Augustus. *Augustus John: Finishing Touches*. London: Jonathan Cape, 1964.

Johnston, Lolo Bob. "The Moscow Art Theater in America." PhD diss., Northwestern University, 1952.

Joseph, May. *Nomadic Identities: The Performance of Citizenship*. Minneapolis: University of Minnesota Press, 1999.

"Joseph Buloff." Internet Broadway Database, https://www.ibdb.com/broadway-cast-staff/joseph-buloff-14313

"Joseph Buloff." Internet Movie Database, http://gb.imdb.com/name/nm0120233/?ref_=filmo_li_st_3

Joyner, Charles W. *Shared Traditions: Southern History and Folk Culture*. Urbana: University of Illinois Press, 1999.

"Jüdisches Künstlertheater: Dybuk." *Rotterdamsch Nieuwblad*, July 28, 1923.

"Jüdisches Künstlertheater." *Niuwe Rotterdamsche Courant*, June 29, 1923, 5.

"Jüdisches Theater." *Der Nachmittag*, November 16, 1922, 3.

Kacyzne, Alter. "Tsu der oyffirung fun Bay nakht afn altn mark bay di Vilner." *Literarishe Bleter*, November 2, 1928, 869–71.

Kadison, Leyb. "A bisl zikhroynes." *Literarishe Bleter* 36 (September 4, 1931): 692–93; 38 (September 18, 1931): 732–33; 39 (October 2, 1931): 772; 42 (October 16, 1931): 800–802; 43 (October 23, 1931): 818; and 45 (November 6, 1931): 853–54.

Kadison, Leyb. "Amatorn un profesioneln." In *Finf un tsvantsik yor folksbine*, edited by Yankev Fishman, B. Levin, and B. Stabinovitsh, 47–48. New York: Posy-Shoulson Press, 1940.

Kadison, Luba, Joseph Buloff, and Irving Genn. *On Stage Off Stage: Memories of a Lifetime in the Yiddish Theatre*. Cambridge, MA: Harvard University Library Judaica Division, 1992.

Kahan, Yitzkhak. "Yankev Waislitz—The Veteran of the Yiddish Stage (to His 50 Years of Theatrical Activities)." Yiddish Melbourne, Monash University. http://future.arts.monash.edu/yiddish-melbourne/download/--documents/almanac-3-yankev-waislitz.pdf

Kaminska, Ida. *My Life, My Theater*. New York: Macmillan, 1973.

Karlinski, Ber. "Baynakht afn altn mark: Tsu der oyffirung fun der Vilner trupe (teater elezium)." *Der Moment*, October 19, 1928, 7.

Karlinski, Ber. "Dos ekho: Tsum 50-ter offirung fun dibek." *Der Moment*, January 28, 1921, 6.

Karner, Doris. "Jüdische Identitäten in der Prager Theaterszene zwischen 1910 und 1939." *Maske und Kothurn*, 40.2–4 (December 1994), 113–24.

Kassow, Samuel D. *Who Will Write Our History: Emanuel Ringelblum, the Warsaw Ghetto, and the Oyneg Shabes Archive*. Bloomington: Indiana University Press, 2007.

Katz, Pinkhas. "Di barimte Vilner teater trupe—oder beyde kuni-lemels." *Forverts*, December 30, 1922, 3.

Katz, Pinkhas. "Ir zayn a Vilner?: Oyb ye, vet ir hobn parnose in Varshe." *Forverts*, March 7, 1924, 3.

Katznelson, "Der koyekh fun di Vilner." *Literarishe Bleter*, February 20, 1931, 15.

Keller, Max. *Light Fantastic: The Art and Design of Stage Lighting*. New York: Prestel, 2010.

Kerr, Alfred. *So liegt der Fall: Theaterkritiken 1919–1933 und im Exil*. Edited by Günther Rühle. Frankfurt am Main: S. Fischer Verlag, 2001.

Khad Gadyo. "Der dibek un 'Fankoni.'" *Der Moment*, March 6, 1921, 4.

Khilinovitsh, B. [Ben Zion, pseud.]. "Der dibek in a nayer geshtalt . . ." *Der Moment*, January 18, 1921, 2.

Kipnis, M. "An emeser dibek . . . (A varshever felieton)." *Haynt*, January 3, 1921, 3.

Klaynman, Dr. Anzelm. "Der Dibek in Nyu York un in Berlin: A por farglaykhende batrakhtungen." *Yidish Teater* 4–5 (March/April 1922): 30–36.

Kligman, Mark. "Jewish Liturgical Music." In *The Cambridge Companion to Jewish Music*, edited by Joshua S. Walden, 84–103. Cambridge: Cambridge University Press, 2015.

Kobrin, Rebecca. *Jewish Bialystok and Its Diaspora*. Bloomington: Indiana University Press, 2010.

Kon, S. "'Shray khine' bay di Vilner." *Vokhnshrift*, March 31, 1933, 6.

Koralnik, Dr. A. "Der Vilner 'Dibek.'" *Der Tog*, January 30, 1924, 5.

Korohodski, Y. "Peretz Hirshbayns literarish-kinstlerishe drame in Yekaterinoslav." *Idishe Tsaytung*, June 24, 1909, 2.

Koss, Andrew Noble. "World War I and the Remaking of Jewish Vilna, 1914–1918." PhD diss., Stanford University, 2010.

Koster, Simon. "Het 'Spel' van de 'Wilnaërs.'" *Het Masker*, July 1922, 157–59.

Kremer, H. "Freydke R. Noach's from Olyka Tells Ansky the Story of a Dybbuk." In *Pinkas ha-Kehilah Olyka: Sefer Yizkor*, 69–72. Tel Aviv: Hotsaat Irgun Yotsey Olyka be-Yisrael, 1972.

Kritikus, Dr. Y. "Di 'Vilner' vern Amerikaner." *Der Amerikaner*, April 16, 1926, 10.

Kruger, Loren. *The National Stage: Theatre and Cultural Legitimation in England, France, and America*. Chicago: University of Chicago Press, 1992.

Krupnik, Baruch. "Jüdisches Künstlertheater." *Jüdische Rundschau*, October 7, 1921, 586–87.

Kuhns, David F. *German Expressionist Theatre: The Actor and the Stage*. Cambridge: Cambridge University Press, 1997.

"Kulturchronik." *Prager Presse*, June 22, 1933, 6.

"Kunst." *Algemeen Handelsblad*, June 24, 1922, 2.

"Kunst en letteren." *Haagsche Courant*, June 23, 1922, 2.

"Kunst en letteren." *Haagsche Courant*, June 26, 1922, 2.

"Kunst und Wissen." *Arbeter-Zeitung*, November 2, 1922, 5.

"Kunst und Wissen." *Arbeter-Zeitung*, November 30, 1922, 6.

Kutner, Shloyme. "Zikhroynes fun der Hirshbayn-trupe." *Teater un Kunst*, February 2, 1923, 6.

Kuznitz, Cecile Esther. *YIVO and the Making of Modern Jewish Culture*. Cambridge: Cambridge University Press, 2014.

Lahad, Ezra. "Halakhakah havilnait—bat shevaim." *Bamah* 22 (1988): 5–29.

Lande, Peter. "Jewish Refugees in Tashkent." April 2007. JewishGen, http://www.jewishgen.org/databases/Holocaust/0136_uzbek.html

Landman, Salcia. "*Der Dibbuk* von An-Ski: Zur Aufführungsgeschichte." In *Der Dibbuk: Dramatische Jüdische Legende*, by An-ski, translated and introduced by Salcia Landman, 117–56. Frankfurt am Main: Deutscher Taschenbuch Verlag, 1976.

Lane, Stewart F. *Jews on Broadway: A Historical Survey of Performers, Playwrights, Composers, Lyricists, and Producers*. New York: McFarland, 2011.

Leach, Robert. *Revolutionary Theatre*. New York: Routledge, 1994.

Led Pensil. "Vos es hot zikh opgeton in teater bay der ershter forshtelung fun di Vilner." *Forverts*, February 1, 1924, 3.

Lee, Steven S. *The Ethnic Avant-Garde: Minority Cultures and World Revolution.* New York: Columbia University Press, 2015.

Legutko, Agnieszka. "Possessed by the Other: Dybbuk Possession and Modern Jewish Identity in Twentieth-Century Jewish Literature and Beyond." PhD diss., Columbia University, 2012.

Lei, Daphne Pi-Wei. *Operatic China: Staging Chinese Identity across the Pacific.* New York: Palgrave Macmillan, 2006.

Lemster, Moyshe. "Shternberg, Yankev." 2010. *YIVO Encyclopedia of Jews in Eastern Europe*, www.yivoencyclopedia.org/article.aspx/Shternberg_Yankev

Lerner, Dovid. "Di Vilner trupe in Brisl." *Literarishe Bleter*, February 16, 1934, 97–98.

Les, A. "Arum teater: Alter Kacyzne's *Ger tsedek* bay di Vilner." *Di Vokh*, January 3, 1930, 18.

"A Lesson in Acting: What the Vilna Troupe Could Teach Our Players," *Daily News*, November 4, 1922.

Lester, Eleanore. "Buloff Sees a 'Miracle' in Future of Yiddish Theatre." *Sentinel*, March 25, 1976, 48.

"Letste teg fun 'Shray khine' in Skala-teater." *Unzer Ekspres*, May 29, 1933, 2.

Levy, Emanuel. *The Habimah: Israel's National Theater, 1917–1977: A Study of Cultural Nationalism.* New York: Columbia University Press, 1979.

Leyeles, A. "Arum teater: 'Mord' bay di Vilner in Amerike teater." *Di Vokh*, November 15, 1929, 19.

Leyko, Małgorzata, ed. *Lódzkie sceny żydowskie*. Łódz: Wydawnictwo Uniwersytetu Łódzkiego, 2000.

Lifson, David S. "The History of the Yiddish Art Theatre Movement in New York from 1918 to 1940." PhD diss., New York University, 1962.

Lifson, David S. *The Yiddish Theater in America.* New York: T. Yoseloff, 1965.

Likht, Dovid. "Baym keyver fun Yehudis Lares." *Literarishe Bleter*, December 12, 1929, 983–84.

Liliput. "Kunst kohanim in der fremd," *Frayhayt*, January 18, 1924, 5.

Lirik, A. S. "Der 'Dibek' in Berlin iz a durkhfal." *Der Tog*, December 16, 1921, 3.

Liulevicius, Vejas G. *War Land on the Eastern Front: Culture, National Identity, and German Occupation in World War I.* Cambridge: Cambridge University Press, 2000.

Lo, Jacqueline, and Helen Gilbert. "Toward a Topography of Cross-Cultural Theatre Praxis." *TDR* 46.3 (Autumn 2002): 31–53.

MacDonald, Laura, and Myrte Halman. "*Geen Grenzen Meer*: An American Musical's Unlimited Border Crossing." *Theatre Research International* 39.3 (October 2014): 198–216.

Makaryk, Irene R., and Marissa McHugh, eds. *Shakespeare and the Second World War: Memory, Culture, Identity.* Toronto: University of Toronto Press, 2012.

"Maks Nordau vegn Dibek." *Teater un Kino*, November 10, 1922, 6.

Mamana, June. "From the Pale of Settlement to *Pacific Overtures*: The Evolution of Boris Aronson's Visual Aesthetic." PhD diss., Tufts University, 1997.

Manger, Itzik. "Araynfir-vort." In *Yidisher teater in Eyrope tsvishn beyde velt milkhomes: Polyn*, edited by Itzik Manger, Yonas Turkow, and Moyshe Perenson, 7–19. New York: Congress for Jewish Culture, 1968.

Manger, Itzik. "Di beyde kuni-lemls: An epizod mit a komentar in azoy fil un azoy fil paragrafn." *Getseylte Verter*, August 23, 1929, 2–3.
Manger, Itzik. "Vilner trupe: Shabsay tsvi." *Unzer Vort*, March 9, 1926, 2–3.
Manor, Giora. "Extending the Traditional Wedding Dance: Inbal's *Yemenite Wedding* and the Beggar's Dance in Habima's *The Dybbuk*." *Dance Research Journal* 17.2/18.1 (Autumn 1985–Spring 1986): 71–75.
Mayzel, Nakhmen, ed. *Briv un redes fun Y. L. Perets*. New York: IKUF, 1944.
Mayzel, Nakhmen. "Der 'Soykher fun Venedik' bay der Vilner trupe." *Literarishe Bleter*, March 8, 1929, 199–200.
Mayzel, Nakhmen. "Di ershte Perets-oyffirung in Varshe." *Haynt*, October 26, 1928, 7.
Mayzel, Nakhmen. "Di Vilner trupe in Varshe." *Literarishe Bleter*, March 30, 1928, 270.
Mayzel, Nakhmen. "Dos letste vort fun di 'Vilner' far zeyer farlozn Poyln." *Literarishe Bleter*, October 31, 1930, 830.
Mayzel, Nakhmen. "Dovid Herman." *Literarishe Bleter*, May 21, 1937, 329–31.
Mayzel, Nakhmen. "Fuftsn yor Vilner trupe." *Literarishe Bleter*, February 20, 1931, 137–38.
Mayzel, Nakhmen. *Geven a mol a lebn: Dos yidishe kultur-lebn in Poyln tsvishn beyde velt-milkhomes*. Buenos Aires: Tsentral-farband fun Poylishe yidn in Argentine, 1951.
Mayzel, Nakhmen. "Mayne-loshn funem Poylishn rezshiser Leon Shiler," *Literarishe Bleter*, March 24, 1933, 209.
Mayzel, Nakhmen. "Peretzs *Baynakht afn altn mark* bay der Vilner trupe." *Literarishe Bleter*, October 19, 1928, 818–20.
Mayzel, Nakhmen. "Peretzs Bay nakht afn altn mark in Moskver yidishn melukheteater, gastshpiln in Berlin." *Literarishe Bleter*, November 9, 1928, 881–82.
Mayzel, Nakhmen. "'Shray, khine' in der Vilner trupe." *Literarishe Bleter*, March 24, 1933, 207.
Mayzel, Nakhmen. "Tsu der oyffirung fun Shaylok bay di Vilner." *Literarishe Bleter*, March 1, 1929, 172.
Mayzel, Nakhmen. "Vilner trupe in kamf far ir kiyum." *Literarishe Bleter*, February 17, 1933, 126.
Mazo, Mordechai. "Przed nowym sezonem trupy wileńskiej: Rozmowa z dyrektorem Mazo." *Nasz Przegląd*, October 10, 1928, 5.
Mazo, Mordechai. "S'volt geven dos ergste." *Literarishe Bleter*, April 24, 1929, 345.
Melman, Marian, "Teatr Żydowski w Warszawi w latach międzywojennych." In *Warszawa II Rzeczypospolitej*, 1:383–96. Warsaw: Państwowe Wydawn. Naukowe, 1968.
Meserve, Walter, and Ruth Meserve. "The Stage History of *Roar, China!*: Documentary Drama as Propaganda." *Theatre Survey* 21.1 (May 1980): 1–13.
Mestel, Yankev. *Literatur un teater*. New York: IKUF, 1962.
Meumann, Max Alexander. "Hamburger Kammerspiele: Gastspiel des Jüdischen Künstlertheaters, Berlin." *Hamburger Fremden-Blatt*, May 8, 1922.
Meyer, Morris. *Idish Teater in London 1902–1942*. London: M. Meyer, 1943.
Midgley, David. "The Romance of the East: Encounters of German-Jewish Writers

with Yiddish-Speaking Communities, 1916–27." In *The Yiddish Presence in European Literature: Inspiration and Interaction*, edited by Ritchie Robertson and Joseph Sherman, 87–98. London: European Humanities Research Centre, 2005.

"Ming Cho Lee." 2008. American Theatre Wing. http://americantheatrewing.org/biography/detail/mingcholee

Miron, Dan. *Tales of Mendele the Book Peddler: Fishke the Lame and Benjamin the Third*. New York: Schocken Books, 1996.

Mishpat Ha-Dibuk: Din Ve-Kheshbon Stenografi. Tel Aviv: Ha-Makhlakhah Le-Sifrut Yafah Ulevikoret Shebe Agudat Ha-Sofrim Vehasifrut Ha-Ivrit, 1926.

M. K. "Dos yidishe teater in Yekaterinoslav." *Idishe Tsaytung*, May 19, 1909, 3.

Mokrzycka-Pokora, Monika. "Andrzej Pronaszko." Culture.pl. http://culture.pl/pl/tworca/andrzej-pronaszko

Mokrzycka-Pokora, Monika. "Stanisława Wysocka." Culture.pl, http://culture.pl/pl/tworca/stanislawa-wysocka

Moossen, Inge. *Theater als Kunst: Sinn und Unsinn des Stanislawski-Systems*. Frankfurt am Main: Haag und Herchen, 1993.

Morevsky, Avrom. *Ahin un tsurik: Zikhroynes un rayoynes fun a yid, an aktyor*. 4 vols. Warsaw: Yidish Bukh, 1960.

Morevsky, Avrom. "Kunst un shund." *Vilner Tog*, December 28, 1928, 4.

Morevsky, Avrom. "Lares—in shotn fun fargangenhayt." *Unzer Veg*, August 13, 1926, 3.

Morevsky, Avrom. "Tsvishn tsvey dibukim." *Ringen* 3–4 (1921): 165–68.

Morgenstern, Soma. "Zur Entstehung der Oper Lulu." In *Alban Berg und seine Idole: Erinnerungen und Briefe*, 130–33. Berlin: Aufbau, 1999.

Most, Andrea. *Theatrical Liberalism: Jews and Popular Entertainment in America*. New York: NYU Press, 2013.

Mukdoni, Dr. Alexander. "Alte bakantn tsvishn di Vilner: Tsum onkumen fun der Vilner trupe." *Morgn Zhurnal*, January 11, 1924, 7.

Mukdoni, Dr. Alexander. "Fun yidishn teater." *Fraynd*, January 1, 1910, 4.

Mukdoni, Dr. Alexander. "Fun yidishn teater: Peretz Hirshbayn's trupe." *Der Fraynd*, March 5, 1910, 4.

Mukdoni, Dr. Alexander. "Der sakhakol vegn Perets Hirshbayn's trupe," *Der Fraynd*, March 10, 1910, 4.

Mukdoni, Dr. Alexander. *Teater*. New York: A. Mukdoni yuviley komitet, 1927.

Mukdoni, Dr. Alexander. *Yitskhok Leybush Perets un dos yidishe teater*. New York: IKUF, 1949.

Mukdoni, Dr. Alexander. "Zikhroynes fun a yidishn teater-kritiker: Yidisher teater in Poyln fun 1909 biz 1915." In *Arkhiv far der geshikhte fun yidishn teater un drame*, edited by Jacob Shatzky, 341–421. Vilna: YIVO, 1930.

Murav, Harriet. *Music from a Speeding Train: Jewish Literature in Post-Revolution Russia*. Stanford, CA: Stanford University Press, 2011.

Musil, Robert. *Sämtliche Werke: Vollständige Ausgaben*. Berlin: e-artnow, 2013. E-book. http://www.beam-ebooks.de/ebook/78705

Nachbush, Noah. *Gems of Yiddish Poetry and Folklore*. Brooklyn: N. Nachbush. Music record.

Nadel, Arno. "Dybuk." *Het Vaderland*, June 17, 1922, 2.

Nahshon, Edna. "Overture: From the Bowery to Broadway." In *New York's Yiddish Theater: From the Bowery to Broadway*, edited by Edna Nahshon, 8–50. New York: Columbia University Press, 2016.

Nahshon, Edna. "Stars, Strikes, and the Yiddish Stage: The Story of the Hebrew Actors' Union." New York: YIVO Institute for Jewish Research, 2009. Exhibition catalog.

Nayman, Yehezkel-Moyshe. "Bay nakht afn altn mark fun Y. L. Peretsn." *Haynt*, October 19, 1928, 8.

Nayman, Yehezkel-Moyshe. "Dos ergste fun der gantser geshikhte: Tsu der shaylok-debate." *Haynt*, April 19, 1929, 321.

Nayman, Yehezkel-Moyshe. "Hateatron hayihudi vihavilnaim." *Bamah* 34 (1942): 12.

Nayman, Yehezkel-Moyshe. "Shaylok bay di Vilner." *Haynt*, March 7, 1929, 3.

"New Stagecraft Lifts Scenes through Floor and Paints Them with Light." *Popular Science* 102.2 (February 1923): 38–39.

"New York 'Dybbuk' Premiere." *New York Times*, May 10, 1936, X5.

Nigal, Gedalyah. *Magic, Mysticism, and Hasidism: The Supernatural in Jewish Thought*. Northvale, NJ: Jason Aronson, 1994.

Niger, Shmuel, ed. *Perets Hirshbayn (tsu zayn zekhtsikstn geboyrntog)*. New York: CYCO, 1948.

Niger, Shmuel. "Di rezshi fun Dibek in Shvarts's Kunst teater." *Der Tog*, September 12, 1921.

Niger, Shmuel. *Y. L. Perets: Zayn lebn, zayn firndikn perzenlekhkayt*. Buenos Aires: Congress for Jewish Culture, 1952.

Nomberg, H. D. "Vokhedike shmuesn: Di Vilner trupe." *Der Moment*, October 5, 1917, 3.

Norman, Yitskhok. *Bereshit Habimah: Nakhum Tsemakh meyased Habimah bekhazon uvema'as*. Jerusalem: Hasifriyah hatsionit, 1966.

Novershtern, Abraham. "Between Dust and Dance: Peretz's Drama and the Rise of Yiddish Modernism." *Prooftexts* 12 (1933): 71–90.

O'Brien, Caraid. "Luba Kadison Buloff, 99, Last Survivor of Yiddish Theater Company." *Jewish Daily Forward*, May 12, 2006, http://forward.com/articles/1388/luba-kadison-buloff—last-survivor-of-yiddish-th/

"Orthodox Rabbis Condemn Theatre." *Sentinel*, July 30, 1926, 20.

Orwin, Donna Tussing, ed. *The Cambridge Companion to Tolstoy*. Cambridge: Cambridge University Press, 2002.

Osborne, John. *Gerhart Hauptmann and the Naturalist Drama*. New York: Routledge, 2005.

Osterwa, Juliusz. "O *Dybuku* Trupy Wileńskiej (1925)." *Pamiętnik Teatralny* 41.1 (1992): 493–94.

Ostrowska, Elżbieta. "Der Dibuk / The Dybbuk." In *The Cinema of Central Europe*, edited by Peter Hames, 25–34. New York: Wallflower Press, 2004.

"Oyfgehert tsu ekzistirn Hirshbayns trupe." *Gut Morgen* (Odessa), July 12, 1910, 3.

Oyslender, Nokhem. *Yidisher teater, 1887–1917*. Moscow: Der emes, 1940.

Pabst, Curt. "Jüdisches Theater." *Zeitung der 10. Armee*, March 7, 1916, 8.

Perelman, Ala Zuskin. *The Travels of Benjamin Zuskin*. Syracuse, NY: Syracuse University Press, 2015.

Peretz, Maya. "Jewish Theatre in Poland before the Second World War: Its Audiences and Its Critics." *Polin: Studies in Polish Jewry* 13 (2000): 356–65.

Peretz, Y. L. *Ale verk*. Vol. 7. New York: Tsiko, 1947.

Peretz, Y. L. *A Night in the Old Marketplace*. Translated by Hillel Halkin. In *The I. L. Peretz Reader*, edited by Ruth R. Wisse, 363–432. New Haven, CT: Yale University Press, 2002.

Peretz, Y. L. *Khurban beit tsadik: Hashiloakh* 11 (May 1903, June 1903): 471–74; 12 (December 1903): 566–70, 529–43.

Peretz, Y. L. "What Our Literature Needs." In *Voices from the Yiddish: Essays, Memoirs, Diaries*, edited by Irving Howe and Eliezer Greenberg, 25–31. Ann Arbor: University of Michigan Press, 1972.

Perle, Yehoshua. "Yidish teater." *Der Moment*, February 7, 1933, 6.

Picon-Vallin, Béatrice. *Le théâtre juif soviétique pendant les années vingt*. Lausanne, Switzerland: La Cité, 1973.

Pinsker, Shachar. *Literary Passports: The Making of Modernist Hebrew Fiction in Europe*. Stanford, CA: Stanford University Press, 2010.

Pinski, Dovid. *Dos idishe drama: Eyn iberblik iber ir entviklung*. New York: S. Drukerman, 1909.

Pinski, Dovid. "Perets Hirshbayn der dramatiker." In *Teater, veltrayzes, zikhroynes*, edited by Shmuel Rozshanski, 316–20. Buenos Aires: Literatur Gezelshaft Baym YIVO in Argentine, 1967.

"The Play in Paris." *Era*, October 19, 1922, 18.

"Plays in Yiddish." *Era*, November 2, 1922, 18.

"Polish Parties Object to Play," *Sentinel*, August 19, 1927, 6.

Prilutski, Noyekh. "Fun yidishn teater." *Unzer Lebn*, March 3, 1910, 3.

Prilutski, Noyekh. *Yidish teater: 1905–1912*. Bialystok: A. Albek, 1921.

Prokop-Janiec, Eugenia. *Polish-Jewish Literature in the Interwar Years*. Translated by Abe Shenitzer. Syracuse, NY: Syracuse University Press, 2003.

Puchner, Martin. *Poetry of the Revolution: Marx, Manifestos, and the Avant-Gardes*. Princeton, NJ: Princeton University Press, 2006.

Rabinovitch, Simon, ed. *Jews and Diaspora Nationalism: Writings on Jewish Peoplehood in Europe and the United States*. Waltham, MA: Brandeis University Press, 2012.

Ran, Leyzer. *Vilna, Jerusalem of Lithuania*. Fourth Annual Avrom-Nokhem Stencl Lecture in Yiddish Studies. Oxford: Oxford Centre for Postgraduate Hebrew Studies, 1987.

Ravitsh, Melekh, ed. *Dos amolike Yidishe Varshe biz der shvel fun dritn khurbm, 1414–1939*. Montreal: Farband fun Varshever yidn in Montreal, 1967.

Rees, Leslie. "This Week at the Playhouse." *Era*, April 4, 1934, 4.

Reich, Tova. "Once Upon a Time in Vilnius." *Washington Post*, March 3, 1991. https://www.washingtonpost.com/archive/entertainment/books/1991/03/03/once-upon-a-time-in-vilnius/9453dd44-a103-475f-b94a-64156b6f1b37/

"Rekhtlozikayt un negishes fartraybn di Vilner trupe fun Varshe." *Haynt*, May 10, 1929, 10.

Reyzen, Avrom. "Di vanderndike yidishe trupe." In *Perets Hirshbayn*, edited by Shmuel Niger, 204–10. New York: Komitet Yoyvl Hirshbayn, 1941.

Reyzen, Zalmen. "Der yidisher teater in Vilna." In *Vilner zamelbukh*, edited by Tsemakh Shabad, 2:165–76. Vilna: M. Rosental, 1918.

Riss, Heidelore. *Ansätze zu einer Geschichte des jüdischen Theaters in Berlin 1889–1936*. Frankfurt am Main: Peter Lang, 2000.

Rogoff, Hillel. "Di Vilner trupe in a realistisher drama: *Di neveyle* fun Perets Hirshbayn." *Forverts*, February 6, 1924, 4.

Rogoff, Hillel. "Di Vilner trupe in Perets Hirshbayn's *Grine felder*." *Forverts*, February 27, 1924, 4.

Rokem, Freddie. "Hebrew Theater from 1889 to 1948." In *Theater in Israel*, edited by Linda Ben-Zvi, 51–84. Ann Arbor: University of Michigan Press, 1996.

Rosenberg, Joel. "The Soul of Catastrophe: On the 1937 Film of S. Ansky's *The Dybbuk*." *Jewish Social Studies* 17.2 (Winter 2011): 1–27.

Rovit, Rebecca. "Theatrical Performance at Auschwitz: A Concert of Words." In *The Last Expression: Art and Auschwitz*, edited by David Mickenberg, Corrine Granof, and Peter Hayes, 104–13. Chicago: Northwestern University Press, 2003.

Rozshanski, Shmuel, ed. *Vilne in der yidisher literature*. Buenos Aires: YIVO in Argentina, 1980.

Rubel, Elinor. "Fishzon's Theater and the Premiere of Peretz's *Nisojen* (*Temptation*) in Warsaw (1906)." In *Teatr żydowski w Polsce: Materiały z międzynarodowej konferencji naukowej, Warszawa, 18–21 października 1993 roku*, edited by Anna Kuligowska-Korzeniewska and Małgorzata Leyko, 113–26. Łódź: Uniwersytetu Łódzkiego, 1998.

Rubin, Reuven. *Rubin: My Life, My Art*. New York: Sabra Books, 1974.

Rumshinsky, Joseph. *Klangen fun mayn lebn*. New York: A. Biderman, 1944.

Safran, Gabriella. "Rapoport, Shloyme Zaynvl." 2010. *YIVO Encyclopedia of Jews in Eastern Europe*, http://www.yivoencyclopedia.org/article.aspx/RapoportShloymeZaynvl

Safran, Gabriella. *Wandering Soul: The Dybbuk's Creator, S. An-sky*. Cambridge, MA: Harvard University Press, 2010.

Sandrow, Nahma. *Vagabond Stars: A World History of Yiddish Theater*. Syracuse, NY: Syracuse University Press, 1996.

Savran, David. "Trafficking in Transnational Brands: The New 'Broadway-Style' Musical." *Theatre Survey* 55.3 (September 2014): 318–42.

Schachter, Allison. *Diasporic Modernisms: Hebrew and Yiddish Literature in the Twentieth Century*. Oxford: Oxford University Press, 2011.

Schack, William. "Introducing Joseph Buloff of Russia." *New York Times*, November 23, 1930, 112.

Schack, William. "The Yiddish Theatre in Travail." *New York Times*, March 30, 1930, X2.

Schiller, Friedrich. "The Stage as a Moral Institution." In *Theatre/Theory/Theatre: The Major Critical Texts from Aristotle and Zeami to Soyinka and Havel*, edited by Daniel Gerould, 250–54. New York: Applause, 2000.

Schiller, Leon. *Droga Przez Teatr*. Warsaw: J. Timoszewicz, 1984.

Schiller, Leon. "'Krzyczcie Chiny!' Na Dzielnej," *Wiadomości Literackie*, March 19, 1933, 6.

Schoell, F. L. "L'Enfant terrible de la Pologne." *La Pologne*, 1931, 580–600.

Schreiber, Baruch David. "The Woman's Voice in the Synagogue." *Journal of Jewish Music and Liturgy* 7 (January 1984): 27–32.

Schwartz, Maurice. "Impresionizm un realism: Velkhe fun di tsvey metodn darf ongevendet vern in der oyffirung fun Anskis dramatishe legende *Der dibek*?" *Unzer Teater* 1.1 (September 1921): 10–12.

Schwartz, Maurice. "Theatre in a Democracy: The Yiddish Art Theatre's Director States a Case and Points a Warning." *New York Times*, December 1, 1940, X1.

Schweitzer, Marlis. *Transatlantic Broadway: The Infrastructural Politics of Global Performance*. New York: Palgrave Macmillan, 2015.

S. D. "Als Figurant en interviewer het Jüdisches Künstlertheater." *Het Vaderland*, August 30, 1922, 4.

Segel, Harold B. *Turn-of-the-Century Cabaret*. New York: Columbia University Press, 1987.

Seidman, Aaron B. "The First Performance of Yiddish Theatre in America." *Jewish Social Studies* 10.1 (January 1948): 67–70.

Seidman, Naomi. *A Marriage Made in Heaven: The Sexual Politics of Hebrew and Yiddish*. Berkeley: University of California Press, 1997.

Senelick, Laurence. *Historical Dictionary of Russian Theatre*. 2nd ed. Lanham, MD: Rowman and Littlefield, 2015.

Senelick, Laurence, ed. *Wandering Stars: Russian Emigré Theatre, 1905–1940*. Iowa City: University of Iowa Press, 1992.

Senelick, Laurence, and Sergei Ostrovsky, eds. *The Soviet Theater: A Documentary History*. New Haven, CT: Yale University Press, 2014.

Senn, Alfred E. *The Great Powers: Lithuania and the Vilna Question, 1920–1928*. Leiden: E. J. Brill, 1966.

Shandler, Jeffrey. *Adventures in Yiddishland: Postvernacular Language and Culture*. Berkeley: University of California Press, 2008.

Sherrod, D. Troy. *Historic Dallas Theatres*. Charleston, SC: Arcadia, 2014.

Shmeruk, Chone. "Aspects of the History of Warsaw as a Yiddish Literary Center." *Polin* 3 (1988): 140–55.

Shneer, David. *Yiddish and the Creation of Soviet Jewish Culture: 1918–1930*. Cambridge: Cambridge University Press, 2004.

Shner (Shinar), Mordkhe. "Varshever yidisher kunst-teater ('VYKT')." In *Yidisher teater in Eyrope tsvishn beyde velt milkhomes: Polyn*, edited by Itzik Manger, Yonas Turkow, and Moyshe Perenson, 53–72. New York: Congress for Jewish Culture, 1968.

Shniur, Chaim. "On a nomen: A bintl zikhroynes vegn der Vilner trupe." *Literarishe Bleter*, August 25, 1929, 661–62.

Shrayer, Maxim D. *An Anthology of Jewish-Russian Literature: Two Centuries of Dual Identity in Prose and Poetry*. New York: Routledge, 2015.

"'Shray khine' in Skala-teater." *Unzer Ekspres*, May 8, 1933.

Shteynbarg, Eliezer. "Moshiakh iz gekumen: Tsur oyffirung funem *Mabul* fun Berger." *Di Frayhayt*, April 15, 1924, 2.

Silberschlag, Eisig. "Hebrew Literature, Modern." In *Encyclopedia Judaica*, 2nd ed., 8:684–738. Detroit: Macmillan Reference USA, 2007.

Silverman, Lisa. *Becoming Austrians: Jews and Culture between the World Wars*. Oxford: Oxford University Press, 2012.

Silverman, Lisa. "Max Reinhardt between Yiddish Theatre and the Salzburg Festival." In *Jews and the Making of Modern German Theatre*, edited by Jeanette R. Malkin and Freddie Rokem, 197–218. Iowa City: University of Iowa Press, 2010.

"Socialities." *South African Jewish Times*, October 16, 1936.

Sosulski, Michael J. *Theater and Nation in Eighteenth-Century Germany*. Aldershot, UK: Ashgate, 2007.

"Special Taxes for Jewish Theatre Productions." *Jewish Telegraphic Agency*, May 14, 1929.

Stamberg, Ursula. "Das Theaterlebn der jüdischen Bevölkerung Brünns." *Maske und Kothurn* 47.3–4 (December 2001): 67–82.

Stein, Wilm. "Verborgene Kunst in Warschau." *Berliner Tageblatt*, February 16, 1921, 2.

Steinlauf, Michael C. "'Fardibekt!': An-sky's Polish Legacy." In *The Worlds of S. An-sky*, edited by Gabriella Safran and Steven J. Zipperstein, 232–51. Stanford, CA: Stanford University Press, 2006.

Steinlauf, Michael C. "Fear of Purim: Y. L. Peretz and the Canonization of Yiddish Theater." *Jewish Social Studies* 1.3 (Spring 1995): 44–65.

Steinlauf, Michael C. "Kaminski Family." 2010. *YIVO Encyclopedia of Jews in Eastern Europe*, http://www.yivoencyclopedia.org/article.aspx/Kaminski_Family

Steinlauf, Michael C. "Między dwoma światami: Opętani tradycją" *Midrasz* 5 (1997): 27–30.

Steinlauf, Michael C. "Polish-Jewish Theater: The Case of Mark Arnshteyn. A Study of the Interplay among Yiddish, Polish, and Polish-Language Jewish Culture in the Modern Period." PhD diss., Brandeis University, 1988.

Stössinger, Felix. "Vom unbekannten Judentum: *Dybuk* im Jüdischen Künstlertheater." *Die Freiheit*, October 28, 1921.

Struck, Hermann. "Das Jüdische Theater in Wilna." *Korrespondenz B*, November 8, 1916.

"Szymon and Helena Syrkus." Culture.pl, http://culture.pl/en/artist/szymon-and-helena-syrkus

"Tadeusz Boy-Żeleński." Culture.pl, http://culture.pl/en/artist/tadeusz-boy-zelenski

Taub, Michael. "Bella Bellarina." Jewish Women's Archive, http://jwa.org/encyclopedia/article/bellarina-bella

Telushkin, Joseph. *Jewish Humor: What the Best Jewish Jokes Say about the Jews*. New York: William Morrow, 1992.

Tennant, Victoria. *Irina Baronova and the Ballets Russes de Monte Carlo*. Chicago: University of Chicago Press, 2014.

"Theater, Kabaret, und Film." *Österreichs Illustrirte Zeitung* 52 (December 28, 1930): 14–15.

"Theater und Art." *Neues Wiener Tagblatt*, February 25, 1930, 9.

"Theater und Kunst." *Czernowitzer Allgemeiner Zeitung*, November 4, 1923, 7.

Thissen, Judith. "Reconsidering the Decline of the New York Yiddish Theatre in the Early 1900s." *Theatre Survey* 44.2 (November 2003): 173–97.

Thomashefsky, Boris. "Thomashevski dertseylt vos es hot zikh ongeton in teater velt mit der Vilner trupe." *Forverts*, December 12, 1923, 3.

Tietze, Hans. *Jakub Steinhardt*. Berlin: J. J. Ottens-Verlag.

Tirkel, Dovid Ber. *Di yugntlekhe bine: Geshikhte fun di idish-hebreishe dramatishe gezelshaftn, 1890–1940*. Philadelphia: Hebrew Literature Society, 1940.

"Tooneel te Berlin: Jüdisches Künstlertheater: S. Anski: *Der Dybuk*." *Algemeen Handelsblad*, December 15, 1921, 7.

"Transylvania Sees New Anti-Jewish Excesses." *Jewish Telegraphic Agency*, May 24, 1927.

Tsanin, M. *Herts Grosbard*. Tel Aviv: Farlag–Di mi un der onshtreng un M. Tsa vi s'iz geven der vuntsh fun Herts Grosbard un zayn tsavoe, 1995.

Tsaytlin, Aron. "Bay di Vilner in Lemberg." *Literarishe Bleter*, August 26, 1927, 658–60.

Turkow, Yonas. "Dovid Herman." *Literarishe Bleter*, May 21, 1937, 333.

Turkow, Yonas. *Farloshene shtern*. Buenos Aires: Tsentral-farband fun Poylishe yidn in Argentine, 1953.

Turkow, Zygmunt. *Di ibergerisene tkufe*. Buenos Aires: Tsentral-farband fun Poylishe yidn in Argentine, 1961.

Turkow-Grudberg, Yitskhok. *Varshe, dos vigele fun yidishn teater*. Warsaw: Yidish Bukh, 1956.

Turkow-Grudberg, Yitskhok. *Yidish teater in Poyln*. Warsaw: Yidish Bukh, 1951.

Turkow-Grudberg, Yitskhok. *Y. L. Perets—der veker: Tsu der 50-ter yortsayt*. Tel Aviv: Farlag Y. L. Peretz, 1965.

United States Holocaust Memorial Museum. "Carl Clauberg." *Holocaust Encyclopedia*, http://www.ushmm.org/wlc/en/article.php?ModuleId=10007061

Vaysblat, Volf. "Vegn a yidishn kinstlerishn teater." *Der Fraynd*, April 13, 1908, 3.

Veidlinger, Jeffrey. *Jewish Public Culture in the Late Russian Empire*. Bloomington: Indiana University Press, 2009.

Veidlinger, Jeffrey. *The Moscow State Yiddish Theater: Jewish Culture on the Soviet Stage*. Bloomington: Indiana University Press, 2000.

Vertovec, Steven. "Conceiving and Researching Transnationalism." *Ethnic and Racial Studies* 22.2 (1999): 447–62.

Vertovec, Steven. "Migration and Other Modes of Transnationalism: Towards Conceptual Cross-Fertilization." *International Migration Review* 37.3 (2003): 641–65.

"Vilna Troupe Give Odd Yiddish Drama: Throng Greets Their First Appearance Here in 'The Dibbuk' at Thomashefsky's Theatre." *New York Times*, January 29, 1924, 17.

"Vilner aktyorn dertseyln vi azoy zeyer barimte trupe iz organizirt gevorn." *Forverts*, January 11, 1924, 1.

"Vilner teater politik in Amerika." *Forverts*, January 18, 1924, 3.

Viorel, Elena. "Deutsches und Jüdisches Theater im Czernowitz der Zwanziger Jahre." In *Teatru şi politică: Teatre minoritare de limba gemană din sud-estul Europei în secolul al 20-lea / Theater und Politik: Deutschsprachige Minderheitentheater in Südosteuropa im 20. Jahrhundert*, edited by Horst Fassel, 117–34. Cluj-Napoca: Presa Universitară Clujeană, 2001.

Vladimirsky, Irena. "The Jews of Kyrgyzstan." Beit Hatfutsot, http://www.bh.org.il/jews-kyrgyzstan/

Waislitz, Jacob. "Der gang in der velt." In *Yidisher teater in Eyrope tsvishn beyde velt milkhomes: Polyn*, edited by Itzik Manger, Yonas Turkow, and Moyshe Perenson, 35–49. New York: Congress for Jewish Culture, 1968.

Waldinger, Roger, and David Fitzgerald. "Transnationalism in Question." *American Journal of Sociology* 109.5 (2004): 1117–95.

Walker, Katharine Sorley. *De Basil's Ballets Russes*. New York: Atheneum, 1983.

Wallas, Armin A. "Jiddisches Theater: Das Gastspiel der Wilnaer Truppe in Wien 1922/23." *Das Jüdische Echo: Zeitschrift für Kultur und Politik* 44 (1995): 179–92.

Waltz, Gwendolyn. "Filmed Scenery on the Live Stage." *Theatre Journal* 58.4 (December 2006): 547–73.

Warnke, Nina. "Going East: The Impact of American Yiddish Plays and Players on the Yiddish Stage in Czarist Russia, 1890–1914." *American Jewish History* 92.1 (March 2004): 1–29.

Warnke, Nina. "Reforming the New York Yiddish Theater: The Cultural Politics of Immigrant Intellectuals and the Yiddish Press, 1887–1910." PhD diss., Columbia University, 2001.

Warnke, Nina. "Theater as Educational Institution: Jewish Immigrant Intellectuals and Yiddish Theater Reform." In *The Art of Being Jewish in Modern Times*, edited by Barbara Kirshenblatt-Gimblett and Jonathan Karp, 23–41. Philadelphia: University of Pennsylvania Press, 2008.

W. B. "Jüdisches Künstlertheater: Neweijle." *De Telegraaf*, July 20, 1922, 9.

Web, Marek. "Yiddish Actors' Union." In *The YIVO Encyclopedia of Jews in Eastern Europe*, edited by Gershon David Hundert, 2:2058–59. New Haven, CT: Yale University Press, 2008.

Weferling, Erich. "Jüdisches Theater in Subat." *Zeitung der 10. Armee*, February 21, 1918, 4.

Weferling, Erich. "Jüdisches Theater in Subat." *Zeitung der 10. Armee*, February 22, 1918, 4.

Weichert, Mikhl. "Di shefe fun Vilner trupes." *Literarishe Bleter*, July 25, 1930, 560–61.

Weichert, Mikhl. "Mayn oyffirung fun Sholem Ash's Kidush Hashem." In *Dos amolike Yidishe Varshe biz der shvel fun dritn khurbm, 1414–1939*, edited by Melekh Ravitsh, 254–62. Montreal: Farband fun Varshever yidn in Montreal, 1967.

Weichert, Mikhl. "Shaylok." *Literarishe Bleter*, March 8, 1929, 197–98.

Weichert, Mikhl. *Zikhroynes*. Vol. 2. Tel Aviv: Farlag Menorah, 1961.

Weinreich, Max. *History of the Yiddish Language*. Vols. 1 and 2. Translated by Shlomo Noble. New Haven, CT: Yale University Press, 2008.

Weinreich, Max, Zalmen Reyzen, and Khayim Broyde, eds. *Di ershte yidishe shprakh-konferets: Barikhtn, dokumentn un opklangen fun der Tsernovitser konferents, 1908*. Vilna: VIVO, 1931.

Weiser, Keith Ian, and Joshua A. Fogel, eds. *Czernowitz at 100: The First Yiddish Language Conference in Historical Perspective*. Lanham, MD: Lexington Books, 2010.

Welch, Robert. *The Abbey Theater 1899–1999: Form and Pressure*. Oxford: Oxford University Press, 1999.

Welsh, Robert Gilbert. "Spirit Control in Yiddish Play: *The Dibuk* by the Vilna Troupe Is Strange Occult Drama." *New York Telegram and Evening Mail*, February 15, 1924, 17.

Werry, Margaret. "'The Greatest Show on Earth': Political Spectacle, Spectacular Politics, and the American Pacific." *Theatre Journal* 57.3 (October 2005): 357.

Wilde, Oscar. *Complete Works of Oscar Wilde*. 3rd ed. Glasgow: HarperCollins, 1994.

Wiles, David, and Christine Dymkowski. *The Cambridge Companion to Theatre History*. Cambridge: Cambridge University Press, 2013.

Wilfred, Thomas. "The Projected Setting." *Educational Theatre Journal* 6.2 (May 1954): 136–44.

Wilmer, S. E. "The Development of National Theatres in Europe in the Eighteenth and Nineteenth Centuries." In *National Theatres in a Changing Europe*, edited by S. E. Wilmer, 9–20. New York: Palgrave Macmillan, 2008.

Wilmeth, Don B., and Christopher Bigsby, eds. *The Cambridge History of American Theatre*. Vol. 3. Cambridge: Cambridge University Press, 2000.

"Wilnaer Künstlertruppe 'Tag und Nacht' von An-skie." *Brünner Tagesboten*, June 12, 1930, 3.

"Wilnaer 'Shver zu sein ein Jud' Scholem Alejchem." *Brünner Tagesboten*, June 13, 1930, 3.

Winter, Curt. "Jüdisches Theater." *Zeitung der 10. Armee*, February 22, 1916, 8.

Wisse, Ruth R. *I. L. Peretz and the Making of Modern Jewish Culture*. Seattle: University of Washington Press, 1991.

Witkowski, Georg. *The German Drama of the Nineteenth Century*. Translated by L. E. Horning. New York: Henry Holt, 1909.

"Wolfe Barzell." Internet Broadway Database. https://www.ibdb.com/broadway-cast-staff/wolfe-barzell-31219

Wolitz, Seth. "Inscribing An-sky's *Dybbuk* in Russian and Jewish Letters." In *The Worlds of S. An-sky*, edited by Gabriella Safran and Steven J. Zipperstein, 164–202. Stanford, CA: Stanford University Press, 2006.

Woods, Leigh. *Transatlantic Stage Stars in Vaudeville and Variety*. New York: Palgrave Macmillan, 2006.

Worrall, Nick. *The Moscow Art Theatre*. New York: Routledge, 1996.

Wróbel, Piotr. "The First World War—The Twilight of Jewish Warsaw." In *The Jews in Warsaw: A History*, edited by Władysław T. Bartoszewski and Antony Polonsky, 278–90. Oxford: Basil Blackwell, 1991.

Wygodski, Jacob. *In shturem: Zikhroynes fun di okupatsye tsaytn*. Vilna: B. Kletskin, 1926.

Yarkhai, A. "Etlekhe verter vegn yudishn teater." *Der Fraynd*, January 10, 1908, 1–2.

Yates, W. E. *Theater in Vienna: A Critical History (1776–1995)*. Cambridge: Cambridge University Press, 1996.

Y. B. "Hinter di kulisn fun der *Kidush-hashem* oyffirung: A shmues mit Mikhl Vaykhert." *Literarishe Bleter*, May 25, 1928, 410–11.

"Yiddish Art Theatre: 'The Dibbuk,' a Strange and Imaginative Folk Play, Acted." *New York Times*, September 2, 1921, 15.

"Yiddish Players Score." *New York Clipper*, November 29, 1922, 14.

Youker, Timothy. "'The Destiny of Words': Documentary Theatre, the Avant-Garde, and the Politics of Form." PhD diss., Columbia University, 2012.

Young, Boaz. *Mayn lebn in teater*. New York: Ikuf farlag, 1950.

"Yuliush Osterva vegn yidishn teater." *Vilner Tog*, February 3, 1925, 3.

Zable, Arnold. *The Fig Tree*. Melbourne: Text Publishing Company, 2002). Kindle ed.

Zable, Arnold. *Wanderers and Dreamers: Tales of the David Herman Theater*. Melbourne: Hyland, 1998.

"Zalmen Hirshfeld." HaBait, http://www.habait.co.il/document/80,62,29.aspx

Zarrilli, Phillip B., Bruce McConachie, Gary Jay Williams, and Carol Fisher Sorgenfrei. *Theatre Histories: An Introduction*. 2nd ed. New York: Routledge, 2010.

Zer-Zion, Shelly. "The Birth of Habima and the Yiddish Art Theatre Movement." In *Jewish Theatre: Tradition in Transition and Intercultural Vistas*, edited by Ahuva Belkin, 73–88. Tel Aviv: Tel Aviv University, 2008.

Zer-Zion, Shelly. "*The Dybbuk* Reconsidered—The Emergence of a Modern Jewish Symbol Between East and West." *Leipziger Beiträge zur jüdischen Geschichte und Kultur* 3 (2005): 175–97.

Zer-Zion, Shelly. "Ha-'Vilner trupe'—prolog la-historiyah shel 'Habima.'" *Bikoret ve-Parshanut*, 41 (2009): 65–92.

Zer-Zion, Shelly. "Theater: Hebrew Theater." 2010. *YIVO Encyclopedia of Jews in Eastern Europe*, http://www.yivoencyclopedia.org/article.aspx/Theater/Hebrew_Theater

Zhitlovski, Khayim. "A por verter vegn Anskis Dibek." *Unzer teater* 1.1 (September 1921): 5–10.

Zohn, Hershel. *The Story of the Yiddish Theatre*. Las Cruces, NM: Zohn, 1979.

Zweig, Arnold. *Jüden auf der deutschen Bühne*. Berlin: Heine-Bund, 1927.

Zylbercweig, Zalmen, ed. *Leksikon fun yidishn teater*. 6 vols. New York, Warsaw, and Mexico City: Farlag Elisheva, 1931–69.

Index

Page numbers in italics refer to the illustrations.